T5-CVP-453

Metal Forming

Fundamentals and Applications

ASM Series in Metal Processing

Series Editor

HAROLD L. GEGEL, FASM
Senior Scientist
Air Force Wright Aeronautical Laboratories

---

1. **Metal Forming: Fundamentals and Applications**
   Taylan Altan, Soo-Ik Oh, Harold L. Gegel

Other volumes in preparation

Metal Forming

Fundamentals and Applications

Taylan Altan
Senior Research Leader
Battelle Columbus Laboratories

Soo-Ik Oh
Principal Research Scientist
Battelle Columbus Laboratories

Harold L. Gegel
Senior Scientist
Air Force Wright Aeronautical Laboratories

AMERICAN SOCIETY FOR METALS
Metals Park, OH 44073

Library of Congress Catalog Card No. 83-70673

ISBN: 0-87170-167-7

SAN 204-7586

Editorial and production coordination by
Carnes Publication Services, Inc.

PRINTED IN THE UNITED STATES OF AMERICA

Series Editor's Foreword

The American Society for Metals is responding to the technical needs of a growing fraternity of scientists, engineers, and production managers of the second- and third-tier industrial base who are being challenged by rapid advances in the technology of automation.

The introduction of computer-aided and robotic technologies into the manufacturing process has caused managers to rethink manufacturing operations in terms of providing the full market value of which they are capable. The up-to-date factory is striving to reach the "ideal" goal of stockless production, which can be achieved only through closer relationships between design and manufacturing and between the designer and the parts vendor. In general, a productivity gap has always existed between vendors and users, because vendors traditionally have not been partners with their customers. The parts and material suppliers must now improve the quality of their products and their productivity to bring their production capabilities in line with the new trends in world manufacturing.

The quality of products produced by the factory of the future will depend on the parts vendor's ability to change from a job-shop mode of production to one of zero lead time with repetitive production of discrete units that are free of defects.

The ASM Process Modeling Activity members are formulating a series of monographs that will link the components of process modeling and focus on its use to facilitate modernization of the vendor industries served by the society.

Although the range of process modeling is very broad, these monographs will focus primarily on the metalworking community. They will be aimed at supporting the continuing education of graduate engineers, and each monograph will have sufficient technical depth to be useful as reference material for university courses at the graduate and upper-undergraduate student levels. The monographs will link equipment or machinery dynamics, material-behavior modeling, numerical methods for process simulation, interface phenomena, and process economics. One of the aims of this series is to underscore the fact that process modeling is intimately associated with process simulation, die (mold) design and manufacturing, and process control.

The theory and examples contained in these monographs provide the basis for understanding the value of computer-aided engineering and manufacturing (CAE/CAM) as a productivity and part-quality enhancement tool. CAE/CAM systems will serve as a direct link between the designer and the parts vendor, making the vendor a "partner" in the total manufacturing operation.

In preparing these monographs, the authors have drawn extensively from the existing literature and the published results of active research programs in processing science. In particular, the Air Force Office of Scientific Research (AFOSR) program on processing science has had significant influence. This research encompassed materials, mechanics, interface phenomena, and equipment characteristics in a unified approach to the modeling of deformation processes. The various components of the modeling system were integrated by means of an interactive computer program that facilitates the simulation of material flow in arbitrarily shaped dies. The analytical models make possible the design of dies based on metal-flow simulation and the development of a process-control algorithm for feedforward control of metalworking presses; furthermore, they provide the means for using process control as a method of guaranteeing quality assurance of net-shape products. Shop-floor validation of process modeling for the design of near-net-shape products having a controlled set of microstructures and properties has been a rewarding result of this research.

It is a pleasure to acknowledge the support provided by AFOSR and, in particular, Dr. T. E. Walsh, Electronic and Materials Science, for his continued support. The stimulation and guidance provided by Dr. Frank Kelley, Dr. H. M. Burte, Dr. N. M. Tallan, and colleagues of the Air Force Wright Aeronautical Laboratories/Materials Laboratory throughout the program is also gratefully acknowledged. Special thanks are also due to Dr. George Dieter, Dean of the College of Engineering at the University of Maryland, and Dr. Roger N. Wright, Professor at Rensselaer Polytechnic Institute, who provided consultative advice. Special recognition must be given to Dr. Shiro Kobayashi, Professor of Mechanical Engineering at the University of California – Berkeley, for his dedicated research which has significantly advanced the analysis of metalworking processes. Finally, it is a pleasure to acknowledge Dr. Taylan Altan, of Battelle Columbus Laboratories, who was the principal investigator for the AFOSR processing science program.

Harold L. Gegel
Series Editor

Preface

Among all manufacturing processes, metal forming technology has a special place because it helps to produce parts of superior mechanical properties with minimum waste of material. In metal forming, the starting material has a relatively simple geometry; this material is plastically deformed in one or more operations into a product of relatively complex configuration. Forming to near net or to net shape dimensions drastically reduces metal removal requirements, resulting in significant material and energy savings. Metal forming usually requires relatively expensive tooling. Thus, the process is economically attractive when a large number of parts must be produced and/or when the mechanical properties required in the finished product can be obtained only by a forming process.

The ever-increasing costs of materials and energy and the trends toward flexible manufacturing require that metal forming processes and tooling be designed and developed with a minimum amount of trial and error. For this reason, the application of CAD/CAM (computer-aided design and manufacturing) as well as CAE (computer-aided engineering) techniques is becoming more commonly accepted in metal forming technology. The practical use of these techniques requires a thorough knowledge of the principal variables of a metal forming process and their interactions. These variables include (*a*) the flow behavior of the formed material under processing conditions; (*b*) tooling geometry and materials; (*c*) friction; (*d*) the mechanics of deformation; (*e*) the characteristics of the forming equipment; (*f*) the product geometry, tolerances, surface finish and mechanical properties; and (*g*) the effect of the process on the environment.

There are many excellent textbooks and technical papers on the basic principles of metal forming. These principles are briefly reviewed in this book, but the major emphasis is on the latest developments in the design of metal forming operations and tooling. The subject is introduced in Chapter 1 with a discussion of the position of metal forming in manufacturing. Chapter 2 considers a metal forming process as a system consisting of several variables that interact with one another. This chapter also includes an over-all review and classification of all metal forming processes. The fundamentals of plastic deformation — i.e., metal flow, flow stress of metals, and yield criteria — are discussed in Chapters 3, 4 and 5. Chapters 6 through 9 cover significant practical variables of metal forming processes such as friction, temperatures, and forming machines and their characteristics. Chapter 10 is devoted to approximate methods of analyzing simple forming operations. Chapters 11 through 17 discuss massive forming processes such as closed-die forging, hot extrusion, cold forging/extrusion, rolling (strip, plate and shapes) and drawing (rod, wire, shapes and tubes). The discussion includes the prediction of stresses and load in each process and the state of the art concerning applications of computer-aided techniques. Chapter 18 covers die materials and die manufacturing. Recent developments in metal forming technology, including CAD/CAM for die design and manufacturing, are discussed in Chapter 19. Finally, Chapter 20 reviews the latest trends in metal flow analysis and simulation. These include the application of recently developed computer programs based on the rigid viscoplastic finite element method.

This book gives a brief classification of sheet forming processes and covers only the massive forming processes in detail. It is hoped that the text will be useful to the practicing metal forming (metallurgical, mechanical or industrial) engineer as well as to undergraduate senior and first-year graduate students.

The preparation of the text has been supported in part by the Processing Science Project, funded by the Air Force Wright Aeronautical Laboratory. Additional funding for the preparation of the figures was provided by the Corporate Technical Development office of the Battelle Memorial Institute. This assistance is gratefully acknowledged. Thanks are due also to Ms. Shirley Timmons, who prepared, with considerable patience, the drafts of the manuscript.

Some of the chapters of this book are based on the results of recent research and development projects conducted at Battelle Columbus Laboratories under the sponsorship of various NASA, Air Force and Army agencies. These research studies were conducted by past and present staff of Battelle's CAD/CAM group as follows: Dr. Nuri Akgerman (Forging, Rolling, NC Machining), Mr. Carl F. Billhardt (Forging, Extrusion, NC Machining), Dr. Vijay Nagpal (Extrusion, Classification of Processes, Die Materials), Dr. G. D. Lahoti (Rolling, Material Properties), Dr. T. L. Subramanian (CAD/CAM, NC Machining), Dr. S. L. Semiatin (Die Materials, Isothermal Forging), Dr. P. S. Raghupathi (Cold Forging, Recent Developments), Dr. Aly Badawy (Forging of Gears, NC Machining) and Mr. Kevin F. Kennedy (Rolling). Many technical papers and reports prepared by these scientists were very helpful in the preparation of this book.

Contents

Metal Forming

Fundamentals and Applications

CHAPTER 1
Metal Forming Processes in Manufacturing

In a manufacturing process, a given material, usually shapeless or of a simple geometry, is transformed into a useful part. This part usually has a complex geometry with well-defined (a) shape, (b) size, (c) accuracy and tolerances, (d) appearance and (e) properties.

CLASSIFICATION OF MANUFACTURING PROCESSES

The manufacture of metal parts and assemblies can be classified, in a simplified manner, into five general areas:[1-1 to 1-3]

1. *Primary shaping* processes, such as casting, melt extrusion, die casting, and pressing of metal powder. In all these processes the material initially has no shape but obtains a well-defined geometry through the process.
2. *Metal forming* processes, such as rolling, extrusion, cold and hot forging, bending and deep drawing, where metal is formed by plastic deformation.
3. *Metal cutting* processes, such as sawing, turning, milling and broaching, where a new shape is generated by removing metal.
4. *Metal treatment* processes, such as heat treating, anodizing and surface hardening, where the part remains essentially unchanged in shape but undergoes changes in properties or appearance.
5. *Joining* processes, including (a) metallurgical joining, such as welding and diffusion bonding, and (b) mechanical joining, such as riveting, shrink fitting and mechanical assembly.

CHARACTERISTICS OF MANUFACTURING PROCESSES

There are four main characteristics of any manufacturing process — namely, geometry, tolerances, production rates, and human and environmental factors.

Geometry. Each manufacturing process is capable of producing a family of geometries. Within this family there are geometries which can be produced only with extraordinary cost and effort. For example, the forging process allows production of parts which can be easily removed from a die set, i.e., upper and lower die. By use of a "split-die" design, it is possible to manufacture forgings with undercuts and with more complex shapes.

Tolerances. No variable, especially no dimensional variable, can be produced exactly as specified by the designer. Therefore, each dimension is associated with a tolerance. Each manufacturing process allows certain dimensional tolerances and surface finishes to be obtained. The quality of these variables can always be improved by use of more sophisticated variations of the process and by means of new developments. For example, through use of the lost wax vacuum casting process it is possible to obtain much more complex parts with tighter tolerances than are possible with ordinary sand casting methods. Dimensional tolerances serve a dual purpose. First, they allow proper functioning of the manufactured part: for example, an automotive brake drum must be round, within limits, to avoid vibrations and to ensure proper functioning of the brakes. The second role of dimensional tolerances is to provide interchangeability. Without interchangeability — the ability to replace a defective part or component (a bearing, for example) with a new one, manufactured by a different supplier — modern mass production would be unthinkable.

Production Rate. The rate of production that can be attained with a given manufacturing operation is probably the most significant feature of that operation, because it indicates the economics of and the achievable productivity with that manufacturing operation. In industrialized countries, manufacturing industries represent 30 to 40% of gross national product. Consequently, manufacturing productivity, i.e., production of discrete parts, assemblies and products per unit time, is the single most important factor which influences the standard of living in a country as well as that country's competitive position in international trade in manufactured goods.

The rate of production or manufacturing productivity can be increased by improving existing manufacturing processes and by introducing new machines and new processes, all of which require new investments. However, the most important ingredient for improving productivity lies in human and managerial resources, because good decisions regarding investments (when, how much and in what) are made by people who are well trained and well motivated. As a result, the present and future manufacturing productivity in a plant, an industry or a nation depends not only on the level of investment in new plants and machinery but also on the level of training and availability of manufacturing engineers and specialists in that plant, industry or nation.

Environmental Factors. Every manufacturing process must be examined in view of (a) its effects on the environment, i.e., in terms of air, water and noise pollution, (b) its interfacing with human resources, i.e., in terms of human safety, physiological effects and psychological effects, and (c) its use of energy and material resources, particularly in view of the changing world conditions concerning scarcity of energy and materials. Consequently, the introduction and use of a manufacturing process must also be preceded by a consideration of these environmental factors.

METAL FORMING PROCESSES IN MANUFACTURING

Metal forming includes (a) massive forming processes such as forging, extrusion, rolling and drawing and (b) sheet forming processes such as brake forming, deep drawing and stretch forming. Among the group of manufacturing processes discussed earlier, metal forming represents a highly significant group of processes for producing industrial and military components and consumer goods.

A common way of classifying metal forming processes is to consider cold (room temperature) and hot (above the recrystallization temperature) forming. Most materials behave differently under different temperature conditions. Usually, the yield stress of a metal increases with increasing strain (or deformation) during cold forming and with increasing strain rate (or deformation rate) during hot forming. However, the general principles governing the forming of metals at various temperatures are basically the same; therefore, classification of forming processes based on initial material temperature does not contribute a great deal to the understanding and improvement of these processes. In fact, tool design, machinery, automation, part handling and lubrication concepts can be best considered by means of a classification based not on temperature but rather on specific input and output geometries and material and production rate conditions.

Complex geometries, in both massive and sheet forming processes, can be obtained equally well by hot or cold forming. Of course, due to the lower yield strength of the deforming material at elevated temperatures, tool stresses and machine loads are, in a relative sense, lower in hot forming than in cold forming.

Forming is especially attractive in cases where (a) the part geometry is of moderate complexity and the production volumes are large, so that tooling costs per unit product can be kept low — for example, in automotive applications; and (b) the part properties and metallurgical integrity are extremely important, in examples such as load-carrying aircraft and jet engine and turbine components.

The design, analysis and optimization of forming processes require (a) analytical knowledge regarding metal flow, stresses and heat transfer as well as (b) technological information related to lubrication, heating and cooling techniques, material handling, die design and manufacture, and forming equipment. A considerable amount of information on the general aspects of metal forming is available in the literature. Some of the books covering this subject are given as References 1-4 to 1-13 at the end of this chapter. Other books and technical articles dealing with more specific subjects are referenced at the end of each chapter of this book.

REFERENCES

1-1. Kienzle, O., "The Principles of Manufacturing Technology" (in German), Werkstattstechnik und Maschinenbau, Vol 46 (1956), No. 5, p 204.

1-2. Lange, K., "The Investigation of Metal Forming Processes as Part of a Technical System", Proc. 10th International Machine Tool Design and Research Conference, Pergamon Press, 1969, p 485.

1-3. Lahoti, G. D., and Altan, T., "Input/Output Relationships in Metal Forming", SME Paper EM75-375, Society of Manufacturing Engineers, Dearborn, MI, 1975.

1-4. Backofen, W. A., *Deformation Processing,* Addison-Wesley, 1972.
1-5. Johnson, W., and Mellor, P. B., *Engineering Plasticity,* Van Nostrand, 1978.
1-6. Slater, R. A. C., *Engineering Plasticity,* John Wiley, 1977.
1-7. Blazynski, T. Z., *Metal Forming – Tool Profiles and Flow,* John Wiley, 1976.
1-8. Prager, W., and Hodge, P. G., Jr., *Theory of Perfectly Plastic Solids,* Dover Publications, 1968.
1-9. Rowe, G. W., *Principles of Industrial Metalworking Processes,* Edward Arnold, 1977.
1-10. Thomsen, E. G., Yang, C. T., and Kobayashi, S., *Mechanics of Plastic Deformation in Metal Processing,* Macmillan Company, 1965.
1-11. Avitzur, B., *Metal Forming – Process and Analysis,* McGraw-Hill, 1968.
1-12. Dieter, G. E., Jr., *Mechanical Metallurgy,* McGraw-Hill, 1961.
1-13. Lange, K. (editor), *Study Book of Forming Technology* (in German), Vol I, II and III, Springer-Verlag, 1972.

CHAPTER 2

Variables, Classification and Description of Metal Forming Processes*

In metal forming, an initially simple part — a billet or a sheet blank, for example — is plastically deformed between tools (or dies) to obtain the desired final configuration. Thus, a simple part geometry is transformed into a complex one, whereby the tools "store" the desired geometry and impart pressure on the deforming material through the tool/material interface. Metal forming processes usually produce little or no scrap and generate the final part geometry in a very short time, usually in one or a few strokes of a press or hammer. As a result, metal forming offers potential savings in energy and material — especially in medium and large production quantities, where tool costs can be easily amortized. In addition, for a given weight, parts produced by metal forming exhibit better mechanical and metallurgical properties and reliability than do those manufactured by casting or machining.

Metal forming is an experience-oriented technology. Throughout the years, a great deal of know-how and experience has been accumulated in this field, largely by trial-and-error methods. Nevertheless, the metal forming industry has been capable of supplying sophisticated products manufactured to very rigid standards from newly developed, difficult-to-form alloys.

The physical phenomena describing a forming operation are difficult to express with quantitative relationships. The metal flow, the friction at the tool/material interface, the heat generation and transfer during plastic flow, and the relationships between microstructure/properties and process conditions are difficult to predict and analyze. Often in producing discrete parts, several forming operations (preforming) are required to transform the initial "simple" geometry into a "complex" geometry, without causing material failure or degrading material properties. Consequently, the most significant ob-

*This chapter has been reproduced from an MCIC report entitled "Variables, Classification and Description of Metal Forming Processes", by V. Nagpal and T. Altan.

jective of any method of analysis is to assist the forming engineer in the design of forming and/or preforming sequences. For a given operation (preforming or finish forming), such design essentially consists of (a) establishing the kinematic relationships (shape, velocities, strain rates, strains) between the deformed and undeformed part, i.e., predicting metal flow; (b) establishing the limits of formability or producibility, i.e., determining whether it is possible to form the part without surface or internal failure; and (c) predicting the forces and stresses necessary to execute the forming operation so that tooling and equipment can be designed or selected.

For the understanding and quantitative design and optimization of metal forming operations it is useful to (a) consider metal forming processes as a system and (b) classify these processes in a systematic way.

METAL FORMING AS A SYSTEM

A metal forming system comprises all the input variables such as the billet or blank (geometry and material), the tooling (geometry and material), the conditions at the tool/material interface, the mechanics of plastic deformation, the equipment used, the characteristics of the final product, and finally the plant environment where the process is being conducted.[2-1]

The "systems approach" in metal forming allows study of the input/output relationships and the effects of process variables on product quality and process economics. The key to a successful metal forming operation, i.e., to obtaining the desired shape and properties, is the understanding and control of metal flow. The direction of metal flow, the magnitude of deformation, and the temperatures involved greatly influence the properties of the formed components. Metal flow determines both the mechanical properties related to local deformation and the formation of defects such as cracks or folds at or below the surface. The local metal flow is in turn influenced by the process variables, which are summarized in Table 2-1.[2-1]

Material Characterization

For a given material composition and deformation/heat treatment history (microstructure), the flow stress, and the workability (or formability) in various directions (anisotropy), are the most important material variables in analysis of a metal forming process.

For a given microstructure, the flow stress, $\bar{\sigma}$, is expressed as a function of strain, $\bar{\epsilon}$; strain rate, $\dot{\bar{\epsilon}}$; and temperature, T:

$$\bar{\sigma} = f(\bar{\epsilon},\dot{\bar{\epsilon}},T) \tag{2-1}$$

To formulate the Constitutive Equation (Equation 2-1) it is necessary to conduct torsion, plane-strain compression, and uniform axisymmetric-compression tests. During any one of these tests, plastic work creates a certain increase in temperature, which must be considered in evaluating and using the test results.

Workability or formability is the capability of a material to deform without failure; it depends on (a) conditions existing during deformation processing (such as temperature, rate of deformation, stresses and strain history) and

Table 2-1. Significant variables in a deformation process

Billet material
Flow stress as a function of strain, strain rate, temperature and microstructure (constitutive equations)
Workability as a function of strain, strain rate, temperature and microstructure (forming limit curves)
Surface conditions
Thermal/physical properties
Initial conditions (composition, temperature, history/microstructure)
Effects of changes in microstructure and composition on flow stress and workability

Tooling
Geometry of tools
Surface conditions
Material/heat treatment/hardness
Temperature
Stiffness and accuracy

Conditions at tool/material interface
Lubricant type and temperature
Insulation and cooling characteristics of the interface layer
Lubricity and frictional shear stress
Characteristics related to lubricant application and removal

Deformation zone
Deformation mechanics, model used for analysis
Metal flow, velocities, strain rates, strains (kinematics)
Stresses (variation during deformation)
Temperatures (heat generation and transfer)

Equipment used
Speed/production rate
Force/energy capabilities
Rigidity and accuracy

Product
Geometry
Dimensional accuracy/tolerances
Surface finish
Microstructure, mechanical and metallurgical properties

Environment
Available manpower
Air, noise and wastewater pollution
Plant and production facilities and control

(b) material variables (such as composition, voids, inclusions and initial microstructure). In hot forming processes, temperature gradients in the deforming material (for example, due to local die chilling) also influence metal flow and failure phenomena.

Tooling and Equipment

The selection of a machine for a given process is influenced by the time, accuracy and load/energy characteristics of that machine. Optimum equipment selection requires consideration of the entire forming system, including lot size, conditions at the plant, environmental effects and maintenance requirements, as well as the requirements of the specific part and process under consideration.

The tooling variables include (a) design and geometry, (b) surface finish, (c) stiffness and (d) mechanical and thermal properties under conditions of use.

Friction and Lubrication at the Tool/Workpiece Interface

The mechanics of interface friction are very complex. One way of expressing friction quantitatively is through a friction coefficient, μ, or a friction shear factor, m. Thus, the frictional shear stress, τ, is

$$\tau = \sigma_n \mu \tag{2-2}$$

or

$$\tau = m\bar{\sigma}/\sqrt{3} = f\bar{\sigma} \tag{2-3}$$

where σ_n is the normal stress at the interface, $\bar{\sigma}$ is the flow stress of the deforming material and f is the friction factor ($= m/\sqrt{3}$). There are various methods of evaluating friction, i.e., estimating the value of μ or m. Tests most commonly used are the ring and spike tests for massive forming and the plane-strain-draw and stretch-draw tests for sheet forming.

Deformation Zone/Mechanics of Deformation

In forming, material is deformed plastically to generate the shape of the desired product. Metal flow is influenced mainly by (a) tool geometry, (b) friction conditions, (c) characteristics of the stock material and (d) thermal conditions existing in the deformation zone. The details of metal flow influence the quality and properties of the formed product and the force and energy requirements of the process. The mechanics of deformation, i.e., the metal flow, strains, strain rates and stresses, can be investigated by using one of the approximate methods of analysis (e.g., finite element, matrix, finite difference, slab or upper bound).

Product Geometry and Properties

The macro- and microgeometry of the product, i.e., its dimensions and surface finish, are influenced by process variables. The processing conditions (temperature, strain and strain rate) determine the microstructural variations taking place during deformation and often influence final product properties. Consequently, a realistic systems approach must include consideration of (a) the relationships between properties and microstructure of the formed material and (b) the quantitative influences of process conditions and heat treatment schedules on microstructural variations.

CLASSIFICATION AND BRIEF DESCRIPTION OF METAL FORMING PROCESSES

The metal forming processes may be classified into two broad categories:

1. Massive forming processes (Table 2-2).
2. Sheet-metal forming processes (Table 2-3).

Table 2-2. Classification of massive forming processes

Forging	Rolling	Extrusion	Drawing
Closed-die forging with flash	Sheet rolling	Nonlubricated hot extrusion	Drawing
Closed-die forging without flash	Shape rolling	Lubricated direct hot extrusion	Drawing with rolls
Coining	Tube rolling	Hydrostatic extrusion	Ironing
Electro-upsetting	Ring rolling		Tube sinking
Forward extrusion forging	Rotary tube piercing		
Backward extrusion forging	Gear rolling		
Hobbing	Roll forging		
Isothermal forging	Cross rolling		
Nosing	Surface rolling		
Open-die forging	Shear forming (flow turning)		
Orbital forging	Tube reducing		
P/M forging			
Radial forging			
Upsetting			

Table 2-3. Classification of sheet metal forming processes

Bending and straight flanging	**Deep recessing and flanging**
Brake bending	Spinning (and roller flanging)
Roll bending	Deep drawing
Surface contouring of sheet	Rubber pad forming
Contour stretch forming (Stretch forming)	Marform process
Androforming	Rubber diaphragm hydroforming
Age forming	**Shallow recessing**
Creep forming	Dimpling
Die-quench forming	Drop hammer forming
Bulging	Electromagnetic forming
Vacuum forming	Explosive forming
Linear contouring	Joggling
Linear stretch forming (Stretch forming)	
Linear roll forming (Roll forming)	

In both cases, the surfaces of the deforming material and of the tools are in contact, and friction between them has a major influence on the process. In massive forming, the input material is in billet, rod or slab form, and a considerable increase in the surface-to-volume ratio occurs in the formed part. In sheet forming, a sheet blank is plastically deformed into a three-dimensional object without any significant changes in sheet thickness and surface characteristics.

Processes which fall under the category of massive forming processes have the following distinguishing features:

- The workpiece undergoes large plastic deformation, resulting in an appreciable change in shape or cross section.
- The portion of the workpiece undergoing permanent (plastic) deformation is generally much larger than the portion undergoing elastic deformation; therefore, elastic recovery after deformation is negligible.

Examples of massive forming processes are extrusion, forging, rolling and drawing.

The characteristics of sheet-metal forming processes are:

- The workpiece is a sheet or a part fabricated from a sheet.
- The deformation usually causes significant changes in shape, but not in cross section, of the sheet.
- In some cases, the magnitudes of permanent plastic and recoverable elastic deformations are comparable; therefore, elastic recovery or springback may be significant.

Examples of processes which fall under the category of sheet-metal forming processes are brake forming, deep drawing, stretch forming and rubber forming.

Some processes can fall under both categories (sheet-metal and massive forming), depending on the configuration of the workpiece. For example, in reducing the thickness of a tube, if the starting workpiece is a thick-wall tube, the reduction (ironing) process would be classified as a massive forming process, whereas if the starting workpiece is a thin can, the ironing process could be considered to be a sheet-metal forming process.

Most significant metal forming processes are listed in Tables 2-2 and 2-3. Massive forming processes, given in Table 2-2, are briefly described in Figures 2-1 to 2-32. Sheet forming processes, given in Table 2-3, are described in Figures 2-33 to 2-50. The description given in each figure also includes the equipment used and the applications of the process.* From a metal deformation point of view, if some processes or their variations are similar, they are grouped under one title, specified as "process variations".

*The descriptions of various metal forming processes and the schematics used to illustrate them have been collected from various sources, which are given at the end of this chapter as References 2-2 to 2-22.

FIGURE 2-1. CLOSED-DIE FORGING WITHOUT FLASH

Definition: In this process, a billet with carefully controlled volume is deformed (hot or cold) by a punch in order to fill a die cavity without any loss of material. The punch and the die may be made of one or several pieces.

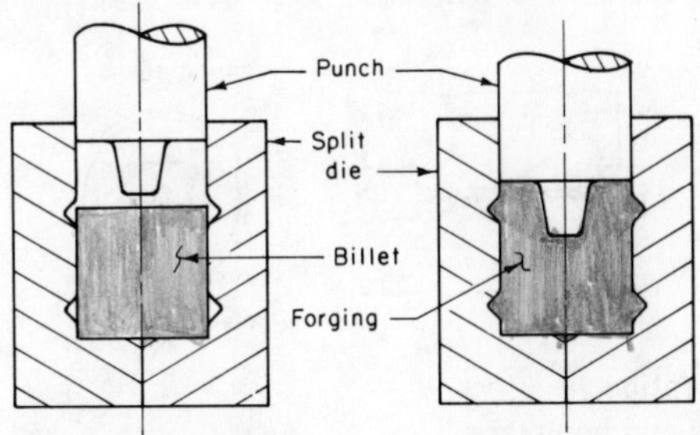

Figure: Closed-die forging without flash

Equipment: Hydraulic presses, multiram mechanical presses

Materials: Carbon and alloy steels, copper alloys, aluminum alloys

Process Variations: Core forging, precision forging, cold and warm forging, PM forging

Applications: Precision forgings; hollow forgings; fittings, elbows, Tee's, etc.

FIGURE 2-2. CLOSED-DIE FORGING WITH FLASH

Definition: In this process, a billet is formed (hot) in dies (usually with two halves) such that the flow of metal from the die cavity is restricted. The excess material is extruded through a restrictive narrow gap and appears as flash around the forging at the die parting line.

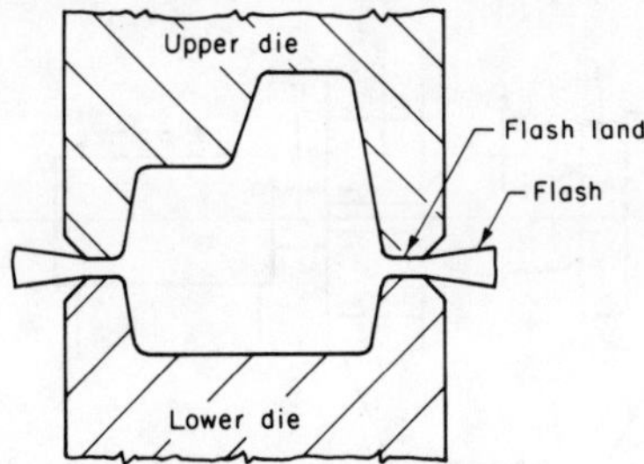

Figure: Closed-die forging with flash

Equipment: Anvil and counterblow hammers, hydraulic, mechanical and screw presses

Materials: Aluminum alloys, magnesium alloys, beryllium, copper alloys, carbon and alloy steels, stainless steels, nickel alloys, titanium and titanium alloys, iron-, cobalt- and nickel-base superalloys, niobium and niobium alloys, tantalum and tantalum alloys, molybdenum and molybdenum alloys, tungsten alloys (all forgeable materials)

Process Variations: Closed-die forging with lateral flash, closed-die forging with longitudinal flash, closed-die forging without flash

Applications: Production of forgings for automobiles, trucks, tractors, off-highway equipment, aircraft, railroad and mining equipment; general mechanical industry and energy-related engineering production

FIGURE 2-3. COINING

Definition: Coining is a closed-die forming operation, usually performed cold, in which all surfaces of the work are confined or restrained, resulting in a well-defined imprint of the die on the workpiece. It is also a *restriking* operation used to sharpen or change an existing radius or profile.

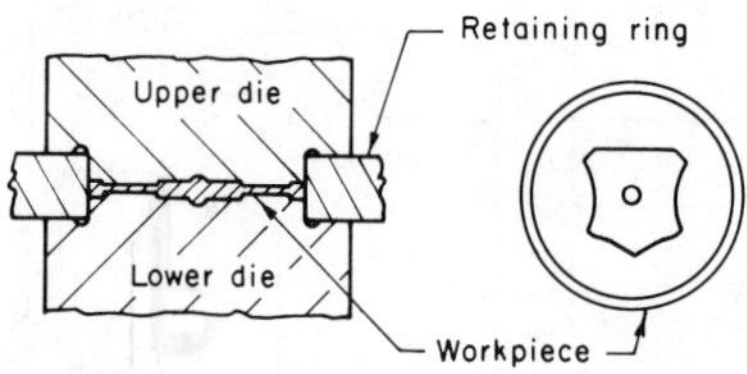

Figure: Coining operation

Equipment: Presses and hammers

Materials: Carbon and alloy steels, stainless steels, heat-resisting alloys, aluminum alloys, copper alloys, silver and gold alloys

Process Variations: Coining without flash, coining with flash, coining in closed die, sizing

Applications: Metallic coins; decorative items, such as patterned tableware, medallions and metal buttons; sizing of automobile and aircraft engine components

FIGURE 2-4. ELECTRO-UPSETTING

Definition: Electro-upsetting is the hot forming process of gathering a large amount of material at one end of a round bar by heating the bar end electrically and pushing it against a flat anvil or shaped die cavity.

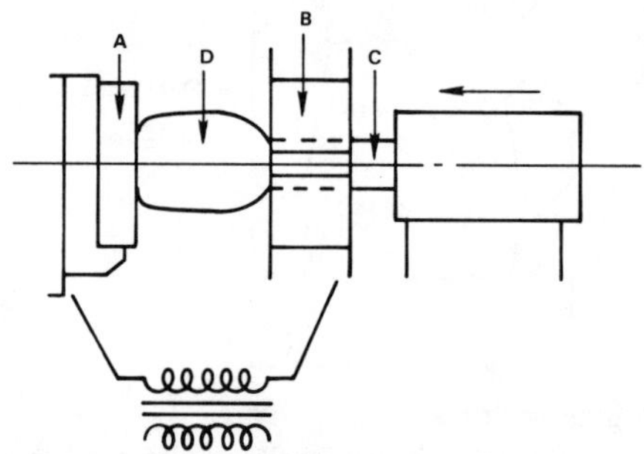

Figure: Electro-upsetting: a = anvil electrode
b = gripping electrode
c = workpiece
d = upset end of workpiece

Equipment: Electric upsetters

Material: Carbon and alloy steels, titanium

Application: Preforms for finished forgings

FIGURE 2-5. FORWARD EXTRUSION FORGING

Definition: In this process, a punch compresses a billet (hot or cold) confined in a container so that the billet material flows through a die in the same direction as the punch.

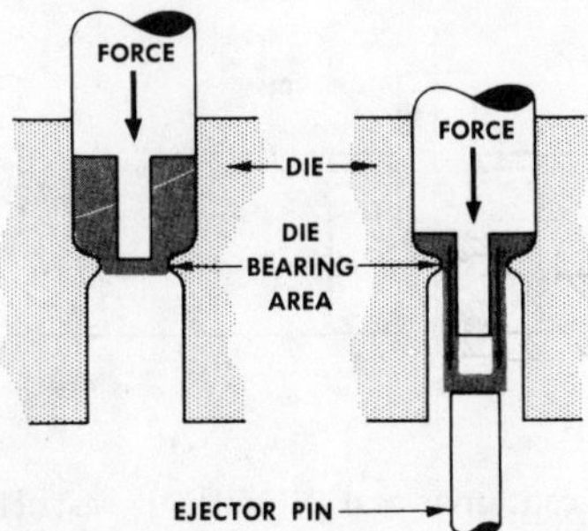

Figure: Forward extrusion forging

Equipment: Mechanical and hydraulic presses

Materials: Carbon and alloy steels, aluminum alloys, copper alloys, magnesium alloys, titanium alloys

Process Variations: Closed-die forging without flash, PM forging

Applications: Stepped or tapered-diameter solid shafts; tubular parts with multiple-diameter cylindrical, conical or other nonround holes

FIGURE 2-6. BACKWARD EXTRUSION FORGING

Definition: In this process, a moving punch applies a steady pressure to a slug (hot or cold) confined in a closed die, and forces the metal to flow around the punch in a direction opposite the direction of punch travel.

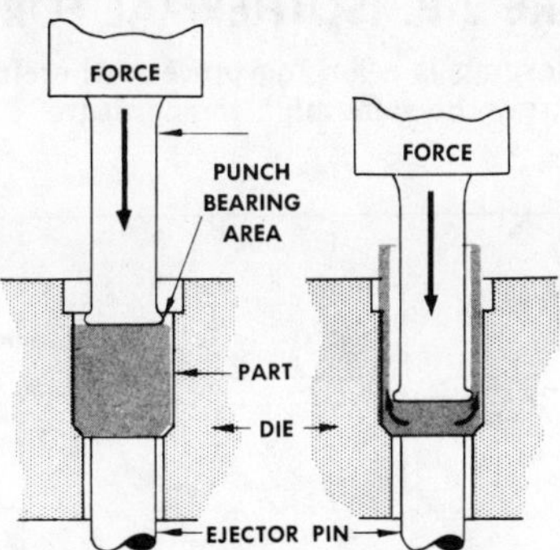

Figure: Backward extrusion forging

Equipment: Mechanical and hydraulic presses

Materials: Carbon and alloy steels, aluminum alloys, copper alloys, magnesium alloys, titanium alloys

Process Variations: Closed-die forging without flash, PM forging

Applications: Hollow parts having a closed end; cupped parts with holes that are cylindrical, conical or of other shapes

FIGURE 2-7. HOBBING

Definition: Hobbing is the process of indenting or coining an impression into a cold or hot die block by pressing with a punch.

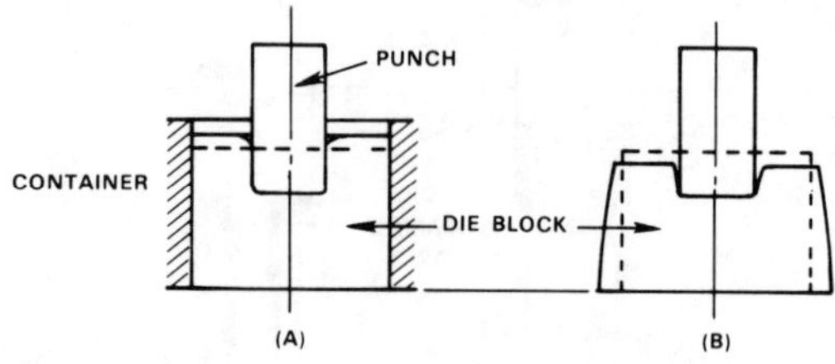

Figure: Hobbing (A) in a container and (B) without restriction
Equipment: Hydraulic presses, hammers
Materials: Carbon and alloy steels
Process Variations: Die hobbing, die typing
Application: Manufacture of dies and molds with relatively shallow impressions

FIGURE 2-8. ISOTHERMAL FORGING

Definition: Isothermal forging is a forging process wherein the dies and the forging stock are at approximately the same high temperature.

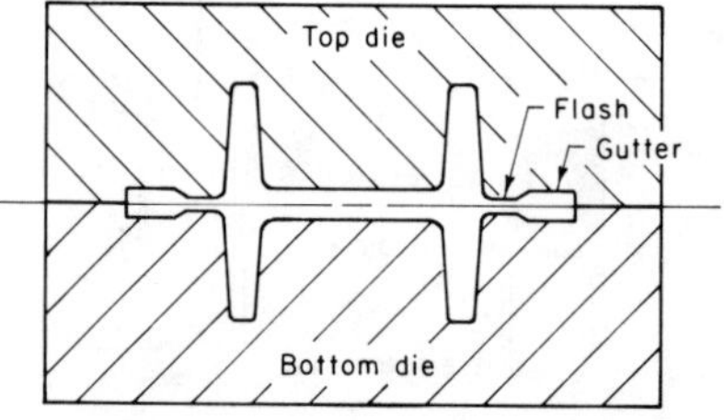

Figure: Isothermal forging with dies and workpiece at approximately the same temperature
Equipment: Hydraulic presses
Materials: Titanium alloys, aluminum alloys
Process Variations: Closed-die forging with or without flash, PM forging
Application: Net- and near-net-shape forgings for the aircraft industry

FIGURE 2-9. NOSING

Definition: Nosing is a hot or cold forming process in which the open end of a shell or tubular component is closed by axial pressing with a shaped die.

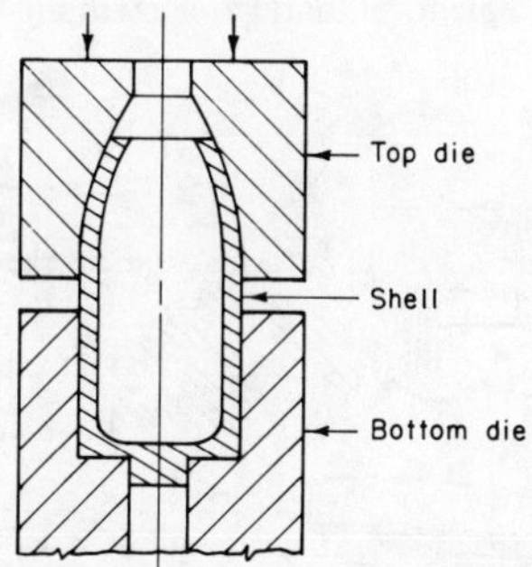

Figure: Nosing of a shell

Equipment: Mechanical and hydraulic presses, hammers

Materials: Carbon and alloy steels, aluminum alloys, titanium alloys

Process Variations: Tube sinking, tube expanding

Applications: Forming of open ends of ammunition shells; forming of gas pressure containers

FIGURE 2-10. OPEN-DIE FORGING

Definition: Open-die forging is a hot forming process in which metal is shaped by hammering or pressing between flat or simple contoured dies.

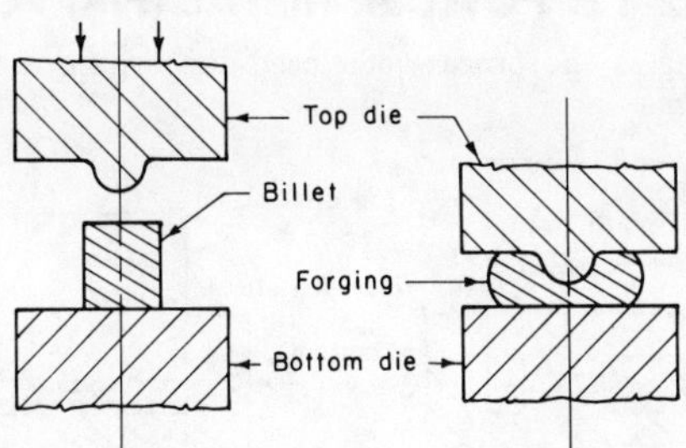

Figure: Open-die forging

Equipment: Hydraulic presses, hammers

Materials: Carbon and alloys steels, aluminum alloys, titanium alloys, all forgeable metals

Process Variations: Slab forging, shaft forging, mandrel forging, ring forging, upsetting between flat or curved dies, drawing out

Applications: Forging ingots; large and bulky forgings; preforms for finished forgings

FIGURE 2-11. ORBITAL FORGING

Definition: Orbital forging is the process of forming shaped parts by incrementally forging (hot or cold) a slug between an orbiting upper die and a nonrotating lower die. The lower die is raised axially toward the upper die, which is fixed axially but whose axis makes orbital, spiral, planetary or straight-line motions.

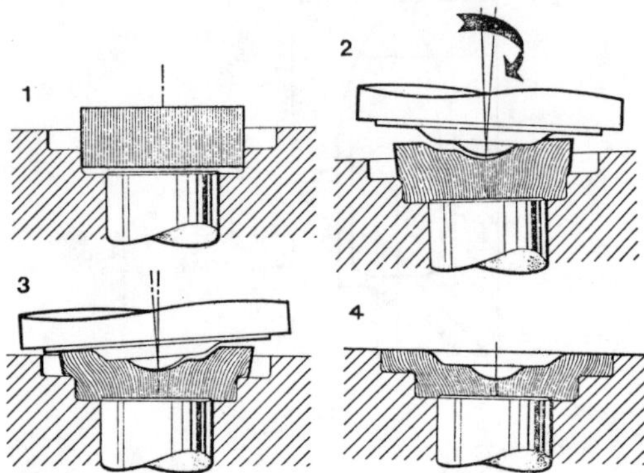

Figure: Various stages in orbital forging process

Equipment: Orbital forging presses

Materials: Carbon and low-alloy steels, stainless steels, aluminum alloys and brasses, all forgeable materials

Process Variations: This process is also called rotary forging, swing forging or rocking die forging. In some cases, the lower die may also rotate.

Applications: Bevel gears, claw clutch parts, wheel disks with hubs, bearing rings, rings of various contours, bearing-end covers

FIGURE 2-12. POWDER METAL (PM) FORGING

Definition: PM forging is the process of closed-die forging (hot or cold) of sintered powder metal preforms.

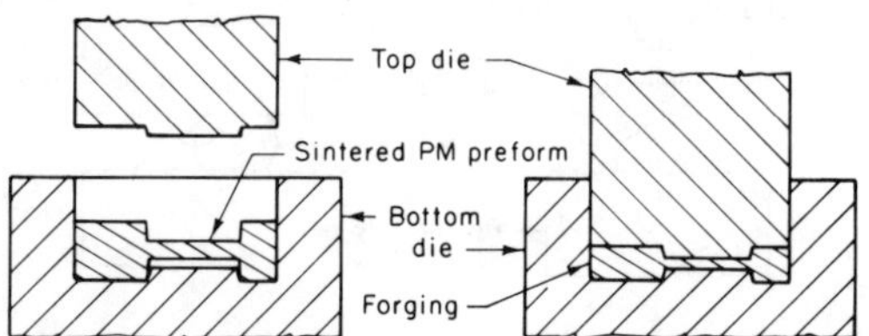

Figure: Forging of a PM preform

Equipment: Hydraulic presses, mechanical presses

Materials: Carbon and alloy steels, stainless steels, cobalt-base alloys, aluminum alloys, titanium alloys, nickel-base alloys

Process Variations: Closed-die forging without flash, closed-die forging with flash

Applications: Forgings and finished parts for automobiles, trucks and off-highway equipment

FIGURE 2-13. RADIAL FORGING

Definition: This hot or cold forming process utilizes two or more radially moving anvils, or dies, for producing solid or tubular components with constant or varying cross sections along their length.

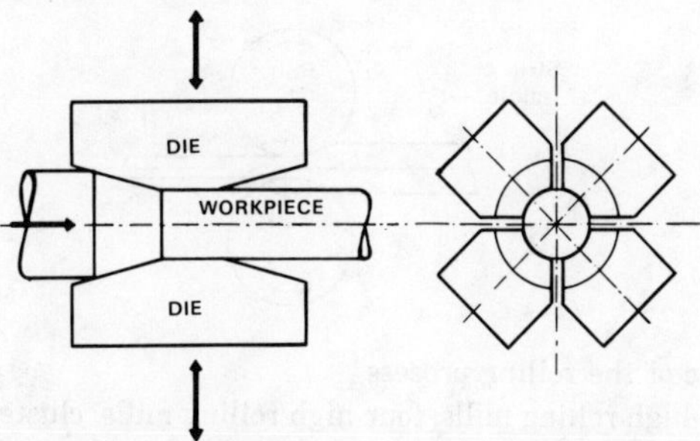

Figure: Radial forging of a shaft

Equipment: Radial forging machines

Materials: Carbon and alloy steels, titanium alloys, tungsten, beryllium and high-temperature superalloys

Process Variations: Rotary swaging

Applications: Reducing the diameters of ingots and bars, forging of stepped shafts and axles, forging of gun and rifle barrels, production of tubular components with and without internal profiles

FIGURE 2-14. UPSETTING

Definition: Upsetting is the process of forming metal (hot or cold) so that the cross-sectional area of a portion, or all, of the stock is increased.

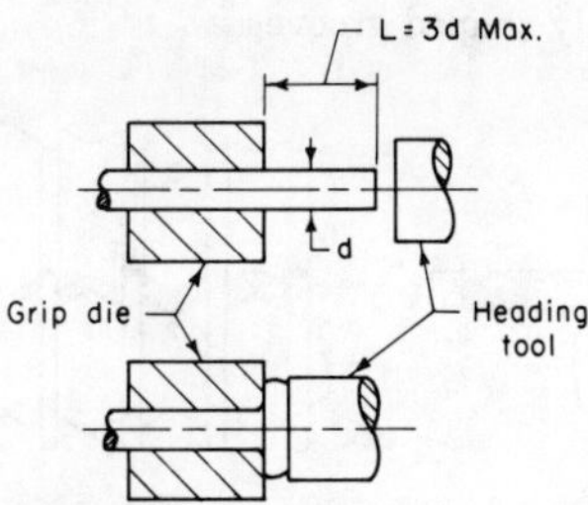

Figure: Upsetting with flat-heading tool

Equipment: Hammers; upsetting machines; hydraulic, mechanical and screw presses

Materials: Carbon and alloy steels, stainless steels, all forgeable materials

Process Variations: Electro-upsetting, upset forging, open-die forging

Applications: Finished forgings, including nuts and bolts; flanged shafts; preforms for finished forgings

FIGURE 2-15. SHEET ROLLING

Definition: Sheet rolling is a hot or cold forming process for reducing the cross-sectional area of the stock with the use of rotating rolls. In general, the rolled material elongates and spreads simultaneously while the cross-sectional area is reduced.

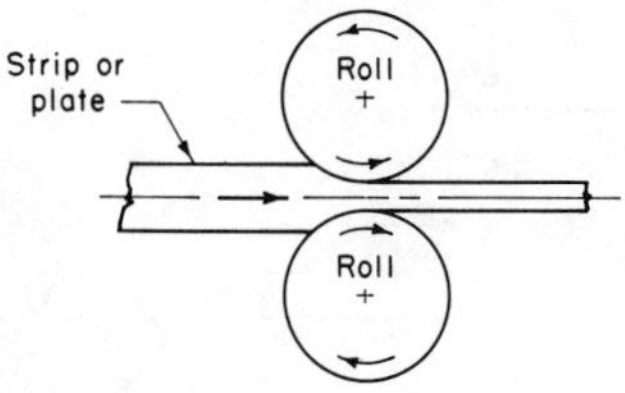

Figure: Schematic of the rolling process

Equipment: Two-high rolling mills, four-high rolling mills, cluster rolling mills, planetary rolling mills

Materials: Carbon and alloy steels, aluminum alloys, copper alloys, titanium alloys, nickel alloys

Process Variations: Strip rolling, plate rolling, slab rolling, temper rolling

Applications: Strip, sheet and plate

FIGURE 2-16. SHAPE ROLLING

Definition: Shape rolling is a cold or hot forming process for reducing as well as shaping the cross section of the metal stock by passing it through a series of rotating sets of rolls with appropriately shaped grooves.

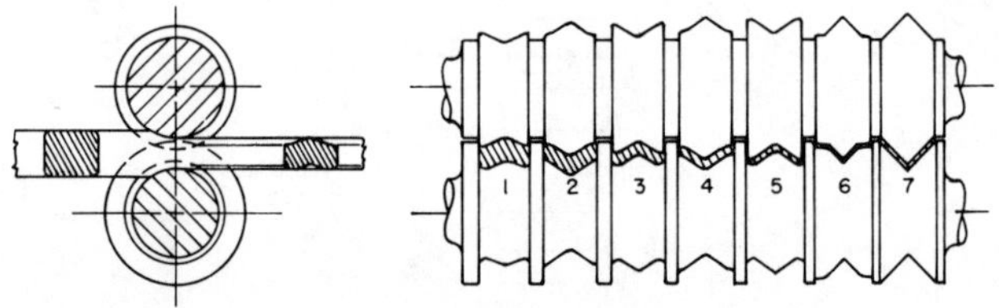

Figure: Roll passes for rolling an angle (L) shape

Equipment: Two-high rolling mills

Materials: Carbon and alloy steels, tool steels, 200 and 400 series stainless steels; superalloys, such as the various Inconels, Hastelloy-X, Waspaloy and A-286; nonferrous materials such as titanium, copper and copper-base alloys

Process Variations: Form rolling

Application: Structural parts, such as T-, L- and U-sections; airfoil sections for blades

FIGURE 2-17. TUBE ROLLING

Definition: Tube rolling is the process of reducing the cross section and/or the diameter of a tube by passing it through powered rolls.

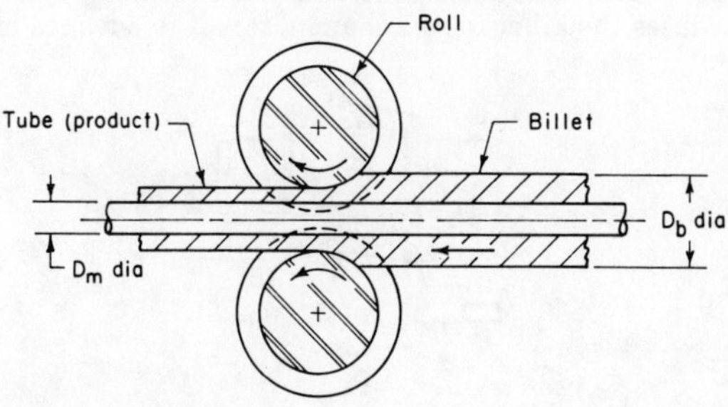

Figure: Tube rolling with a mandrel
Equipment: Two-high rolling mills
Materials: Carbon and alloy steels, copper alloys, aluminum alloys
Process Variations: Tube rolling with mandrel, tube rolling without mandrel
Application: Seamless tubes for various industries

FIGURE 2-18. RING ROLLING

Definition: Ring rolling is a process whereby a hollow circular blank (cold or hot) is formed into a ring. A main roll presses on the outside diameter of the blank, which is supported by a mandrel on the inside diameter. Shaped cross sections are obtained by appropriate contouring of the mandrel and the roll. The height of the ring is controlled by auxiliary rolls.

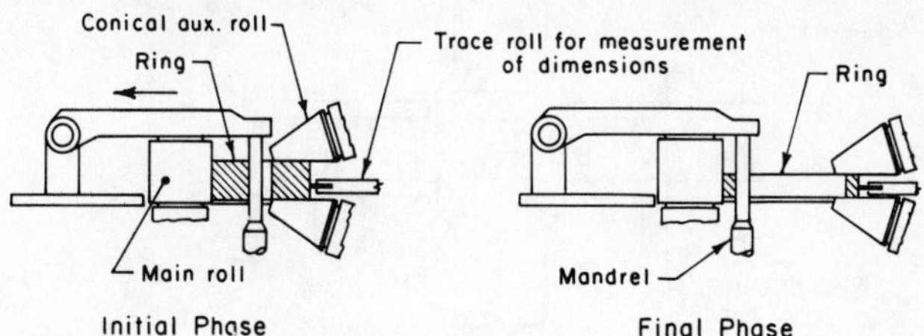

Figure: Principles of ring rolling
Equipment: Ring rolling machines or mills
Materials: Carbon and alloy steels, aluminum alloys, titanium alloys, nickel alloys
Applications: Rings of all types, flanges, bearing races, gear rims, wheel bearings, commutator rings, rings for jet engines, nuclear reactor components

FIGURE 2-19. ROTARY TUBE PIERCING

Definition: In this process, a hollow is formed by peripherally rolling a cylindrical hot billet over a conical piercer point. The billet is driven by a pair of cone-shape rolls, set askew to the longitudinal axis of the billet. The frictional load between the rolls and the billet causes the billet to rotate and forces it to advance longitudinally over the piercer point.

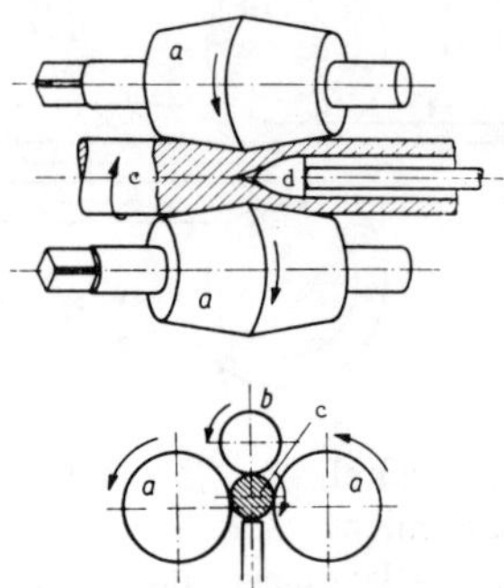

Figure: Rotary tube piercing process: a. double-conical working rolls
b. guide roll
c. billet
d. conical piercer point

Equipment: Tube piercing mills
Materials: Carbon and alloy steels
Process Variations: Mannesman tube piercing process
Application: Manufacture of seamless tubes

FIGURE 2-20. GEAR ROLLING

Definition: Gear rolling is the process of forming gear teeth on a hot or cold blank by rolling it between driven toothed die wheels.

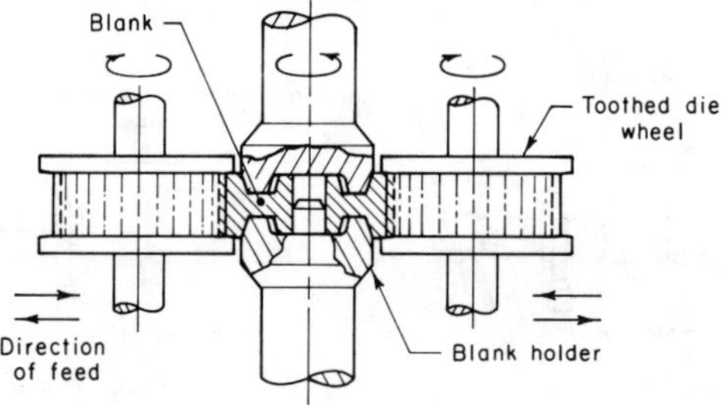

Figure: Schematic of gear rolling process
Equipment: Gear rolling machines
Materials: Carbon and alloy steels
Process Variations: Sprocket rolling, thread rolling
Applications: Gears, sprockets

FIGURE 2-21. ROLL FORGING OR REDUCER ROLLING

Definition: In this process, the desired shape is produced by rolling the hot billet between two rotating dies having appropriately profiled grooves.

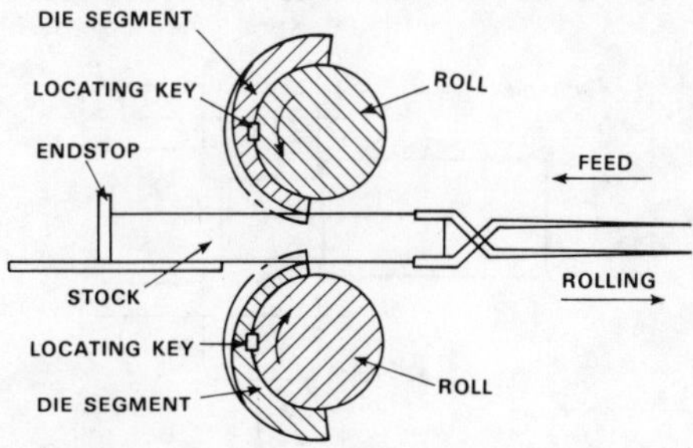

Figure: Schematic of the roll forging operation
Equipment: Reducer rolls
Materials: Carbon and alloy steels, aluminum alloys
Application: Preforms for forging long and thin parts

FIGURE 2-22. CROSS ROLLING OR WEDGE ROLLING

Definition: In this process, a round billet is inserted transversely between rolls having appropriate impressions or between straight wedge-shape tools. When rolls are used, the rolls rotate in the same direction and drive the billet. In cross rolling with two straight wedge-shape tools, the tools move in opposite directions and rotate and form the billet.

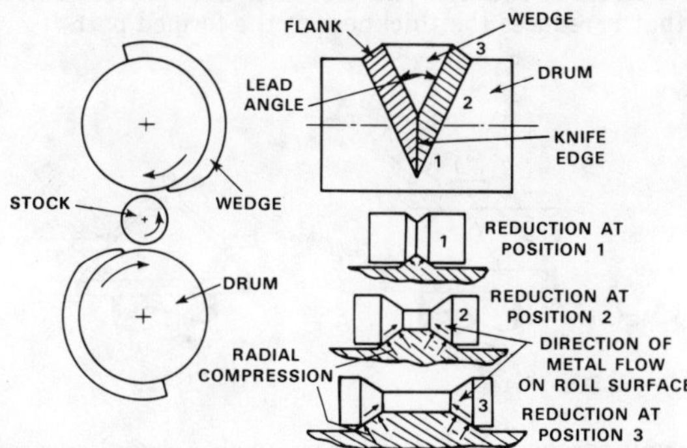

Figure: Principle of operation in cross rolling
Equipment: Two- and three-roll cross rolling machines, transverse rolling machines
Materials: Carbon and alloy steels, aluminum alloys, brasses
Process Variations: Transverse rolling
Applications: Preforms for finish forging; axially symmetrical parts, such as stepped shafts with or without tapers; cluster gear blanks

FIGURE 2-23. SURFACE ROLLING

Definition: In this process, two rolls are pressed radially against a rotating part and moved axially to smooth and polish the part surface. At the same time, compressive stresses are introduced on the part surface to improve fatigue life.

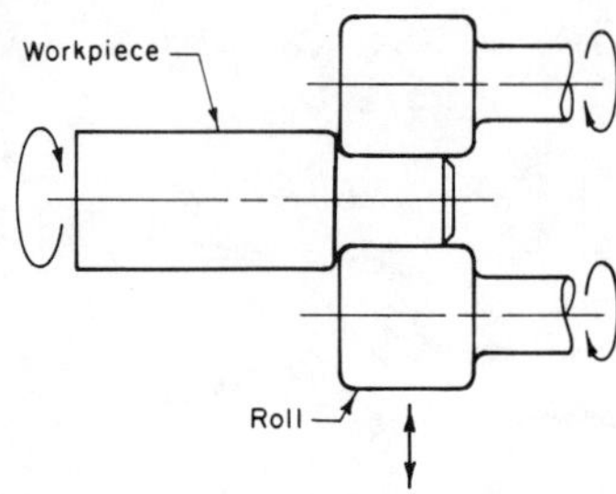

Figure: Schematic of surface rolling

Equipment: Surface rolling machines, lathes with special attachments

Materials: Steels, aluminum alloys, brasses

Application: Surface polishing of shafts and bearing surfaces

FIGURE 2-24. SHEAR FORMING (FLOW TURNING)

Definition: Shear forming is a process for hot or cold seamless shaping of dished parts by the combined forces of rotation and pressure. This process differs from spinning principally in that it reduces the thickness of the formed part.

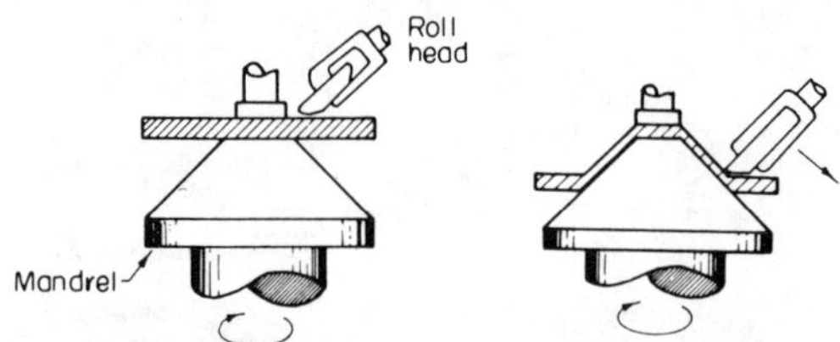

Figure: Shear forming from a plate: (left) start, (right) partially or completely formed part

Equipment: Shear forming machines

Materials: Steels, aluminum alloys, copper, titanium alloys

Process Variations: Cone shear forming, tube shear forming, roll extrusion

Applications: Hardware items such as tumblers; components used in the aerospace industry, such as rocket noses; dish-shape parts produced in small and moderate quantities

FIGURE 2-25. TUBE REDUCING (ROCKING)

Definition: In this process, the cross-sectional area of a tube is reduced by rolling the tube over a tapered mandrel using semicircular dies with tapering grooves. These dies do not rotate, but rock back and forth. The mandrel and the tube are rotated between strokes and move forward at the same time.

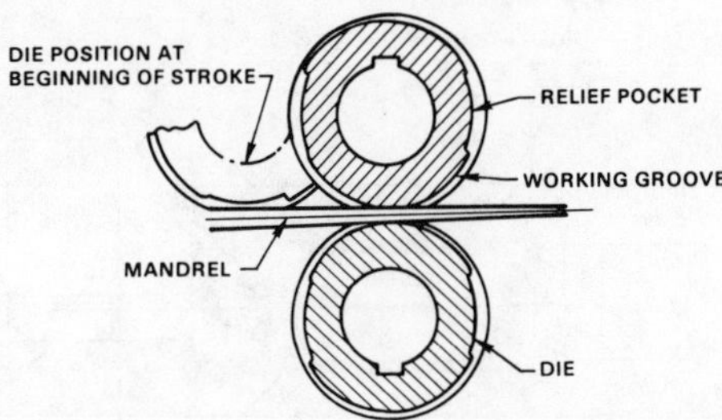

Figure: Die, mandrel, and tube relationship during tube reducing

Equipment: Tube reducing mills, "HPTR" cold tube reducers

Materials: Carbon and alloy steels, titanium alloys, tantalum alloys, niobium alloys

Applications: Widely used as a process intermediate between extrusion of the blank and the final drawing operation, or as a tube-finishing process

FIGURE 2-26. NONLUBRICATED HOT EXTRUSION

Definition: In this process, the product of desired cross section is obtained by forcing a heated billet through a die without lubricating the billet, the container or the die. In the direct extrusion process, the product is extruded in the direction of ram movement. When the product is extruded in a direction opposite that of ram travel, the process is called indirect extrusion.

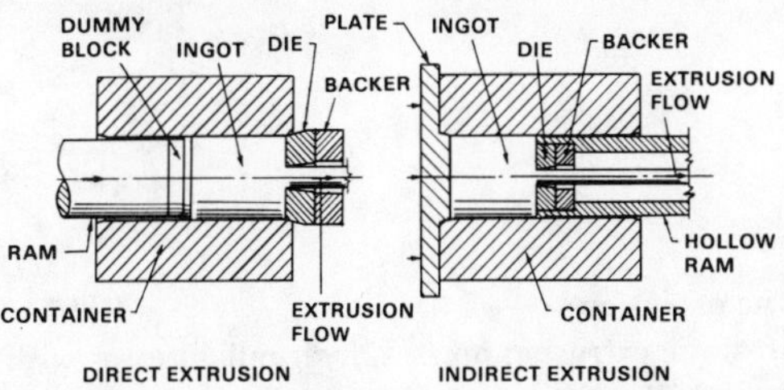

Figure: Tooling and metal flow for direct and indirect extrusion processes

Equipment: Hydraulic presses

Materials: Copper alloys, lead alloys, aluminum alloys, magnesium alloys, zinc alloys

Applications: Extrusion of rod, tube and complex shapes

FIGURE 2-27. LUBRICATED DIRECT HOT EXTRUSION

Definition: In this process, the heated billet is forced through a die, using some form of lubrication, to obtain a product of desired cross section. Glass is the most widely used lubricant for extruding long lengths from steels and high-temperature alloys on a production basis.

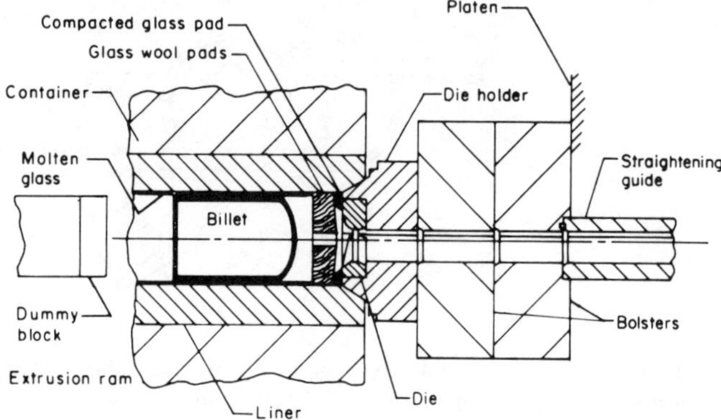

Figure: Hot extrusion setup using glass lubrication

Equipment: Hydraulic and mechanical presses

Materials: Carbon and alloy steels, titanium alloys, beryllium, niobium alloys, tantalum alloys, tungsten alloys, molybdenum alloys, nickel- and cobalt-base superalloys

Process Variations: Sejournet process, hot extrusion using graphite-based greases

Applications: Extrusion of bar, tube and other complex sections

FIGURE 2-28. HYDROSTATIC EXTRUSION

Definition: Hydrostatic extrusion is the process of extruding a cold or warm billet through a die wherein a pressurized fluid, in place of the ram, is used for pushing the billet.

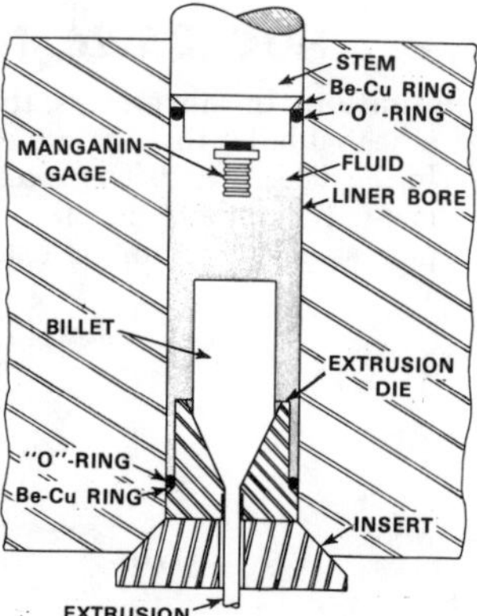

Figure: Hydrostatic extrusion

Equipment: Hydrostatic extrusion presses, hydraulic presses with special tooling

Materials: Carbon and alloy steels, aluminum alloys, magnesium alloys, copper alloys, clad materials, high-temperature and refractory materials, composites

Process Variations: Hydrafilm (thick-film) extrusion, continuous hydrostatic extrusion

Applications: This process is in the developmental stage. Its potential applications are: wire, tube and sections of aluminum alloys and clad materials; steel tubing and complex profiles, such as gears; copper tubes and sections; extrusion of brittle materials.

FIGURE 2-29. DRAWING

Definition: Drawing is the process of reducing the cross-sectional area and/or the shape of a rod, bar, tube or wire (cold or hot) by pulling through a die.

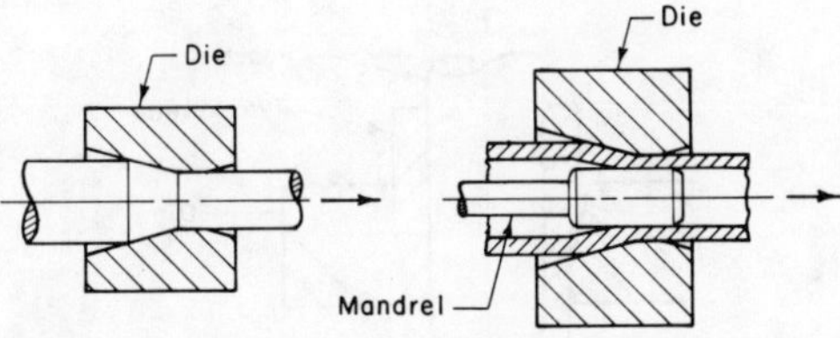

Figure: Drawing of (left) rod or wire and (right) tube

Equipment: Bull blocks, draw benches, wiredrawing machines

Materials: Carbon steels, alloy steels (including stainless steels), copper and copper alloys, aluminum and aluminum alloys, titanium alloys, niobium alloys, tungsten alloys, tantalum alloys, cobalt alloys, beryllium, niobium, zircaloy-2, TD nickel, chromium

Process Variations: Rod drawing, wiredrawing, tube drawing with stationary mandrel, tube drawing with floating mandrel, drawing of shapes

Applications: Round and shaped wire, rod, and tube

FIGURE 2-30. DRAWING THROUGH ROLLS

Definition: This process consists of reducing the cross-sectional area of a rod, bar, strip, tube or wire (cold or hot) by pulling through undriven rolls.

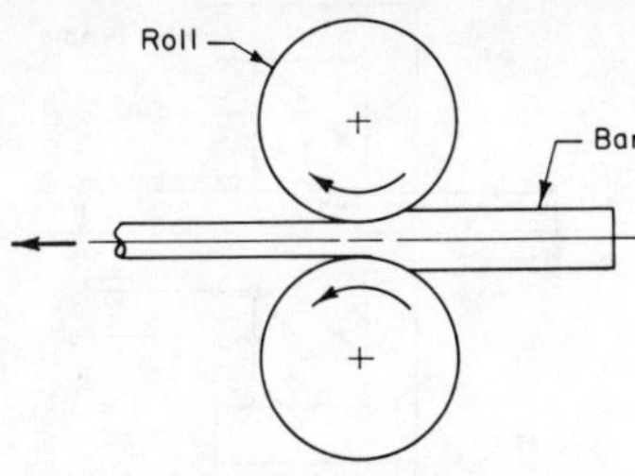

Figure: Drawing of a bar through rolls

Equipment: Drawbenches, wire shaping mills

Materials: Carbon steels, alloy steels, copper and copper alloys, aluminum and aluminum alloys

Process Variations: Steckel rolling; drawing of tubes through rolls with floating mandrel, with moving mandrel or without mandrel

Applications: Rod, bar, strip, tube and wire products for various uses

FIGURE 2-31. IRONING (OR DRAWING)

Definition: Ironing is the process of smoothing and thinning the wall of a shell or cup (cold or hot) by forcing the shell through a die with a punch.

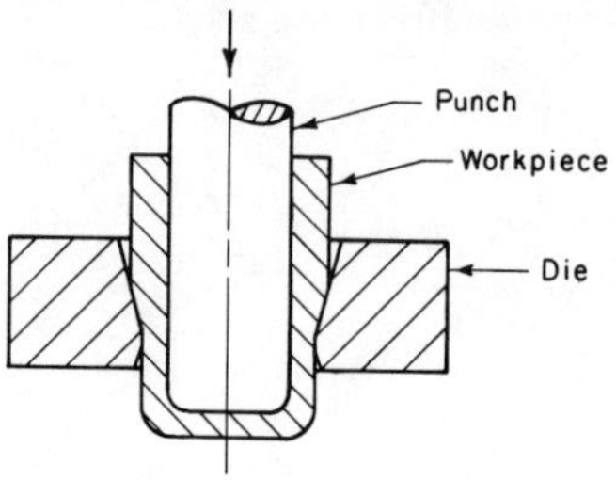

Figure: Schematic of ironing

Equipment: Mechanical presses, hydraulic presses

Materials: Carbon and alloy steels, aluminum and aluminum alloys, titanium alloys

Applications: Shells/cups for various uses

FIGURE 2-32. TUBE SINKING

Definition: Tube sinking is the process of sizing the outside diameter of a tube by drawing the tube (cold or hot) through a die without supporting the tube internally with a mandrel.

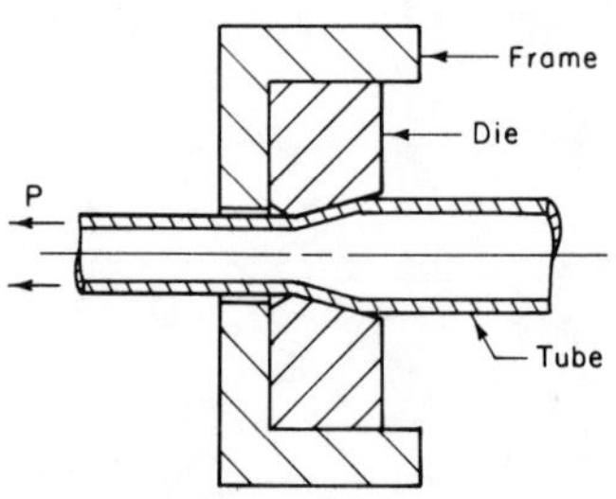

Figure: Tube sinking process

Equipment: Drawbenches

Materials: Carbon steels, alloy steels (including stainless steels), copper and copper alloys

Application: Tubes

FIGURE 2-33. BRAKE BENDING

Definition: Brake bending is a forming operation widely used for forming flat sheets into linear sections, such as angles, channels and hats. There are two typical brake-forming setups: air bending and die bending. In air bending, the workpiece is supported only at the outer edges so that the length of the ram stroke determines the bend angle of the part. In die bending, the sheet is forced into a female die cavity of the required part angle.

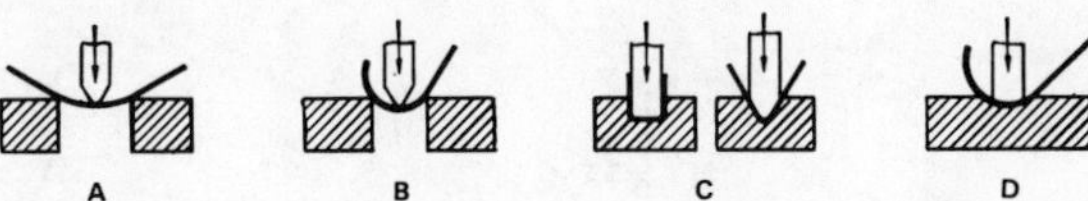

Figure: Typical brake-bending operations: (A) air bending, (B) air rounding, (C) die bending, (D) die rounding

Equipment: Mechanical press brakes, hydraulic press brakes

Materials: Carbon and alloy steels, aluminum alloys, titanium alloys, iron-, nickel- and cobalt-base superalloys, molybdenum alloys, beryllium and tungsten

Process Variations: Brake forming with elastic (urethane) dies, folding (bending of sheet held on one side only)

Application: Production of linear shapes from sheet and plate

FIGURE 2-34. ROLL BENDING (THREE-ROLL FORMING)

Definition: Roll bending gives a curvature to a sheet, bar or shaped section by bending it between two or three cylindrical rolls that can be adjusted.

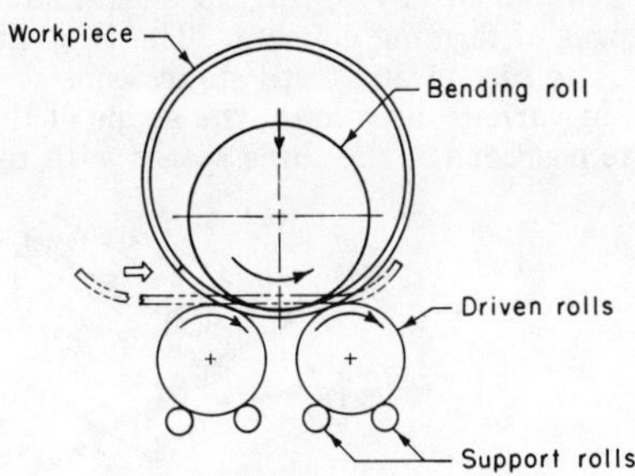

Figure: Roll bending

Equipment: Roll-bending machines, pinch-roll-type machines, pyramid-roll-type machines

Materials: Carbon and alloy steels, aluminum alloys, titanium alloys

Process Variations: Roller leveling

Applications: Cylinders for pressure tanks; boilers; corrugated pipe; cones for hoppers; regular and irregular shapes from structural sections for submarines, aircraft and nuclear reactors

FIGURE 2-35. ROLL FORMING (CONTOUR ROLL FORMING)

Definition: This process is used to produce long components of various cross sections. The sheet metal is formed by passing it through a succession of progressively shaped power-driven contoured rolls.

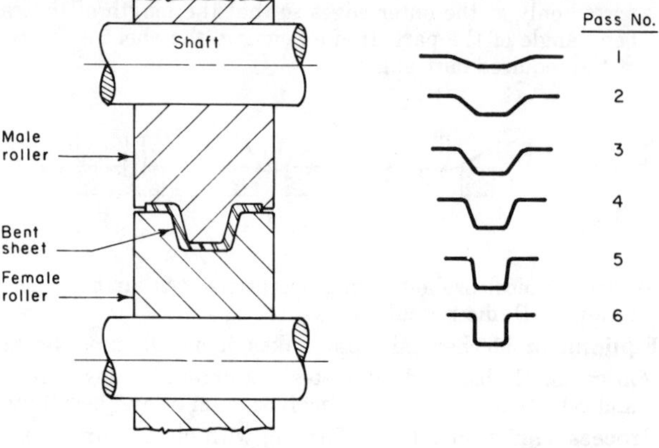

Figure: Roll forming

Equipment: Roll forming machines

Materials: Carbon and alloy steels, aluminum alloys, titanium alloys, iron-, nickel- and cobalt-base superalloys, molybdenum alloys, niobium alloys

Process Variations: Edge rolling

Application: Production of large quantities of complex structural shapes from sheet

FIGURE 2-36. ANDROFORMING

Definition: Androforming is used to form sheet-metal parts with compound curvatures. The contours are established by pulling the sheet material with a set of gripper jaws through three stages of forming elements. The first stage consists of a pair of straight forming dies. The second and third stages consist of contoured dies which can be cam controlled in various directions. The shape of the formed sheet is determined by adjusting the positions of the three stages with respect to each other.

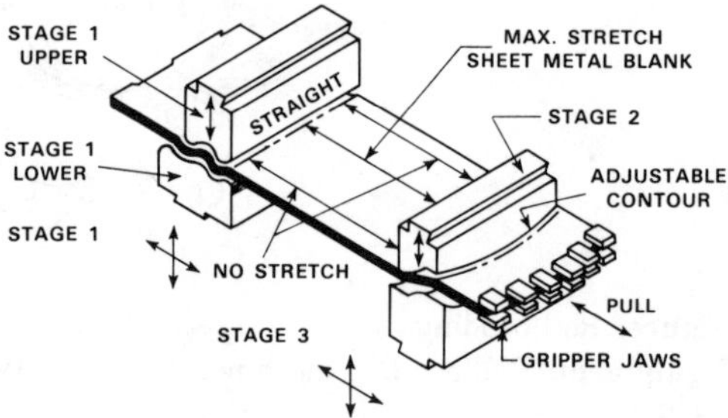

Figure: Movement of material in androforming

Equipment: Androforming machines

Materials: Alloy steels, aluminum alloys, titanium alloys, iron-, nickel- and cobalt-base superalloys, molybdenum alloys, niobium alloys

Application: Forming of double contours in long sheet-metal panels

FIGURE 2-37. AGE FORMING

Definition: In this process, panels to be shaped are restrained on a fixture of required contour and heat treated or aged at a specified temperature for a prescribed period of time. During aging of the part, the material yields to the stress introduced by the action of holding it in the fixture, and retains the contour when removed from the fixture after aging.

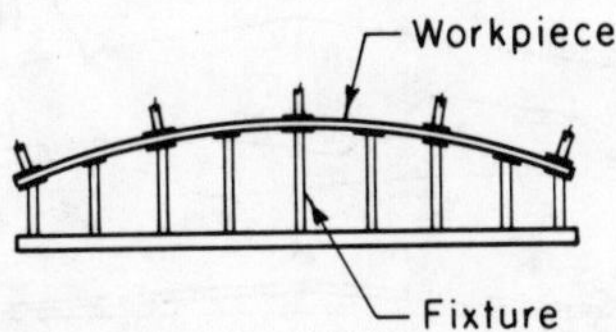

Figure: Age forming
Equipment: Special age forming fixtures/furnaces
Materials: Aluminum and titanium alloys
Application: Imparting contours to panels and sheets in small quantities

FIGURE 2-38. CREEP FORMING

Definition: Pressure is applied to the irregularly shaped or preformed part placed against a heated die. In contact with the hot die, the part is heated and assumes the desired shape against the die by slow creep deformation.

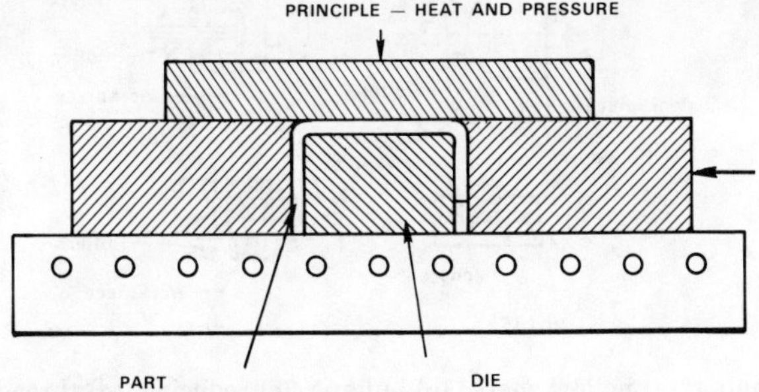

Figure: Schematic of creep forming
Equipment: Special creep forming presses
Materials: Aluminum and titanium
Process Variations: Age forming, hot die forming
Application: Forming of parts for the aerospace industry

FIGURE 2-39. DIE-QUENCH FORMING

Definition: In die-quench forming, the heated workpiece is formed between cold dies under high forming pressure without allowing it to contract during forming. The percentage of stretch introduced in the metal is proportional to the coefficient of thermal expansion of the alloy at the processing temperature.

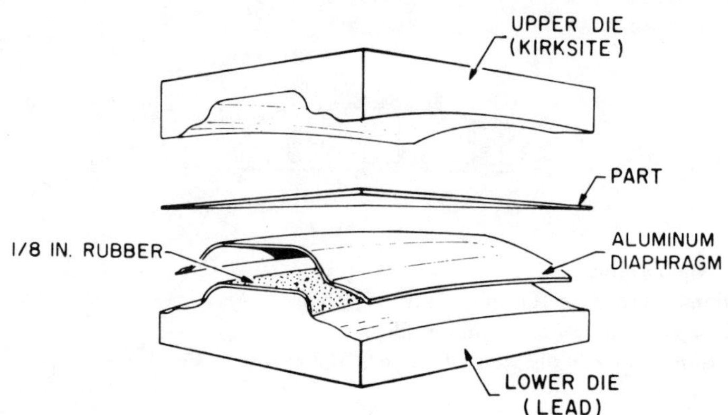

Figure: Die-quench die with aluminum diaphragm

Equipment: Hydraulic presses

Materials: Aluminum and titanium alloys

Process Variations: Hydrodynamic die-quench forming

Applications: Forming of complex parts that are to be formed free from warpage and residual stresses; shaping of integrally stiffened skins

FIGURE 2-40. SPINNING

Definition: Spinning is the process of shaping seamless dished parts by the combined forces of rotation and pressure. Spinning does not result in any change in thickness.

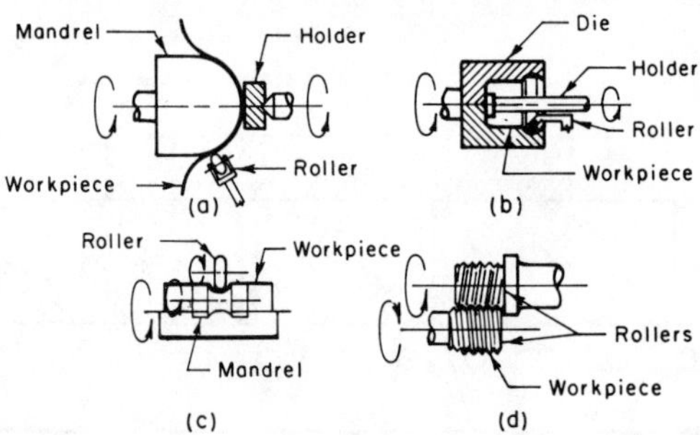

Figure: Spinning: (a) hollow shape, (b) bulging, (c) reducing, (d) threading

Equipment: Modified lathes, spinning machines

Materials: Carbon and alloy steels, aluminum alloys, titanium alloys, iron-, nickel- and cobalt-base superalloys, molybdenum alloys, niobium alloys, beryllium and tungsten

Applications: Forming of flanges, rolled rims, cups, cones and double-curved surfaces of revolution, such as bells

FIGURE 2-41. DEEP DRAWING

Definition: In deep drawing, a sheet blank (hot or cold), usually subjected to a peripheral hold-down pressure, is forced by a punch into and through a die to form a deep recessed part having a wall thickness substantially the same as that of the blank. This process is used to produce cylindrical or prismatic cups with or without a flange on the open end. Cups or tubes can be sunk or redrawn to increase their length and to reduce their lateral dimensions.

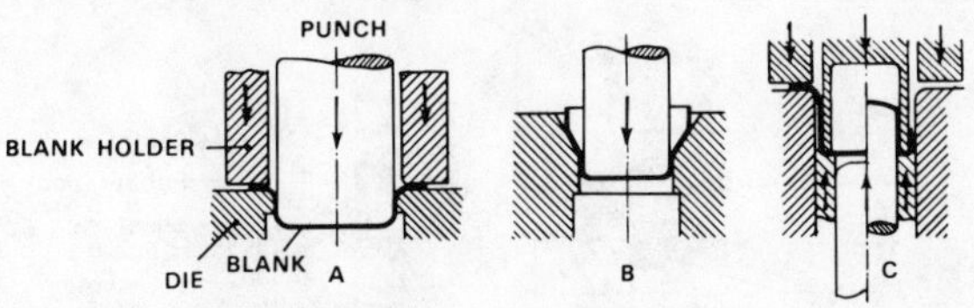

Figure: Deep drawing: (A) first draw, (B) redraw, (C) reverse draw

Equipment: Hydraulic presses, mechanical presses, eyelet-type transfer presses

Materials: Carbon and alloy steels, aluminum alloys, titanium alloys, iron-, nickel- and cobalt-base superalloys, molybdenum alloys, niobium alloys, tungsten

Process Variations: Deep drawing with multiple acting punch, deep drawing with rigid contour punch, rubber forming without blank holder, rubber forming with blank holder (marform process), drawing against liquid (aqua-draw process), explosive forming, hydroforming

Applications: Drawing of deep and shallow cups, shells, cartridge cases, cans

FIGURE 2-42. MARFORM PROCESS

Definition: In the Marform process, the blank is gripped between a blank holder and a rubber pad contained inside a retainer ring attached to the ram. As the ram moves down, the blank is drawn over the punch (form block) under the hydrostatic pressure exerted on the incompressible but pliable rubber pad.

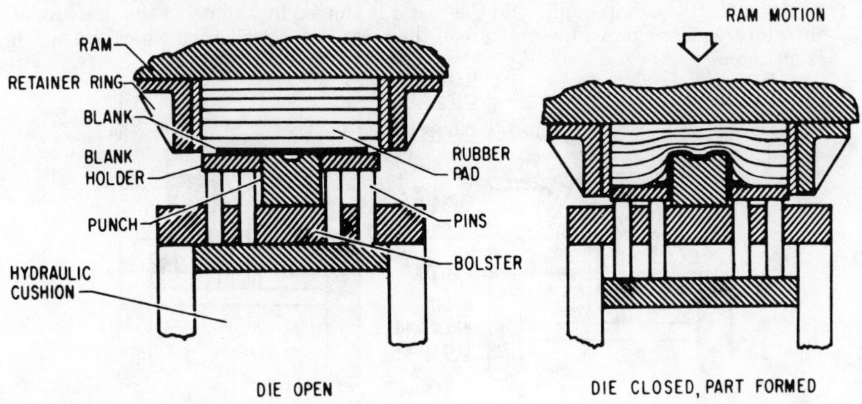

Figure: Marform technique

Equipment: Hydraulic presses, special machines

Materials: Carbon and alloy steels; aluminum alloys

Process Variations: Hydroforming process, Hi-draw technique, rubber-diaphragm forming, SAAB rubber-diaphragm forming

Application: Deeply recessed parts with or without flanges

FIGURE 2-43. RUBBER PAD FORMING (GUERIN PROCESS)

Definition: This is a forming operation for producing shallow parts. A rubber pad is attached to the press slide and becomes the mating die for a punch, or group of punches, which has been placed on the press bed or plate. The rubber pad is confined in a container (pad holder), and the entire slide with attached pad holder is forced against the tools, usually by hydraulic pressure. As the slide descends, the pliable but virtually incompressible rubber fills the space between the slide and the dies and forces the metal to take the exact contours of the dies.

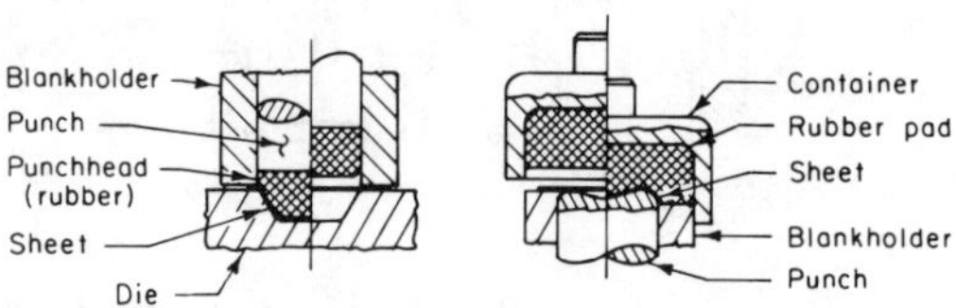

Figure: Rubber pad forming: (left) with rubber punch, (right) with rubber pad

Equipment: Hydraulic presses, special machines, drop hammers

Materials: Carbon and alloy steels, aluminum alloys, titanium alloys, iron-, nickel- and cobalt-base superalloys, molybdenum alloys, niobium alloys

Process Variations: Verson-Wheelon process (rubber-bag forming), drop hammer forming with trapped rubber, rubber flanging, rubber die forming

Applications: Recessed parts such as taillight reflectors, toaster shells, fuselage stiffeners; parts with inside and outside flanges

FIGURE 2-44. RUBBER-DIAPHRAGM HYDROFORMING

Definition: In rubber-diaphragm hydroforming, the blank is held between a diaphragm, which closes the ram pressure chamber, and a blank holder. A male punch works against the diaphragm, and the metal is shaped by balancing the pressure of the ram chamber against the pressure of the press base chamber on which the punch is mounted.

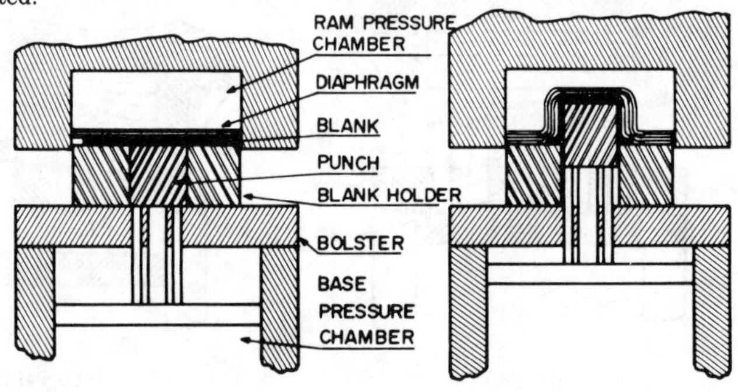

Figure: Rubber-diaphragm hydroforming

Equipment: Double-action hydraulic presses, special machines

Materials: Carbon and alloy steels, aluminum alloys

Process Variation: Hi-draw technique, Marform process

Application: Deeply recessed parts with or without flanges

FIGURE 2-45. DIMPLING

Definition: Dimpling is a process for producing small conical flanges around holes in sheet-metal parts that are to be assembled with flush or flat-headed rivets. Dimpling is most commonly applied to sheets that are too thin for countersinking.

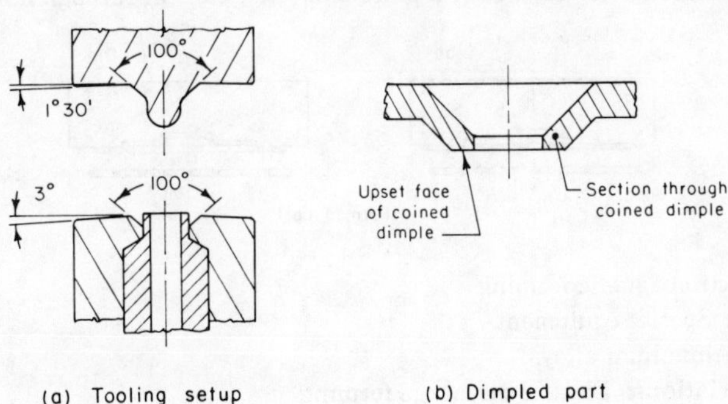

Figure: Ram-coin dimpling

Equipment: Special dimpling machines

Materials: Alloy steels, aluminum alloys, titanium alloys, iron-, nickel- and cobalt-base superalloys, beryllium and tungsten

Process Variations: Radius dimpling, coin dimpling, flanging

Application: Sheet-metal parts requiring assembly with flush or flat-headed rivets

FIGURE 2-46. DROP HAMMER FORMING

Definition: Drop hammer forming is a process for producing shapes by the progressive deformation of sheet metal in matched dies under repetitive blows of a gravity drop or power drop hammer.

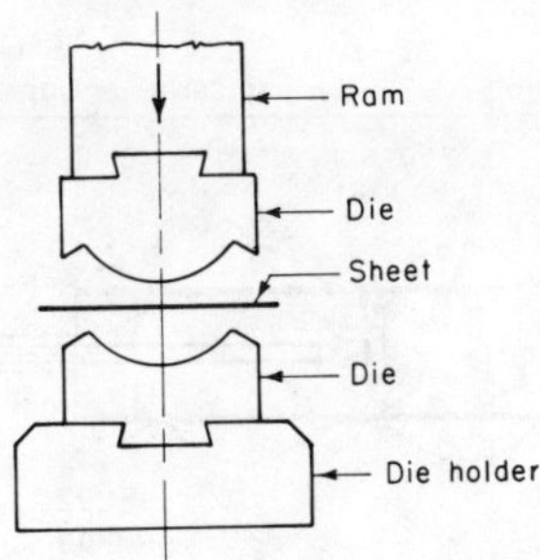

Figure: Drop hammer forming

Equipment: Hammers

Materials: Carbon and alloy steels, aluminum alloys, titanium alloys

Process Variations: Coining, forming to size

Applications: Configurations most commonly formed by drop hammer forming include shallow, smoothly contoured, double-curvature parts; shallow-beaded parts; and parts with irregular and comparatively deep recesses

FIGURE 2-47. ELECTROMAGNETIC FORMING (MAGNETIC PULSE FORMING)

Definition: Electromagnetic forming is a process for forming metal by direct application of an intense, transient magnetic field. The workpiece is formed without mechanical contact by the passage of a pulse of electric current through a forming coil.

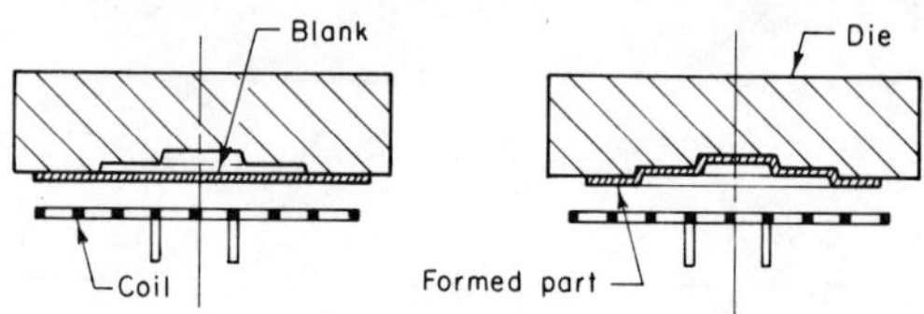

Figure: Electromagnetic forming

Equipment: Special equipment

Materials: Aluminum alloys

Process Variations: Electric discharge forming

Applications: Used primarily for single-step assembly of tubular parts to each other or to other components; it is used to a lesser extent for shaping of tubular parts and shallow forming of flat stock.

FIGURE 2-48. EXPLOSIVE FORMING

Definition: Explosive forming changes the shape of a metal blank or preform by the instantaneous high pressure that results from the detonation of an explosive.

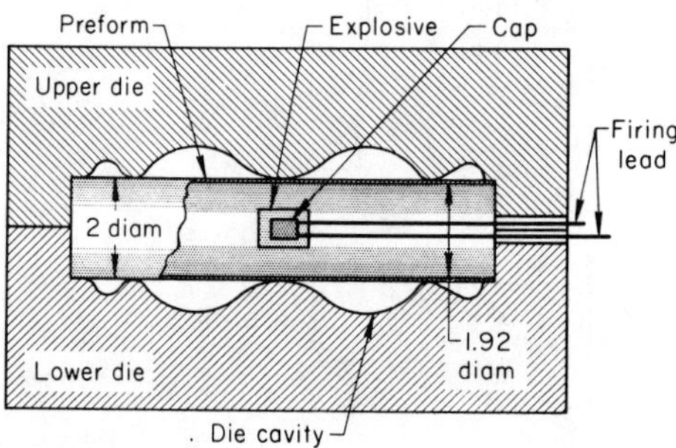

Figure: Confined system for explosive forming (dimensions here are in inches)

Equipment: Special explosive forming equipment

Materials: Aluminum alloys

Applications: Forming of thin-wall tubing to contours with close tolerances; forming of metal plate

FIGURE 2-49. JOGGLING

Definition: Joggling is the process of making an offset in a flat plane by two parallel bends in opposite directions at the same angle. Joggling permits flush connections to be made between sheets, plates, or structural sections.

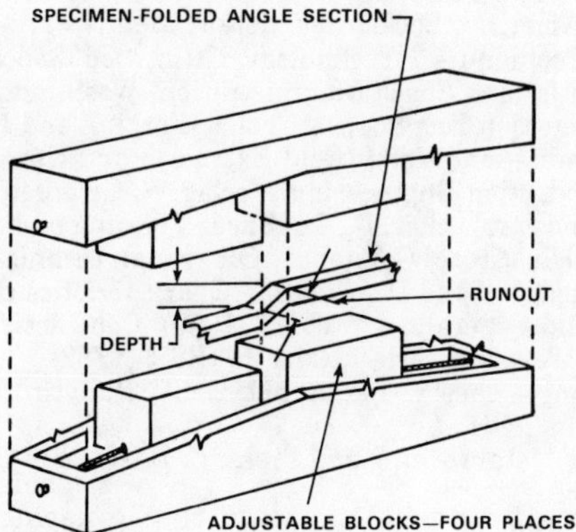

Figure: Universal joggle die

Equipment: Mechanical presses, hydraulic presses

Materials: Alloy steels, aluminum alloys, titanium alloys, iron-, nickel- and cobalt-base superalloys, molybdenum alloys, niobium alloys, beryllium and tungsten

Application: Forming of aerospace parts

FIGURE 2-50. BULGING

Definition: In bulging, an internal pressure is applied so as to form a tube to the desired shape, The internal pressure can be delivered by expanding a segmented punch through a fluid or an elastomer.

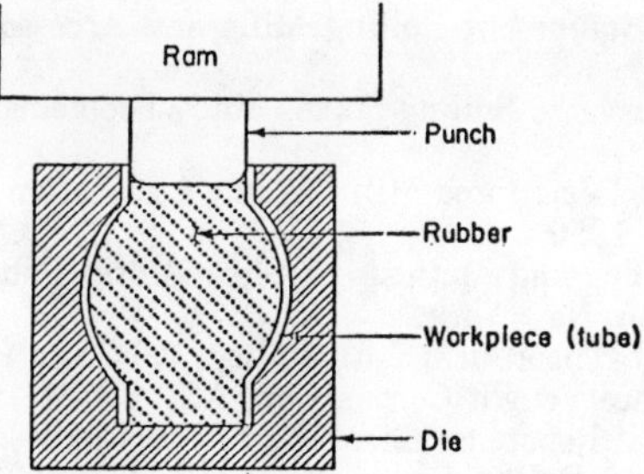

Figure: Rubber-bulging setup

Equipment: Mechanical presses, hydraulic presses

Materials: Carbon and alloy steels, aluminum alloys

Process Variations: Die forming, free forming, bulging by buckling, bulging with steel balls, bulging with internal fluid pressure, explosive (magnetic/electric) bulging

Application: Contoured tubes and shells

REFERENCES

2-1. Altan, T., Lahoti, G. D., and Nagpal, V., "Systems Approach in Massive Forming and Application to Modeling of Forging Processes", J. Applied Metalworking, ASM, Vol 1, No. 1, p 29.

2-2. Metals Handbook, Eighth Edition, Vol 1 (Properties and Selection of Metals) and Vol 4 (Forming), American Society for Metals, Metals Park, OH.

2-3. "Metal-Forming Techniques", Technology Utilization Report, NASA SP-5017, National Aeronautics and Space Administration, Washington, DC, May 1965.

2-4. Dictionary of Production Engineering, Vol 1 (Forging and Drop Forging), Vol 3 (Sheet Metal Forming) and Vol 5 (Cold Extrusion and Upsetting), International Institution for Production Engineering, Verlag W. Girardet, Essen.

2-5. Henning, H. J., and Strohecker, D. E., "Shear Forming and Spinning of Metals", Battelle Memorial Institute, Columbus, OH, Final Technical Report on Survey of Current Knowledge of the Deformation Characteristics of Beryllium and Refractory Metals and Superalloys (Feb 10, 1966), Contract No. 65-02590 for the Bureau of Naval Weapons, Code RRMA-24 (RSIC 1782).

2-6. "Cold Roll Forming – Theory and Application", Bulletin 709/872, The Yoder Company, Cleveland, OH.

2-7. "Computations for Metalworking and Presses", E. W. Bliss Company, Press Div., Hastings, MI.

2-8. Deformation Processing of Stainless Steels", D. E. Strohecker *et al*, NASA Technical Memorandum NASA TM X-53569, Oct 1966.

2-9. "Ultrasonic Activation Aids Tube Production", Tooling and Production, Vol 32, No. 2, May 1966, p 96.

2-10. Altan, T., *et al*, Forging Equipment, Materials and Practices, MCIC-HB-03, Metals and Ceramics Information Center, Battelle Columbus Laboratories, Columbus, OH, 1973.

2-11. Lahoti, G. D., and Altan, T., "Design of Dies for Radial Forging of Rods and Tubes", Technical Paper MF76-390, Society of Manufacturing Engineers, Dearborn, MI.

2-12. Richardson, B. D., Fiorentino, R. J., and Sabroff, A. M., "Comparison of Hydrostatic and Conventional Methods of Extrusion and Drawing", Technical Paper MF68-217, American Society of Tool and Manufacturing Engineers, Dearborn, MI.

2-13. Aluminum, Vol 3 (Fabrication and Finishing), edited by K. R. Van Horn, American Society for Metals, Metals Park, OH, 1967, pp 81-112.

2-14. Byrer, T. G., Design Guide for Use of Structural Shapes in Aircraft Applications, Technical Report AFML-TR-73-211, Sept 1973.

2-15. Geleji, A., Forge Equipment Rolling Mills and Accessories, Akademiai Kiado, Budapest, 1967.

2-16. Egan, P. F., "Transverse Rolling Solves Many Problems", Metal Forming, April 1967, pp 99-107.

2-17. Beyon, R. E., Roll Design and Mill Layout, Association of Iron and Steel Engineers, Pittsburgh, 1956.

2-18. Sachs, G., Principles and Methods of Sheet-Metal Fabricating, Reinhold Publishing Corporation, New York.

2-19. Wood, W. W., *et al*, Theoretical Formability, Vol I and II, Vought Aeronautics – a division of Chance Vought Corporation, ASD TR 61-191, 1961.

2-20. Wood, W. W., Final Report on Sheet-Metal Forming Technology, Vol 1, Chance Vought Corporation, Dallas, Contract No. AF 33(657)-7314, ASD Project No. 7-871, 1963.

2-21. Hoischen, H., "Cold Hobbing of Impressions for Forging Dies" (in German), Industrie-Anzeiger, Vol 89, No. 56, July 14, 1967, p 1256.

2-22. Lange, K., Lehrbuch der Umformtechnik/Textbook of Forming Technology (in German), Springer-Verlag, Berlin, 1972.

CHAPTER 3
Plastic Deformation: Strain and Strain Rate

The purpose of applying plasticity theory in metal forming is to investigate the mechanics of plastic deformation in metal forming processes. Such investigation allows the analysis and prediction of (a) metal flow (velocities, strain rates and strains), (b) temperatures and heat transfer, (c) local variation in material strength or flow stress and (d) stresses, forming load, pressure and energy. Thus, the mechanics of deformation provides the means for determining how the metal flows, how the desired geometry can be obtained by plastic forming and what are the expected mechanical properties of the part produced by forming.

In order to arrive at a "manageable" mathematical description of metal deformation, several simplifying (but reasonable) assumptions are made:

- Elastic deformations are neglected. However, when necessary, elastic recovery (for example, in the case of springback in bending) and elastic deflection of tooling (in the case of precision forming to very close tolerances) must be considered.
- The deforming material is considered to be a continuum (metallurgical aspects such as grains, grain boundaries and dislocations are not considered).
- Uniaxial tensile or compression test data are correlated with flow stress in multiaxial deformation conditions.
- Anisotropy and Bauschinger effects are neglected.
- Volume remains constant.
- Friction is expressed by a simplified expression such as Coulomb's law or by a constant shear stress. This will be discussed later.

LOCAL DEFORMATIONS AND THE VELOCITY FIELD

The local displacement of volume elements is described by a "velocity field", e.g., velocities, strain rates and strains. To simplify analysis, it is often

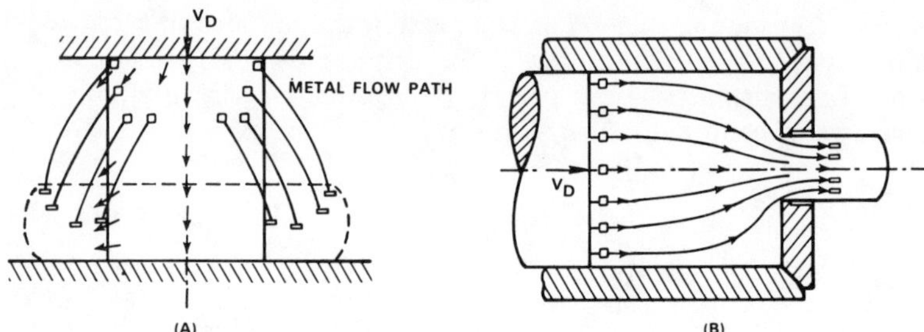

Figure 3-1. Metal flow in certain forming processes: (A) nonsteady-state upset forging, (B) steady-state extrusion.[3-1]

assumed that the "velocity field" is independent of material properties. Obviously, this is not correct. If large strain ($\bar{\epsilon}$) or temperature (θ) gradients are present the material will not flow in exactly the same way as a strictly homogeneous material would flow. The softer portions — where, for example, the temperatures are higher than in other regions of the deformation zone — would flow more easily than would the rest of the deforming material.

In *steady-state flow* (kinematically), the velocity field remains unchanged, as is the case in the extrusion process (Figure 3-1B); in *nonsteady-state flow,* the velocity field changes continuously with time, as is the case in upset forging (Figure 3-1A).[3-1]

STRAINS

In order to investigate metal flow quantitatively, it is necessary to define the strains (or deformations), strain rates (deformation rates) and velocities (displacements per unit time). Figure 3-2 illustrates the deformation of an infinitesimal rectangular block, abcd, into a parallelogram, a′b′c′d′, after a small amount of plastic deformation. Although this illustration is in two dimensions, the principles apply also to three-dimensional cases.[3-1,3-2]

The coordinates of a point are initially x and y (and z in three dimensions). After a small amount of deformation, the same point has the coordi-

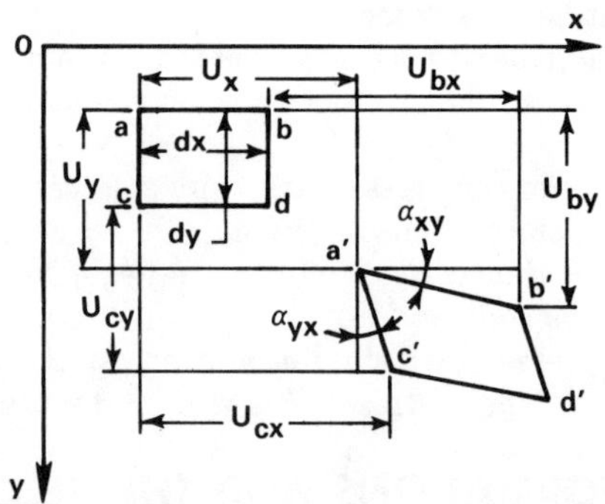

Figure 3-2. Displacements in the x-y plane.

nates x′ and y′ (and z′ in 3-D). By neglecting the higher-order components, we can determine the magnitude of the displacement of point b, u_{bx}, as a function of the displacement of point a. This value, u_{bx}, is different from the displacement of point a, u_x, about the variation of the function u_x over length dx, i.e.:

$$u_{bx} = u_x + \frac{\partial u_x}{\partial x} dx \tag{3-1}$$

We note that u_x also depends on y and z.

The relative elongation of length ab (which is originally equal to dx), or the strain in the x direction, ϵ_x, is now:

$$\epsilon_x = (u_{bx} - u_x)/dx, \quad \text{or}$$

$$\epsilon_x = \left(u_x + \frac{\partial u_x}{\partial x} dx - u_x\right) \Big/ dx = \frac{\partial u_x}{\partial x} \tag{3-2a}$$

Similarly, in the y and z directions:

$$\epsilon_y = \frac{\partial u_y}{\partial y}; \quad \epsilon_z = \frac{\partial u_z}{\partial z} \tag{3-2b}$$

The angular variations due to the small deformation considered in Figure 3-2 are infinitesimally small. Therefore, tan $\alpha_{xy} = \alpha_{xy}$ and tan $\alpha_{yx} = \alpha_{yx}$. Thus:

$$\alpha_{xy} = (u_{by} - u_y)/(u_{bx} + dx - u_x) \tag{3-3}$$

The expression for u_{bx} is given in Equation 3-1, and that for u_{by} can be obtained similarly, as:

$$u_{by} = u_y + \frac{\partial u_y}{\partial y} dy \tag{3-4}$$

Using Equations 3-1 and 3-4, and considering that $\partial u_x/\partial x = \epsilon_x$ is considerably smaller than 1, Equation 3-3 leads to:

$$\alpha_{xy} = \frac{\partial u_y}{\partial x} \tag{3-5a}$$

and, similarly:

$$\alpha_{yx} = \frac{\partial u_x}{\partial y} \tag{3-5b}$$

Thus, the total angular deformation in the xy plane, or the shear strain, γ_{xy}, is:

$$\gamma_{xy} = \alpha_{xy} + \alpha_{yx} = \frac{\partial u_y}{\partial x} + \frac{\partial u_x}{\partial y} \tag{3-6a}$$

Similarly:

$$\gamma_{yz} = \frac{\partial u_y}{\partial x} + \frac{\partial u_z}{\partial y} \tag{3-6b}$$

and

$$\gamma_{xz} = \frac{\partial u_z}{\partial x} + \frac{\partial u_x}{\partial z} \tag{3-6c}$$

VELOCITIES AND STRAIN RATES

The distribution of velocity components (v_x, v_y, v_z) within a deforming material describes the metal flow in that material. The velocity is the variation of displacement in time, or, in the x, y and z directions:[3-2,3-3]

$$v_x = \frac{\partial u_x}{\partial t}; \quad v_y = \frac{\partial u_y}{\partial t}; \quad v_z = \frac{\partial u_z}{\partial t} \tag{3-7}$$

The strain rates, i.e., the variations of strain with time, are:

$$\dot{\epsilon}_x = \frac{\partial \epsilon_x}{\partial t} = \frac{\partial}{\partial t}\frac{\partial (u_x)}{\partial x} = \frac{\partial}{\partial x}\left(\frac{\partial u_x}{\partial t}\right) = \frac{\partial v_x}{\partial x}$$

Similarly:

$$\dot{\epsilon}_x = \frac{\partial v_x}{\partial x}; \quad \dot{\epsilon}_y = \frac{\partial v_y}{\partial y}; \quad \dot{\epsilon}_z = \frac{\partial v_z}{\partial z} \tag{3-8a}$$

$$\dot{\gamma}_{xy} = \frac{\partial v_x}{\partial y} + \frac{\partial v_y}{\partial x} \tag{3-8b}$$

$$\dot{\gamma}_{yz} = \frac{\partial v_y}{\partial z} + \frac{\partial v_z}{\partial y} \tag{3-8c}$$

$$\dot{\gamma}_{xz} = \frac{\partial v_x}{\partial z} + \frac{\partial v_z}{\partial x} \tag{3-8d}$$

The state of deformation in a plastically deforming metal is fully described by the displacements, u, velocities, v, strains, ϵ, and strain rates, $\dot{\epsilon}$ (in an x,y,z coordinate system). It is possible to express the same values in an x′,y′,z′ system, provided that the angle of rotation from x,y,z to x′,y′,z′ is known. Thus, in every small element within a plastically deforming body, it is possible to orient the coordinate system such that the element is not subject to "shear" but only to compression or tension. In this case, the strains γ_{xy}, γ_{yz} and γ_{xz} all equal zero, and the element deforms along the "principal axes of deformation".

In uniaxial tension and compression tests (no necking, no bulging), deformation is also in the directions of "principal axes".

The assumption of volume constancy, made earlier, neglects the elastic strains. This assumption is reasonable in most forming processes where the amount of plastic strain is much larger than the amount of elastic strain. This assumption can also be expressed, for deformation along principal axes, as follows:

$$\epsilon_x + \epsilon_y + \epsilon_z = 0 \tag{3-9}$$

and

$$\dot{\epsilon}_x + \dot{\epsilon}_y + \dot{\epsilon}_z = 0 \tag{3-10}$$

HOMOGENEOUS DEFORMATION

We consider "frictionless" upset forging of a rectangular block in Figure 3-3. The upper die is moving downward, at velocity V_D. The coordinate axes x, y and z have their origins on the lower platen, at the center of the lower rectangular surface.

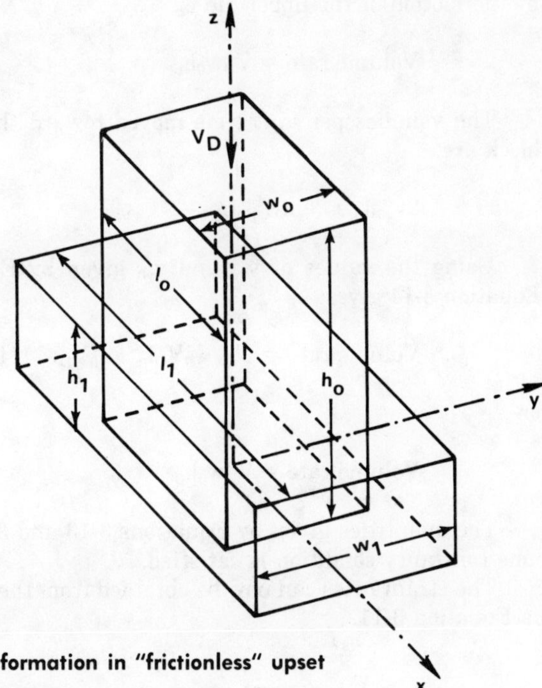

Figure 3-3. Homogeneous deformation in "frictionless" upset forging.

The initial and final dimensions of the block are designated by the subscripts 0 and 1, respectively. The instantaneous height of the block during deformation is h. The velocity components, v_x, v_y and v_z, describing the motion of each particle within the deforming block, can be expressed as linear functions of the coordinates x, y and z as follows:

$$v_x = V_D x/2h; \quad v_y = V_D y/2h; \quad v_z = -V_D z/h \tag{3-11}$$

In order to demonstrate that the velocity field described by Equation 3-11 is "acceptable", it is necessary to prove that these velocities satisfy (a) the volume constancy and (b) the boundary conditions.[3-4]

Satisfaction of the boundary conditions can be shown by considering the initial shape of the block before deformation (Figure 3-3). At the origin of coordinates, all velocities must be equal to zero. This condition is satisfied because, at the origin, for x = y = z = 0, we have, from Equation 3-11, $v_x = v_y = v_z = 0$. At the boundaries:

$$\text{At } x = l_0/2; \quad \text{velocity in x direction:} \quad v_{x0} = V_D l_0/4h_0 \tag{3-12a}$$

$$\text{At } y = w_0/2; \quad \text{velocity in y direction:} \quad v_{y0} = V_D w_0/4h_0 \tag{3-12b}$$

$$\text{At } z = h_0; \quad \text{velocity in z direction:} \quad v_{z0} = -V_D \tag{3-12c}$$

It can easily be shown that the volume constancy is also satisfied. At the start of deformation, the volume rate or the volume per unit time displaced by the motion of the upper die is:

$$\text{Volume rate} = V_D w_0 h_0 \tag{3-13}$$

The volumes per unit time moved toward the sides of the rectangular block are:

$$2v_{x0}h_0w_0 + 2v_{y0}l_0h_0 \tag{3-14}$$

Using the values of v_{x0} and v_{y0} given by Equations 3-12a and 3-12b, Equation 3-14 gives:

$$\text{Volume rate} = 2h_0(w_0V_Dl_0 + l_0V_Dw_0)/4h_0 \tag{3-15a}$$

or

$$\text{Volume rate} = V_D w_0 h_0 \tag{3-15b}$$

The quantities given by Equations 3-13 and 3-15 are equal, i.e., the volume constancy condition is satisfied.

The strain rates can now be obtained from the velocity components given in Equation 3-11:[3-4,3-5]

$$\dot{\epsilon}_x = \frac{\partial v_x}{\partial x} = V_D/2h \tag{3-16a}$$

Similarly:

$$\dot{\epsilon}_y = V_D/2h; \quad \dot{\epsilon}_z = -V_D/h \tag{3-16b}$$

It can be easily seen that:

$$\dot{\gamma}_{xy} = \dot{\gamma}_{xz} = \dot{\gamma}_{yz} = 0$$

In homogeneous deformation, the shear strain rates are equal to zero. The strains can be obtained by integration with respect to time, t.

In the height direction:

$$\epsilon_z = \int_{t_0}^{t_1} \dot{\epsilon}_z dt = \int_{t_0}^{t_1} -\frac{V_D}{h} dt \tag{3-17}$$

For small displacements, $dh = -V_D dt$. Thus, Equation 3-17 gives:

$$\epsilon_h = \epsilon_z = \int_{h_0}^{h_1} \frac{dh}{h} = \ln \frac{h_1}{h_0} \tag{3-18a}$$

Other strains can be obtained similarly:

$$\epsilon_l = \epsilon_x = \ln \frac{l_1}{l_0}; \quad \epsilon_b = \epsilon_y = \ln \frac{w_1}{w_0} \tag{3-18b}$$

Volume constancy in terms of strains can be verified from:

$$V = h_0 w_0 l_0 = h_1 w_1 l_1 \rightarrow \frac{h_0 w_0 l_0}{h_1 w_1 l_1} = 1,$$

or, taking the natural logarithm,

$$\ln \frac{h_0}{h_1} + \ln \frac{b_0}{b_1} + \ln \frac{l_0}{l_1} = \epsilon_h + \epsilon_b + \epsilon_l = 0 \tag{3-19}$$

PLASTIC (TRUE) STRAIN AND ENGINEERING STRAIN

The results of Equation 3-18 can also be obtained through a different approach.[3-5] In the theory of strength of materials — during uniform elongation in tension, for example — the infinitesimal engineering strain, de, is considered with respect to original length, l_0, or:

$$de = \frac{dl}{l_0} \rightarrow e = \int_{l_0}^{l_1} \frac{dl}{l_0} = \frac{l_1 - l_0}{l_0} \tag{3-20}$$

In the theory of metal forming plasticity, the initial condition cannot be used as a frame of reference; therefore, the change in length must be related to instantaneous length, or:

$$d\epsilon = \frac{dl}{l} \rightarrow \epsilon = \int_{l_0}^{l_1} \frac{dl}{l} = \ln \frac{l_1}{l_0} \tag{3-21}$$

Equations 3-20 and 3-21 give:

$$\epsilon = \ln \frac{l_1}{l_0} = \ln (e + 1) \tag{3-22}$$

The relations between ϵ and e can be illustrated by considering the following example uniform deformations, where a bar is uniformly (or homogeneously) compressed to half its original length or is elongated to twice its original length:

	Compression, for $l_1 = l_0/2$	Tension, for $l_1 = 2l_0$
$\epsilon = \ln \frac{l_1}{l_0}$	−0.693	+0.693
$e = \frac{l_1 - l_0}{l_0}$	−0.5	+1

REFERENCES

3-1. Lange, K. (editor), *Study Book of Forming Technology* (in German), Vol 1 (Fundamentals), Springer-Verlag, New York, 1972.
3-2. Backofen, W. A., "Deformation Processing", Addison-Wesley Publishing Company, 1972.
3-3. Rowe, G. W., "Principles of Industrial Metalworking Processes", Edward Arnold Publishers, London, 1977.
3-4. Johnson, W., and Mellor, P. B., "Engineering Plasticity", Van Nostrand Reinhold Co., London, 1975.
3-5. Thomsen, E. G., Yang, C. T., and Kobayashi, S., "Mechanics of Plastic Deformation in Metal Processing", The Macmillan Company, New York, 1965.

CHAPTER 4
Plastic Deformation: Simple State of Stress

For understanding the stresses and the forces involved in metal forming processes it is useful (a) to become familiar with the concept of flow stress and (b) to start with the study of plastic deformation under conditions where a simple state of stress exists.

FLOW STRESS OF METALS

For studying the plastic deformation behavior of a given metal, it is appropriate to consider uniform or homogeneous deformation conditions. The yield stress of a metal under uniaxial conditions, as a function of strain, $\bar{\epsilon}$, strain rate, $\dot{\bar{\epsilon}}$, and temperature, θ, can also be considered as the "flow stress". The metal starts "flowing" or deforming plastically when the applied stress (in uniaxial tension without necking or in uniaxial compression without bulging) reaches the value of the "yield stress" or "flow stress".

The flow stress, $\bar{\sigma}$, is important because in metal forming processes the forming loads and stresses depend on (a) part geometry, (b) friction and (c) the flow stress of the deforming material. The flow stress of a metal is influenced by:

- Factors *unrelated* to the deformation process, such as chemical composition, metallurgical structure, phases, grain size, segregation and prior strain history.
- Factors explicitly *related* to the deformation process, such as temperature of deformation, θ, degree of deformation or strain, $\bar{\epsilon}$, and rate of deformation or strain rate, $\dot{\bar{\epsilon}}$.

Thus, the flow stress, $\bar{\sigma}$, can be expressed as a function of temperature, θ, strain, $\bar{\epsilon}$, strain rate, $\dot{\bar{\epsilon}}$, and microstructure, S:

$$\bar{\sigma} = f(\theta, \bar{\epsilon}, \dot{\bar{\epsilon}}, S) \tag{4-1}$$

In hot forming of metals at temperatures above the recrystallization temperature, the influence of strain on flow stress is insignificant, and the influence of strain rate (i.e., rate of deformation) becomes increasingly important. Conversely, at room temperature (i.e., in cold forming), the effect of strain rate on flow stress is negligible, and the effect of strain on flow stress (i.e., strain hardening) is most important. The degree of dependency of flow stress on temperature varies considerably among different materials. Therefore, temperature variations in a forming operation can have quite different effects on load requirements and on metal flow for different materials. For instance, a drop of approximately 100 F in the hot forming temperature (from 1700 to 1600 F) would result in a 40% increase in flow stress for titanium alloy Ti-8Al-1Mo-1V. The increase in flow stress that would result from the same temperature drop, 100 F within the hot working range (from 2200 to 2100 F), would be only about 15% for AISI type 4340 steel.[4-1]

To be useful in metal forming analyses, the flow stresses of metals must be determined experimentally for the $\bar{\varepsilon}$, $\dot{\bar{\varepsilon}}$ and θ conditions, which exist in metal forming processes. The methods most commonly used for obtaining flow stress data are tensile, uniform compression and torsion tests.

TENSILE TEST

The tensile test is commonly used for determining the mechanical properties of metals. However, the material properties determined in this test are basically useful for designing components and not for producing parts by a metal forming process. The main reason for this is that tensile data, i.e., flow stress data obtained in a tensile test, are only valid for relatively small amounts of plastic strains. Flow stress data, however, must be valid for large amounts of strains, encountered in metal forming processes, so that these data are useful in metal forming analysis.

Two methods of representing tensile data are illustrated in Figure 4-1.[4-2] In the classical engineering stress-strain diagram (Figure 4-1A) the

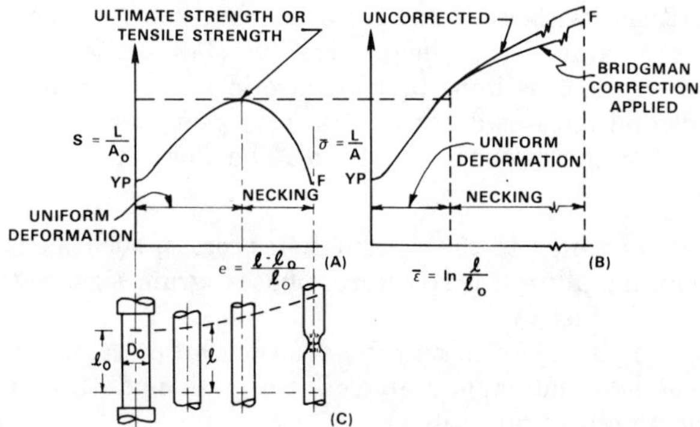

Figure 4-1. Representation of data in a tensile test: (A) engineering stress-strain curve; (B) true stress-strain curve; (C) schematic of dimensional change of the specimen during the test.[4-2]

stress is obtained by dividing the instantaneous tensile load, L, by the original cross-sectional area of the specimen, A_0. This stress is then plotted against the engineering strain, $e = (l - l_0)/l_0$. During deformation the specimen elongates initially in a uniform fashion. When the load reaches its maximum value, necking starts and the uniform uniaxial stress conditions cease to exist. Deformation is then concentrated only at the neck region while the rest of the specimen remains rigid. Figure 4-1(B) illustrates the true stress-strain representation of the same tensile data. In this case, before necking occurs, the following relationships are valid:

$$\begin{aligned} \bar{\sigma} &= \text{true stress (or flow stress)} \\ &= \text{instantaneous load/instantaneous area} \\ &= L/A \end{aligned} \qquad (4\text{-}2)$$

and

$$\bar{\epsilon} = \text{true strain} = \ln(l/l_0) = \ln(A_0/A) \qquad (4\text{-}3)$$

The instantaneous load in tension is given by $L = A\bar{\sigma}$. The criterion for necking can be formulated as the condition that L be maximum or that:[4-2]

$$\frac{dL}{d\bar{\epsilon}} = 0 \qquad (4\text{-}4)$$

Near but slightly before the attainment of maximum load, the uniform deformation conditions, i.e., Equations 4-2 and 4-3, are valid.[4-2] From Equation 4-3:

$$A = A_0(e)^{-\bar{\epsilon}}, \quad \text{or}$$

$$L = A\bar{\sigma} = A_0\bar{\sigma}(e)^{-\bar{\epsilon}} \qquad (4\text{-}5)$$

Combining Equations 4-4 and 4-5 gives:

$$\frac{dL}{d\bar{\epsilon}} = 0 = A_0\left(\frac{d\bar{\sigma}}{d\bar{\epsilon}}(e)^{-\bar{\epsilon}} - \bar{\sigma}(e)^{-\bar{\epsilon}}\right) \qquad (4\text{-}6)$$

or

$$\frac{d\bar{\sigma}}{d\bar{\epsilon}} = \bar{\sigma} \qquad (4\text{-}7)$$

As will be discussed later, very often the flow stress curve, $\bar{\sigma} - \bar{\epsilon}$, obtained at room temperature can be expressed in the form of an exponential equation:

$$\bar{\sigma} = K(\bar{\epsilon})^n \qquad (4\text{-}8)$$

where K and n are constants.

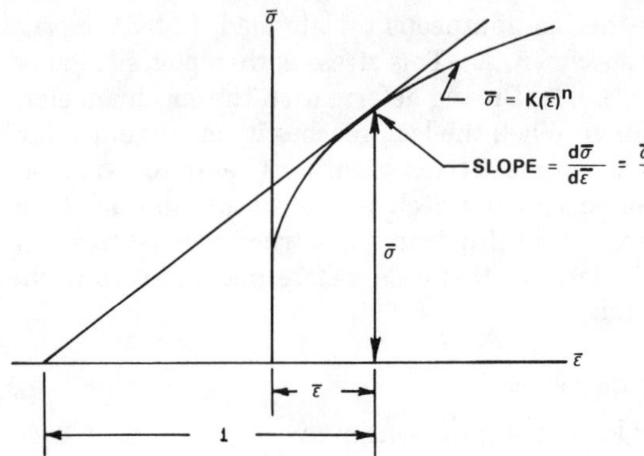

Figure 4-2. Schematic representation of conditions of necking in simple tension.[4-2]

Combining Equations 4-7 and 4-8 gives:

$$\frac{d\bar{\sigma}}{d\epsilon} = Kn(\bar{\epsilon})^{n-1} = \bar{\sigma} = K(\bar{\epsilon})^n \tag{4-9}$$

or

$$\bar{\epsilon} = n \tag{4-10}$$

This condition is shown schematically in Figure 4-2. From this figure and from Equation 4-10 it is evident that at low forming temperatures, where Equation 4-8 is valid, a material with a large n, or strain hardening coefficient, has greater formability — i.e., sustains a larger amount of uniform deformation in tension — than a material with a smaller n. It should be noted, however, that this statement is not correct for materials and conditions where the flow stress cannot be expressed by Equation 4-8.

The calculation of true stress after the necking strain (Figure 4-1B) requires a correction because a triaxial state of stress is induced. Such a correction, derived by Bridgeman, is given by:[4-2]

$$\sigma_s = \bar{\sigma} = \frac{L}{\pi r^2}\left[\left(1 + \frac{2R}{r}\right)\ln\left(1 + \frac{r}{2R}\right)\right]^{-1} \tag{4-11}$$

The quantities r and R are defined in Figure 4-3.[4-2] It can be clearly seen that, for evaluation of Equation 4-11, the values of r and R must be measured continuously during the test. This is quite cumbersome and prone to error. Therefore, other tests, which provide $\bar{\sigma} - \bar{\epsilon}$ data at larger strains relative to the tensile test, are used for metal forming applications.

COMPRESSION TEST

The compression test is used for determining flow-stress data (true stress/true strain relationships) for metals at various temperatures and strain rates.[4-1] In this test the flat platens and the cylindrical sample are main-

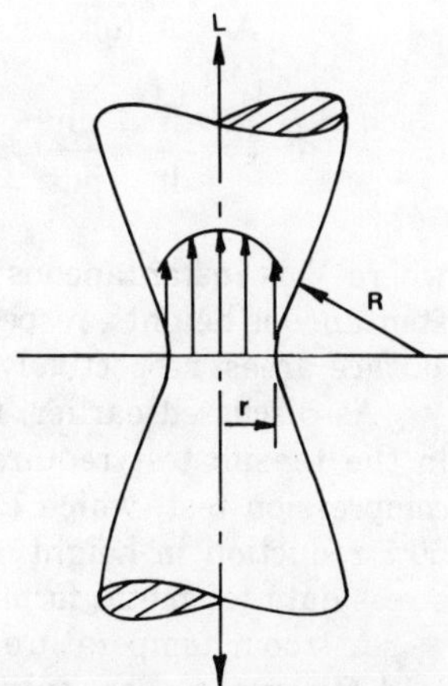

Figure 4-3. Axial stress distribution in the necked portion of a tensile specimen.[4-2]

tained at the same temperature so that die chilling, with its influence on metal flow, is prevented. To be applicable without errors or corrections, the cylindrical sample must be upset without any barreling, i.e., the state of uniform stress in the sample must be maintained as shown in Figure 4-4. Barreling is prevented by using adequate lubrication, e.g., Teflon or machine oil at room temperature and, at hot working temperatures, graphite in oil for aluminum alloys and glass for steel, titanium and high-temperature alloys.[4-3] The load and displacement, or sample height, are measured during the test. From this information the flow stress is calculated at each stage of deformation, or for increasing strain.

Similar to the uniform elongation portion of the tensile test, the following relationships are valid for the uniform compression test:

$$\bar{\epsilon} = \ln \frac{h_0}{h} = \ln \frac{A}{A_0} \tag{4-12}$$

$$\bar{\sigma} = \frac{L}{A} \tag{4-13}$$

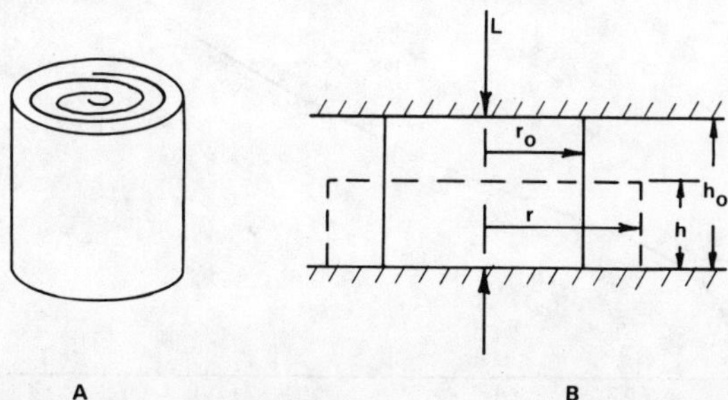

Figure 4-4. Compression test specimen: (A) view of specimen, showing lubricated shallow grooves at ends; (B) shape of specimen before and after test.

$$A = A_0(e)^{\bar{\epsilon}} \tag{4-14}$$

$$\dot{\bar{\epsilon}} = \frac{d\bar{\epsilon}}{dt} = \frac{dh}{hdt} = \frac{V}{h} \tag{4-15}$$

where V is instantaneous deformation velocity; h_0 and h are initial and instantaneous heights, respectively; and A_0 and A are initial and instantaneous surface areas, respectively.

As discussed earlier, the flow stress values determined at high strains in the tensile test require a correction because of necking. Therefore, the compression test, which can be conducted without barreling at up to about 50% reduction in height ($\bar{\epsilon}$ = 0.693 or more), is widely used to obtain flow stress data for metal forming applications.

At room temperature the flow stresses of most metals (except that of lead, for example) are only slightly strain-rate dependent. Therefore, any testing machine or press can be used for the compression test, regardless of its ram speed. Adequate lubrication of the platens is usually accomplished by using lubricants such as Teflon, molybdenum disulfide or high-viscosity oil and by machining grooves on both flat faces of the compression specimen, to hold the lubricant (Figure 4-4). A typical load-displacement curve obtained in uniform compression of an aluminum alloy (Al 1100, annealed) at room temperature in a testing machine is shown in Figure 4-5. The $\bar{\sigma}$-$\bar{\epsilon}$ data obtained from this curve are shown in Figure 4-6.[4-4]

At hot working temperatures, i.e., above the recrystallization temperature, the flow stresses of nearly all metals are very much strain-rate dependent. Therefore, whenever possible, these temperature range compression tests are conducted on a machine which provides a velocity-displacement profile such that the condition $\dot{\bar{\epsilon}}$ = velocity/sample height can be maintained throughout the test. Used for this purpose are mechanical cam-activated presses called plastometer or hydraulic programmable testing machines (MTS, for ex-

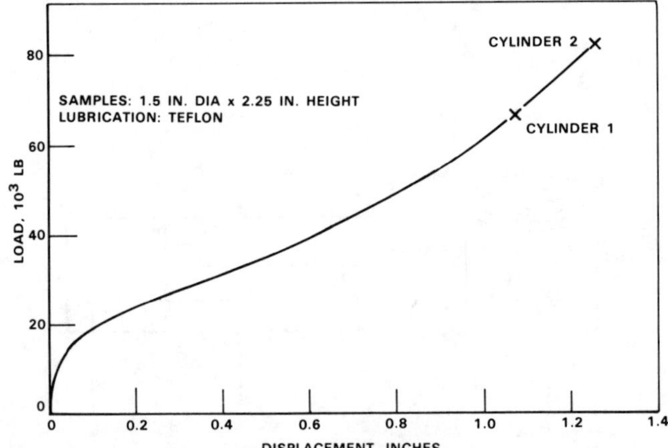

Figure 4-5. Load-displacement curve obtained in uniform upsetting of annealed 1100 aluminum cylinders.[4-4]

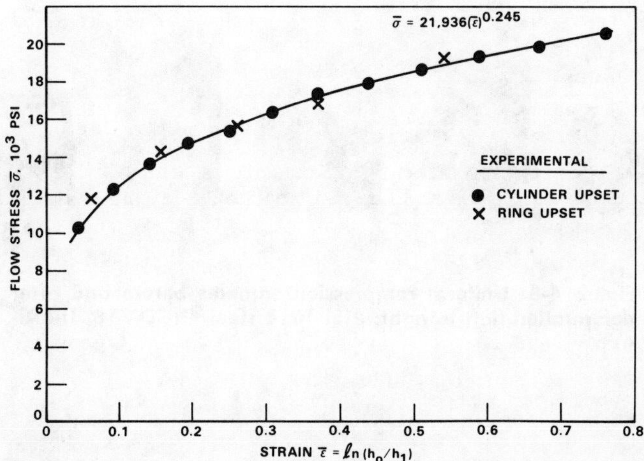

Figure 4-6. Flow stress-strain ($\bar{\sigma}$-$\bar{\epsilon}$) curve for annealed 1100 aluminum obtained from uniform cylinder and ring-upset tests.(4-4)

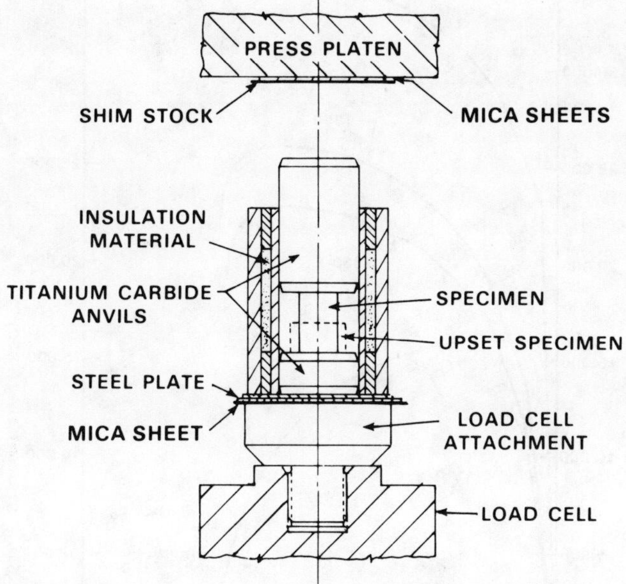

Figure 4-7. Press setup and fixture used in heating and compression of cylinders and rings.

ample).(4-5) In order to maintain nearly isothermal and uniform compression conditions, the test is conducted in a furnace or a fixture such as that shown in Figure 4-7. The specimens are lubricated with appropriate lubricants — for example, oil graphite for temperatures up to 800 F and glass for temperatures up to 2300 F. The fixture and the specimens are heated to test

Figure 4-8. Uniform compression samples before and after deformation (left to right: AISI 1018 steel, INCO 718, Ti-6Al-4V).

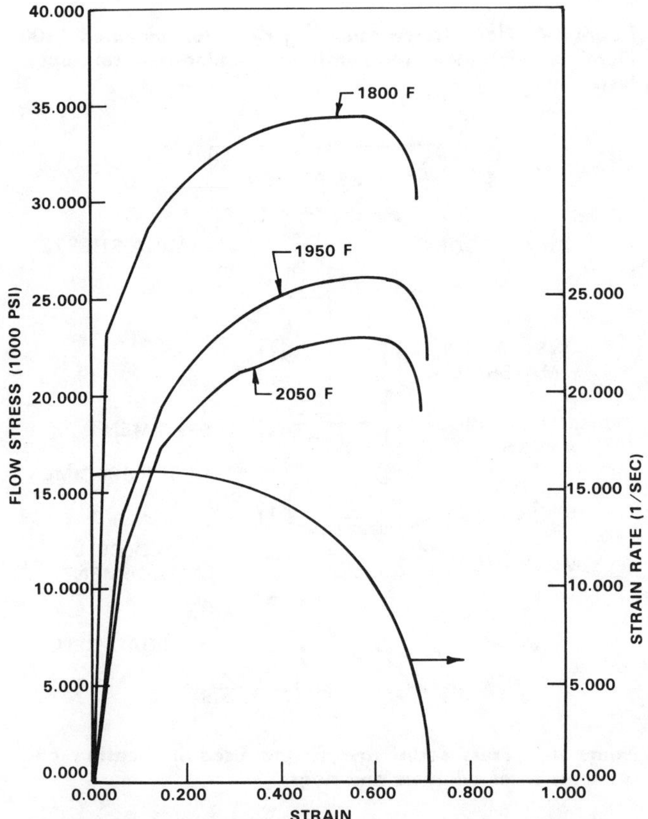

Figure 4-9. Flow stress vs. strain, and strain rate vs. strain, for type 403 stainless steel at 1800, 1950 and 2050 F (tests were conducted in a mechanical press where $\dot{\varepsilon}$ was not constant).[4-3]

temperature and then the test is initiated. Examples of hot formed compression samples are shown in Figure 4-8. Examples of high-temperature $\bar{\sigma}$-$\bar{\epsilon}$ data are given in Figures 4-9 and 4-10.

RING TEST

The ring test consists of compressing a flat ring-shape specimen to a known reduction (Figure 4-11). The changes in internal and external diameters of the forged ring are very much dependent on the friction at the tool/specimen interface.[4-4] If friction were equal to zero the ring would deform in the same way as a solid disk, with each element flowing radially outward at a rate proportional to its distance from the center. With increasing deformation, the internal diameter of the ring is reduced if friction is large, and is increased if friction is low. Thus, the change in the internal diameter represents a simple method for evaluating interface friction. This is discussed in detail in Chapter 6.

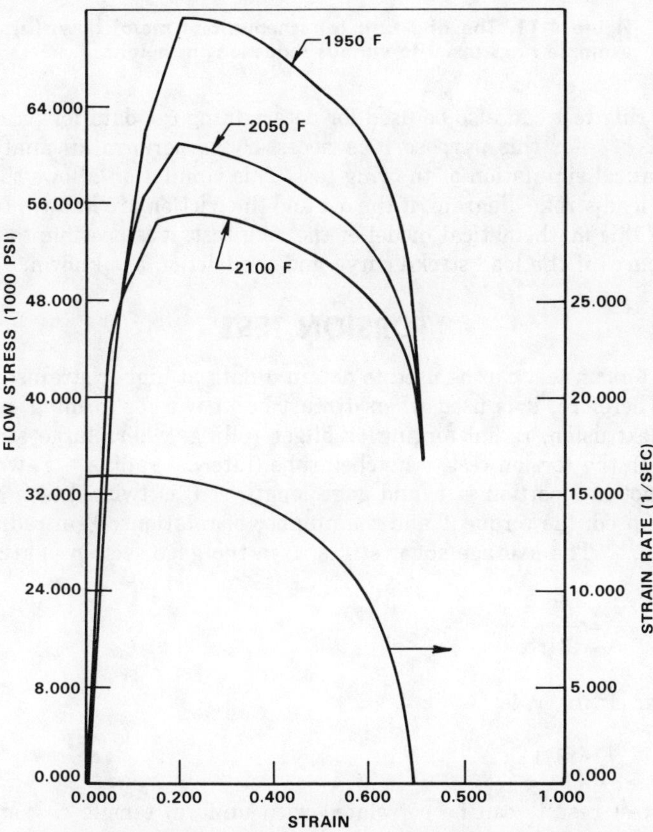

Figure 4-10. Flow stress vs. strain, and strain rate vs. strain, for Waspaloy at 1950, 2050 and 2100 F (tests were conducted in a mechanical press where $\dot{\bar{\epsilon}}$ was not constant).[4-3]

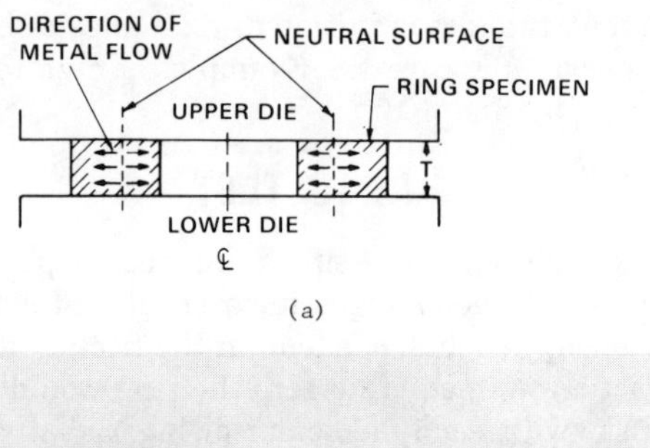

(a)

(b)

Figure 4-11. The ring test: (a) schematic of metal flow; (b) example rings upset to various reductions in height.

The ring test can also be used for determining $\bar{\sigma}$-$\bar{\epsilon}$ data for practical applications.[4-3] For this purpose it is necessary to perform an analysis or a mathematical simulation of the ring test. This simulation allows the prediction of a load-stroke diagram, if the $\bar{\sigma}$-$\bar{\epsilon}$ and the friction are known. Inversely, by using this mathematical model of the ring test, it is possible to calculate the $\bar{\sigma}$-$\bar{\epsilon}$ curve if the load-stroke curve and the friction are known.

TORSION TEST

The torsion test can be used to obtain $\bar{\sigma}$ data at higher strains up to $\bar{\epsilon}$ = 2 to 4. Therefore, it is used when $\bar{\sigma}$ must be known for forming operations such as extrusion, radial forging or pilger rolling, where large strains are present. In the torsion test, a notched tube (internal radius = r, wall thickness at notched portion = t, and gage length = l) is twisted at a given rotational speed; the torque T and the number of rotations, θ (in radians), are measured.[4-6] The average shear stress, τ, in the gage section is given by:

$$\tau = \frac{T}{2\Pi r^2 t} \tag{4-16}$$

The shear strain, γ, is:

$$\gamma = r\theta / l \tag{4-17}$$

Torsion test results can be correlated with uniform tensile or compression results as follows:

$$\tau = \frac{\bar{\sigma}}{\sqrt{3}} \tag{4-18}$$

and

$$\gamma = \int d\gamma = \sqrt{3} \int d\bar{\epsilon} = \sqrt{3}\,\bar{\epsilon} \tag{4-19}$$

Equations 4-18 and 4-19 are obtained from the Von Mises flow rule, which will be discussed later.

REPRESENTATION OF FLOW STRESS DATA

A typical $\bar{\sigma}$-$\bar{\epsilon}$ curve, obtained at temperatures below the recrystallization temperature, i.e., in the cold forming range, is similar to that shown in Figure 4-6. Here the strain hardening is pronounced, and $\bar{\sigma}$ for most materials is not appreciably affected by $\dot{\bar{\epsilon}}$. At hot working temperatures, most $\bar{\sigma}$-$\bar{\epsilon}$ curves are similar to those given in Figure 4-9 or 4-10. Obviously, values of $\bar{\sigma}$ are higher for stronger materials. At cold forming temperatures, $\bar{\sigma}$ increases with increasing $\bar{\epsilon}$ and reaches a "saturation" stress at values of $\bar{\epsilon}$ larger than 0.8 or 1.0. At hot working temperatures, $\bar{\sigma}$ increases with increasing $\dot{\bar{\epsilon}}$ and with decreasing temperature, θ. At constant $\dot{\bar{\epsilon}}$, $\bar{\sigma}$ versus $\bar{\epsilon}$ increases first, then decreases because of internal heat generation and thermal softening. In all tests, the test temperature is not constant in a strict sense. Because of plastic deformation, a temperature increase, $\Delta\theta$, takes place. This can be estimated as:

$$\Delta\theta = \frac{A\bar{\epsilon}\bar{\sigma}}{c\rho} \tag{4-20}$$

where A is a conversion factor, c is heat capacity and ρ is density.

Most materials, when tested at room temperature in the work-hardening range, are not affected by moderate strain rates; hence the speed of loading need not be controlled too closely. Approximate stress-strain relationships for a limited region of strain can often be given by an exponential equation of the form:

$$\bar{\sigma} = K(\bar{\epsilon})^n \tag{4-21}$$

where K and n are constants.

Equation 4-21 is illustrated graphically in Figure 4-12.[4-2] The slope of the curve on log-log coordinates is n, and $K = \bar{\sigma}$ when $\bar{\epsilon} = 1$. It may be noted

(text continued on page 71)

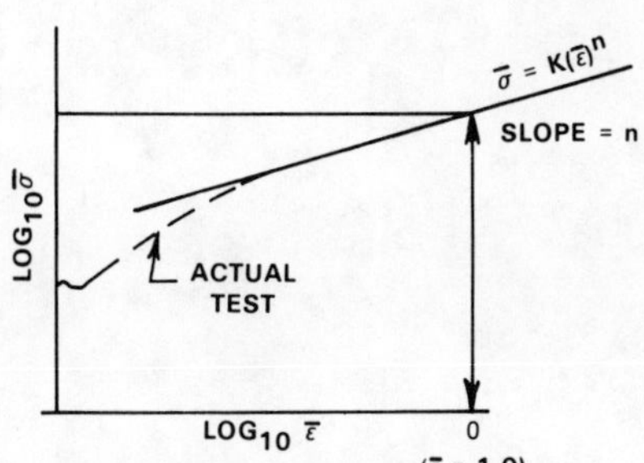

Figure 4-12. Effective stress vs. effective strain curve in log-log scale.

Table 4-1. Summary of K and n values describing the flow stress–strain relation, $\bar{\sigma} = K(\bar{\epsilon})^n$, for various steels

Steel	Composition(a), %												Material history(b)	Temperature		Strain rate, 1/s	Strain range	K, 10^3 psi	n
	C	Mn	P	S	Si	N	Al	V	Ni	Cr	Mo	W		F	C				
Armco iron	0.02	0.03	0.021	0.010	Tr								A	68	20	(c)	0.1-0.7	88.2	0.25
1006	0.06	0.29	0.02	0.042	Tr	0.004							A	68	20	(c)	0.1-0.7	89.6	0.31
1008	0.08	0.36	0.023	0.031	0.06	0.007							A	68	20	(c)	0.1-0.7	95.3	0.24
	0.07	0.28			0.27								A	68	20	(c)	0.1-0.7	95.3	0.17
1010	0.13	0.31	0.010	0.022	0.23	0.004							A	68	20	(c)	0.1-0.7	103.8	0.22
1015	0.15	0.40	0.01	0.016	Tr								F,A	32	0	30	0.2-0.7	91.4	0.116
1015	0.15	0.40	0.01	0.016	Tr								F,A	390	200	30	0.2-0.6	73.7	0.140
1015(d)	0.15	0.40	0.045	0.045	0.25								A	68	20	1.6		113.8	0.10
1015(d)	0.15	0.40	0.045	0.045	0.25								A	572	300	1.6		115.2	0.11
1020	0.22	0.44	0.017	0.043	Tr	0.005							A	68	20	(c)	0.1-0.7	108.1	0.20
1035	0.36	0.69	0.025	0.032	0.27	0.004							A	68	20	(c)	0.1-0.7	130.8	0.17
													A	68	20	1.6		139.4	0.11
													A	572	300	1.6		122.3	0.16
1045(d)	0.45	0.65	0.045	0.045	0.25								A	68	20	1.6		147.9	0.11
													A	68	20	1.5		137.9	0.14
													A	572	300	1.6		126.6	0.15
1050(e)	0.51	0.55	0.016	0.041	0.28	0.0062	0.03						A	68	20	(c)	0.1-0.7	140.8	0.16
													A	68	20	1.6		163.5	0.09

											A	572	300	1.6		102.4	0.15
5120(e)	0.18	1.13	0.019	0.023	0.27			0.86			A	68	20	(c)	0.1-0.7	126.6	0.18
											A	68	20	1.6		116.6	0.09
											A	572	300	1.6		98.1	0.16
5140	0.41	0.67	0.04	0.019	0.35			1.07			A	68	20	(c)	0.1-0.7	125.1	0.15
											A	68	20	1.6		133.7	0.09
											A	572	300	1.6		112.3	0.12
D2 tool steel(e)	1.60	0.45			0.24	0.46		11.70	0.75	0.59	A	68	20	(c)	0.2-1.0	191.0	0.157
L6 tool steel	0.56					0.14	1.60	1.21	0.47		A	68	20	(c)	0.2-1.0	170.2	0.128
W1-1.0C special	1.05	0.21			0.16						A	68	20	(c)	0.2-1.0	135.6	0.179
302 SS	0.08	1.06	0.037	0.005	0.49		9.16	18.37			HR,A	32	0	10	0.25-0.7	185.7	0.295
											HR,A	390	200	30	0.25-0.7	120.8	0.278
											HR,A	750	400	30	0.25-0.7	92.7	0.279
302 SS	0.053	1.08	0.027	0.015	0.27		10.2	17.8			A	68	20	(c)	0.1-0.7	210.5	0.6
304 SS(e)	0.030	1.05	0.023	0.014	0.47		10.6	18.7			A	68	20	(c)	0.1-0.7	210.5	0.6
316 SS	0.055	0.92	0.030	0.008	0.49		12.9	18.1	2.05		A	68	20	(c)	0.1-0.7	182.0	0.59
410 SS	0.093	0.31	0.026	0.012	0.33			13.8			A	68	20	(c)	0.1-0.7	119.4	0.2
											A	68	20	1.6		137.9	0.09
431 SS	0.23	0.38	0.020	0.006	0.42		1.72	16.32			A	68	20	(c)	0.1-0.7	189.1	0.11

(a) Tr = trace. (b) A = annealed, F = forged, HR = hot rolled. (c) Low-speed testing machine; no specific rate given. (d) Composition given is nominal (analysis not given in original reference). (e) Approximate composition.

Table 4-2. Summary of K and n values describing the flow stress–strain relation, $\bar{\sigma} = K(\bar{\epsilon})^n$, for various aluminum alloys

Alloy	Al	Cu	Si	Fe	Composition, % Mn	Mg	Zn	Ti	Cr	Pb	Material history(a)	Temperature F	C	Strain rate, 1/s	Strain range	K, 10^3 psi	n
1100	99.0	0.10	0.15	0.50	0.01	0.01					CD,A	32	0	10	0.25-0.7	25.2	0.304
1100	Rem	0.01	0.10	0.16	0.01	0.01	0.03				A	68	20	(b)	0.2-1.0	17.3	0.297
EC	99.5	0.01	0.092	0.23	0.026	0.033	0.01				A(c)	68	20	4	0.2-0.8	22.4	0.204
2017	Rem	4.04	0.70	0.45	0.55	0.76	0.22			0.06	A	68	20	(b)	0.2-1.0	45.2	0.180
2024(d) ..	Rem	4.48	0.60	0.46	0.87	1.12	0.20			0.056	A	68	20	(b)	0.2-1.0	56.1	0.154
5052	Rem	0.068	0.10	0.19	0.04	2.74	0.01	0.003			A(e)	68	20	4	0.2-0.8	29.4	0.134
5052(d) ..	Rem	0.09	0.13	0.16	0.23	2.50	0.05				A	68	20	(b)	0.2-1.0	55.6	0.189
5056	Rem	0.036	0.15	0.22	0.04	4.83	0.01		0.14		A(e)	68	20	4	0.2-0.7	57.0	0.130
5083	Rem	0.01	0.10	0.16	0.77	4.41	0.01	0.002	0.13		A	68	20	4	0.2-0.8	65.2	0.131
5454	Rem	0.065	0.12	0.18	0.81	2.45	<0.01	0.002			A(e)	68	20	4	0.2-0.8	49.9	0.137
6062	Rem	0.03	0.63	0.20	0.63	0.68	0.065	0.08				68	20	(b)	0.2-1.0	29.7	0.122

(a) CD = cold drawn, A = annealed. (b) Low-speed testing machine; no specific rate given. (c) Annealed for 4 h at 752 F (400 C). (d) Approximate composition. (e) Annealed for 4 h at 788 F (420 C).

Table 4-3. Summary of K and n values describing the flow stress–strain relation, $\bar{\sigma} = K(\bar{\epsilon})^n$, for various copper alloys

Alloy(a)	Composition(b), %									Temperature		Material history(c)	Strain rate, 1/s	Strain range	K, 10^3 psi	n
	Cu	Si	Fe	Sb	Sn	Zn	S	Pb	Ni	F	C					
CDA110	99.94		0.0025	0.0003			0.0012	0.0012	0.001	64	18	HR,A	2.5	0.25-0.7	65.5	0.328
CDA110										68	20	F	(d)	0.2-1.0	54.0	0.275
CDA230	84.3					15.7				68	20	A	(d)	0.2-1.0	76.7	0.373
CDA260	70.8					29.2				68	20	A	(d)	0.2-1.0	98.1	0.412
CDA260	70.05		Tr		Tr	Rem				390	200	HR,A		0.25-0.7	71.7	0.414
CDA272	63.3					36.7				68	20	A	(d)	0.2-1.0	103.9	0.394
CDA377	58.6		Tr			39.6		1.7		68	20	A	(d)	0.2-1.0	115.3	0.334
CDA521(e) ..	91.0				9.0					68	20	F	(d)	0.2-1.0	130.8	0.486
CDA647	97.0	0.5							2.0	68	20	F	(d)	0.2-1.0	67.2	0.282
CDA757	65.1					22.4		<0.05	12.4	68	20	A	(d)	0.2-1.0	101.8	0.401
CDA794	61.7		Tr			20.6		Tr	17.5	68	20	A	(d)	0.2-1.0	107.0	0.336

(a) CDA = Copper Development Association. (b) Tr = trace. (c) HR = hot rolled, A = annealed, F = forged. (d) Low-speed testing machine; no specific rate given. (e) Approximate composition.

Table 4-4. Summary of C (ksi) and m values describing the flow stress–strain rate relation, $\bar{\sigma} = C(\dot{\epsilon})^m$, for steels at various temperatures (C is in 10^3 psi)

Steel	Material history	Strain rate range, 1/s	Strain	C	m	C	m	C	m	C	m	C	m
		Test temperature, F (C):		**1110 (600)**		**1470 (800)**		**1830 (1000)**		**2190 (1200)**			
1015 0.15 C, trace Si, 0.40 Mn, 0.01 P, 0.016 S	Forged, annealed	0.2-30	0.2	36.8	0.112								
			0.25			19.9	0.105	17.0	0.045	7.2	0.137		
			0.4	40.6	0.131								
			0.5			21.5	0.104	18.8	0.058	6.8	0.169		
			0.6	40.0	0.121								
			0.7	39.5	0.114	21.1	0.109	18.3	0.068	5.7	0.181		
		Test temperature, F (C):		**1650 (900)**		**1830 (1000)**		**2010 (1100)**		**2190 (1200)**			
1016 0.15 C, 0.12 Si, 0.68 Mn, 0.034 S, 0.025 P	Hot rolled, annealed	1.5-100	0.10	16.6	0.092	13.4	0.100	9.9	0.124	7.5	0.143		
			0.30	22.7	0.082	18.2	0.085	13.3	0.115	9.4	0.153		
			0.50	23.7	0.087	18.2	0.105	12.7	0.146	8.5	0.191		
			0.70	23.1	0.099	16.1	0.147	11.9	0.166	7.5	0.218		
1016 0.15 C, 0.12 Si, 0.68 Mn 0.034 S, 0.025 P	Hot rolled, annealed		0.05	11.8	0.133	10.7	0.124	9.0	0.117	6.4	0.150		
			0.1	16.5	0.099	13.7	0.099	9.7	0.130	7.1	0.157		
			0.2	20.8	0.082	16.5	0.090	12.1	0.119	9.1	0.140		
			0.3	22.8	0.085	18.2	0.088	13.4	0.109	9.5	0.148		
			0.4	23.0	0.084	18.2	0.098	12.9	0.126	9.1	0.164		
			0.5	23.9	0.088	18.1	0.109	12.5	0.141	8.2	0.189		
			0.6	23.3	0.097	16.9	0.127	12.1	0.156	7.8	0.205		
			0.7	22.8	0.104	17.1	0.127	12.4	0.151	8.1	0.196		
		Test temperature, F (C):		**1600 (870)**		**1800 (980)**		**2000 (1090)**		**2200 (1205)**		**2150 (1180)**	
1018				25.2	0.07	15.8	0.152	11.0	0.192	9.2	0.20		
1025 0.25 C, 0.08 Si, 0.45 Mn, 0.012 P, 0.025 S	Forged, annealed	3.5-30	0.25			33.7	0.004	16.2	0.075	9.3	0.077		
			0.50			41.4	−0.032	17.2	0.080	9.6	0.094		
			0.70			41.6	−0.032	17.5	0.082	8.8	0.105		
1043	Hot rolled, as received	0.1-100	0.3/0.5/0.7									10.8	0.21
		Test temperature, F (C):		**1650 (900)**		**1830 (1000)**		**2010 (1100)**		**2190 (1200)**			
1045(a) 0.46 C, 0.29 Si, 0.73 Mn, 0.018 P, 0.021 S, 0.08 Cr, 0.01 Mo, 0.04 Ni			0.05	25.4	0.080	15.1	0.089	11.2	0.100	8.0	0.175		
			0.10	28.9	0.082	18.8	0.103	13.5	0.125	9.4	0.168		
			0.20	33.3	0.086	22.8	0.108	15.4	0.128	10.5	0.167		
			0.30	35.4	0.083	24.6	0.110	15.8	0.162	10.8	0.180		
			0.40	35.4	0.105	24.7	0.134	15.5	0.173	10.8	0.188		
		Test temperature, F (C):		**1110 (600)**		**1470 (800)**		**1830 (1000)**		**2190 (1200)**			
[illegible]	[illegible]	[illegible]				29.4	0.087	14.9	0.126	7.4	0.145		

			0.30	23.3	0.114	16.9	0.123	12.6	0.135	8.9	0.158		
0.014 S, 0.013 P, 0.12 Cr,			0.50	23.3	0.118	16.4	0.139	12.0	0.158	8.6	0.180		
0.09 Ni			0.70	21.3	0.132	14.9	0.161	10.4	0.193	7.8	0.207		
1060(a)			0.05	16.2	0.128	10.8	0.168	8.7	0.161	6.5	0.190		
0.56 C, 0.26 Si, 0.28 Mn,			0.10	18.3	0.127	13.2	0.145	10.1	0.149	7.5	0.165		
0.014 S, 0.013 P, 0.12 Cr,			0.20	21.8	0.119	16.1	0.125	12.1	0.126	8.5	0.157		
0.09 Ni			0.30	23.3	0.114	17.1	0.125	12.8	0.132	8.8	0.164		
			0.40	23.7	0.112	16.8	0.128	12.5	0.146	8.8	0.171		
			0.50	23.6	0.110	16.6	0.133	12.7	0.143	8.7	0.176		
			0.60	22.8	0.129	17.1	0.127	11.7	0.169	8.4	0.189		
			0.70	21.3	0.129	16.2	0.138	10.7	0.181	7.8	0.204		
1095(a)	Hot rolled,	1.5-100	0.10	18.3	0.146	13.9	0.143	9.8	0.159	7.1	0.184		
1.00 C, 0.19 Si, 0.17 Mn,	annealed		0.30	21.9	0.133	16.6	0.132	11.7	0.147	8.0	0.183		
0.027 S, 0.023 P, 0.10 Cr,			0.50	21.8	0.130	15.7	0.151	10.6	0.176	7.3	0.209		
0.09 Ni			0.70	21.0	0.128	13.6	0.179	9.7	0.191	6.5	0.232		
		Test temperature, F (C):		**1705 (930)**		**1830 (1000)**		**1940 (1060)**		**2075 (1135)**		**2190 (1200)**	
1115	Hot rolled,	4.4-23.1	0.105	16.3	0.088	13.0	0.108	10.9	0.112	9.1	0.123	7.6	0.116
0.17 C, 0.153 Si, 0.62 Mn,	as received		0.223	19.4	0.084	15.6	0.100	12.9	0.107	10.5	0.129	8.6	0.122
0.054 S, 0.032 P			0.338	20.4	0.094	17.3	0.090	14.0	0.117	11.2	0.138	8.8	0.141
			0.512	20.9	0.099	18.0	0.093	14.4	0.127	11.0	0.159	8.3	0.173
			0.695	20.9	0.105	16.9	0.122	13.6	0.150	9.9	0.198	7.6	0.196
		Test temperature, F (C):		**1650 (900)**		**1830 (1000)**		**2010 (1100)**		**2190 (1200)**			
Alloy steel			0.05	16.6	0.102	12.2	0.125	9.4	0.150	7.4	0.161		
0.35 C, 0.27 Si, 1.49 Mn,			0.10	19.9	0.091	14.8	0.111	11.5	0.121	8.1	0.149		
0.041 S, 0.037 P, 0.03 Cr,			0.20	23.0	0.094	17.6	0.094	13.5	0.100	9.4	0.139		
0.11 Ni, 0.28 Mo			0.30	24.9	0.092	19.1	0.093	14.4	0.105	10.2	0.130		
			0.40	26.0	0.088	19.6	0.095	14.5	0.112	10.4	0.139		
			0.50	25.9	0.091	19.6	0.100	14.4	0.112	10.1	0.147		
			0.60	25.9	0.094	19.5	0.105	14.2	0.122	9.7	0.159		
			0.70	25.5	0.099	19.2	0.107	13.9	0.126	9.2	0.165		
4337(a)	Hot rolled,	1.5-100	0.10	22.1	0.080	16.6	0.109	12.1	0.115	8.2	0.165		
0.35 C, 0.27 Si, 0.66 Mn,	annealed		0.30	28.1	0.077	20.8	0.098	15.0	0.111	10.7	0.138		
0.023 S, 0.029 P, 0.59 Cr,			0.50	29.2	0.075	21.8	0.096	15.7	0.112	11.3	0.133		
2.45 Ni, 0.59 Mo			0.70	28.1	0.080	21.3	0.102	15.5	0.122	11.3	0.135		
926(a)	Hot rolled,	1.5-100	0.10	22.9	0.109	17.1	0.106	11.8	0.152	8.6	0.168		
0.61 C, 1.58 Si, 0.94 Mn,	annealed		0.30	28.2	0.101	20.4	0.106	14.3	0.140	10.1	0.162		
0.038 S, 0.035 P, 0.12 Cr,			0.50	27.8	0.104	20.0	0.120	13.8	0.154	9.1	0.193		
0.27 Ni, 0.06 Mo			0.70	25.8	0.112	18.2	0.146	11.8	0.179	7.5	0.235		
50100(a)			0.05	16.1	0.155	12.4	0.155	8.2	0.175	6.3	0.199		
1.00 C, 0.19 Si, 0.17 Mn,			0.10	18.6	0.145	14.1	0.142	9.5	0.164	6.8	0.191		
0.027 S, 0.023 P, 0.10 Cr,			0.20	20.9	0.135	15.9	0.131	11.4	0.141	8.1	0.167		
0.09 Ni			0.30	21.8	0.135	16.6	0.134	11.7	0.142	8.0	0.174		

(continued)

Table 4-4. (continued)

Steel	Material history	Strain rate range, 1/s	Strain	C	m	C	m	C	m	C	m	C	m
50100(a), *continued*			0.40	22.0	0.134	16.8	0.134	11.2	0.155	8.4	0.164		
1.00 C, 0.19 Si, 0.17 Mn,			0.50	21.5	0.131	15.6	0.150	11.1	0.158	7.4	0.199		
0.027 S, 0.023 P, 0.10 Cr,			0.60	21.3	0.132	14.6	0.163	10.0	0.184	7.0	0.212		
0.09 Ni			0.70	20.9	0.131	13.5	0.176	9.7	0.183	6.7	0.220		
52100	Hot rolled,	1.5-100	0.10	20.9	0.123	14.3	0.146	9.5	0.169	6.7	0.203		
1.06 C, 0.22 Si, 0.46 Mn,	annealed		0.30	25.5	0.107	17.7	0.127	12.0	0.143	8.3	0.171		
0.019 S, 0.031 P, 1.41 Cr,			0.50	25.9	0.107	17.7	0.129	12.3	0.143	8.3	0.178		
0.17 Ni			0.70	23.3	0.131	16.8	0.134	12.0	0.148	7.7	0.192		
		Test temperature, F(C):		**1650 (900)**		**1830 (1000)**		**2010 (1100)**		**2190 (1200)**			
Mn-Si steel			0.05	19.2	0.117	14.8	0.119	9.7	0.172	7.5	0.181		
0.61 C, 1.58 Si, 0.94 Mn,			0.10	22.6	0.112	17.1	0.108	11.8	0.151	8.7	0.166		
0.038 S, 0.035 P, 0.12 Cr,			0.20	25.7	0.108	19.5	0.101	13.5	0.139	9.7	0.160		
0.27 Ni, 0.06 Mo			0.30	27.6	0.108	20.5	0.109	14.8	0.126	10.0	0.161		
			0.40	27.6	0.114	20.2	0.114	14.4	0.141	9.5	0.179		
			0.50	27.2	0.113	19.8	0.125	14.1	0.144	9.1	0.188		
			0.60	26.0	0.121	18.8	0.137	12.8	0.162	8.2	0.209		
			0.70	24.7	0.130	17.8	0.152	11.9	0.178	7.5	0.228		
Cr-Si steel			0.05	19.9	0.118	23.9	0.104	15.1	0.167	10.0	0.206		
0.47 C, 3.74 Si, 0.58 Mn,			0.10	19.9	0.136	25.6	0.120	16.8	0.162	11.1	0.189		
8.20 Cr, 0.20 Ni			0.20	19.9	0.143	27.6	0.121	18.5	0.153	11.9	0.184		
			0.30	19.9	0.144	28.4	0.119	19.1	0.148	12.1	0.182		
			0.40	19.3	0.150	28.2	0.125	18.9	0.150	12.1	0.178		
			0.50	18.5	0.155	26.6	0.132	18.5	0.155	11.8	0.182		
			0.60	17.5	0.160	25.2	0.142	17.5	0.160	11.5	0.182		
			0.70	16.1	0.163	23.3	0.158	16.1	0.162	10.7	0.199		
D3(a)	Hot rolled,	1.5-100	0.10	39.2	0.087	29.0	0.108	21.0	0.123	14.6	0.121		
2.23 C, 0.43 Si, 0.37 Mn,	annealed		0.30	43.7	0.087	30.4	0.114	21.0	0.139	13.9	0.130		
			[illegible]	[illegible]	[illegible]	[illegible]	[illegible]	[illegible]	0.155	[illegible]	0.124		

[illegible]											
0.018 P, 0.020 S, 5.29 Cr,			0.3	31.0	0.179	15.1	0.265	10.8	0.305	11.6	0.267
0.04 Ni, 1.35 Mo, 0.027 N,			0.4	25.9	0.204	12.3	0.295	12.5	0.287	11.8	0.269
0.83 V											
		Test temperature, F (C):		**1650 (900)**		**1830 (1000)**		**2010 (1100)**		**2190 (1200)**	
H-26(a)	Hot rolled,	1.5-100	0.10	46.7	0.058	37.4	0.072	26.2	0.106	18.7	0.125
0.80 C, 0.28 Si, 0.32 Mn,	annealed		0.30	49.6	0.075	38.1	0.087	26.0	0.121	18.3	0.140
4.30 Cr, 0.18 Ni, 0.55 Mo,			0.50	44.6	0.096	33.7	0.102	23.6	0.131	16.2	0.151
18.40 W, 1.54 V			0.70	39.1	0.115	27.9	0.124	20.1	0.149	13.8	0.162
		Test temperature, F (C):		**1110 (600)**		**1470 (800)**		**1830 (1000)**		**2190 (1200)**	
301 SS(a)	Hot rolled,	0.8-100	0.25			40.5	0.051	16.3	0.117	7.6	0.161
0.08 C, 0.93 Si, 1.10 Mn,	annealed		0.50			39.3	0.062	17.8	0.108	7.6	0.177
0.009 P, 0.014 S, 16.99 Cr,			0.70			37.8	0.069	17.4	0.102	6.6	0.192
6.96 Ni, 0.31 Mo, 0.93 Al,											
0.02 N, 0.063 Se											
302 SS	Hot rolled,	310-460	0.25	26.5	0.147	25.1	0.129	11.0	0.206	4.6	0.281
0.07 C, 0.71 Si, 1.07 Mn,	annealed		0.40	31.3	0.153	30.0	0.121	13.5	0.188	4.7	0.284
0.03 P, 0.005 S, 18.34 Cr,			0.60	17.5	0.270	45.4	0.063	16.8	0.161	4.1	0.310
9.56 Ni											
302 SS	Hot rolled,	0.2-30	0.25	52.2	0.031	36.6	0.042	23.1	0.040	12.8	0.082
0.08 C, 0.49 Si, 1.06 Mn,	annealed		0.40	58.9	0.022	40.4	0.032	24.7	0.050	13.6	0.083
0.037 P, 0.005 S, 18.37 Cr,			0.60	63.2	0.020	41.9	0.030	24.9	0.053	13.5	0.091
9.16 Ni			0.70	64.0	0.023	42.0	0.031	24.7	0.052	13.4	0.096
		Test temperature, F (C):		**1650 (900)**		**1830 (1000)**		**2010 (1100)**		**2190 (1200)**	
302 SS		1.5-100	0.05	24.6	0.023	16.8	0.079	13.7	0.093	9.7	0.139
0.07 C, 0.43 Si, 0.48 Mn,			0.10	28.4	0.026	21.2	0.068	15.6	0.091	11.1	0.127
18.60 Cr, 7.70 Ni			0.20	33.6	0.031	25.2	0.067	18.1	0.089	12.5	0.120
			0.30	35.3	0.042	26.3	0.074	19.5	0.089	13.5	0.115
			0.40	35.6	0.055	26.9	0.084	19.9	0.094	14.2	0.110
			0.50	35.6	0.060	27.0	0.093	19.6	0.098	14.2	0.115
			0.60	34.1	0.068	26.4	0.092	19.3	0.102	13.8	0.118
			0.70	33.6	0.072	25.7	0.102	18.9	0.108	13.9	0.120

(continued)

Table 4-4. (continued)

Steel	Material history	Strain rate range, 1/s	Strain	C	m	C	m	C	m	C	m	C	m
		Test temperature, F (C):		**1110 (600)**		**1470 (800)**		**1830 (1000)**		**2190 (1200)**		**1650 (900)**	
309 SS	Hot drawn,	200-525	0.25			39.4	0.079			8.7	0.184		
0.13 C, 0.42 Si, 1.30 Mn,	annealed		0.40			45.1	0.074			9.6	0.178		
0.023 P, 0.008 S, 22.30 Cr,			0.60			48.1	0.076			9.5	0.185		
12.99 Ni													
310 SS	Hot drawn,	310-460	0.25	50.3	0.080	32.3	0.127	27.5	0.101	12.0	0.154		
0.12 C, 1.26 Si, 1.56 Mn,	annealed		0.40	56.5	0.080	32.2	0.142	22.8	0.143	10.8	0.175		
0.01 P, 0.009 S, 25.49 Cr,			0.60	61.8	0.067	21.9	0.212	9.7	0.284	4.5	0.326		
21.28 Ni													
316 SS	Hot drawn,	310-460	0.25	13.5	0.263	22.2	0.149	6.4	0.317	8.0	0.204		
0.06 C, 0.52 Si, 1.40 Mn,	annealed		0.40	28.8	0.162	26.8	0.138	3.7	0.435	7.4	0.227		
0.035 P, 0.005 S, 17.25 Cr,			0.60	39.3	0.128	30.1	0.133	6.1	0.365	6.5	0.254		
12.23 Ni, 2.17 Mo													
403 SS	Hot rolled,	0.8-100	0.25			26.3	0.079	15.4	0.125	7.3	0.157		
0.16 C, 0.37 Si, 0.44 Mn,	annealed		0.50			26.9	0.076	16.0	0.142	7.8	0.152		
0.024 P, 0.007 S, 12.62 Cr			0.70			24.6	0.090	15.3	0.158	7.5	0.155		
SS	Hot rolled,	0.8-100	0.25			28.7	0.082	17.2	0.082	11.9	0.079		
0.12 C, 0.12 Si, 0.29 Mn,	annealed		0.50			29.1	0.093	20.7	0.073	11.6	0.117		
0.014 P, 0.016 S, 12.11 Cr,			0.70			28.7	0.096	22.5	0.067	11.2	0.131		
0.50 Ni, 0.45 Mo													
SS	Hot rolled,	3.5-30	0.25					19.5	0.099	8.9	0.128	28.3	0.114
0.08 C, 0.45 Si, 0.43 Mn,	annealed		0.50					22.3	0.097	9.5	0.145	34.9	0.105
0.031 P, 0.005 S, 17.38 Cr,			0.70					23.2	0.098	9.2	0.158	37.1	0.107
0.31 Ni													
		Test temperature, F (C):		**1600 (870)**		**1700 (925)**		**1800 (980)**		**2000 (1095)**		**2100 (1150)**	
Maraging 300				43.4	0.077	36.4	0.095	30.6	0.113	21.5	0.145	18.0	0.165
		Test temperature, F (C):		**2200 (1205)**									
Maraging 300				12.8	0.185								

(a) Approximate composition.

Table 4-5. Summary of C (ksi) and m values describing the flow stress–strain rate relation, $\bar{\sigma} = C(\dot{\bar{\varepsilon}})^m$, for aluminum alloys at various temperatures

Alloy	Material history	Strain rate range, 1/s	Strain	C	m	C	m	C	m	C	m	C	m
	Test temperature, F (C):			**390 (200)**		**570 (300)**		**750 (400)**		**930 (500)**		**1110 (600)**	
Super-pure	Cold rolled,	0.4-311											
99.98 Al, 0.0017 Cu,	annealed 1/2 h		0.288	5.7	0.110	4.3	0.120	2.8	0.140	1.6	0.155	0.6	0.230
0.0026 Si, 0.0033 Fe,	at 1110 F		2.88	8.7	0.050	4.9	0.095	2.8	0.125	1.6	0.175	0.6	0.215
0.006 Mn													
	Test temperature, F (C):			**465 (240)**		**645 (360)**		**825 (480)**					
EC	Annealed 3h	0.25-63											
0.01 Cu, 0.026 Mn,	at 750 F		0.20	10.9	0.066	5.9	0.141	3.4	0.168				
0.033 Mg, 0.092 Si,			0.40	12.3	0.069	6.3	0.146	3.3	0.169				
0.23 Fe, 0.01 Zn,			0.60	13.1	0.067	6.4	0.147	3.2	0.173				
99.5 Al			0.80	13.8	0.064	6.7	0.135	3.4	0.161				
	Test temperature, F (C):			**390 (200)**		**750 (400)**		**930 (500)**					
1100	Cold drawn,	0.25-40											
99.0 Al (min), 0.10 Cu,	annealed		0.25	9.9	0.066	4.2	0.115	2.1	0.211				
0.15 Si, 0.50 Fe,			0.50	11.6	0.071	4.4	0.132	2.1	0.227				
0.01 Mn, 0.01 Mg			0.70	12.2	0.075	4.5	0.141	2.1	0.224				
	Test temperature, F (C):			**300 (150)**		**480 (250)**		**660 (350)**		**840 (450)**		**1020 (550)**	
1100(a)	Extruded, an-	4-40											
0.10 Cu, 0.20 Si,	nealed 1 h at		0.105	11.4	0.022	9.1	0.026	6.3	0.055	3.9	0.100	2.2	0.130
0.02 Mn, 0.46 Fe,	750 F		0.223	13.5	0.022	10.5	0.031	6.9	0.061	4.3	0.098	2.4	0.130
0.01 Zn, Rem Al			0.338	15.0	0.021	11.4	0.035	7.2	0.073	4.5	0.100	2.5	0.141
			0.512	16.1	0.024	11.9	0.041	7.3	0.084	4.4	0.116	2.4	0.156
			0.695	17.0	0.026	12.3	0.041	7.4	0.088	4.3	0.130	2.4	0.155
	Test temperature, F (C):			**390 (200)**		**750 (400)**		**930 (500)**					
2017	Cold drawn,	0.2-30											
94.95 Al, 3.50 Cu,	annealed		0.250	34.5	0.014	14.8	0.110	5.8	0.126				
0.10 Si, 0.50 Fe,			0.500	32.2	−0.025	13.2	0.121	5.2	0.121				
0.50 Mn, 0.45 Mg			0.700	29.5	−0.038	12.5	0.128	5.1	0.119				
	Test temperature, F (C):			**570 (300)**		**660 (350)**		**750 (400)**		**840 (450)**		**930 (500)**	
2017(a)	Solution treated	0.4-311											
0.89 Mg, 4.17 Cu,	1 h at 950 F,		0.115	10.8	0.695	9.1	0.100	7.5	0.110	6.2	0.145	5.1	0.155
0.61 Si, 0.41 Fe, 0.80 Mn,	water quenched		2.660	10.0	0.100	9.2	0.100	7.7	0.080	6.8	0.090	4.6	0.155
0.052 Zn, 0.01 Pb,	annealed 4 h												
92.9 Al	at 750 F												

(continued)

Table 4-5. (continued)

Alloy	Material history	Strain rate range, 1/s	Strain	C	m	C	m	C	m	C	m	C	m
		Test temperature, F (C):		**465 (240)**		**645 (360)**		**825 (480)**					
5052	Annealed 3 h	0.25-63											
0.068 Cu, 0.04 Mn,	at 790 F		0.20	14.3	0.038	8.9	0.067	5.6	0.125				
2.74 Mg, 0.10 Si,			0.40	15.9	0.035	9.3	0.071	5.3	0.130				
0.19 Fe, 0.01 Zn,			0.60	16.8	0.035	9.0	0.068	5.1	0.134				
0.003 Ti, Rem Al			0.80	17.5	0.038	9.4	0.068	5.6	0.125				
5056	Annealed 3 h	0.25-63											
0.036 Cu, 0.04 Mn,	at 790 F		0.20	42.6	−0.032	20.9	0.138	11.7	0.200				
4.83 Mg, 0.15 Si,			0.40	44.0	−0.032	20.8	0.138	10.5	0.205				
0.22 Fe, 0.01 Zn,			0.60	44.9	−0.031	19.9	0.143	10.3	0.202				
0.14 Cr, Rem Al			0.70	45.6	−0.034	20.3	0.144	10.3	0.203				
5083	Annealed 3 h	0.25-63											
0.01 Cu, 0.77 Mn,	at 790 F		0.20	43.6	−0.006	20.5	0.095	9.3	0.182				
4.41 Mg, 0.10 Si,			0.40	43.6	−0.001	19.7	0.108	8.3	0.208				
0.16 Fe, 0.01 Zn,			0.60	41.9	0.003	18.8	0.111	8.5	0.201				
0.13 Cr, 0.002 Ti,			0.80	40.2	0.002	19.1	0.105	9.7	0.161				
Rem Al													
5454	Annealed 3 h	0.25-63											
0.065 Cu, 0.81 Mn,	at 790 F		0.20	33.6	−0.005	16.8	0.093	10.8	0.182				
2.45 Mg, 0.12 Si,			0.40	36.0	−0.009	16.3	0.104	10.7	0.188				
0.18 Fe, <0.01 Zn,			0.60	36.9	−0.009	16.0	0.102	10.0	0.191				
0.002 Ti, Rem Al			0.80	37.0	−0.009	16.2	0.097	10.2	0.183				
		Test temperature, F (C):		**750 (400)**		**840 (450)**		**930 (500)**		**1020 (550)**			
7075(a)	Solution treated 1 h	0.4-311											
89.6 Al, 1.31 Cu,	at 870 F, water		0.115	10.0	0.090	6.0	0.135	3.9	0.150	2.9	0.170		
2.21 Mg, 0.21 Si,	quenched, aged		2.66	9.7	0.115	6.2	0.120	4.8	0.115	2.7	0.115		
0.30 Fe, 0.34 Mn,	at 285 F for												
5.75 Zn, 0.01 Pb	16 h												

(a) Approximate composition.

Table 4-6. Summary of C (ksi) and m values describing the flow stress–strain rate relation, $\bar{\sigma} = C(\dot{\epsilon})^m$, for copper alloys at various temperatures

Alloy	Material history	Strain rate range, 1/s	Strain	C	m	C	m	C	m	C	m	C	m
		Test temperature, F (C):		**570 (300)**		**840 (450)**		**1110 (600)**		**1380 (750)**		**1650 (900)**	
Copper	Cold drawn,	4-40	0.105	20.2	0.016	17.0	0.010	12.7	0.050	7.6	0.096	4.7	0.134
0.018 P, 0.0010 Ni, 0.0003 Sn,	annealed 2 h		0.223	26.5	0.018	22.5	0.004	16.8	0.043	9.7	0.097	6.3	0.110
0.0002 Sb, 0.0005 Pb	at 1110 F		0.338	30.2	0.017	25.1	0.008	18.9	0.041	10.0	0.128	6.1	0.154
0.0010 Fe, 0.0020 Mn,			0.512	32.2	0.025	26.6	0.014	19.4	0.056	8.5	0.186	5.5	0.195
<0.0005 Mg, <0.0005 As,			0.695	34.4	0.024	26.8	0.031	19.0	0.078	8.2	0.182	5.2	0.190
<0.0001 Bi, 0.0014 S, less													
than 0.003 O_2, Se + Te not													
detected													
		Test temperature, F (C):		**800 (427)**									
OFHC Copper				26.7	0.0413								
		Test temperature, F (C):		**750 (400)**		**930 (500)**		**1110 (600)**					
CDA 110	Hot rolled,	0.25-40	0.25	23.0	0.046	12.9	0.136	6.6	0.160				
99.94 Cu, 0.0003 Sb, 0.0012 Pb	annealed		0.50	27.4	0.049	13.7	0.150	6.9	0.168				
0.0012 S, 0.0025 Fe, 0.001 Ni			0.70	28.8	0.057	13.3	0.165	6.8	0.176				
		Test temperature, F (C):		**390 (200)**		**750 (400)**		**1110 (600)**		**1470 (800)**			
CDA 220	Extruded, cold	0.1-10	0.25	41.0	0.017	34.1	0.018	22.6	0.061	11.2	0.134		
90.06 Cu, 0.033 Fe, 0.004 Pb,	drawn 30%;		0.50	46.7	0.029	39.9	0.032	24.4	0.084	11.0	0.156		
0.003 Sn, Rem Zn	annealed 650 C,		0.70	48.1	0.034	40.7	0.024	24.6	0.086	11.4	0.140		
	90 min												
CDA 260	Hot rolled,	3.5-30	0.25			34.9	0.036	16.0	0.194	7.1	0.144		
70.05 Cu, trace Fe + Sn,	annealed		0.50			42.3	0.031	14.8	0.237	7.0	0.148		
Rem Zn			0.70			42.4	0.045	14.3	0.228	6.3	0.151		
CDA 280	Hot rolled,	3.5-30	0.25	49.0	0.028	26.9	0.083	7.6	0.189	3.1	0.228		
60.44 Cu, 0.01 Pb, 0.02 Fe,	annealed		0.50	58.6	0.027	28.6	0.075	5.4	0.281	2.8	0.239		
trace Sn, Rem Zn			0.70	60.3	0.027	26.7	0.081	4.7	0.291	2.7	0.220		
CDA 365	Hot rolled,	3.5-30	0.25	45.8	0.038	28.6	0.065	9.8	0.106	2.4	0.166		
59.78 Cu, 0.90 Pb, 0.02 Fe,	annealed		0.50	57.2	0.032	28.9	0.085	8.5	0.137	2.1	0.197		
trace Sn, Rem Zn			0.70	59.1	0.035	26.6	0.078	8.4	0.113	1.8	0.222		

Table 4-7. Summary of C (ksi) and m values describing the flow stress–strain rate relation, $\bar{\sigma} = C(\dot{\varepsilon})^m$, for titanium alloys at various temperatures

Alloy	Material history	Strain rate range, 1/s	Strain	C	m	C	m	C	m	C	m	C	m	C	m	C	m
		Test temperature, F (C):		**68 (20)**		**392 (200)**		**752 (400)**		**1112 (600)**		**1472 (800)**		**1652 (900)**		**1832 (1000)**	
Type 1	Annealed 15 min	0.25-16.0	0.2	92.8	0.029	60.9	0.046	39.8	0.074	25.3	0.097	12.8	0.167	5.4	0.230	3.0	0.387
0.04 Fe, 0.02 C,	at 1200 F in		0.4	113.7	0.029	73.3	0.056	48.8	0.061	29.6	0.115	14.6	0.181	5.5	0.248	3.6	0.289
0.005 H_2, 0.01 N_2,	high vacuum		0.6	129.6	0.028	82.2	0.056	53.9	0.049	32.1	0.105	14.9	0.195	5.5	0.248	3.5	0.289
0.04 O_2, Rem Ti			0.8	142.5	0.027	87.7	0.058	56.3	0.042	32.7	0.099	15.4	0.180	5.9	0.186	3.2	0.264
			1.0	150.6	0.027	90.7	0.054	56.6	0.044	32.5	0.099	15.9	0.173	5.9	0.167	3.0	0.264
Type 2	Annealed 15 min	0.25-16.0	0.2	143.3	0.021	92.7	0.043	54.5	0.051	33.6	0.092	17.5	0.167	6.9	0.135	4.2	0.220
0.15 Fe, 0.02 C,	at 1200 F in		0.4	173.2	0.021	112.1	0.042	63.1	0.047	36.3	0.101	18.4	0.190	7.2	0.151	4.9	0.167
0.005 H_2, 0.02 N_2,	high vacuum		0.6	193.8	0.024	125.3	0.045	65.6	0.047	36.9	0.104	18.4	0.190	7.8	0.138	4.5	0.167
0.12 O_2, Rem Ti			0.8	208.0	0.023	131.9	0.051	66.0	0.045	37.0	0.089	18.4	0.190	7.6	0.106	3.9	0.195
			1.0	216.8	0.023	134.8	0.056	65.3	0.045	36.9	0.092	18.6	0.190	6.8	0.097	3.7	0.167
		Test temperature, F (C):		**1110 (600)**		**1290 (700)**		**1470 (800)**		**1650 (900)**							
Unalloyed	Hot rolled,	0.1-10	0.25	23.4	0.062	14.3	0.115	8.2	0.236	1.8	0.324						
0.03 Fe, 0.0084 N,	annealed 800 C,		0.50	27.9	0.066	17.8	0.111	10.0	0.242	2.1	0.326						
0.0025 H, Rem Ti	90 min		0.70	30.1	0.065	20.0	0.098	12.2	0.185	2.5	0.316						
		Test temperature, F (C):		**68 (20)**		**392 (200)**		**752 (400)**		**1112 (600)**		**1472 (800)**		**1652 (900)**		**1832 (1000)**	
Ti-5Al-2.5 Sn	Annealed 30 min	0.25-16.0	0.1	173.6	0.046	125.6	0.028	97.6	0.028								
5.1 Al, 2.5 Sn, 0.06 Fe,	at 1470 F in		0.2	197.9	0.048	138.8	0.022	107.4	0.026	86.1	0.025	58.5	0.034	44.2	0.069	5.4	0.308
			0.3	215.6	0.046	147.4	0.021	112.5	0.027	92.8	0.020						

			[illegible]									46.8	0.025				
			1.0											35.2	0.056	5.3	0.280
Ti-6Al-4V	Annealed 120 min	0.25-16.0	0.1	203.3	0.017	143.8	0.026	119.4	0.025								
6.4 Al, 4.0 V, 0.14 Fe,	at 1200 F in		0.2	209.7	0.015	151.0	0.021	127.6	0.022	94.6	0.064	51.3	0.146	23.3	0.143	9.5	0.131
0.05 C, 0.01 H_2,	high vacuum		0.3	206.0	0.015	152.0	0.017	126.2	0.017	91.2	0.073						
0.015 N_2, 0.1 O_2, Rem Ti			0.4					118.7	0.014	84.6	0.079	39.8	0.175	21.4	0.147	9.4	0.118
			0.5							77.9	0.080						
			0.6									30.4	0.205	20.0	0.161	9.6	0.118
			0.8									26.6	0.199	19.5	0.172	9.3	0.154
			0.9									24.9	0.201				
			1.0											20.3	0.146	8.9	0.192
	Test temperature, F (C):			**1550 (843)**		**1750 (954)**		**1800 (982)**									
Ti-6Al-4V				38.0	0.064	12.3	0.24	9.4	0.29								
	Test temperature, F (C):			**68 (20)**		**392 (200)**		**752 (400)**		**1112 (600)**		**1472 (800)**		**1652 (900)**		**1832 (1000)**	
Ti-13V-11Cr-3Al	Annealed 30 min	0.25-16.0	0.1	173.1	0.041												
3.6 Al, 14.1 V, 10.6 Cr,	at 1290 F in		0.2	188.2	0.037	150.5	0.030	136.5	0.035	118.4	0.040	65.4	0.097	44.6	0.147	32.4	0.153
0.27 Fe, 0.02 C,	high vacuum		0.3	202.3	0.034												
0.014 H_2, 0.03 N_2,			0.4	215.2	0.029	174.2	0.024	153.9	0.030	107.5	0.039	59.5	0.096	42.1	0.139	30.9	0.142
0.11 O_2, Rem Ti			0.5	226.3	0.026	181.1	0.023										
			0.6			183.5	0.026	147.9	0.046	92.8	0.045	56.7	0.088	40.9	0.127	29.2	0.155
			0.7			181.4	0.029										
			0.8					136.3	0.045	84.7	0.036	53.9	0.081	39.3	0.125	27.8	0.167
			0.9									52.9	0.080				
			1.0											38.8	0.127	28.0	0.159

Table 4-8. Summary of C (ksi) and m values describing the flow stress–strain rate relation, $\bar{\sigma} = C(\dot{\bar{\epsilon}})^m$, for various materials

Material	Material history	Strain rate range, 1/s	Strain	C	m	C	m	C	m	C	m	C	m	C	m	C	m
	Test temperature, F (C):			**72 (22)**		**230 (110)**		**335 (170)**		**415 (215)**		**500 (260)**		**570 (300)**			
Lead			0.115	2.0	0.040	1.56	0.065	1.21	0.085	0.70	0.130	0.47	0.160	0.40	0.180		
99.98 Pb, 0.003 Cu,			2.66	4.0	0.055	1.47	0.100	1.04	0.125	0.55	0.135	0.36	0.180	0.28	0.225		
0.003 Fe, 0.002 Zn,																	
0.002 Ag																	
	Test temperature, F (C):			**390 (200)**		**570 (300)**		**750 (400)**		**930 (400)**							
Magnesium	Extruded, cold			(13)		(14)		(13)		(14)							
0.010 Al, 0.003 Zn,	drawn 15%,	0.1-10	0.25	19.1	0.069	9.8	0.215	4.1	0.263	1.7	0.337						
0.008 Mn, 0.004 Si,	annealed 550 C		0.50	17.2	0.093	8.4	0.211	4.0	0.234	1.7	0.302						
0.003 Cu, 0.0008 Ni,	90 min		0.70	15.5	0.094	8.3	0.152	4.3	0.215	2.1	0.210						
Rem Mg																	
	Test temperature, F (C):			**1975 (1080)**		**2030 (1166)**											
U-700				26.6	0.21	22.1	0.21										
	Test temperature, F (C):			**68 (20)**		**392 (200)**		**752 (400)**		**1112 (600)**		**1472 (800)**		**1652 (900)**		**1832 (1000)**	
Zirconium	Annealed 15	0.25-16.0	0.2	117.4	0.031	74.0	0.052	40.2	0.050	23.8	0.069	16.8	0.069	6.8	0.227	4.6	0.301
99.8 Zr, 0.009 Hf,	min at 1380 F		0.3	143.7	0.022	92.2	0.058										
0.008 Al, 0.038 Fe,	in high vacuum		0.4	159.5	0.017	105.1	0.046	54.4	0.085	29.4	0.09	18.2	0.116	7.1	0.252	4.0	0.387
0.0006 H_2, 0.0025 N_2,			0.5	169.3	0.017	112.8	0.041	58.2	0.093								
0.0825 O_2, 0.0 Ni			0.6			118.5	0.042	60.2	0.095	31.3	0.089	18.8	0.118	7.2	0.264	4.0	0.387
			0.7					61.9	0.095								
			0.8							32.0	0.081	19.4	0.101	6.9	0.252	4.1	0.403
			1.0							32.1	0.085	19.7	0.108	6.9	0.252	4.1	0.403
Zircaloy 2	Annealed 15	0.25-16.0	0.1	96.8	0.031	65.9	0.046										
98.35 Zr, 0.015 Hf,	min at 1380 F		0.2	136.9	0.025	105.8	0.035	58.3	0.065	30.4	0.049	16.6	0.147	7.5	0.325	3.9	0.362
1.4 Zn, 0.01 Al,	in high vacuum		0.3	178.5	0.034	131.4	0.035	67.9	0.056								
0.06 Fe, 0.045 Ni,			0.4	202.7	0.027	145.4	0.036	73.5	0.056	37.8	0.053	18.7	0.172	7.8	0.342	4.0	0.387
0.0006 H_2, 0.0023 N_2,			0.5			154.2	0.034	77.3	0.057								
0.0765 O_2			0.6					79.9	0.055	39.2	0.059	18.8	0.178	7.2	0.387	4.0	0.387
			0.8							40.4	0.057	18.8	0.178	7.9	0.342	4.8	0.333
			1.0							40.7	0.053	18.8	0.178	8.5	0.310	4.8	0.333
	Test temperature, F (C):			**68 (20)**		**212 (100)**		**392 (200)**		**572 (300)**		**932 (500)**		**1292 (900)**		**1652 (900)**	
Uranium	Annealed 2 hr	0.25-16.0	0.2	151.0	0.043	113.0	0.042	77.4	0.034	45.9	0.044	31.9	0.051	16.0	0.081	4.5	0.069
99.8 U, 0.0012 Mn,	at 1110 F in		0.4	173.9	0.033	132.7	0.049	91.0	0.031	53.3	0.047	33.1	0.059	16.1	0.089	4.5	0.069
0.0012 Ni, 0.00074 Cu,	high vacuum		0.6	184.9	0.023	143.1	0.047	98.1	0.032	56.0	0.056	33.4	0.054	16.1	0.089	4.5	0.069
0.00072 Cr, 0.0001 Co,			0.8	189.8	0.018	149.5	0.048	102.0	0.036	58.3	0.057	33.3	0.049	16.2	0.097	4.5	0.069
0.0047 H_2, 0.0041 N_2,			1.0							59.0	0.056	32.5	0.055	16.4	0.097	4.5	0.069
0.1760 O_2 (free of																	

from the schematic diagram of Figure 4-12 that, at small strains, an experimentally determined curve may depart from the curve given by Equation 4-14. In that case, other values of n and K may be specified for different ranges of effective strain. Typical values of n and K are given in Tables 4-1 to 4-3 for various metals.[4-1] It should be noted that other forms of stress-strain curves for room-temperature forming, i.e., cold forming, have been suggested. Some of these are:

$$\text{Ludwik:} \quad \bar{\sigma} = a + b(\bar{\epsilon})^c \tag{4-22}$$

where a, b and c are arbitrary constants. This form approximates the stress-strain curves for annealed materials, but tends to underestimate stress where strains are small (<0.2) and to overestimate actual stress for larger strains. For heavily prestrained materials, $c \simeq 1$.

$$\text{Voce:} \quad \bar{\sigma} = a + [b - a][1 - \exp(-c\bar{\epsilon})] \tag{4-23}$$

This gives a good fit, but is not suitable for use in analysis because of its complexity.

Table 4-9. Average flow stress values determined in the uniform compression test that might be used in practical load-predicting applications

Material	Flow stress, 10^3 psi	Temperature, F	Strain range (ln), h_0/h_1	Strain rate range, 1/s
403 stainless steel	33.0	1800	0.3-0.7	10.0-14.0
	25.0	1950	0.3-0.7	10.0-14.0
	21.0	2050	0.3-0.7	10.0-14.0
Waspaloy	62.0	1950	0.2-0.4	13.0-15.0
	56.0	1950	0.4-0.6	10.0-13.0
	52.0	2050	0.1-0.3	12.0-15.0
	48.0	2050	0.3-0.6	10.0-13.0
	46.0	2100	0.1-0.3	13.0-15.0
	42.0	2100	0.3-0.6	10.0-13.0
Ti-6Al-2Sn-4Zr-2Mo	56.0	1600	0.1-0.4	13.0-15.0
	52.0	1600	0.4-0.6	10.0-13.0
	52.0	1675	0.1-0.4	13.0-15.0
	46.0	1675	0.4-0.6	10.0-13.0
	38.0	1750	0.1-0.4	13.0-15.0
	34.0	1750	0.4-0.6	10.0-13.0
Inconel 718	54.0	2000	0.1-0.4	13.0-15.0
	48.0	2000	0.4-0.6	10.0-13.0
	46.0	2100	0.1-0.4	13.0-15.0
	40.0	2100	0.4-0.6	10.0-13.0
Ti-8Mo-8V-2Fe-3Al	40.0	1650	0.1-0.6	10.0-15.0
	28.0	1850	0.1-0.6	10.0-15.0
	24.0	2000	0.1-0.6	10.0-15.0
AISI 4340	25.0	1900	0.2-0.7	10.0-14.0
	21.0	2000	0.3-0.8	12.0-17.0

Table 4-10. Average flow stress values obtained from ring compression tests suggested for use in practical applications

Material	Flow stress(a), 10^3 psi	Temperature, F	Strain rate range, 1/s	Frictional shear factor, m	Contact time, s	Ring dimensions(b)
6061 Al	9	800	18-22	0.4	0.038	A
	9	800	15-17	0.31	0.047	B
	7	800	10-13	0.53	0.079	C
Ti-7Al-4Mo	48	1750	13	0.42	0.033	D
	30	1750	18-23	0.42	0.044	E
	30	1750	15-18	0.7	0.056	F
403 SS	37	1800	25-28	0.23	0.029	D
	33	1800	25-27	0.24	0.037	E
	33	1800	16-18	0.34	0.047	F
403 SS	32	1950	20	0.28	0.06	F
	28	1950	16	0.29	0.07	F
	25	2050	20	0.35	0.06	F
	19	2050	16	0.43	0.07	F
Waspaloy	55	2100	20	0.18	0.06	F
	50	2100	13-16	0.21-0.24	0.07-0.09	F
17-7PH SS	34	1950	13-20	0.22-0.28	0.06-0.09	F
	22	2100	16-20	0.35	0.06-0.07	F
	18	2100	13	0.31	0.09	F
Ti-6Al-4V	43	1700	20	0.30	0.06	F
	35	1700	13-16	0.29-0.34	0.07-0.09	F
	27	1750	16-20	0.32-0.46	0.06-0.07	F
	20	1750	13	0.38	0.09	F
Inconel 718	65	2000	16-20	0.17-0.18	0.06-0.07	F
	58	2000	13	0.18	0.09	F
	50	2100	20	0.33	0.06	F
	48	2100	13-16	0.29-0.30	0.07-0.09	F
Ti-8Al-1Mo-1V	50	1750	13-16	0.22-0.26	0.07-0.09	F
	47	1750	20	0.27	0.06	F
	40	1800	13-16	0.27-0.32	0.07-0.09	F
	27	1800	20	0.27	0.06	F
7075 Al	19	700	13-20	0.36-0.42	0.06-0.09	G
	16	800	13-20	0.31-0.49	0.06-0.09	G
Udimet	65	2050	14-17	0.4	(c)	F

(a) At 10 to 30% reduction. (b) Dimensions, OD:ID:thickness, in inches: A = 6:3:0.5, B = 6:3:1.0, C = 6:3:2.0, D = 3:1.5:0.25, E = 3:1.5:0.5, F = 3:1.5:1.0, G = 5:3:1. (c) Not measured.

Swift: $$\bar{\sigma} = c\,(a + \bar{\epsilon})^n \qquad (4\text{-}24)$$

This is a more realistic equation than Equation 4-21. However, algebraic manipulations resulting from such an expression may be difficult.

For strain-rate-sensitive materials, the most commonly used expression is:

$$\bar{\sigma} = C(\dot{\bar{\epsilon}})^m \qquad (4\text{-}25)$$

The coefficients C and m of this curve would be obtained at various temperatures and strains, so that C and m would have different values at a given temperature for various strains. As examples, C and m values for some metals are given in Tables 4-4 through 4-8.[4-1] For predicting forces and stresses in practical forming operations, very often it is sufficient to specify an average or maximum value of $\bar{\sigma}$ to be used in equations for predicting the maximum forming load. In such practical cases, use of a constant average value for $\bar{\sigma}$ is justified. If $\bar{\epsilon}$ and $\dot{\bar{\epsilon}}$ are not accurately known, then the value of C in Equation 4-25 may be used as an approximation for $\bar{\sigma}$. Such values for hot working temperatures are given for a few materials in Tables 4-9 and 4-10.[4-3] The data given in Table 4-9 were obtained with uniform isothermal compression tests. The data in Table 4-10 were obtained in nonisothermal ring tests. In these tests the ring dimensions are also important, because the average ring specimen temperature varies during the test and is influenced by heat transfer and thickness of the ring.

REFERENCES

4-1. Altan, T., and Boulger, F. W., "Flow Stress of Metals and Its Application in Metal Forming Analyses", Trans. ASME, J. Engr. Ind., Nov 1973, p 1009.

4-2. Thomsen, E. G., Yang, C. T., and Kobayashi, S., "Mechanics of Plastic Deformation in Metal Processing", The Macmillan Company, New York, 1965.

4-3. Douglas, J. R., and Altan, T., "Flow Stress Determination for Metals at Forging Rates and Temperatures", Trans. ASME, J. Engr. Ind., Feb 1975, p 66.

4-4. Lee, C. H., and Altan, T., "Influence of Flow Stress and Friction Upon Metal Flow in Upset Forging of Rings and Cylinders", Trans. ASME, J. Engr. Ind., Aug 1972, p 775.

4-5. Altan, T., Semiatin, S. L., and Lahoti, G. D., "Determination of Flow Stress Data for Practical Metal Forming Analysis", Annals of CIRP, Vol 30, No. 1, 1981, p 129.

4-6. Lahoti, G. D., and Altan, T., "Prediction of Temperature Distributions in Axisymmetric Compression and Torsion", J. Engr. Materials Technology, April 1975, p 113.

CHAPTER 5
Plastic Deformation: Complex State of Stress and Flow Rules

In simple homogeneous (uniaxial) compression or tension, the metal flows plastically when the stress, σ, reaches the value of the flow stress, $\bar{\sigma}$, or when the flow rule in uniaxial deformation is:

$$|\sigma| = \frac{F}{A} = \bar{\sigma} \tag{5-1}$$

where F and A are instantaneous force and area, respectively.

In a multiaxial state of stress, plastic flow (yielding) depends on a combination of all stresses.[5-1,5-2] There are two major "hypotheses" or criteria for plastic flow:

1. Tresca or shear stress criterion of yield or plastic flow.
2. von Mises or distortion energy criterion of yield or plastic flow.

THE TRESCA YIELD CRITERION

The Tresca yield criterion states that plastic flow starts when the maximum shear stress, τ_{max}, reaches a certain critical value, k, or when $|\tau_{max}| =$ k, where k is the shear flow stress which is characteristic of a given material and its microstructure and depends on shear strain rate, strain and deformation temperature.

As in the case of strains, stresses also have principal axes, as illustrated by means of the Mohr circle in Figure 5-1. The Mohr circle represents the stresses in a plane whose coordinate axes are chosen to be the shear stress τ (ordinate) and the normal stress σ (abscissa). In the physical x-y plane the "principal" stresses are perpendicular to each other, and in the direction of "principal" stresses the shear stresses are zero, as can be seen in Figure 5-

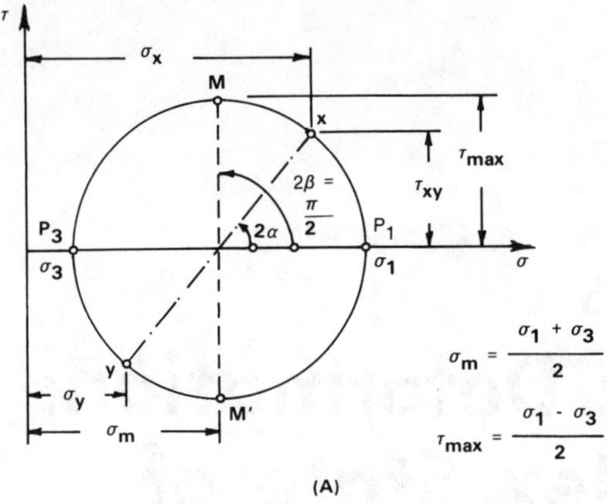

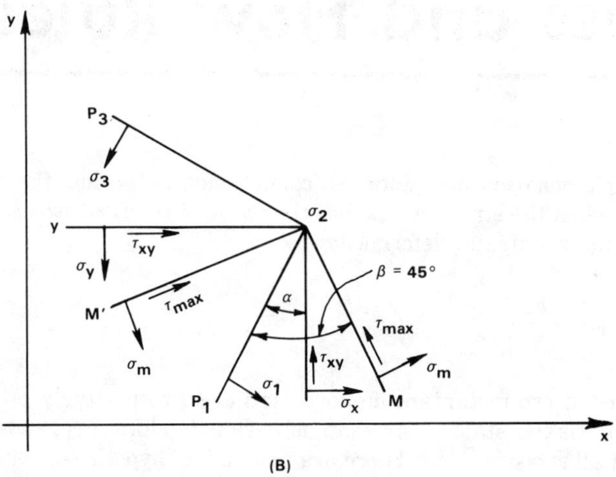

Figure 5-1. Representation of state of stress through the Mohr circle.

1B. In the Mohr circle representation, i.e., in the τ-σ plane, the maximum principal stress, σ_1, and the minimum principal stress, σ_3, define the size of the Mohr circle (Figure 5-1A). The subscripts 1 and 3 are arbitrary and indicate only that $\sigma_3 \leq \sigma_2 \leq \sigma_1$.

As can be seen in Figure 5-1, the largest shear stress, τ_{max}, acting on the τ-σ plane is given by one radius of the Mohr circle.[5-3] Thus:

$$\tau_{max} = (\sigma_1 - \sigma_3)/2 \tag{5-2}$$

The states of stress, which cause plastic deformation, are illustrated with the Mohr circle of radius k.

For the uniaxial tensile test (no necking, and $\sigma_2 = \sigma_3 = 0$), plastic flow starts when (Figure 5-2):

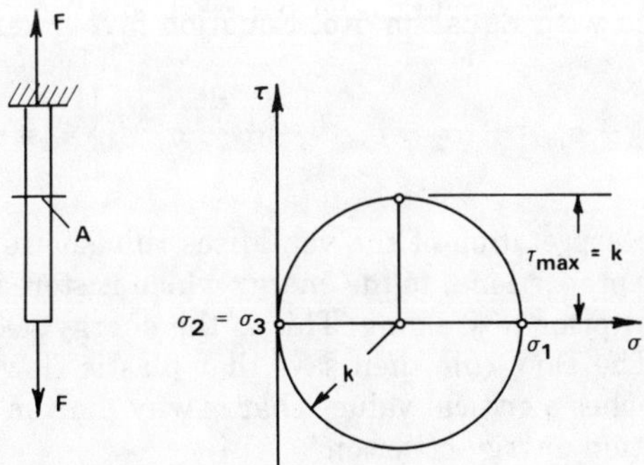

Figure 5-2. Mohr circle for uniaxial tension.[5-2]

$$\sigma_1 = \frac{L}{A} = \bar{\sigma} = 2k, \quad \text{or} \quad k = \frac{\bar{\sigma}}{2} \tag{5-3}$$

where L is tensile force and A is the instantaneous cross-sectional area of the sample. Thus, the Tresca flow rule can be expressed as:

$$\sigma_1 - \sigma_3 = \bar{\sigma} \tag{5-4}$$

Equation 5-4 shows that, according to Tresca's rule, plastic flow starts if the difference of maximum (σ_1) and minimum (σ_3) principal stresses is equal to $\bar{\sigma}$. Figure 5-1 shows that the position of the circle, i.e., the hydrostatic stress, is not important for plastic flow. The mean principal stress is:

$$\sigma_m = (\sigma_1 + \sigma_2 + \sigma_3)/3 \tag{5-5}$$

and the hydrostatic pressure is:

$$p = -\sigma_m \tag{5-6}$$

THE VON MISES YIELD CRITERION

The von Mises flow rule considers all the stresses acting on the deforming body and can be expressed as follows. The start of flow (yielding) must depend on a combination of normal and shear stresses, which does not change its value when transformed from one coordinate system into another.[5-2,5-4] In terms of principal stresses, the von Mises rule is:

$$\left\{\frac{1}{2}[(\sigma_1 - \sigma_2)^2 + (\sigma_2 - \sigma_3)^2 + (\sigma_1 - \sigma_3)^2]\right\}^{1/2} = \bar{\sigma} \tag{5-7a}$$

In a general way:

$$\left\{\frac{1}{2}[(\sigma_x - \sigma_y)^2 + (\sigma_y - \sigma_z)^2 + (\sigma_z - \sigma_x)^2 + 3(\tau_{xy}^2 + \tau_{yz}^2 + \tau_{zx}^2)]\right\}^{1/2} = \bar{\sigma} \tag{5-7b}$$

or, when combined with Equation 5-5, Equation 5-7a gives:

$$\left\{\frac{3}{2}\left[(\sigma_1 - \sigma_m)^2 + (\sigma_2 - \sigma_m)^2 + (\sigma_3 - \sigma_m)^2\right]\right\}^{1/2} = \bar{\sigma} \tag{5-7c}$$

A physical interpretation of the von Mises rule shows that the left side of Equation 5-7 is proportional to the energy which is stored in the elastically deformed material prior to yielding. This is the energy necessary for elastic volume change. The flow rule then says that plastic flow starts when this elastic energy reaches a critical value. That is why the von Mises rule is also called the "distortion energy criterion".

COMPARISON OF TRESCA AND VON MISES CRITERIA

In uniaxial tension or compression, i.e., for $\sigma_1 = L/A$ and $\sigma_2 = \sigma_3 = 0$, Equation 5-7a gives:

$$\sqrt{\frac{1}{2}\,2\sigma_1^2} = \bar{\sigma}, \quad \text{or} \quad \sigma_1 = \bar{\sigma} \tag{5-8}$$

Comparison of Equations 5-8 and 5-4 indicates that both yield criteria, Tresca and von Mises, give the same result under uniaxial flow conditions; or, from Equation 5-3:

$$\tau_{max} = \frac{1}{2}\sigma_1 = \frac{1}{2}\bar{\sigma} \tag{5-9}$$

In pure shear, the situation is different. As can be seen in Figure 5-3, pure shear exists for $\sigma_3 = -\sigma_1$, $\sigma_2 = 0$. The Tresca criterion gives, using Equation 5-4: $\tau_{max} = \sigma_1 = \bar{\sigma}/2$. The von Mises criterion gives, from Equation 5-7a:

$$\bar{\sigma} = \sqrt{\frac{1}{2}(\sigma_1^2 + \sigma_1^2 + 4\sigma_1^2)} = \sqrt{3}\,\sigma_1 \tag{5-10}$$

In addition, as can be seen in Figure 5-3:

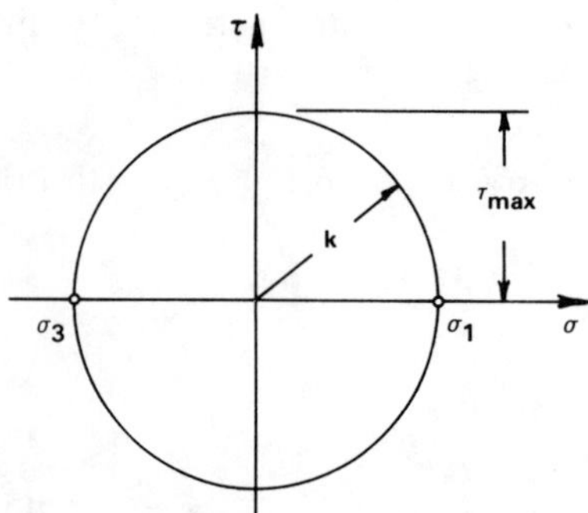

Figure 5-3. Mohr circle for pure shear.[5-2]

$$\tau_{max} = \sigma_1 = \frac{\bar{\sigma}}{\sqrt{3}} = 0.577\,\bar{\sigma} \tag{5-11}$$

Thus, in pure shear, there is a 15% difference between values of τ_{max} obtained from the Tresca and von Mises rules. Experiments (with combined shear and tension) indicate that the von Mises rule is a better criterion (closer to reality) than Tresca's flow rule.

When the stresses at a given point in the metal reach a certain level, as specified by a flow rule (Tresca or von Mises), then plastic flow, i.e., plastic deformation, starts. Analysis of plastic deformation requires a certain relation between the applied stresses and the velocity field (kinematics as described by velocity, ϵ and $\dot{\epsilon}$ fields). Such a relation exists between the stresses (in principal axes) and strain rates, as follows:

$$\dot{\epsilon}_1 = \lambda(\sigma_1 - \sigma_m) \tag{5-12a}$$

$$\dot{\epsilon}_2 = \lambda(\sigma_2 - \sigma_m) \tag{5-12b}$$

$$\dot{\epsilon}_3 = \lambda(\sigma_3 - \sigma_m) \tag{5-12c}$$

Equations 5-12a, b and c are called "plasticity equations".[5-1,5-2,5-4] The variable λ depends on direction of plastic flow, temperature, material, strain and strain rate. The plasticity equations — for example, Equation 5-12a — can also be expressed in the form:

$$d\epsilon_1 = \frac{3}{2}\frac{d\bar{\epsilon}}{\bar{\sigma}}(\sigma_1 - \sigma_m) \tag{5-13}$$

where $\bar{\epsilon}$ and $\bar{\sigma}$ denote effective stress and strain. Equation 5-13 can also be expressed as:

$$\dot{\epsilon}_1 = \frac{3}{2}\frac{\dot{\bar{\epsilon}}}{\bar{\sigma}}(\sigma_1 - \sigma_m) \tag{5-14}$$

POWER AND ENERGY OF DEFORMATION

The plastic deformation processes are irreversible. The mechanical energy, consumed during deformation, is transformed largely into heat. It is useful to consider again the homogeneous deformation of a block (Figure 5-4). The following relations, derived in Chapter 3, hold here also:[5-2]

$$\epsilon_h = \epsilon_1 = \ln\frac{h}{h_0}; \quad \dot{\epsilon}_1 = \frac{v_h}{h}$$

$$\epsilon_2 = \ln\frac{w}{w_0}; \quad \dot{\epsilon}_2 = \frac{v_w}{w}$$

$$\epsilon_3 = \ln\frac{l}{l_0}; \quad \dot{\epsilon}_3 = \frac{v_l}{l}$$

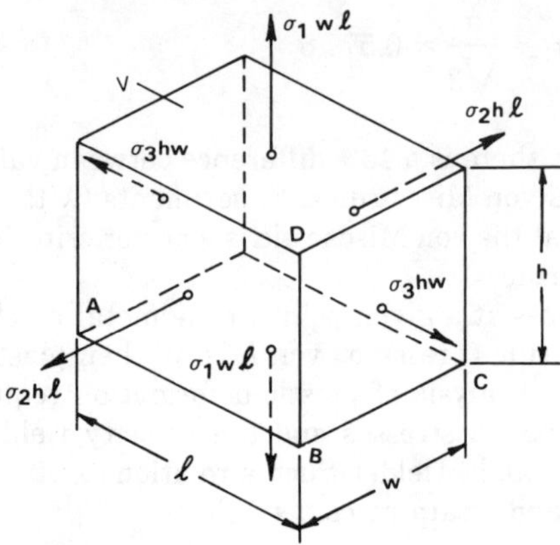

Figure 5-4. Homogeneous deformation of a block.

Following Figure 5-4, the instantaneous power of deformation (force times velocity) is given by:

$$\begin{aligned} P &= \sigma_1 wlv_h + \sigma_2 hlv_w + \sigma_3 whv_l \\ &= \sigma_1 wlh\dot{\epsilon}_1 + \sigma_2 wlh\dot{\epsilon}_2 + \sigma_3 wlh\dot{\epsilon}_3 \\ &= (\sigma_1\dot{\epsilon}_1 + \sigma_2\dot{\epsilon}_2 + \sigma_3\dot{\epsilon}_3)V \end{aligned} \tag{5-15}$$

where V is the volume of the deforming block. It follows that the energy of deformation, E, is:

$$E = V\int_{t_0}^{t_1}(\sigma_1\dot{\epsilon}_1 + \sigma_2\dot{\epsilon}_2 + \sigma_3\dot{\epsilon}_3)dt \tag{5-16}$$

With $\dot{\epsilon}dt = d\epsilon$, Equation 5-16 can also be written as:

$$E = V\left(\int_0^{\epsilon_1}\sigma_1 d\epsilon_1 + \int_0^{\epsilon_2}\sigma_2 d\epsilon_2 + \int_0^{\epsilon_3}\sigma_3 d\epsilon_3\right) \tag{5-17}$$

EFFECTIVE STRAIN AND EFFECTIVE STRAIN RATE

The flow stress, $\bar{\sigma}$, is determined from a uniaxial test (compression or homogeneous tension). Under multiaxial deformation conditions, it is necessary to relate uniaxial material behavior to multiaxial material behavior.

Considering an element and the principal directions, the deformation energy, dW, expended during a time element Δt, is:

$$dW = (\sigma_1 d\epsilon_1 + \sigma_2 d\epsilon_2 + \sigma_3 d\epsilon_3)V \tag{5-18}$$

or, divided by dt, the deformation power, P, is:

$$P = \frac{dW}{dt} = (\sigma\dot{\epsilon}_1 + \sigma_2\dot{\epsilon}_2 + \sigma_3\dot{\epsilon}_3)V \tag{5-19}$$

The effective strain, $\bar{\epsilon}$, and strain rate, $\dot{\bar{\epsilon}}$ (both indicated with overbar), are defined as:

$$dW = \bar{\sigma}d\bar{\epsilon}V \tag{5-20}$$

or

$$P = \bar{\sigma}\dot{\bar{\epsilon}}V \tag{5-21}$$

Equations 5-19 and 5-21 give:

$$\bar{\sigma}\dot{\bar{\epsilon}} = \sigma_1\dot{\epsilon}_1 + \sigma_2\dot{\epsilon}_2 + \sigma_3\dot{\epsilon}_3 \tag{5-22}$$

From volume constancy, in Chapter 3, it was shown that:

$$\dot{\epsilon}_1 + \dot{\epsilon}_2 + \dot{\epsilon}_3 = 0 \tag{5-23a}$$

or

$$\sigma_m(\dot{\epsilon}_1 + \dot{\epsilon}_2 + \dot{\epsilon}_3) = 0 \tag{5-23b}$$

Equations 5-23 and 5-22 give:

$$\bar{\sigma}\dot{\bar{\epsilon}} = \dot{\epsilon}_1(\sigma_1 - \sigma_m) + \dot{\epsilon}_2(\sigma_2 - \sigma_m) + \dot{\epsilon}_3(\sigma_2 - \sigma_m) \tag{5-24}$$

Using the one form of the von Mises rule, Equation 5-7c, Equation 5-24 gives:

$$\dot{\bar{\epsilon}} = \frac{\dot{\epsilon}_1(\sigma_1 - \sigma_m) + \dot{\epsilon}_2(\sigma_2 - \sigma_m) + \dot{\epsilon}_3(\sigma_3 - \sigma_m)}{\left\{\frac{3}{2}[(\sigma_1 - \sigma_m)^2 + (\sigma_2 - \sigma_m)^2 + (\sigma_3 - \sigma_m)^2]\right\}^{1/2}} \tag{5-25}$$

Using the plasticity Equations 5-12a, b and c, which give $\sigma_1 - \sigma_m = \dot{\epsilon}_1/\lambda$, etc., Equation 5-25 can be reduced to:

$$\dot{\bar{\epsilon}} = \sqrt{\frac{2}{3}(\dot{\epsilon}_1^2 + \dot{\epsilon}_2^2 + \dot{\epsilon}_3^2)} \tag{5-26}$$

or, by integration, to:

$$\bar{\epsilon} = \int_{t_0}^{t_1} \dot{\bar{\epsilon}}dt \tag{5-27}$$

Equations 5-20 and 5-27 show how to calculate the effective strain rate and the effective strain in principal directions.

REFERENCES

5-1. Thomsen, E. G., Yang, C. T., and Kobayashi, S., "Mechanics of Plastic Deformation in Metal Processing", The Macmillan Company, New York, 1965.
5-2. Lange, K. (editor), "Study Book of Forming Technology" (in German), Vol 1 (Fundamentals), Springer-Verlag, New York, 1972.
5-3. Backofen, W. A., "Deformation Processing", Addison-Wesley Publishing Co., 1972.
5-4. Johnson, W., and Mellor, P. B., "Engineering Plasticity", Van Nostrand Reinhold Co., London, 1975.

CHAPTER 6

Friction in Metal Forming

In metal forming, the flow of metal is caused by the pressure transmitted from the dies to the deforming workpiece. Therefore, the frictional conditions at the material/die interface greatly influence metal flow, formation of surface and internal defects, stresses acting on the dies, and load and energy requirements. There are three basic types of lubrication that govern the frictional conditions in metal forming:[6-1,6-2]

1. Under "dry" conditions, no lubricant is present at the interface and only the oxide layers present on the die and workpiece materials may act as a "separating" layer. In this case friction is high, and such a situation is desirable in only a few selected forming operations, such as hot rolling of plates and slabs and nonlubricated extrusion of aluminum alloys.
2. "Hydrodynamic" conditions exist when a thick layer of lubricant is present between the dies and the workpiece. In this case the friction conditions are governed by the viscosity of the lubricant and by the relative velocity between the die and the workpiece. The viscosities of most lubricants decrease rapidly with increasing temperature. Consequently, in most practical high-speed forming operations, such as strip rolling and wiredrawing, the hydrodynamic conditions exist only within a certain regime of velocities, where the interface temperatures are relatively low.[6-2]
3. "Boundary" lubrication is the most widely encountered situation in metal forming. Increases in temperature at the interface and the relatively high forming pressures do not usually allow the presence of a hydrodynamic lubrication regime. Boundary lubrication, on the other hand, does not lend itself to reliable analysis. Consequently, most of the knowledge on metal forming lubrication is empirical, with very little analysis-based information.

CHARACTERISTICS OF LUBRICANTS USED IN METAL FORMING

In metal forming, friction is controlled by use of appropriate lubricants for given applications. The lubricant is expected to have certain characteristics and to perform some, if not most, of the following significant functions:[6-1]

- Reduce the sliding friction between the dies and the workpiece. This is achieved by using a lubricant of high lubricity.
- Act as a parting agent and prevent sticking and galling of the workpiece to the dies.
- Possess good insulating properties, especially in hot forming, so as to reduce heat losses from the workpiece to the dies.
- Possess inertness to prevent or minimize reaction with the dies and the workpiece materials at the forming temperatures used.
- Be nonabrasive so as to reduce erosion of the die surface and die wear.
- Be free of polluting and poisonous components and not produce unpleasant or dangerous gases.
- Be easily applicable to and removable from dies and workpiece.
- Be commercially available at reasonable cost.

No single lubricant can fulfill all of the requirements listed above and no single method can evaluate all of these characteristics simultaneously. Therefore, various testing methods exist for evaluation of one or more lubricant characteristics.

LUBRICITY AND FRICTIONAL SHEAR STRESS

In most forming applications, the lubricity of a lubricant is the single most significant factor since it directly determines the interface friction, which in turn influences the stresses, the forming load and the forming energy. In order to evaluate the performances of various lubricants and to be able to predict forming pressures, it is necessary to express the interface friction quantitatively, in terms of a factor or a coefficient.[6-3] The frictional shear stress, τ, is most commonly expressed as:

$$\tau = \sigma_n \mu \tag{6-1}$$

or

$$\tau = f\bar{\sigma} = \frac{m}{\sqrt{3}}\bar{\sigma} \tag{6-2}$$

where $0 \le m \le 1$.

Equation 6-1 indicates that the frictional shear stress τ is proportional to the normal stress σ_n at the die/material interface and the friction coefficient μ. Equation 6-2 expresses that τ is dependent on the flow stress of the deforming material, $\bar{\sigma}$, and the friction factor f or the shear factor m.* Recent studies in forming mechanics indicate that Equation 6-2 represents the frictional shear stress in metal forming adequately and offers advantages in evaluating friction and in performing stress and load calculations. For various forming conditions, the values of m vary as follows:

- m = 0.05 to 0.15 in cold forming of steels, aluminum alloys and copper, using conventional phosphate-soap lubricants or oils.
- m = 0.2 to 0.4 in hot forming of steels, copper and aluminum alloys with graphite-base (graphite-water or graphite-oil) lubricants.
- m = 0.1 to 0.3 in hot forming of titanium and high-temperature alloys with glass lubricants.
- m = 0.7 to 1.0 when no lubricant is used, e.g., in hot rolling of plates or slabs and in nonlubricated extrusion of aluminum alloys.

In determining the friction factor, f, or the shear factor, m, for hot forming, in addition to lubrication effects, the effects of die chilling or heat transfer from the hot material to colder dies must be considered. Therefore, the lubrication tests used for determining friction factors must include both lubrication and die-chilling effects. Consequently, in hot forming, a good test must satisfy as well as possible the following requirements.

- The specimen and die temperatures must be approximately the same as those encountered in the actual hot forming operation.
- The contact time between specimen and tools under pressure must be approximately the same as in the forming operation of interest.
- The ratio of the new generated deformed surface area to the original surface area of the undeformed specimen must be approximately the same as in the process investigated.
- The relative velocity between deforming metal and dies should have approximately the same magnitude and direction as in the forming process.

THE RING COMPRESSION TEST

Lubricity, as defined by the friction factor, f, or the shear factor, m, is most commonly measured by using the ring test.[6-4,6-5] In the ring test, a flat ring-shape specimen is compressed to a known reduction (Figure 6-1). The change in internal and external diameters of the forged ring is very much dependent on the friction at the tool/specimen interface. If friction were equal to zero, the ring would deform in the same way as a solid disk, with each element flowing radially outward at a rate proportional to its distance from the center. With increasing deformation, the internal diameter of the ring is reduced if friction is high, and is increased if friction is low. Thus, the change in the internal diameter represents a simple method for evaluating interface friction.

---

*The shear factor "m" in Equation 6-2 is not to be confused with the exponent "m" in the simple exponential law, $\bar{\sigma} = C(\dot{\bar{\epsilon}})^m$, used to express the strain-rate dependency of flow stress, discussed in Chapter 4.

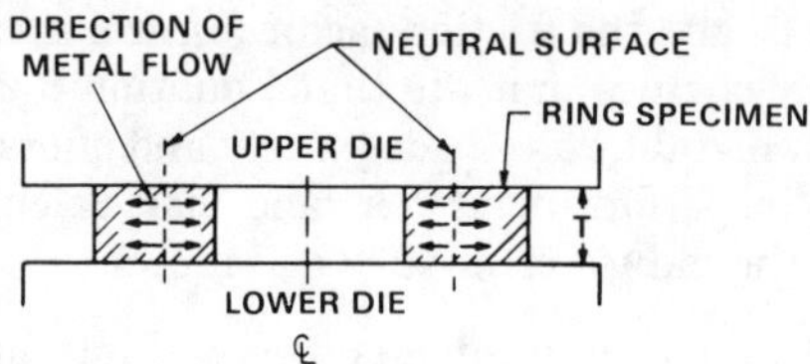

Figure 6-1. Metal flow in ring compression test.

The ring test has an advantage when applied to the study of friction. In order to measure friction with this test, the force necessary to deform the ring and the flow stress of the specimen material do not have to be known. Thus, evaluation of test results is greatly simplified. To obtain the magnitude of the friction factor, the internal diameter of the compressed ring must be compared with the values predicted by using various friction factors, f, or shear factors, m. Several theoretical analyses are available for this purpose.[6-3,6-6,6-7] In one of these analyses a computer program has been developed for mathematically simulating the metal flow in ring compression with bulging.[6-3] Thus, ring dimensions for various reductions in height and shear factors, m, can be determined. The results are plotted in the form of "theoretical calibration curves", as can be seen in Figure 6-2, for rings having OD:ID:thickness ratios of 6:3:2, 6:3:1 and 6:3:0.5. The internal diameters used in this figure are the diameters at the internal bulge. In determining the value of the shear factor, m, for a given experimental condition, the mea-

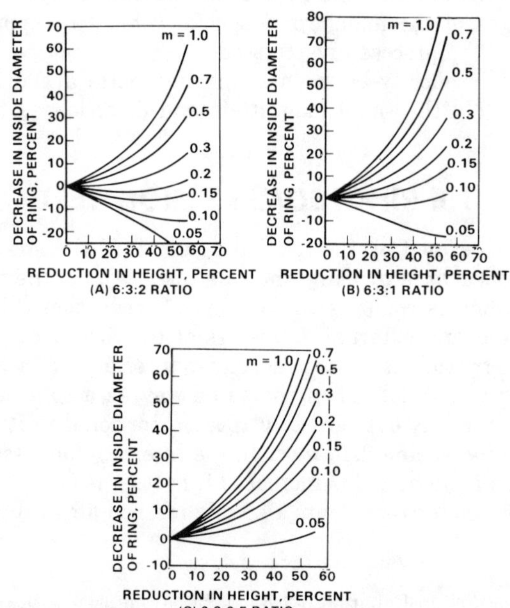

Figure 6-2. Theoretical calibration curves for upsetting rings having indicated OD:ID:thickness ratios.

Table 6-1. Values of frictional shear factor, m, obtained from ring tests conducted in a mechanical press (temperature of the dies ≃300 F; surface finish ≃25 micro-in.)[6-5]

Material	Specimen tempera-ture, F	Frictional shear factor (m)	Contact time, s	Ring ratio(a)	Lubrication system
6061 Al	800	0.4	0.038	6:3:0.5	(b)
	800	0.31	0.047	6:3:1	(b)
	800	0.53	0.079	6:3:2	(b)
Ti-7Al-4Mo	1750	0.42	0.033	3:1.5:0.25	(c)
	1750	0.42	0.044	3:1.5:0.5	(c)
	1750	0.7	0.056	3:1.5:1	(c)
403 SS	1800	0.23	0.029	3:1.5:0.25	(c)
	1800	0.24	0.039	3:1.5:0.5	(c)
	1800	0.34	0.047	3:1.5:1	(c)
	1950	0.28	0.06	3:1.5:1	(c)
	2050	0.35	0.06	3:1.5:1	(c)
Waspaloy	2100	0.18	0.06	3:1.5:1	(c)
17-7PH SS	1950	0.28	0.06	3:1.5:1	(c)
	2100	0.35	0.06	3:1.5:1	(c)
Ti-6Al-4V	1700	0.3	0.06	3:1.5:1	(c)
	1750	0.46	0.06	3:1.5:1	(c)
Inconel 718	2000	0.18	0.06	3:1.5:1	(c)
	2100	0.33	0.06	3:1.5:1	(c)
Ti-8Al-1Mo-1V	1750	0.27	0.06	3:1.5:1	(c)
	1800	0.27	0.06	3:1.5:1	(c)
Udimet	2050	0.4	0.06	3:1.5:1	(c)
7075 Al	700	0.37	0.06	5:3:1	(b)
	800	0.31	0.06	5:3:1	(b)

(a) Ring dimensions in inches, OD:ID:thickness. (b) Caustic precoat + graphite coating Dag 137 (Acheson) on the specimens and graphite spray Deltaforge 43 (Acheson) on the dies. (c) Glass-base coating Deltaforge 347 (Acheson) on the specimens and graphite spray Deltaforge 43 (Acheson) on the dies.

sured dimensions (reduction in height and variation in internal diameter) are placed on the appropriate calibration figure. From the position of that point with respect to theoretical curves given for various values of "m", the value of the shear factor, m, which existed in the experiment is obtained.

In a recent study, ring compression tests were conducted for various materials in a 500-ton mechanical press with a nominal speed of 90 strokes per minute and a total stroke of 10 in.[6-5] The results of these tests are summarized in Table 6-1. The data in Table 6-1 do not represent the optimum values for frictional shear factor, m, but illustrate the order of magnitude of "m" encountered in practical operations in mechanical presses. Similar data for various lubricants and for forging in different machines are available in the literature.[6-1,6-5]

REFERENCES

6-1. Schey, J. A. (editor), "Metal Deformation Processes: Friction and Lubrication", Marcel Dekker, New York, 1970; superseded by Schey, J. A., "Tribology in Metalworking:

Lubrication, Friction and Wear", American Society for Metals, Metals Park, OH, 1983.

6-2. Altan, T., "Heat Generation and Temperatures in Wire and Rod Drawing", Wire Journal, March 1970, p 54.

6-3. Lee, C. H., and Altan, T., "Influence of Flow Stress and Friction Upon Metal Flow in Upset Forging of Rings and Cylinders", Trans. ASME, J. Engr. Industry, Vol 94, No. 3, Aug 1972, p 775.

6-4. Male, A. T., and DePierre, V., "The Validity of Mathematical Solutions for Determining Friction from the Ring Compression Test", Trans. ASME, J. Lubrication Technology, Vol 92, 1970, p 389.

6-5. Douglas, J. R., and Altan, T., "Flow Stress Determination for Metals at Forging Rates and Temperatures", Trans. ASME, J. Engr. Industry, Feb 1975, p 66.

6-6. Avitzur, B., "Metalforming: Processes and Analyses", McGraw-Hill, New York, 1968.

6-7. Hawkyard, J. B., and Johnson, W., "An Analysis of the Changes in Geometry of a Short Hollow Cylinder During Axial Compression", Int. J. Mech. Sci., 1967, Vol 9, p 163.

CHAPTER 7

Temperatures in Metal Forming

In metal forming processes, both plastic deformation and friction contribute to heat generation. Approximately 90 to 95% of the mechanical energy involved in the process is transformed into heat.[7-1] In some continuous forming operations such as drawing and extrusion, performed at high speeds, temperature increases of several hundred degrees may be involved.[7-2] A part of the generated heat remains in the deformed material, another part flows into tooling, while still an additional part may flow into the undeformed portion of the material. The temperatures developed in the process influence lubrication conditions, tool life and the properties of the final product, and, most significantly, determine the maximum deformation speed which can be used for producing sound products without excessive tool damage. Thus, temperatures generated during plastic deformation greatly influence the productivity of metal forming processes.

HEAT GENERATION AND HEAT TRANSFER IN METAL FORMING PROCESSES

In metal forming, the magnitudes and distribution of temperatures depend mainly on:

- The initial material and die temperatures.
- Heat generation due to plastic deformation and friction at the die/material interface.
- Heat transfer between the deforming material and the dies and between the material and the environment (air or coolant).

In processes such as forging and extrusion, where large amounts of coolants are not present, the heat losses to the environment, through radiation and conduction, can be neglected. Thus, tne average instantaneous temperature in the deforming metal, θ_A, can be estimated by:[7-3]

$$\theta_A = \theta_S + \theta_D + \theta_F - \theta_T \tag{7-1}$$

where θ_S is the initial stock (or part) temperature, θ_D is the temperature increase due to plastic deformation, θ_F is the temperature increase due to interface friction, and θ_T is the temperature drop due to heat transfer into the dies.

The temperature increase due to deformation, θ_D, in a time interval Δt is given by:

$$\theta_D = \frac{A\bar{\sigma}\dot{\bar{\epsilon}}\Delta t}{c\rho}\beta = \frac{\bar{\sigma}\Delta\bar{\epsilon}}{Jc\rho}\beta \tag{7-2}$$

where $\bar{\sigma}$ is the flow stress of the deforming material, $\dot{\bar{\epsilon}}$ is the effective strain rate, $\Delta\bar{\epsilon}$ is the effective strain generated during Δt, A is a conversion factor between mechanical and thermal energies, c is the specific heat of the deforming material, ρ is the specific weight of the deforming material, and β is the fraction of deformation energy transformed into heat ($0 \leq \beta \leq 1$); usually, $\beta = 0.95$.

The temperature increase due to friction, θ_F, is given by:

$$\theta_F = \frac{Af\bar{\sigma}vF\Delta t}{c\rho V_a} \tag{7-3}$$

where, in addition to the symbols already described, f is the friction factor at the material/tool interface, such that frictional shear stress $\tau = f\bar{\sigma}$, v is the velocity at the material/tool interface, F is the surface area at the material/tool interface, and V_a is the volume which is subject to temperature increase.

In actual forming operations, there is a temperature gradient in the deforming material and in the dies. The temperatures are usually high at the material/die interface, where friction generates heat, and they decrease toward the inside of the material and the die, as shown in Figure 7-1. In many applications and for practical purposes it is sufficient to estimate an average temperature in the deforming material, by neglecting the temperature gradients. In such a case, the deforming material can be considered to be a thin plate with an average uniform temperature, which is cooled between two dies from both sides. In nearly all forming processes the dies are colder than the deforming material. Thus, the heat balance gives:

$$-c\rho V_a d\theta = \alpha F(\theta - \theta_1)dt \tag{7-4}$$

where c is heat capacity (material), ρ is specific gravity (material), V_a is the average volume under consideration (material), θ is the instantaneous average temperature of the material, α is the heat transfer coefficient between the material and the dies, F is the surface area of contact between the material and the dies, θ_1 is the temperature of the die surfaces contacting the material, and t is cooling time.

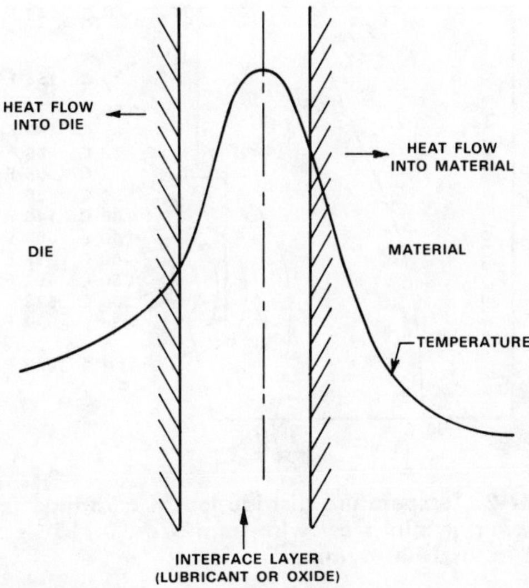

Figure 7-1. Schematic illustration of temperatures at the die/material interface.

Integration of Equation 7-4 gives:

$$\theta = \theta_1 + (\theta_0 - \theta_1)\exp\left(\frac{-\alpha t}{c\rho h}\right) \tag{7-5}$$

where h is material thickness between the dies and θ_0 is initial material temperature.

Equation 7-5 describes the variation of the average material temperature, θ, during cooling of the material, which is assumed to be a thin plate cooled between two die surfaces. Equation 7-5 does not include any temperature increases due to deformation and friction which occur during die formation. The final average material temperature is:

$$\theta_a = \theta_D + \theta + \theta_F \tag{7-6}$$

where θ_D, θ and θ_F are defined by Equations 7-2, 7-5 and 7-3, respectively.

Temperature increases encountered in forming operations for producing discrete parts, such as die forging, upsetting and deep drawing, are quite different from the temperature increases found in quasicontinuous deformation processes such as wiredrawing, rolling and extrusion. In forming operations of the former type, e.g., in cold forging, the metal flow is kinematically nonsteady state. Deformation takes place in a relatively short period of time, i.e., from several milliseconds to a fraction of a second. The deforming material is in contact with the dies during this short period. After the part has been formed and removed from the die, the dies can cool off during a considerable period of time, until the next part is loaded into them.

In continuous forming operations, e.g., wiredrawing, the metal flow is

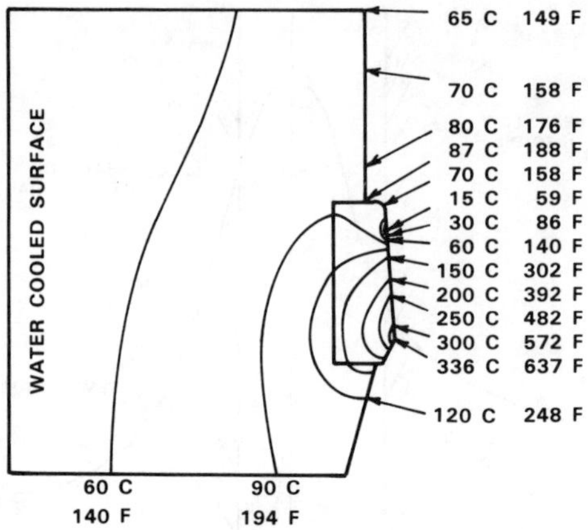

Figure 7-2. Temperature distribution in a carbide insert die in drawing of mild steel wire from $d_0 = 0.115$ in. to $d_1 = 0.1004$ in. at 1400 ft/min.[7-4]

nearly steady state. The deforming material is continuously in contact with the die and there is a cumulative temperature increase in the die. This temperature increase significantly influences die life, production rate and the quality of the drawn material.

TEMPERATURES IN QUASICONTINUOUS FORMING OPERATIONS

A good example of a quasicontinuous forming operation is wiredrawing. Figure 7-2 shows the temperature distribution in a carbide wiredrawing die, obtained in drawing of a steel wire at a drawing speed of 1400 ft/min.[7-4] The magnitudes and distribution of these temperatures depend on the material drawn, the drawing speed and the type of cooling used.

It is possible to estimate the temperatures that occur in drawing and other forming processes by using computer-aided numerical techniques. For example, in drawing through a single die, heat is generated by deformation

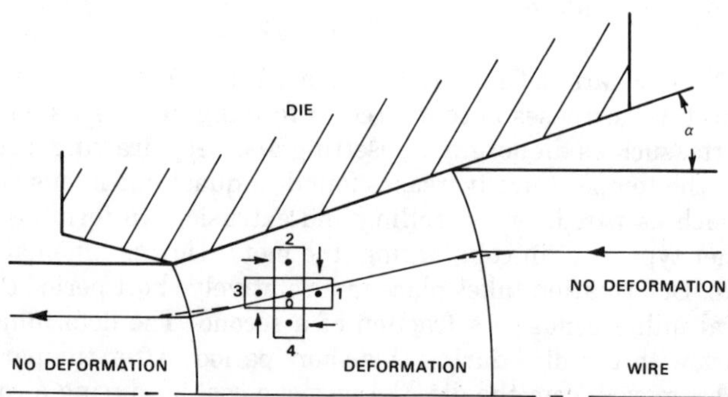

Figure 7-3. Metal flow and configuration of volume elements used in numerical solution of heat conduction.

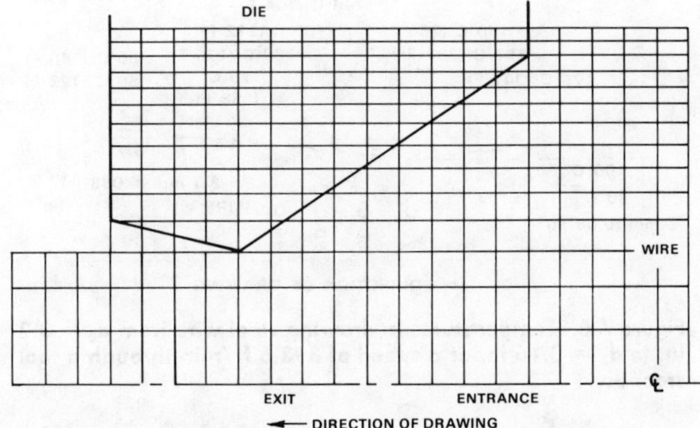

Figure 7-4. Illustration of the grid system used for numerical calculation of temperatures in drawing.

and friction. Some of the generated heat remains in the drawn material and some is transmitted to the die and to the other parts of the material. Thus, the problem involves determination of the simultaneous heat generation, transportation and conduction. The numerical method for solving this problem approximates the heat generation and simultaneous heat conduction in two consecutive steps during equal time increments, Δt. Repetition of these two steps gives the temperature distribution as a function of time. This method gives both the nonsteady- and the steady-state temperatures, because the drawing process is essentially simulated numerically by carrying out calculations for consecutive time elements, Δt, using a digital computer.[7-5,7-6]

Metal flow in drawing and heat transfer between a volume element and its vicinity are illustrated in Figure 7-3, where a volume element moves by following a flow line.[7-7] Deformation takes place under the die in the zone defined by the two entrance and exit boundaries of the plastic deformation zone. For a volume element the temperature increase due to deformation in a time interval Δt is given by Equation 7-2. The temperature increase due to friction is given by Equation 7-3.

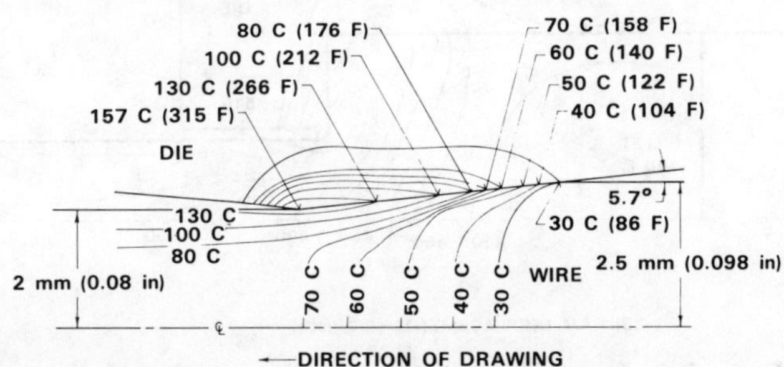

Figure 7-5. Temperatures in drawing steel wire from $d_0 = 0.2$ in. to $d_1 = 0.16$ in. at a speed of 196.8 ft/min through a tool steel die.

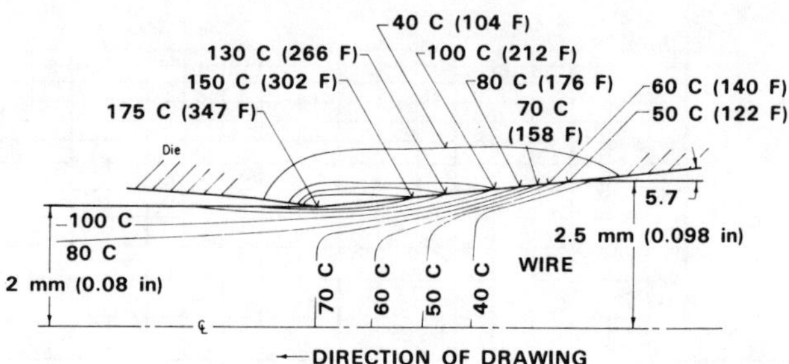

Figure 7-6. Temperatures in drawing steel wire from $d_0 = 0.2$ in. to $d_1 = 0.16$ in. at a speed of 393.6 ft/min through a tool steel die.

During a time interval Δt, conduction heat transfer takes place between the volume element "0" (Figure 7-3) and the adjacent volume elements "1", "2", "3" and "4". The temperature change in the volume element "0" after conduction during time interval Δt is calculated by solving the conduction-difference equations. In order to derive the difference equations of conduction and to calculate the local temperature changes, the drawn material and the die are divided into a grid system (Figure 7-4). The temperature increases

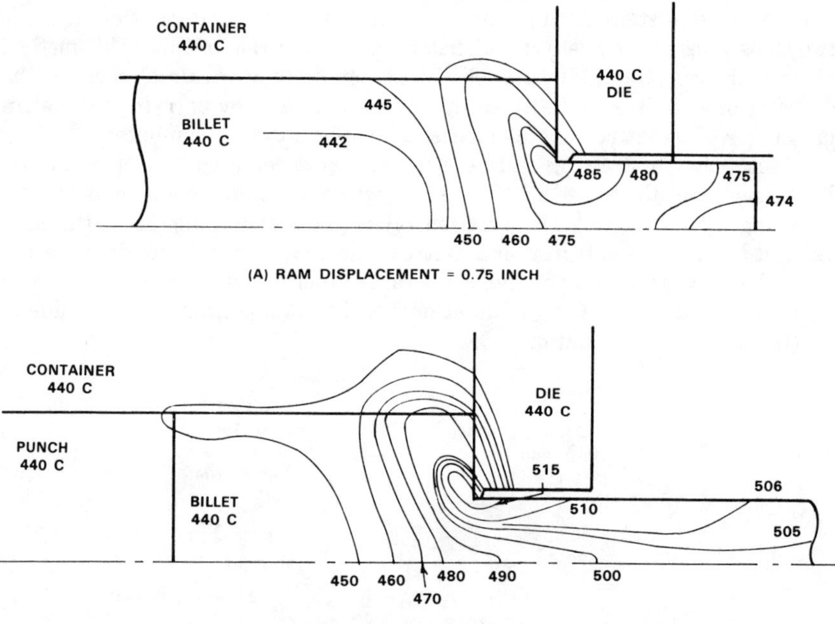

Figure 7-7. Temperature distributions in extrusion of aluminum alloy 5052 rod through a flat die (reduction, 5:1; ram speed, 74.4 in./min; billet diameter, 2.8 in.; billet length, 5.6 in.; initial billet and tooling temperatures, 440 C).[7-6]

and the heat transfer are calculated for each grid point.

Example temperature distributions, calculated for wiredrawing, are shown in Figures 7-5 and 7-6.[7-7] In these two examples, the only process variable that is changed is drawing speed. It can be seen that, as expected, die temperatures increase with increasing drawing speed. Similar calculations are also made for other "continuous" processes. Figure 7-7 illustrates the variation of the temperature field in hot extrusion of an aluminum alloy at various stages of ram displacement, using a constant ram speed.[7-6]

TEMPERATURES IN OPERATIONS USED FOR FORMING DISCRETE PARTS

In forming operations used for producing discrete parts, the metal flow is nonsteady state. Contact between the deforming metal and the dies is intermittent. The length of contact time and the nature of the heat transfer at the die/material interface influence temperatures very significantly. A simple example of an operation involving nonsteady-state metal flow is the cold upsetting of a cylinder. In this process, much as in wiredrawing (as discussed earlier), a grid system is established for calculation of temperatures (Figure 7-8). For various points, indicated in Figure 7-8, temperatures were calculated for cold upsetting of a steel cylinder initially at room temperature.[7-8] The calculated results for the grid points $P_{1,1}$, $P_{1,5}$ and $P_{1,8}$ in Figure 7-8 are

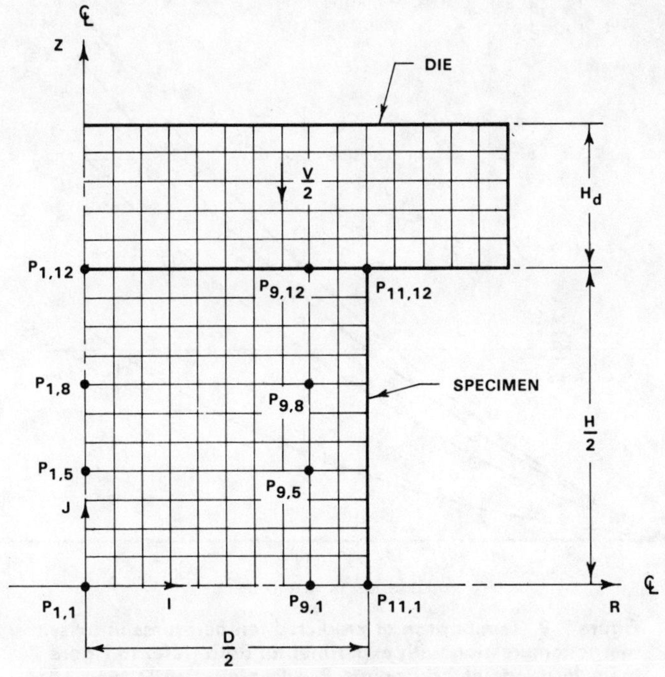

Figure 7-8. Grid system for calculating velocity and temperature fields in compression of cylinders.[7-8]

compared with experimental data in Figure 7-9. As expected, temperatures increase with increasing deformation.

In hot forming operations, the contact time under pressure between the deforming material and the dies is the most significant factor influencing temperature conditions. This is illustrated in Figure 7-10, where the load-displacement curves are given for hot forging of a steel part using different types of forging equipment.(7-9) These curves illustrate that, due to strain rate and temperature effects, for the same forging process, different forging loads and energies are required by different machines. For the hammer, the forging load is initially higher due to strain-rate effects, but the maximum load is lower than for either hydraulic or screw presses. The reason for this is that in the presses the extruded flash cools rapidly, whereas in the hammer the flash temperature remains nearly the same as the initial stock temperature.

Thus, in hot forming, not only the material and the formed shape but also the type of equipment used (rate of deformation and die-chilling effects) determine the metal flow behavior and the forming load and energy required for the process. Surface tearing and cracking or development of shear bands in the formed material often can be explained by excessive chilling of the

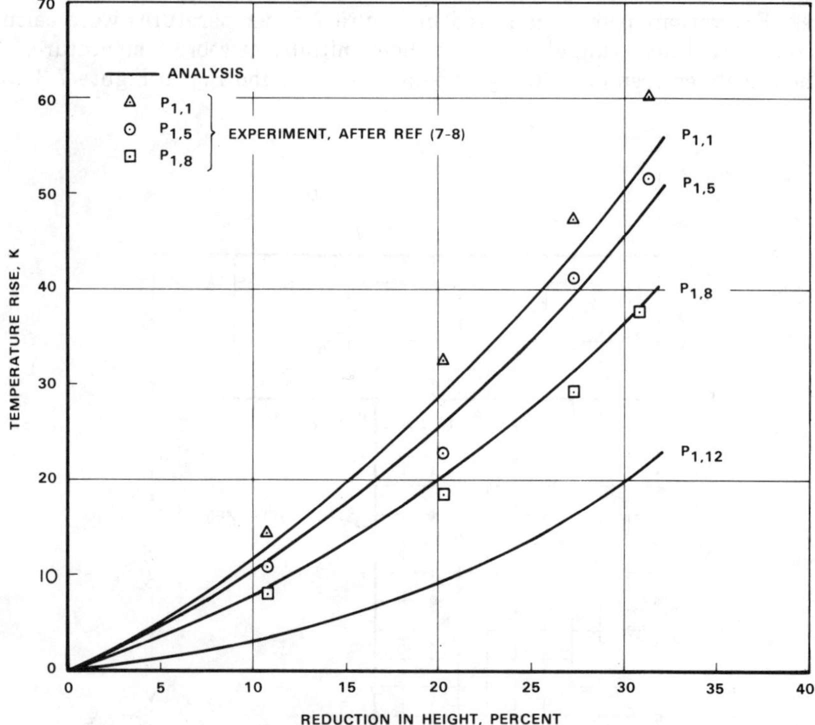

Figure 7-9. Comparison of predicted temperatures in axisymmetric compression with experimental data (refer to Figure 7-8 for locations of grid points $P_{i,j}$) (material, AISI type 1015 steel; specimen dimensions, 20 mm diam by 30 mm high; initial temperatures, 293 K).(7-8)

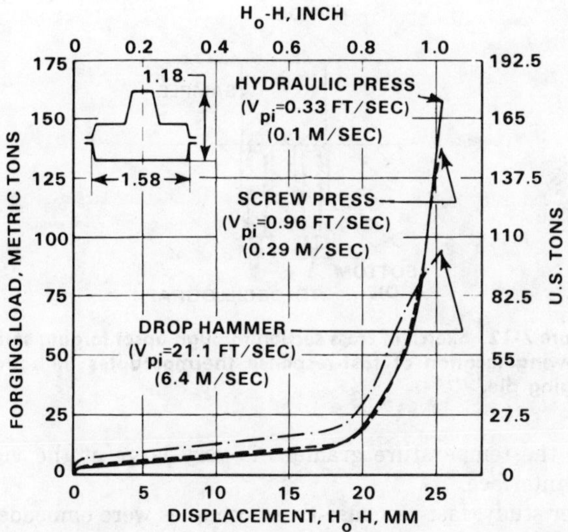

Figure 7-10. Load-versus-displacement curves obtained in closed-die forging of an axisymmetric steel part (dimensions in inches) at 2012 F in three different machines with different initial velocities, V_{pi}.[7-9]

surface layers of the formed part near the die/material interface.

Often it is desirable to measure the temperatures at the material/die interface in hot forming operations. A thermocouple for measuring interface temperatures in hot forming must exhibit very fast response (a few milliseconds), accuracy, minimum interference with heat flow, and the ability to sustain high normal and shear stresses under high temperatures. Such thermocouples are available and were used for measuring die temperatures in forging of steel.[7-10] The results are given in Figure 7-11. These results clearly

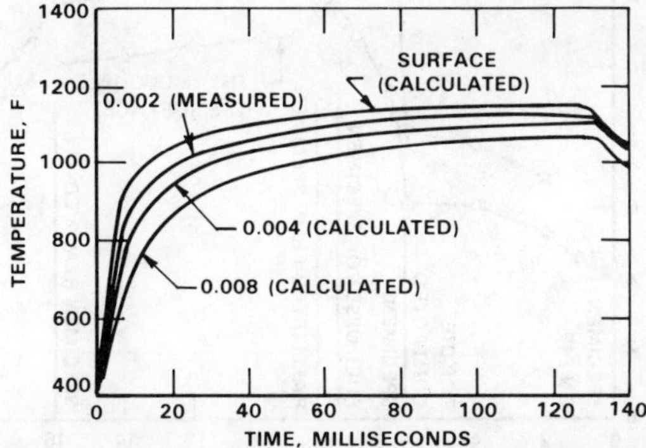

Figure 7-11. Temperatures at the surface and at various depths in the forging die obtained in forging of 1040 steel without a lubricant (samples 1.125 in. high; reduction in height, 75%; sample temperature, 2050 F; die temperature, 450 F).[7-10]

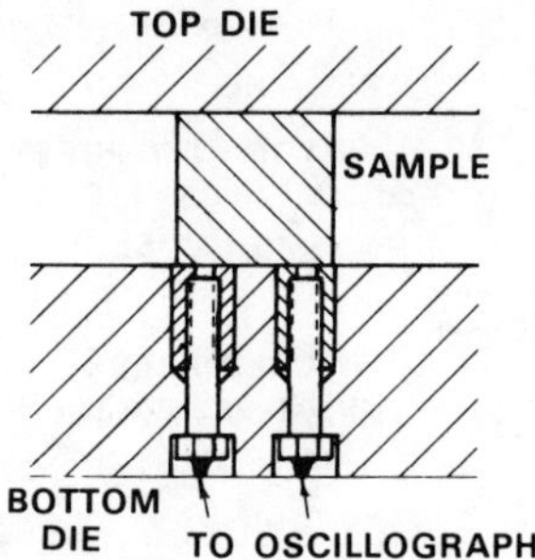

Figure 7-12. Sketch of cross section through upset forging setup, showing location of fast-response thermocouples in bottom forging die.[(7-11)]

indicate that the temperature gradient is very large at the vicinity of the die/material interface.

In another study, fast-response thermocouples were embedded in the bottom flat die of the upset tooling, as shown in Figure 7-12. The outputs of the thermocouples were recorded on a light-beam oscillograph along with the load

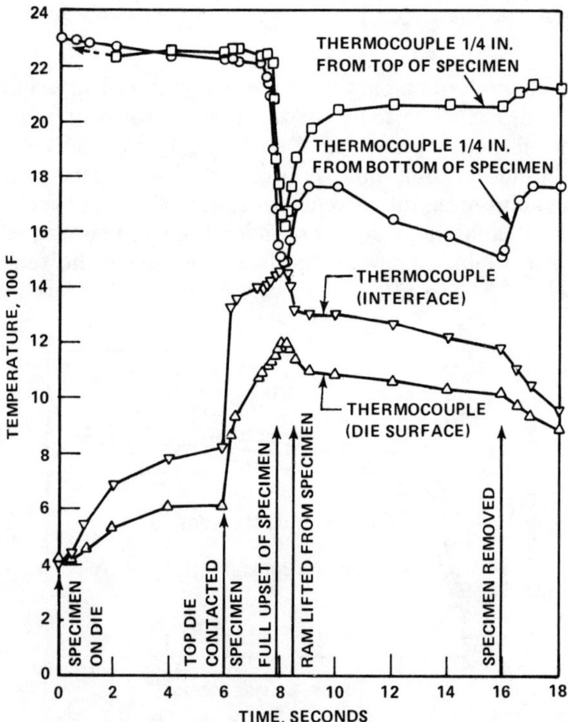

Figure 7-13. Variations in temperature at various locations in forging of 1020 steel billets (3 in. diam by 3 in. high) to 1-in. thickness at 2250 F between dies at 400 F.

required to upset the specimens and the movement of the press ram as determined by potentiometric displacement transducers.[7-3] Figure 7-13 shows the temperature-time traces for four thermocouples — two in the die and two in the 1020 steel billet forged at 2250 F (1230 C). These data show that the interface (or insulated) thermocouple measures the billet surface temperature, but only under load. Evidently, a high contact pressure is necessary to ensure good thermal contact between the billet surface and the thermocouple junction. After the load had been removed, the interface thermocouple indicated a decrease in temperature while the thermocouple placed in the sample actually showed an increase in temperature at the bottom of the forging. It is interesting that the rate of the temperature drop, as indicated by the interface thermocouple, decreases significantly once the upper ram and the pressure are removed. As can be expected, the rate of temperature drop further increases after the sample is removed from the die.

The results shown in Figure 7-13 indicate that, during forging of steel at 2250 F (1230 C) with dies initially at 400 F (204 C), die surface temperatures can reach approximately 1200 F (650 C) in a fraction of a second while the billet temperature at the interface drops to 1450 F (790 C). These data agree with the measurements shown in Figure 7-11. Similar measurements made during forging of aluminum alloy 6061 showed essentially the same trend of temperature variations with time. With the billet at 800 F (430 C) and the dies at 400 F (204 C), the interface temperature reached 700 F (370 C). These data demonstrate how rapidly temperatures change in hot forming, especially under pressure contact.

REFERENCES

7-1. Farren, W. S., and Taylor, G. I., "The Heat Developed During Plastic Extrusion of Metals", Proc. Royal Society, Series A, Vol 107, 1925, pp 422-451.

7-2. Lahoti, G. D., and Altan, T., "Prediction of Metal Flow and Temperatures in Axisymmetric Deformation Process", in "Advances in Deformation Processing", by J. J. Burke and V. Weiss (editors), Plenum Publishing Corp., 1978.

7-3. Altan, T., and Gerds, A. F., "Temperature Effects in Closed-Die Forging", ASM Technical Report No. C70-30.1, Oct 1970.

7-4. Ranger, A. E., "An Electrical Analogue for Estimating Die Temperature During Wire Drawing", J. Iron and Steel Inst., Vol 185, 1957, pp 383-388.

7-5. Altan, T., and Kobayashi, S., "A Numerical Method for Estimating Temperature Distributions in Extrusion Through Conical Dies", Trans. ASME, J. Engr. Industry, Vol 90, No. 1, 1968, pp 107-118.

7-6. Altan, T., Lee, C. H., and Akgerman, N., "Approximate Calculation of Velocity and Temperature Distributions in Axisymmetric Extrusion and Drawing", in Proc. First North American Metalworking Research Conference, McMaster University, Hamilton, Ontario, Canada, 1973, pp 107-127.

7-7. Altan, T., "Heat Generation and Temperatures in Wire and Rod Drawing", Wire Journal, March 1970, p 54.

7-8. Lahoti, G. D., and Altan, T., "Prediction of Temperature Distributions in Axisymmetric Compression and Torsion", ASME, J. Engr. Materials and Technology, Vol 97, 1975, pp 113-120.

7-9. Altan, T., *et al*, "Forging Equipment, Materials and Practices", MCIC Handbook HB-03, Battelle, Columbus, OH, 1973.

7-10. Vigor, C. W., and Hornaday, J. W., "A Thermocouple for Measurement of Temperature Transients in Forging Dies", in "Temperature, Its Measurement and Control", Vol 3, Part 2, Reinhold, New York, 1961, p 625.

CHAPTER 8
Principles of Forming Machines

In a practical sense, each forming process is associated with at least one type of forming machine (or "equipment", as it is sometimes called in practice). The introduction of a new process invariably depends on the cost effectiveness and production rate of the machine associated with that process. Therefore, capabilities of the machine associated with the new process are of paramount consideration. The forming (industrial, mechanical or metallurgical) engineer must also have specific knowledge of forming machines so that he can:

- Use existing machinery more efficiently.
- Define with accuracy the existing plant capacity.
- Better communicate with, and at times request improved performance from, the machine builder.
- If necessary, develop in-house proprietary machines and processes not available in the machine-tool market.

INTERACTION BETWEEN PROCESS REQUIREMENTS AND FORMING MACHINES

The behavior and characteristics of the forming machine influence:[8-1]

- The flow stress and workability of the deforming material.
- The temperatures in the material and in the tools, especially in hot forming.
- The load and energy requirements for a given product geometry and material.
- The "as formed" tolerances of the parts.
- The production rate.

The interaction between the principal machine and process variables is illustrated in Figure 8-1 for hot forming processes conducted in presses.[8-1] As can be seen at left in Figure 8-1, the flow stress, $\bar{\sigma}$, the interface friction conditions, and the forging geometry (dimensions, shape) determine (a) the load, L_p, at each position of the stroke and (b) the energy, E_p, required by the forming process. The flow stress, $\bar{\sigma}$, increases with increasing deformation rate, $\dot{\bar{\epsilon}}$, and with decreasing temperature, θ. The magnitudes of these variations depend on the specific forming material. The frictional conditions deteriorate with increasing die chilling.

As indicated by lines connected to the temperature block, for a given initial stock temperature, the temperature variations in the part are largely influenced by (a) the surface area of contact between the dies and the part, (b) the part thickness or volume, (c) the die temperature, (d) the amount of heat generated by deformation and friction and (e) the contact time under pressure.

The velocity of the slide under pressure, V_p, determines mainly the contact time under pressure, t_p, and the deformation rate, $\dot{\bar{\epsilon}}$. The number of strokes per minute under no-load conditions, n_0, the machine energy, E_M, and the deformation energy, E_p, required by the process influence the slide velocity under load, V_p, and the number of strokes under load, n_p; n_p determines the maximum number of parts formed per minute (i.e., the production rate) provided that feeding and unloading of the machine can be carried out at that speed.

The relationships illustrated in Figure 8-1 apply directly to hot forming of discrete parts in hydraulic, mechanical and screw presses, which will be

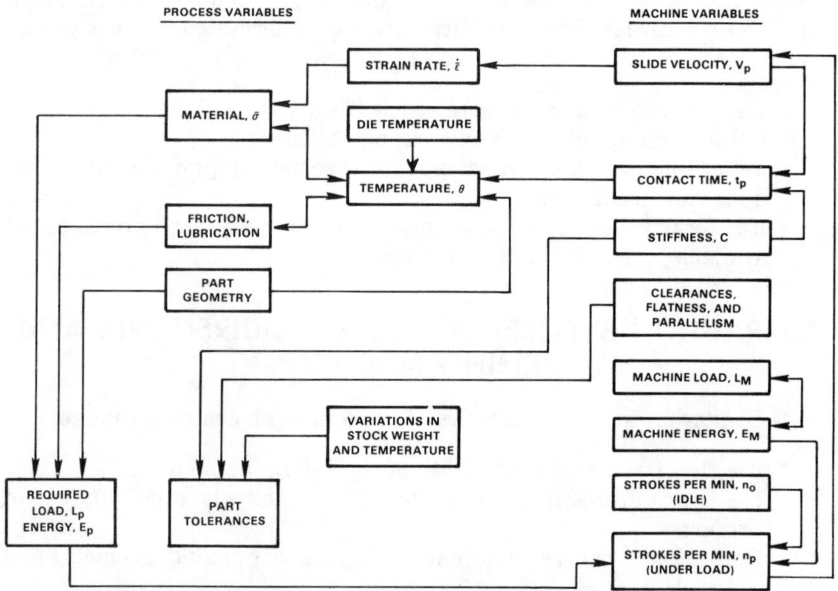

Figure 8-1. Relationships between process and machine variables in hot forming processes conducted in presses.[8-1]

discussed later. However, in principle, most of the same relationships apply also in other hot forming processes such as hot extrusion and hot rolling.

For a given material, a specific forming operation (such as closed-die forging with flash, forward or backward extrusion, upset forging, bending, etc.) requires a certain variation of the forming load over the slide displacement (or stroke). This fact is illustrated qualitatively in Figure 8-2, which shows load-versus-displacement curves characteristic of various forming operations. For a given part geometry, the absolute load values will vary with the flow stress of the material as well as with frictional conditions. In the forming operation, the equipment must supply the maximum load as well as the energy required by the process.

CLASSIFICATION AND CHARACTERISTICS OF FORMING MACHINES

The various forming processes, discussed in Chapter 2, are associated with a large number of forming machines. These include:

- Rolling mills for plate, strip and shapes.

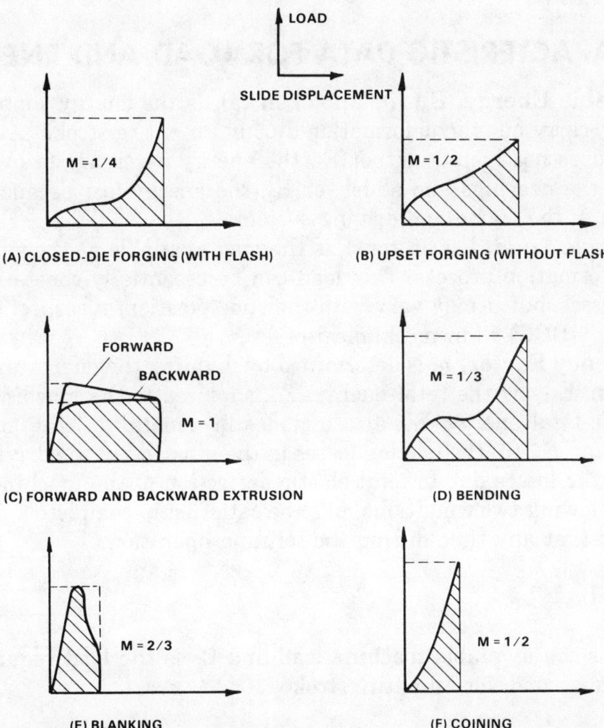

Figure 8-2. Load-versus-displacement curves for various forming operations (energy = load × displacement × M, where M is a factor characteristic of the specific forming operation).[8-1]

- Machines for profile rolling from strip.
- Ring rolling machines.
- Thread rolling and surface rolling machines.
- Magnetic and explosive forming machines.
- Draw benches for tube and rod; wire and rod drawing machines.
- Machines for pressing-type operations, i.e., presses.

Among those listed above, "pressing"-type machines are most widely used and applied for a different variety of processes. These machines can be classified into three types:[8-2,8-3]

- Load-restricted machines (hydraulic presses).
- Stroke-restricted machines (crank and eccentric presses).
- Energy-restricted machines (hammers and screw presses).

The significant characteristics of these machines comprise all machine design and performance data which are pertinent to the machine's economic use.[8-1] These characteristics include:

- Characteristics for load and energy.
- Time-related characteristics.
- Characteristics for accuracy.

CHARACTERISTIC DATA FOR LOAD AND ENERGY

Available Energy, E_M (in ft·lb or m·kg), is the energy supplied by the machine to carry out the deformation during an entire stroke. Available energy, E_M, does not include either E_f, the energy necessary to overcome the friction in the bearings and slides, or E_d, the energy lost because of elastic deflections in the frame and driving system.

Available Load, L_M (in tons), is the load available at the slide to carry out the deformation process. This load can be essentially constant as in hydraulic presses, but it may vary with the slide position in respect to "bottom-dead-center" (BDC) as in mechanical presses.

Efficiency Factor, η, is determined by dividing the energy available for deformation, E_M, by the total energy, E_T, supplied to the machine, i.e., $\eta = E_M/E_T$. The total energy, E_T, also includes in general: (a) the losses in the electric motor, E_e, (b) the friction losses in the gibs and in the driving system, E_f, and (c) the losses due to total elastic deflection of the machine, E_d.

The following two conditions must be satisfied to complete a forming operation: first, at any time during the forming operation,

$$L_M \geq L_P \tag{8-1}$$

where L_M is the available machine load and L_P is the load required by the process; and second, for an entire stroke,

$$E_M \geq E_P \tag{8-2}$$

where E_M is the available machine energy and E_P is the energy required by the process.

If the condition expressed by the former inequality above (8-1) is not fulfilled in a hydraulic press, the press will stall without accomplishing the required deformation. In a mechanical press the friction clutch would slip and the press run would stop before reaching the Bottom Dead Center position. If the condition expressed by the latter inequality (8-2) is not satisfied, either the flywheel will slow down to unacceptable speeds in a mechanical press or the part will not be formed completely in one blow in a screw press or hammer.

TIME-DEPENDENT CHARACTERISTIC DATA

Number of Strokes Per Minute, n, is the most important characteristic of any machine, because it determines the production rate.

Contact Time Under Pressure, t_p, is the time during which the part remains in the die under deformation load. This value is especially important in hot forming. The heat transfer between the hotter formed part and the cooler dies is most significant under pressure. Extensive studies conducted on workpiece and die temperatures in hot forming clearly showed that the heat-transfer coefficient is much larger under forming pressure than under free contact conditions. With increasing contact time under pressure, die wear increases. In addition, cooling of the workpiece results in higher forming load requirements.

Velocity Under Pressure, V_p, is the velocity of the slide under load. This is an important variable because it determines (a) the contact time under pressure and (b) the rate of deformation or the strain rate. The strain rate influences the flow stress of the formed material and consequently affects the load and energy required in hot forming.

CHARACTERISTIC DATA FOR ACCURACY

Under *unloaded* conditions, the stationary surfaces and their relative positions are established by (a) clearances in the gibs, (b) parallelism of upper and lower beds, (c) flatness of upper and lower beds, (d) perpendicularity of slide motion with respect to lower bed and (e) concentricity of tool holders. The machine characteristics influence the tolerances in formed parts. For instance, in backward extrusion a slight nonparallelism of the beds, or a slight deviation of the slide motion from ideal perpendicularity, would result in excessive bending stresses on the punch and in nonuniform dimensions in extruded products.

Under *loaded* conditions, the tilting of the ram and the ram and frame deflections, particularly under off-center loading, might result in excessive wear of the gibs, in thickness deviations in the formed part and in excessive tool wear. In order to reduce off-center loading and ram tilting, the center of loading of a part, i.e., the point where the resultant total forming load vector is applied, should be placed under the center of loading of the forming machine.

In presses (mechanical, hydraulic or screw), where the press frame and the drive mechanism are subject to loading, the stiffness, C, of the press is also a significant characteristic. The stiffness is the ratio of the load, L_M, to the total elastic deflection, d, between the upper and lower beds of the press, i.e.:

$$C = L_M/d \tag{8-3}$$

In mechanical presses, the total elastic deflection, d, includes the deflection of the press frame ($\simeq$25 to 35% of the total) and the deflection of the drive mechanism ($\simeq$65 to 75% of the total). The main influences of stiffness, C, on the forming process can be summarized as follows:

- Under identical forming load, L_M, the deflection energy, E_d, i.e., the elastic energy stored in the press during load buildup, is smaller for a stiffer press (larger C). The deflection energy is given by:

$$E_d = dL_M/2 = L_M^2/2C \tag{8-4}$$

- The higher the stiffness, the lower the deflection of the press. Consequently, the variations in part thickness due to volume or temperature changes in the stock are also smaller in a stiffer press.
- Stiffness influences the velocity-versus-time curve under load. Since a less stiff machine takes more time to build up and remove pressure, the contact time under pressure, t_p, is longer. This fact contributes to the reduction of tool life in hot forming.

The stiffness of a press is increased by using larger components in press design. Therefore, greater press stiffness is directly associated with increased costs and it should not be specified unless it can be justified by expected gains in part tolerances or tool life.

REFERENCES

8-1. Altan, T., *et al,* "Forging Equipment, Materials and Practices", Metals and Ceramics Information Center, HB03, 1973.
8-2. Kienzle, O., "Characteristics of Data in Machine Tools for Closed-Die Forging" (in German), Werkstattstechnik, Vol 55, 1965, p 509.
8-3. Kienzle, O., "The Characteristic Data on Presses and Hammers" (in German), Werkstattstechnik and Maschinenbau, Vol 43, 1953, p 1.

CHAPTER 9
Presses and Hammers for Cold and Hot Forming of Discrete Parts

Presses and hammers are very widely used in hot and cold forming of discrete parts. The understanding of the operational fundamentals of these basic machines is very helpful in the selection and optimal use of all types of metal forming machinery.

There are basically three types of presses: hydraulic, mechanical and screw presses. These machines are used for hot and cold forging, cold extrusion, sheet metal forming, and coining. Hammers are more limited in use, and are employed mostly for hot forging, coining, and some sheet metal forming operations.[9-1]

HYDRAULIC PRESSES

The operation of hydraulic presses is relatively simple and is based on the motion of a hydraulic piston guided in a cylinder.[9-2 to 9-4] Hydraulic presses are essentially load-restricted machines, i.e., their capability for carrying out a forming operation is limited mainly by the maximum available load. The following important features are offered by hydraulic presses:

- In direct-driven hydraulic presses, the maximum press load is available at any point during the entire ram stroke. In accumulator-driven presses, the available load decreases slightly depending on the length of the stroke and the load-displacement characteristics of the forming process.
- Since the maximum load is available during the entire stroke, relatively large energies are available for deformation. This is why the hydraulic press is ideally suited for extrusion-type forming operations requiring a nearly constant load over a long stroke.
- Within the capacity of a hydraulic press, the maximum load can be limited to protect the tooling. It is not possible to exceed the set load,

because a pressure-release valve limits the fluid pressure acting on the ram.

- Within the limits of the machine, the ram speed can be varied continuously at will during an entire stroke cycle. Adequate control systems can regulate the ram speed with respect to forming pressure or product temperature. This control feature can offer a considerable advantage in optimizing forming processes.

DRIVE SYSTEMS FOR HYDRAULIC PRESSES

The operational characteristics of a hydraulic press are essentially determined by the type and design of its hydraulic drive system. As shown in Figure 9-1, two types of hydraulic drive systems give different time-dependent characteristic data:[9-5,9-6]

1. *Direct-driven presses* usually employ hydraulic oil as the working medium. In earlier vertical press designs, at the start of the downstroke the upper ram falls under gravity and oil is drawn from the reservoir into the ram cylinder through the suction of this fall. When the ram contacts the workpiece, the valve between the ram cylinder and the reservoir is closed and the pump builds up pressure in the ram cylinder. This mode of operation results in relatively long dwell times prior to the start of deformation. As illustrated in Figure 9-1(B), during the downstroke in modern direct-driven presses a residual pressure is maintained in the return cylinders or in the return line by means of a pressure relief valve. Thus, the upper ram is forced down against pressure and the dwell inherent in the free fall is eliminated. When the press stroke is completed, i.e., when the upper ram reaches

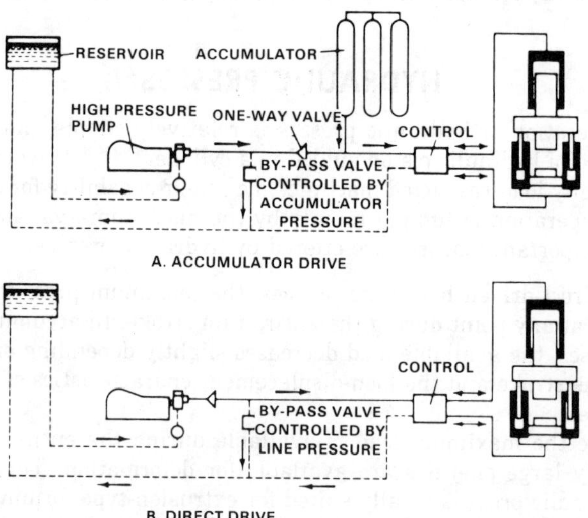

Figure 9-1. Schematic illustration of drives for hydraulic presses.[9-1]

a predetermined position, or when the pressure reaches a certain value, the oil pressure on the ram cylinder is released and diverted to lift the ram.

2. *Accumulator-driven presses* usually employ a water-oil emulsion as the working medium and use nitrogen, steam or air-loaded accumulators to keep the medium under pressure. The sequence of operations is essentially similar to that for the direct-driven press except that the pressure is built up by means of the pressurized water-oil emulsion in the accumulators. Consequently, the rate of penetration, i.e., the ram speed under load, is not directly dependent on the pump characteristics and can vary depending on the pressure in the accumulator, the compressibility of the pressure medium and the resistance of the workpiece to deformation. Toward the end of the forming stroke, as deformation progresses, the working medium expands, the force required to form the material increases and the speed of penetration and the load available at the ram decrease.

In both direct and accumulator drives, as the pressure builds up and the working medium is compressed, a certain slowdown in penetration rate occurs. This slowdown is larger in direct oil-driven presses, mainly because oil is more compressible than a water emulsion.

The approach and initial deformation speeds are higher in accumulator-driven presses. This improves the hot forming conditions by reducing contact times, but wear in hydraulic elements of the system also increases. Sealing problems are somewhat less severe in direct-oil drives, and control and accuracy in manual operation are in general about the same for both types of drives.

From a practical point of view, in a new installation, the choice between direct or accumulator drive is decided by the economics of operation. Usually, the accumulator drive is more economical if one accumulator system can be used by several presses, or if very large press capacities (10,000 to 50,000 tons) are considered.

The frame of a hydraulic press must carry the full forming load exerted by the hydraulic cylinder on the press bed. The load-carrying capability of the frame is achieved by using various designs such as cast (or welded) structures prestressed by forged tie rods, or laminated plates assembled through large transverse pins.

As can be seen in Figure 9-2, the two principal types of press construction are designated as "pull-down" and "push-down" designs.[9-7] The conventional push-down design is often selected for four-column presses of all sizes. The cylinder cross-head and base platen are rigidly connected by four columns that take up the press load and simultaneously guide the moving piston-ram assembly. Considerable elastic deflections are exhibited under off-center loading. This type of press requires a relatively tall shop building. In the pull-down design, the base platen rests on a foundation. The cylinder cross-head, located below floor level, is rigidly connected to the press columns. This assembly is movable and is guided in the bed platen. The center of gravity of the press is low, at approximately floor level, and the over-all static and dynamic stiffness of the press is increased accordingly.[9-8] Pull-down presses are

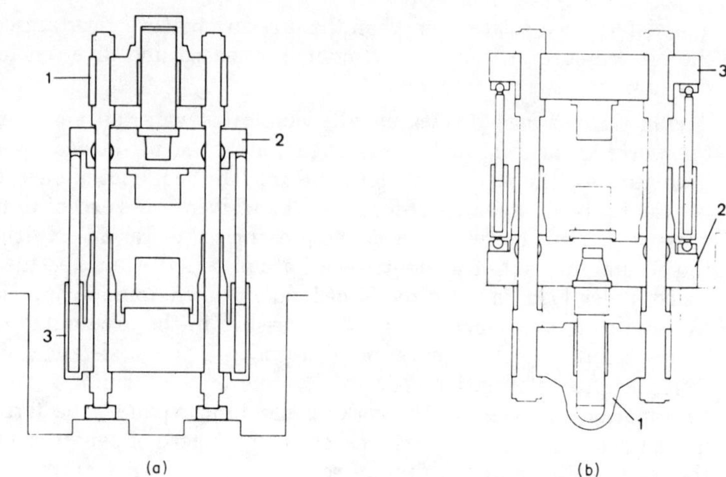

Figure 9-2. Schematic illustration of two types of hydraulic press drives. (a) Push-down drive: 1 — stationary cylinder cross head, 2 — moving piston-ram assembly, 3 — stationary press bed with return cylinders. (b) Pull-down drive: 1 — movable cylinder-frame assembly, 2 — press bed with return cylinders, 3 — moving cross head.[9-1]

particularly suitable for installation in low buildings. Most of the hydraulic and auxiliary equipment may then be accommodated beneath floor level. This arrangement is particularly favorable for direct-oil drives since it minimizes

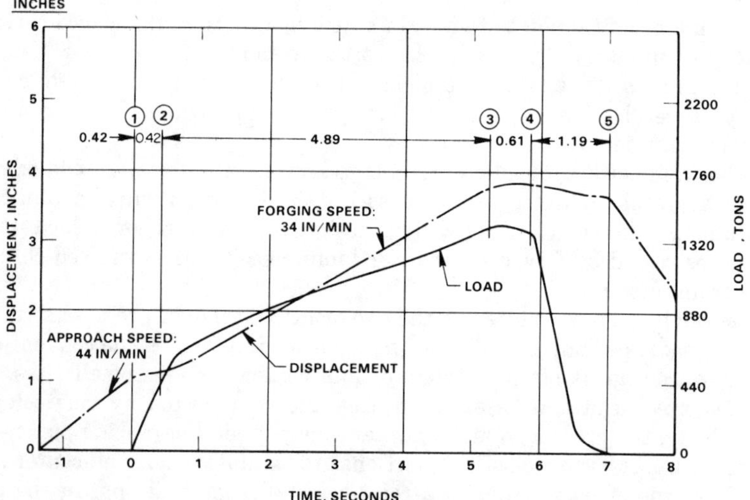

Figure 9-3. Load- and displacement-versus-time curves obtained on a 2500-ton hydraulic press in upsetting with direct drive: (1) start of deformation, (2) initial dwell, (3) end of deformations, (4) dwell before pressure release, (5) ram lift.

fire hazard and reduces the length of piping between the pumping system and the press cylinder.

CHARACTERISTICS OF HYDRAULIC PRESSES

In direct-driven hydraulic presses, the maximum press load is established by the pressure capability of the pumping system and is available throughout the entire press stroke. Thus, hydraulic presses are ideally suited for extrusion-type operations requiring very large amounts of energy. With adequate dimensioning of the pressure system, an accumulator-driven press exhibits only a slight reduction in available press load as the forming operation proceeds.

In comparison with direct drive, the accumulator drive usually offers higher approach and penetration speeds and a shorter dwell time prior to forging. However, the dwell at the end of processing and prior to unloading is larger in accumulator drives. This is illustrated in Figures 9-3 and 9-4, where the load and displacement variations are given for a forming process using a 2500-ton hydraulic press equipped with either accumulator or direct-drive systems.

MECHANICAL CRANK AND ECCENTRIC PRESSES

The drive system used in most mechanical presses (crank or eccentric) is based on a slider-crank mechanism that translates rotary motion into reciprocating linear motion. The eccentric shaft is connected through a clutch and brake system directly to the flywheel (Figure 9-5). In designs for larger capacities, the flywheel is located on the pinion shaft, which drives the eccentric shaft (Figure 9-6). The constant clutch torque, M, is available at the eccentric

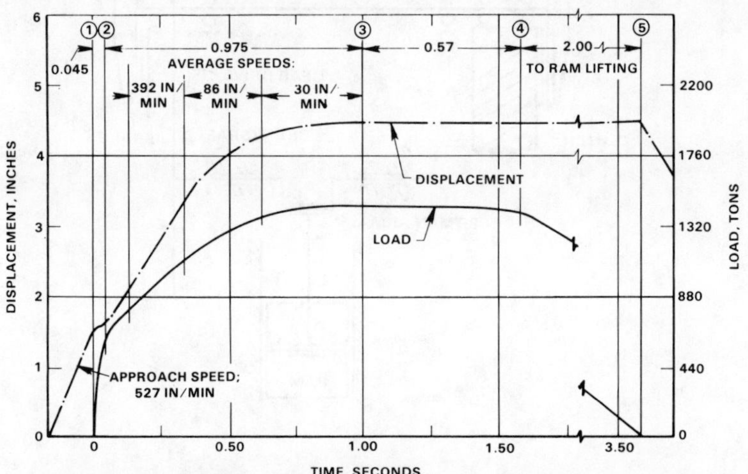

Figure 9-4. Load- and displacement-versus-time curves obtained on a 2500-ton hydraulic press in upsetting with accumulator drive: (1) start forming, (2) initial dwell, (3) end of forming, (4) dwell before pressure release, (5) ram lift.

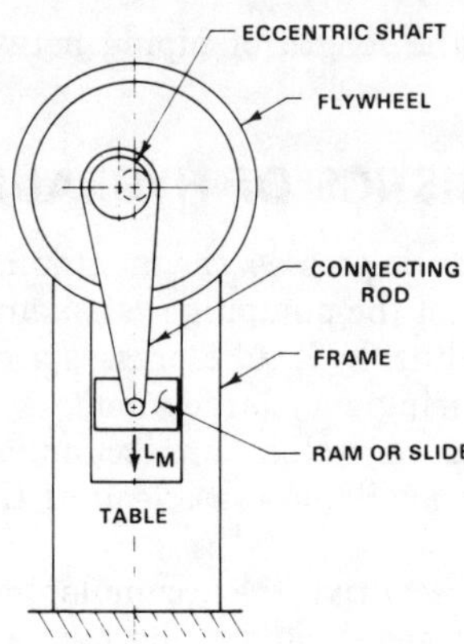

Figure 9-5. Schematic of a mechanical press with eccentric drive (clutch and brake on eccentric shaft).

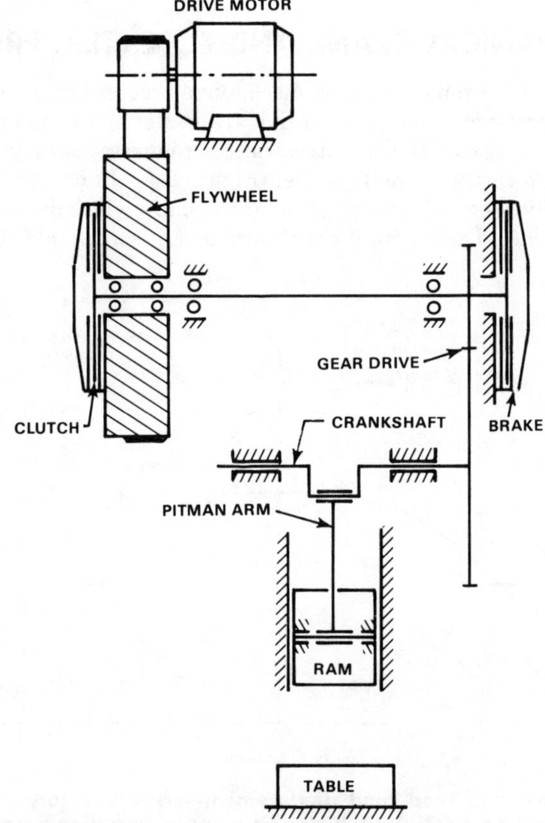

Figure 9-6. Schematic of a crank press with pinion-gear drive (clutch and brake are on pinion shaft; for large capacities this design is more stable and provides high flywheel energy).

shaft, which transmits the torque and the flywheel energy to the slide through the pitman arm or connecting rod, as illustrated in Figure 9-5. The flywheel, which is driven by an electric motor and "V" belts, stores energy that is used only during a small portion of the crank revolution, namely, during deformation of the formed material.[9-1]

Figure 9-7 shows the basic slider-crank mechanism. The clutch at the flywheel transmits the constant torque, M, to the eccentric (or crank) shaft. The force diagram gives the relations between the torque, M, the force on the connecting rod, P, and the tangential force, T:

$$T = P \sin(\alpha + \beta) \tag{9-1}$$

and

$$M = rT \tag{9-2}$$

Usually, the ratio, λ, of crank radius r to connecting-rod length l is small, about:

$$\lambda = \frac{r}{l} = \frac{1}{10} \quad \text{or} \quad \frac{\sin\beta}{\sin\alpha} = \frac{1}{10} \tag{9-3}$$

Using Equation 9-1 and considering that the total press stroke is S = 2r, the machine load, L_M, acting on the ram is:

$$L_M = P\cos\beta = \frac{T\cos\beta}{\sin(\alpha+\beta)} = \frac{2M\cos\beta}{S\sin(\alpha+\beta)} \tag{9-4}$$

When the angles α and β approach 0, i.e., toward Bottom Dead Center (BDC), L_M may go to infinity for constant torque, M. This is illustrated in Figure 9-8.

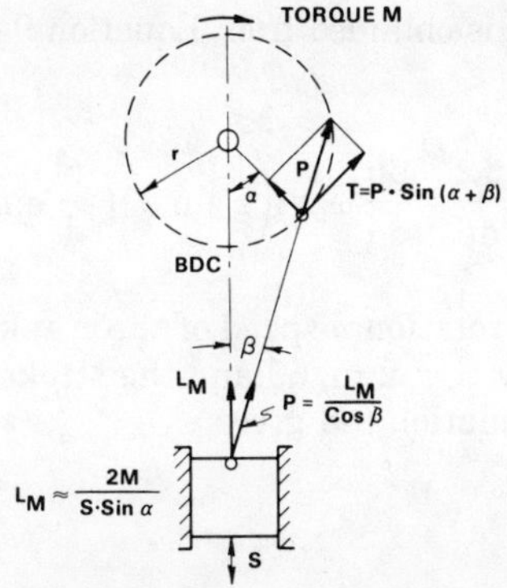

Figure 9-7. The basic slider-crank mechanism used in crank presses: S = stroke, BDC = bottom dead center, α = crank angle before bottom dead center (BDC), L_M = machine load.

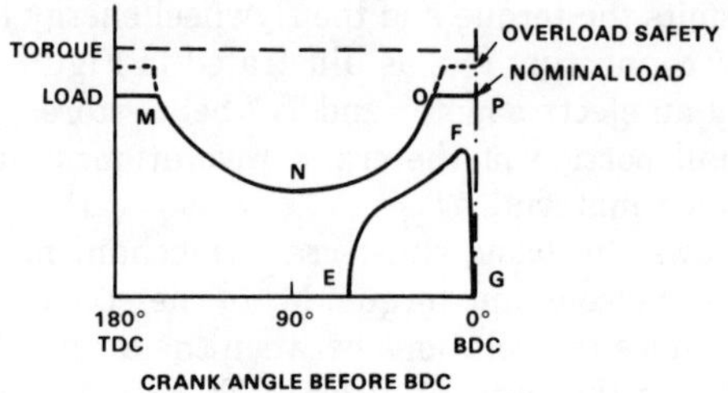

Figure 9-8. Variations of clutch torque and machine load with crank angle in an eccentric or crank press.

The stroke position, i.e., the distance, h, from BDC, as a function of the crank angle, α, can be derived, from the geometric relationships illustrated in Figure 9-7, to be:

$$h = (r + l) - (r \cos \alpha + \sqrt{l^2 - r^2 \sin^2 \alpha}), \quad \text{or}$$

$$h = r(1 - \cos \alpha) + l\left(1 - \sqrt{1 - \left(\frac{r}{l}\right)^2 \sin^2 \alpha}\right) \tag{9-5}$$

Using the binomial expansion, the term under the square root sign can be approximated as $1 - (r/l)^2 \sin^2 \alpha/2$.

Thus, Equation 9-5 can be transformed into:

$$h = r(1 - \cos \alpha) + \frac{r^2}{2l} \sin^2 \alpha \tag{9-6}$$

For small values of α, i.e., near BDC, Equation 9-6 is approximated as:

$$h = r(1 - \cos \alpha) = \frac{S}{2}(1 - \cos \alpha) \tag{9-7}$$

The ram velocity, V, is obtained from Equation 9-6 by differentiation with respect to time, t:

$$V = \frac{dh}{dt} = \frac{dh}{d\alpha}\frac{d\alpha}{dt} = \frac{dh}{d\alpha}\omega = \left(r \sin \alpha + \frac{r^2}{l} \sin \alpha \cos \alpha\right)\omega \tag{9-8}$$

where, with n being the rotational speed of the crank in revolutions per minute, the angular velocity $\omega = 2\pi n/60$ and the stroke $S = 2r$. Neglecting the second small term in Equation 9-8 gives:

$$V = \frac{S\pi n}{60} \sin \alpha \tag{9-9}$$

Using the geometric relationships of Figure 9-7, the ram velocity can be expressed as:

$$V = \frac{\pi n}{30} h \sqrt{\frac{S}{h} - 1} \tag{9-10}$$

Thus, with Equations 9-6 and 9-10 the displacement, h, and the velocity, V, at each point of the ram stroke can be calculated. Figure 9-9 illustrates the variation of these values with the crank angle α before BDC.

LOAD AND ENERGY IN MECHANICAL PRESSES

With the symbols used in Figure 9-7, the ram or machine load, L_M, is given by Equation 9-4. Considering that angle β is much smaller than angle α, L_M can be approximated as:

$$L_M = \frac{2M}{S \sin \alpha} \tag{9-11}$$

As shown in Figure 9-8, Equation 9-11 illustrates the variation of the slide load, L_M, with the crank angle, α, before bottom dead center, BDC, for given values of torque, M, and stroke, S, of the press. The torque, M, at the clutch has a constant value for which the drive machanism (i.e., eccentric shaft, pinion gear, clutch, brake, etc.) is designed. Thus, from Equation 9-11 it can be seen that, as the slide approaches the BDC, i.e., as angle α approaches zero, the available machine load, L_M, may become infinitely large without exceeding the constant clutch torque, M, i.e., without causing the friction clutch to slip.

From the observations made so far, the following conclusions may be drawn:

- Crank and eccentric presses are displacement-restricted machines. The slide velocity, V, and the available slide load, L_M, vary according to the position of the slide before BDC. Most manufacturers in the United States rate their presses by specifying the nominal load at 1/4 or 1/8 in. before BDC. For different applications, the nominal load may be

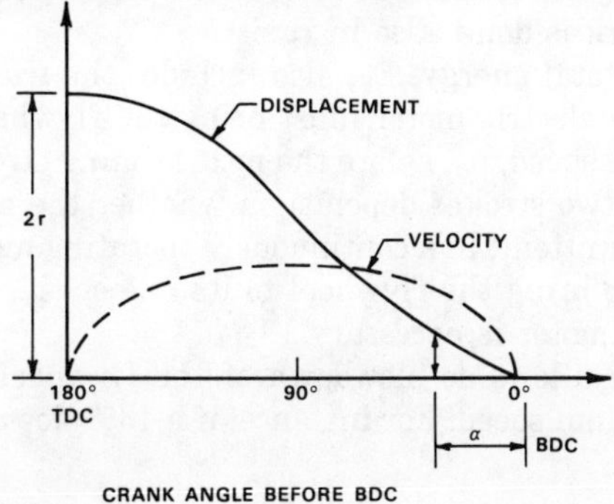

Figure 9-9. Displacement and velocity in a simple slider-crank mechanism (stroke = 2r).

specified at different positions before BDC according to the standards established by the American Joint Industry Conference.[9-9]

- If the load required by the forming process is smaller than the load available at the press (i.e., if curve EFG in Figure 9-8 remains below curve NOP), the process can be carried out provided that the flywheel can supply the necessary energy per stroke.
- For small angles α before BDC, within the OP portion of curve NOP in Figure 9-8, the slide load, L_M, can become larger than the nominal press load if no overload safety (hydraulic or mechanical) is available on the press. In this case, the press stalls, the flywheel stops and the entire flywheel energy is transformed into deflection energy by straining the press frame, the pitman arm and the drive mechanism. Usually, the press can then be freed only by burning out the tooling.
- If the load curve EFG exceeds the press load NOP (Figure 9-8) before point 0 is reached, then the friction clutch slides and the press slide stops, but the flywheel continues to turn. In this case the press can be freed by increasing the air pressure on the clutch and by reversing the flywheel rotation if the slide has stopped before BDC.

The energy needed for the forming operation during each stroke is supplied by the flywheel, which slows down to a permissible percentage — usually 10 to 20% — of its idle speed. The total energy stored in a flywheel is:

$$E_{FT} = \frac{I\omega^2}{2} = \frac{I}{2}\left(\frac{\pi n}{30}\right)^2 \tag{9-12}$$

where I is the moment of inertia of the flywheel, ω is the angular velocity in radians per second and n is the rotational speed of the flywheel in revolutions per minute. The total energy, E_S, used during one stroke is:

$$E_S = \frac{1}{2} I(\omega_0^2 - \omega_1^2) = \frac{I}{2}\left(\frac{\pi}{30}\right)^2 (n_0^2 - n_1^2) \tag{9-13}$$

where ω_0 is initial angular velocity, ω_1 is angular velocity after the work is done, n_0 is initial flywheel speed in revolutions per minute and n_1 is flywheel speed after the work is done, also in rpm.

Note that the total energy, E_S, also includes the friction and elastic deflection losses. The electric motor must bring the flywheel from its lowered speed, n_1, to its idle speed, n_0, before the next forming stroke starts. The time available between two strokes depends on whether the mode of operation is continuous or intermittent. In a continuously operating mechanical press, less time is available to bring the flywheel to its idle speed, and consequently a higher-horsepower motor is necessary.

Very often the allowable slowdown of the flywheel is given as a percentage of the nominal speed. For instance, if a 13% slowdown is permissible, then:

$$\frac{n_0 - n_1}{n_0} = \frac{13}{100}, \quad \text{or} \quad n_1 = 0.87\, n_0$$

The percentage energy supplied by the flywheel is obtained by using Equations 9-12 and 9-13 to arrive at:

$$\frac{E_S}{E_{FT}} = \frac{n_0^2 - n_1^2}{n_0^2} = 1 - (0.87)^2 = 0.25$$

The simple calculations given above illustrate that for a 13% slowdown of the flywheel, 25% of the flywheel energy will be used during one stroke.

As an example, the variation of load, displacement and flywheel speed in upset forming of a copper sample under a 1600-ton mechanical press is illustrated in Figure 9-10. This press was instrumented with strain bars attached to the frame for measuring load, an inductive transducer (LVDT) for measuring ram displacement, and a dc tachometer for measuring flywheel speed.[9-10] In Figure 9-10 it can be seen that, due to frictional and inertial losses in the press drive, the flywheel slows down (by about 5 rpm) before deformation begins. The flywheel requires 3.24 s to recover its idling speed, i.e., in forming this part the press can be operated at a maximum speed of 18 (60/3.24) strokes per minute. For each mechanical press there is a unique relationship between strokes per minute, or production rate, and the available energy per stroke. As shown in Figure 9-11, the strokes per minute available on the machine decreases with increasing energy required per stroke. This relationship can be determined experimentally by upsetting samples which require various amounts of deformation energy and by measuring load, displacement and flywheel recovery time. The energy consumed by each sample is obtained by calculating the surface area under the load-displacement curve.

TIME-DEPENDENT CHARACTERISTICS OF MECHANICAL PRESSES

The number of strokes per minute, n, was discussed as part of the energy considerations. As can be seen in Equation 9-9, the ram velocity is directly

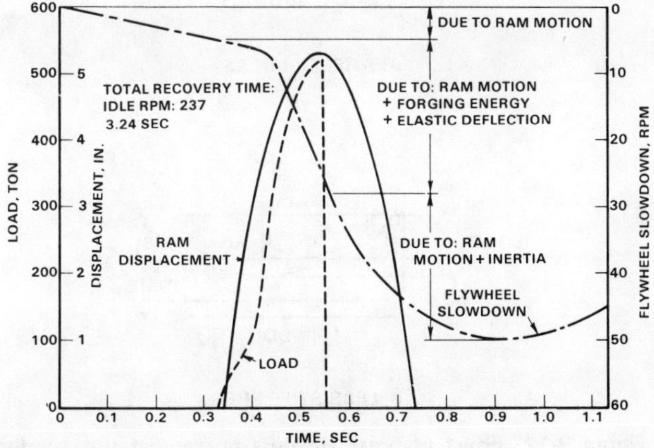

Figure 9-10. Flywheel slowdown, ram displacement and forming load in upsetting of copper samples in a 1600-ton mechanical press.[9-10]

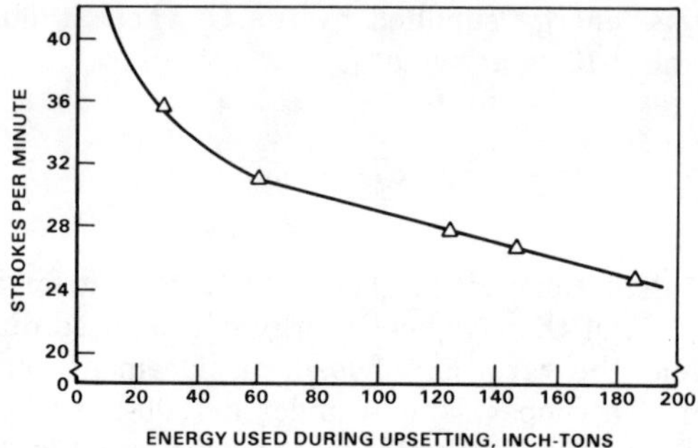

Figure 9-11. Variation of strokes per minute with the energy available for forming in a 500-ton mechanical press.[9-1]

proportional to the number of strokes per minute, n, and to the press stroke, S. Thus, for a given press, i.e., a given stroke, the only way to increase ram velocity during deformation is to increase the stroking rate, n.

For a given idle-flywheel speed, the contact time under pressure, t_p, and the velocity under pressure, V_p, depend mainly on the dimensions of the slide-crank mechanism and on the total stiffness, C, of the press. The effect of press stiffness on contact time under pressure, t_p, is illustrated in Figure 9-12. As the load builds up, the press deflects elastically. A stiffer press (larger C) requires less time, t_{p1}, for pressure build-up and also less time t_{p2}, for pressure release, as shown in Figure 9-12(A). Consequently, the total contact time under pressure ($t_p = t_{p1} + t_{p2}$) is less for a stiffer press.[9-1]

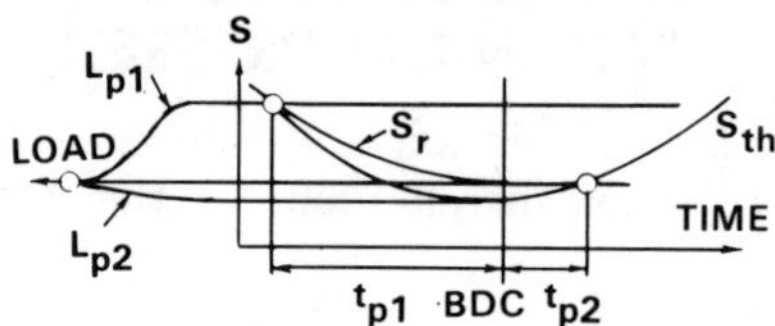

A. STIFFER PRESS

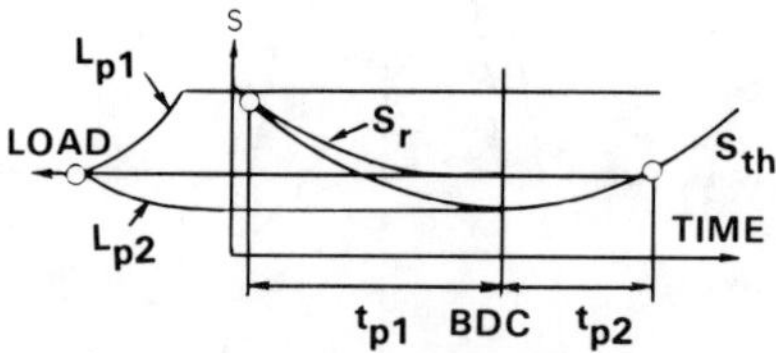

B. LESS STIFF PRESS

Figure 9-12. Effect of press stiffness on contact time under pressure (S_{th} = theoretical displacement-time curve, S_r = real displacement-time curve under load.[9-1]

ACCURACY OF MECHANICAL PRESSES

The working accuracy of an eccentric press is substantially characterized by two features: the tilting angle of the ram under off-center loading and the total deflection under load or stiffness of the press. Tilting of the ram produces skewed surfaces and an offset on the part; stiffness influences the thickness tolerance.[9-11] Under off-center loading conditions, two- or four-point presses perform better than single-point presses because the tilting of the ram and the reduction forces into the gibways are minimized. Assuming the total deflection under load for a one-point eccentric press to be 100%, the following distributions of total deflection were obtained from measurements under nominal load on one- and two-point presses of the same capacity:[9-11]

	Deflection, %	
	One-point eccentric press	**Two-point eccentric press**
Slide + pitman arm	30	21
Frame	33	31
Drive shaft + bearings	37	33
Total deflection	100	85

It is interesting to note that a large percentage of the total deflection is in the drive mechanism, i.e., slide, pitman arm, drive shaft, and bearings.

CRANK PRESSES WITH MODIFIED DRIVES

The velocity-versus-stroke and the load-versus-stroke characteristics of crank presses can be modified by using different press drives. A well-known variation of the crank press is the knuckle joint design (Figure 9-13). This design is capable of generating high forces with a relatively small crank drive. In the knuckle joint drive, the ram velocity slows down much more rapidly toward the BDC than in the regular crank drive. This machine is successfully used for cold forming and coining applications.

A recently developed mechanical press drive uses a four-bar linkage mechanism, as shown in Figure 9-14.[9-12] In this mechanism, the load-stroke and velocity-stroke behavior of the slide can be established, at the design stage, by adjusting the length of one of the four links or by varying the connection point of the slider link with the drag link. Thus, with this press it is possible to maintain the maximum load, as specified by press capacity, over a relatively long deformation stroke. Using a conventional slider-crank-type press, this capability can be achieved only by using a much larger-capacity press. A comparison is illustrated in Figure 9-15, where the load-stroke curves for a four-bar linkage press and a conventional slider-crank press are shown. It can be seen that a slider-crank press equipped with a 1700 ton-inch torque drive can generate a force of about 1500 tons at 1/32 in. before BDC. The four-bar press equipped with a 600 ton-inch drive generates a force of about 750 tons at the same location. However, in both machines a 200-ton force is available at 6 in. before BDC. Thus, a 750-ton, four-bar press could perform the same forming operation, requiring 200 tons over 6 in., as a 1500-ton eccentric press. The four-bar press, which was originally developed for sheet

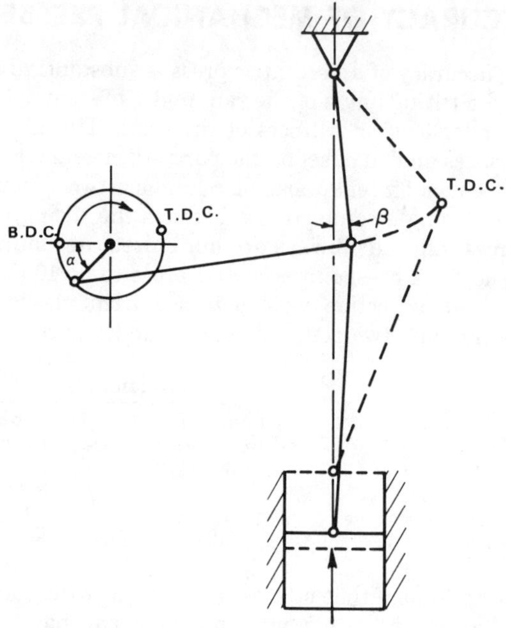

Figure 9-13. Schematic of a toggle (or knuckle) joint mechanical press.

metal forming and cold extrusion, is well suited for extrusion-type forming operations, where a nearly constant load is required over a long stroke.

SCREW PRESSES

The screw press uses a friction, gear, electric or hydraulic drive to accelerate the flywheel and the screw assembly, and it converts the angular kinetic energy into the linear energy of the slide or ram. Figure 9-16 shows two basic designs of screw presses.[9-13]

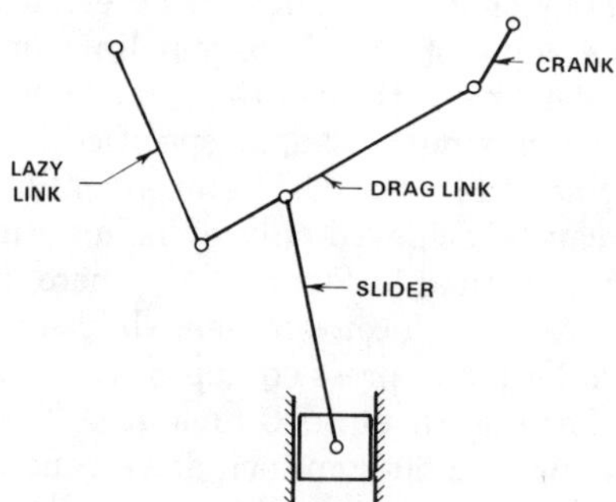

Figure 9-14. Four-bar linkage mechanism for mechanical press drives.[9-12]

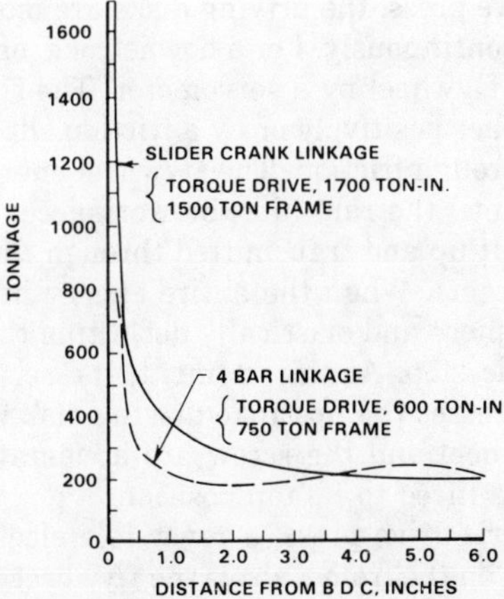

Figure 9-15. Load-stroke curves for a 750-ton four-bar linkage press and a 1500-ton slider-crank press.(9-12)

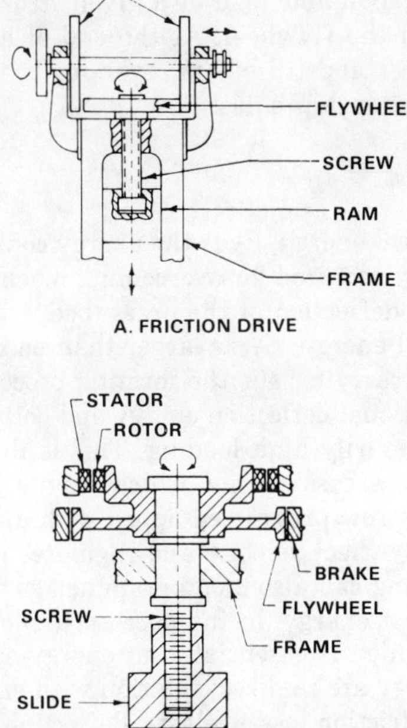

Figure 9-16. Two widely used screw press drives.

In the friction-drive press, the driving disks are mounted on a horizontal shaft and are rotated continuously. For a downstroke, one of the driving disks is pressed against the flywheel by a servomotor. The flywheel, which is connected to the screw either positively or by a friction slip clutch, is accelerated by this driving disk through friction. The flywheel energy and the ram speed continue to increase until the ram hits the workpiece. Thus, the load necessary for forming is built up and transmitted through the slide, the screw and the bed to the press frame. When the entire energy in the flywheel is used in deforming the workpiece and elastically deflecting the press, the flywheel, the screw and the slide stop. At this moment, the servomotor activates the horizontal shaft and presses the upstroke driving disk wheel against the flywheel. Thus, the flywheel and the screw are accelerated in the reverse direction and the slide is lifted to its top position.

In the direct-electric-drive press, a reversible electric motor is built directly on the screw and on the frame, above the flywheel. The screw is threaded into the ram or slide and does not move vertically. To reverse the direction of flywheel rotation, the electric motor is reversed after each downstroke and upstroke.

LOAD AND ENERGY IN SCREW PRESSES

In a screw press the load is transmitted through the slide, screw and bed to the press frame. The available load at a given stroke position is supplied by the energy stored in the flywheel. At the end of a stroke, the flywheel and the screw come to a standstill before reversing the direction of rotation. Thus, the following relationship holds:

$$E_T = E_P + E_F + E_d \tag{9-14}$$

where E_T is total flywheel energy, E_P is the energy consumed by the forming process, E_F is the energy required for overcoming machine friction, and E_d is the energy required for deflection of the press (bed + columns + screw).

If the total flywheel energy, E_T, is larger than necessary for overcoming machine losses and for carrying out the forming process, the excess energy is transformed into additional deflection energy and both the die and the press are subjected to unnecessarily high loading. This is illustrated in Figure 9-17.[9-1] To annihilate the excess energy, which results in increased die wear and noise, the modern screw press is equipped with an energy-metering device that controls the flywheel velocity and regulates the total flywheel energy. The energy metering can also be programmed so that the machine supplies different amounts of energy during successive blows.

In a screw press, which is essentially an energy-bound machine (like a hammer), load and energy are in direct relation with each other. For a given press (i.e., for the same friction losses, elastic deflection properties and available flywheel energy), the load available at the end of the stroke depends mainly on the deformation energy required by the process (i.e., on the shape, temperature and material of the workpiece). Thus, for a constant flywheel energy, low deformation energy, E_p, results in high end load, L_M, and high deformation energy, E_p, results in low end load, L_M. These relations are il-

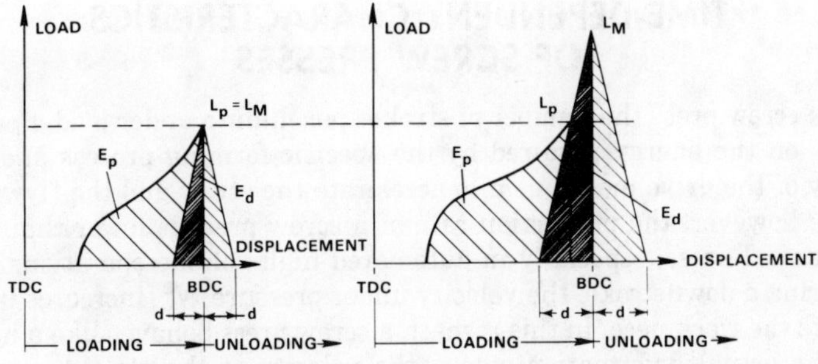

Figure 9-17. Load-energy relationships in forming in a press (E_p = energy required by process, L_M = maximum machine load, E_d = elastic deflection energy, d = press deflection).

lustrated in the "load-energy diagram" of a screw press, as shown in Figure 9-18.[9-14]

The screw press can sustain maximum loads, L_{max}, up to 160 to 200% of its nominal load, L_M. In this sense, the nominal load of a screw press is set rather arbitrarily. The significant information about the press load is obtained from its load-energy diagram (see Figure 9-18). The load-energy curve has a parabolic shape because the deflection energy, E_d, is given by a second-order equation:

$$E_d = L_M^2/2C \tag{9-15}$$

where L_M is machine load and C is total press stiffness.

A screw press designed for a forming operation, where large energies, E_M, are needed, can also be used for operations where smaller energies are required. Here, however, a friction clutch is installed between the flywheel and the screw. When the ram load reaches the nominal load, this clutch starts slipping and uses up a part of the flywheel energy as frictional heat energy, E_c, at the clutch. Consequently, the maximum load at the end of the downstroke is reduced from L to L_{max} and the press is protected from overloading (Figure 9-18). Screw presses used for coining are designed for hard blows (i.e., die-to-die blows without any workpiece) and do not have a friction slip clutch on the flywheel.

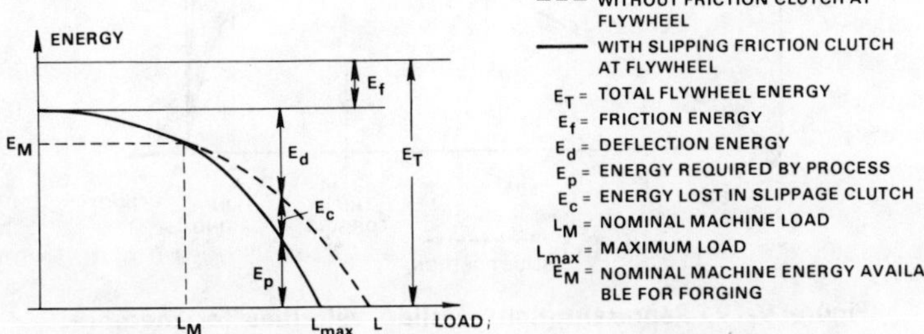

Figure 9-18. Schematic of load-energy relationship in a screw press.[9-14]

TIME-DEPENDENT CHARACTERISTICS OF SCREW PRESSES

In a screw press the number of strokes per minute under load, n_p, largely depends on the energy required by the specific forming process and on the capacity of the drive mechanism to accelerate the screw and the flywheel. In general, however, the production rate of a screw press is lower than that of a mechanical press, especially in automated high-volume operations.

During a downstroke, the velocity under pressure, V_p, increases until the slide hits the workpiece. In this respect, a screw press behaves like a hammer. After the actual deformation starts, the velocity of the slide decreases depending on the energy requirements of the process. Thus, the velocity, V_p, is greatly influenced by the geometry of the stock and of the part. As illustrated in Figure 9-19, this is quite different from the conditions found in mechanical presses, where the ram velocity is established by the press kinematics and is not influenced significantly by the load and energy requirements of the process.

ACCURACY IN SCREW PRESS OPERATION

In general, the dimensional accuracies of press components under unloaded conditions, such as parallelism of slide and bed surfaces, clearances in the gibs, etc., have basically the same significance in the operation of all presses — hydraulic, mechanical and screw presses.

The off-center loading capacity of the press influences the parallelism of upset surfaces. This capacity is increased in modern presses by use of long gibs and by finish forming at the center, whenever possible. The off-center loading capacity of a screw press is less than that of a mechanical press or a hammer.

A screw press is operated like a hammer, i.e., the top and bottom dies

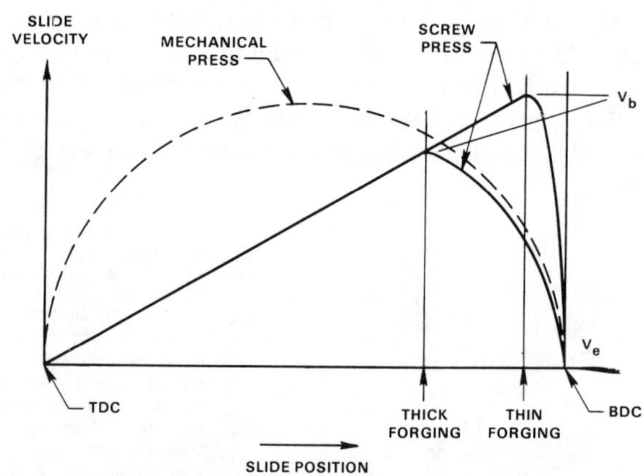

Figure 9-19. Representation of slide velocities for mechanical and screw presses in forming a thick and a thin part (V_b, V_e = velocity at beginning and end of forming, respectively).[(9-1)]

"kiss" at each blow. Therefore, the stiffness of the press, which affects the load and energy characteristics, does not influence the thickness tolerances in the formed part.

VARIATIONS IN SCREW PRESS DRIVES

In addition to direct friction and electric drives (Figure 9-16), there are several other types of mechanical, electric and hydraulic drives that are commonly used in screw presses. A relatively new screw press drive is shown in Figure 9-20.[9-15] A flywheel (1), supported on the press frame, is driven by one or several electric motors and rotates at a constant speed. When the stroke is initiated, an air-operated clutch (2) engages the rotating flywheel against the stationary screw (3). This feature is similar to what is used to initiate the stroke of an eccentric forging press. On engagement of the clutch, the screw is rapidly accelerated and reaches the speed of the flywheel. As a result, the ram (4), which acts like a giant nut, moves downward. During this downstroke, the air is compressed in the pneumatic lift-up cylinders (5). The downstroke is terminated by controlling either the ram position, by means of a position switch, or the maximum load on the ram, by disengaging the clutch

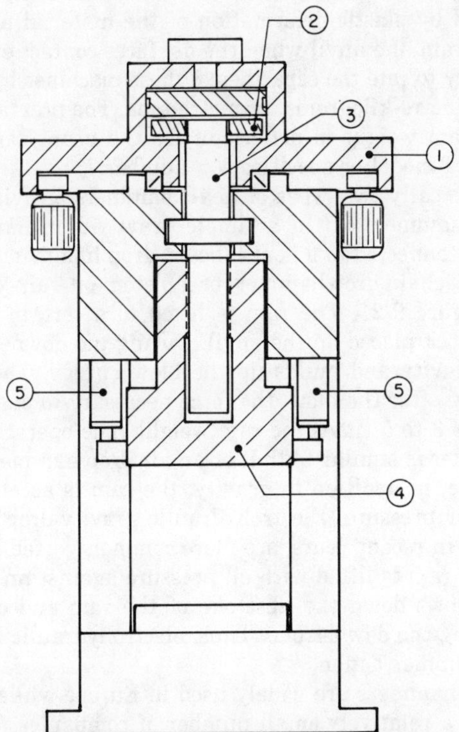

Figure 9-20. A new screw press drive which combines the characteristics of mechanical and screw presses (1 — flywheel, 2 — air-operated clutch, 3 — screw, 4 — ram, 5 — lift-up cylinders).[9-15]

and the flywheel from the screw when the preset forming load is reached. The ram is then lifted by the lift-up cylinders, releasing the elastic energy stored in the press frame, the screw and the lift-up cylinders. At the end of the upstroke, the ram is stopped and held in position by a hydraulic brake.

This press provides several distinct benefits: a high and nearly constant ram speed throughout the stroke, full press load at any position of the stroke, high deformation energy, overload protection, and short contact time between the workpiece and the tools. The press can also be equipped with variable-speed motors so that different flywheel and ram speeds are available. Thus, it offers considerable flexibility and can be used for hot as well as cold forming operations.

HAMMERS

The hammer is the least expensive and most versatile type of equipment for generating load and energy to carry out a forming process. Hammers are primarily used for hot forging, for coining, and, to a limited extent, for sheet metal forming of parts manufactured in small quantities — for example, in the aircraft/airframe industry. The hammer is an energy-restricted machine. During a working stroke, the deformation proceeds until the total kinetic energy is dissipated by plastic deformation of the material and by elastic deformation of the ram and anvil when the die faces contact each other. Therefore, it is necessary to rate the capacities of these machines in terms of energy, i.e., foot-pounds, metre-kilograms, or metre-tons. The practice of specifying a hammer by its ram weight is not useful for the user. Ram weight can be regarded only as a model or specification number.

There are basically two types of anvil hammers: gravity-drop hammers and power-drop hammers.[9-1] In a simple gravity-drop hammer, the upper ram is positively connected to a board (board drop hammer), a belt (belt drop hammer), a chain (chain drop hammer) or a piston (oil-, air- or steam-lift drop hammer); see Figure 9-21. The ram is lifted to a certain height and then dropped on the stock placed on the anvil. During the downstroke, the ram is accelerated by gravity and builds up the blow energy. The upstroke takes place immediately after the blow; the force necessary to ensure quick lift-up of the ram can be 3 to 5 times the ram weight. The operation principle of a power-drop hammer is similar to that of an air drop hammer (Figure 9-21D). In the downstroke, in addition to gravity, the ram is accelerated by steam, cold air or hot air pressure. Electrohydraulic gravity-drop hammers, introduced in the U.S. in recent years, are more commonly used in Europe.[9-16] In this hammer, the ram is lifted with oil pressure against an air cushion. The compressed air slows down the upstroke of the ram and contributes to its acceleration during the downstroke. Thus, electrohydraulic hammer also has a minor power hammer action.

Counterblow hammers are widely used in Europe while their use in the U.S. is limited to a relatively small number of companies. The principles of two types of counterblow hammers are illustrated in Figure 9-22. In both designs, the upper ram is accelerated downward by steam, cold air or hot air.[9-17] At the same time, the lower ram is accelerated upward by a steel

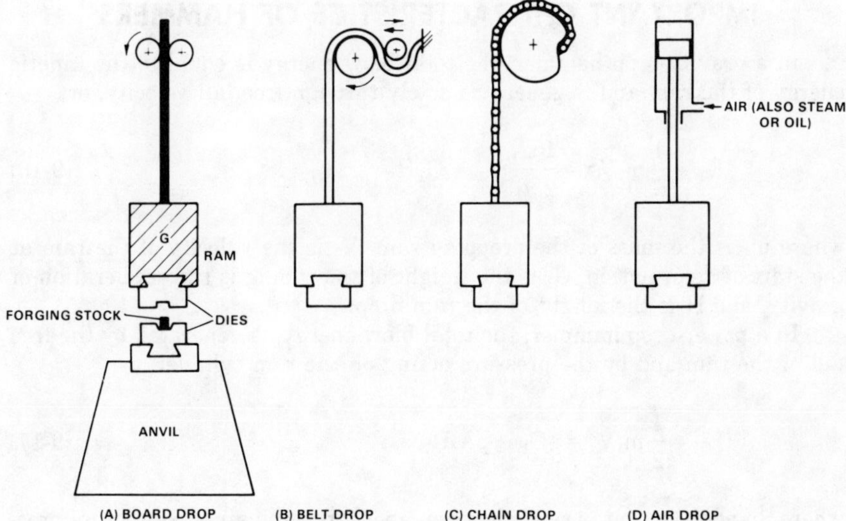

Figure 9-21. Principles of various types of gravity-drop hammers.[9-1]

band (for smaller capacities) or by a hydraulic coupling system (for larger capacities). The lower ram, including the die assembly, is approximately 10% heavier than the upper ram. Therefore, after the blow, the lower ram accelerates downward and pulls the upper ram back up to its starting position. The combined speed of the rams is about 25 ft/s; both rams move with exactly half of the total closure speed. Due to the counterblow effect, relatively little energy is lost through vibration in the foundation and environment. Therefore, for comparable capacities, a counterblow hammer requires a smaller foundation than an anvil hammer.

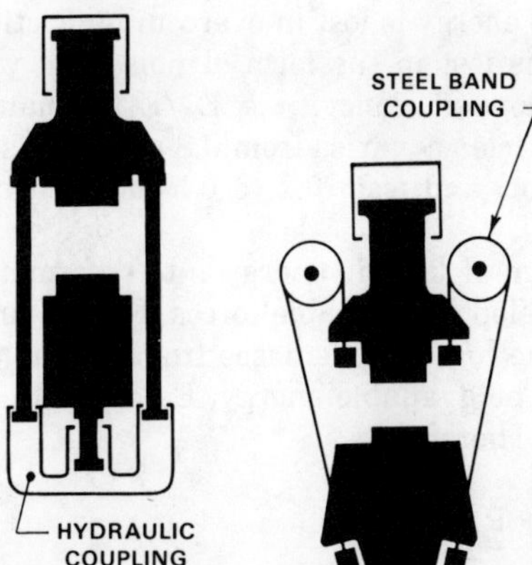

Figure 9-22. Principles of operation of two types of counterblow hammers.[9-1]

IMPORTANT CHARACTERISTICS OF HAMMERS

In a gravity-drop hammer, the total blow energy is equal to the kinetic energy of the ram and is generated solely through free-fall velocity, or:

$$E_T = \frac{1}{2} m_1 V_1^2 = \frac{1}{2} \frac{G_1}{g} V_1^2 = G_1 H \tag{9-16}$$

where m_1 is the mass of the dropping ram, V_1 is the velocity of the ram at the start of deformation, G_1 is the weight of the ram, g is the acceleration of gravity, and H is the height of the ram drop.

In a power-drop hammer, the total blow energy, is generated by the free fall of the ram and by the pressure acting on the ram cylinder, or:

$$E_T = \frac{1}{2} m_1 V_1^2 = (G_1 + pA)H \tag{9-17}$$

where, in addition to the symbols given above, p is the air, steam, or oil pressure acting on the ram cylinder in the downstroke and A is the surface area of the ram cylinder.

In counterblow hammers, when both rams have approximately the same weight, the total energy per blow is given by:

$$E_T = 2\left(\frac{m_1 V_1^2}{2}\right) = \frac{m_1 V_t^2}{4} = \frac{G_1 V_t^2}{4g} \tag{9-18}$$

where m_1 is the mass of one ram, V_1 is the velocity of one ram, V_t is the actual velocity of the blow of the two rams, which is equal to $2V_1$, and G_1 is the weight of one ram.

During a working stroke, the total nominal energy, E_T, of a hammer is not entirely transformed into useful energy available for deformation, E_A. Some small amount of energy is lost in overcoming friction of the guides, and a significant portion is lost in the form of noise and vibration to the environment. Thus, the blow efficiency, $\eta = E_A/E_T$, of hammers is always less than one. The blow efficiency varies from 0.8 to 0.9 for soft blows (small load and large displacement) and from 0.2 to 0.5 for hard blows (high load and small displacement).

The transformation of kinetic energy into deformation energy during a working blow can develop considerable forces. For instance, consider a deformation blow where the load, P, increases from P/3 at the start to P at the end of the stroke, h. The available energy, E_A, is the surface area under the curve in Figure 9-23. Therefore:

$$E_A = \frac{P/3 + P}{2} h = \frac{4Ph}{6} \tag{9-19}$$

Consider a hammer with a total nominal energy, E_T, of 35,000 ft·lb and a blow efficiency, η, of 0.4; here, $E_A = E_T\eta = 14{,}000$ ft·lb. With this value,

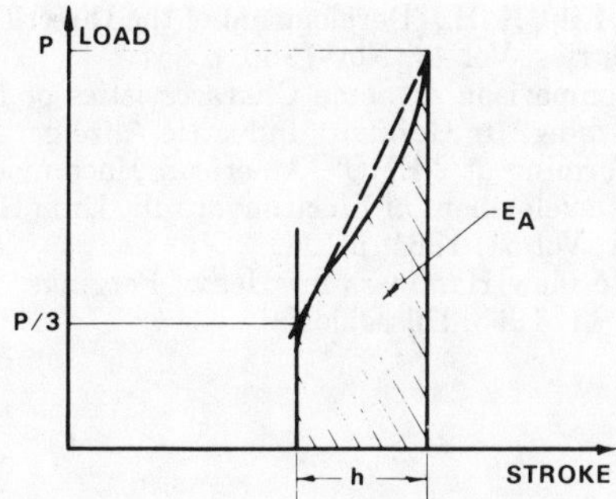

Figure 9-23. Example of a load-stroke curve in a hammer blow (E_A = energy available for forging = $E_T\eta$).[9-1]

for a working stroke, h, of 0.2 in., Equation 9-19 gives:

$$P = \frac{6E_A}{4h} = 1{,}260{,}000 \text{ lb} = 630 \text{ tons}$$

If the same energy were dissipated over a stroke, h, of 0.1-in., the load, P, would reach approximately double the calculated value. The simple hypothetical calculations given above illustrate the capabilities of relatively inexpensive hammers in exerting high forming loads.

REFERENCES

9-1. Altan, T., "Characteristics and Applications of Various Types of Forging Equipment", SME Technical Report MFR72-02, Society of Manufacturing Engineers, Dearborn, MI.

9-2. Geleji, A., "Forge Equipment, Rolling Mills and Accessories" (in English), Akademiai Kiado, Budapest, 1967.

9-3. Mueller, E., Hydraulic Forging Presses, Springer-Verlag, Berlin, 1969.

9-4. Peters, K. H., "Design Features of the Hydraulic Press and Its Field of Application", Sheet Metal Industries, Vol 46, March 1969, pp 221-226.

9-5. Hutson, C., "An Investigation Into Press Driving Systems", Metal Forming, Vol 35, March 1968, pp 79-85.

9-6. Riemenschneider, F., and Nickrawietz, K., "Drives for Forging Presses" (in German), Stahl und Eisen, Vol 79, 1959, p 494.

9-7. Kirschbaum, Z., "A Comparative Study of the Stability and Economic Construction of Pushdown, Pulldown, and Horizontal Double-Opposed Forging Presses", Iron and Steel, Feb 1968, p 46.

9-8. Pahnke, H. J., "Technical and Economical Limitations of Conventional Four-Column Top Drive Forging Presses", SME Paper MF70-589.

9-9. Hamilton, E., "Power Presses, Their Design and Characteristics", Sheet Metal Industries, Vol 37, July 1960, pp 501-513.

9-10. Altan, T., and Nichols, D. E., "Use of Standardized Copper Cylinders for Determining Load and Energy in Forging Equipment", ASME Transactions, Journal of Engineering for Industry, Vol 94, Aug 1972, p 769.

9-11. Rau, G., "A Die Forging Press With a New Drive", Metal Forming, July 1967, pp 194-198.

9-12. Spachner, S. A., "Use of a Four-Bar Linkage as a Slide Drive for Mechanical Presses", SME Paper MF70-216.

9-13. Bohringer, H., and Kilp, K. H., "Development of the Direct-Drive Percussion Press", Sheet Metal Industries, Vol 43, Nov 1966, p 857.
9-14. Klaprodt, Th., "Comparison of Some Characteristics of Mechanical and Screw Presses for Die Forging" (in German), Industrie-Anzeiger, Vol 90, 1968, pp 1423.
9-15. Altan, T., "Metalforming at 2.EMO", American Machinist, Jan 1978, p 132.
9-16. Brauer, W., "The Development of Electrohydraulic Drop Hammers" (in German), Werkstattstechnik, Vol 51, 1961, p 105.
9-17. Kuhn, R., "Counterblow Hammers for Heavy Forgings" (in German), Kleipzig Fachberichte, No. 11, 1963, Düsseldorf.

CHAPTER 10

Approximate Methods of Analysis and Application to Simple Forming Operations

The major process variables involved in metal forming and their influences on metal forming operations were discussed in Chapter 2. The major objectives of analyzing a metal forming operation are:

- Establish the kinematic relationships (shape, velocities, strain rates and strains) between the undeformed part (billet, blank or preform) and the deformed part (product), i.e., predict metal flow during the forming operation.
- Establish the limits of formability or producibility, i.e., determine whether it is possible to perform the forming operation without causing any surface or internal failures (cracks or folds) in the deforming material.
- Predict the stresses, the forces and the energy necessary to carry out the forming operation. This information is necessary for tool design and for selecting the appropriate equipment, with adequate force and energy capabilities, to perform the forming operation.

There are several different approximate methods, both analytical and numerical, for analyzing metal forming problems. None of these methods is perfect, because of the assumptions made in developing the mathematical approach. In addition, every method of analysis requires as input (a) a description of the material behavior under the process conditions, i.e., flow stress data, and (b) a quantitative value to describe the friction i.e., the friction factor, m, or the friction coefficient, μ. These two quantities themselves — flow stress and friction — must be determined by experiment and are difficult to obtain accurately. Thus, any errors in flow stress measurements or uncertainties in the value of the friction factor are expected to influence the accuracy of the results of analysis. Nearly all of the available methods of analysis fail to consider temperature gradients which are present in the deforming material during hot forming operations. As a result, the effects of temperatures on flow stress and metal flow during hot forming often are not considered adequately.

The most widely known methods of analysis are the "slab" or "Sachs" method, the uniform energy method, the slip-line method, the upper bound method, the finite element method, the finite difference method and the visioplasticity method. The capabilities and characteristics of various methods are summarized in Table 10-1.[10-1] Details of some are given in the well-known metal forming textbooks, listed as references in Chapter 1.

In this chapter, only the slab and upper bound methods will be considered, because they are relatively easy to apply to practical metal forming problems. In using both methods, the following reasonable assumptions are made:

- The deforming material is isotropic and incompressible.
- The elastic deformations of the deforming material and of the tool are neglected.
- The inertial forces are small and are neglected.
- The frictional shear stress, τ, is constant at the die/material interface, and $\tau = f\bar{\sigma} = m\bar{\sigma}/\sqrt{3}$, as discussed in Chapter 6.
- The material flows according to the von Mises rule, as discussed in Chapter 5.
- The flow stress, $\bar{\sigma}$, and the temperature are constant within the analyzed portion of the deforming material.

The basic approach for the practical use of both slab and upper bound methods is as follows:

1. Estimate or assume a velocity or metal flow field.
2. For this velocity field, estimate the average strains, strain rates and temperatures within each distinct zone of the velocity field.

Table 10-1. Summary of various analysis methods[10-1]

Method	Input		Output				Comments
	Flow stress	Friction	Velocity field	Stress field	Temperature field	Stresses on tools	
Slab	Average	(a)(b)	No	Yes	No	Yes	Ignores redundant work
Uniform energy	Average	(b)	No	No	No	Average	Redundant work can be included approximately
Slip line	Average	(a)(b)	Yes	Yes	No	Yes	Valid for plane-strain problems
Upper bound	Distribution	(b)	Yes	No	No	Average	Gives upper bound on loads, can determine free boundaries
Hill's	Distribution	(a)(b)	Yes	No	No	Average	Can treat 3-D problems
Finite difference	Distribution	(a)(b)	Yes	Yes	Yes	Yes	Requires considerable computer time
Finite element	Distribution	(a)(b)	Yes	Yes	Yes	Yes	Same as above
Matrix	Distribution	(a)(b)	Yes	Yes	Yes	Yes	Treats rigid/plastic material
Weighted residuals	Distribution	(a)(b)	Yes	Yes	Yes	Yes	Very general approach

(a) $\tau = \mu\sigma_n$. (b) $\tau = m\bar{\sigma}/\sqrt{3}$.

3. Thus, estimate an average value of the flow stress, $\bar{\sigma}$, within each distinct zone of deformation.
4. Knowing $\bar{\sigma}$ and friction, derive or apply the necessary equations for predicting the stress distribution and the forming load (in the slab method) or the forming load and the average forming pressure (in the upper bound method).

APPLICATION OF SLAB METHOD TO PLANE-STRAIN UPSETTING

The Velocity Field

In this case, deformation is homogeneous and takes place in the x-z plane (Figure 10-1). The velocity field was defined in Chapter 3, and is given below, where V_D is the velocity of the top die. The velocities in the z, x and y directions are:

$$v_z = -V_D z/h; \quad v_x = V_D x/h; \quad v_y = 0 \tag{10-1}$$

The strain rates are:

$$\dot{\epsilon}_z = \partial v_z/\partial z = -V_D/h \tag{10-2a}$$

$$\dot{\epsilon}_x = \partial v_x/\partial x = V_D/h = -\dot{\epsilon}_z \tag{10-2b}$$

$$\dot{\epsilon}_y = \partial v_y/\partial y = 0 \tag{10-2c}$$

It can also be shown easily that $\dot{\gamma}_{xz} = \dot{\gamma}_{yz} = 0$.

The strains are:

$$\epsilon_z = \ln\frac{h}{h_0}; \quad \epsilon_x = -\epsilon_z; \quad \epsilon_y = 0 \tag{10-3}$$

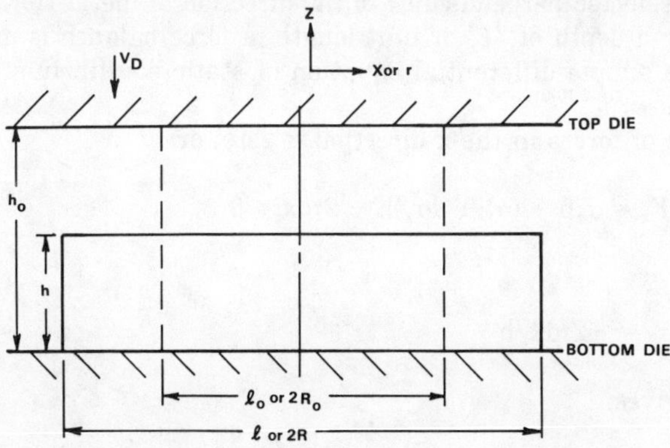

Figure 10-1. Changes in shape during upsetting (plane strain: l_0, x, 1; axisymmetric: R_0, r, R).

The effective strain rate is obtained from Equation 5-26 of Chapter 5:

$$\dot{\bar{\epsilon}} = \sqrt{2(\dot{\epsilon}_x^2 + \dot{\epsilon}_z^2)/3} = \frac{2}{\sqrt{3}}|\dot{\epsilon}_x| = \frac{2}{\sqrt{3}}|\dot{\epsilon}_z| \tag{10-4}$$

The effective strain is:

$$\bar{\epsilon} = \frac{2}{\sqrt{3}}|\epsilon_z| \tag{10-5}$$

The slab analysis assumes that the stresses in the metal flow direction and in the directions perpendicular to the metal flow direction are principal stresses, i.e.,:

$$\sigma_z = \sigma_1; \quad \sigma_x = \sigma_3; \quad \sigma_y = \sigma_2 \tag{10-6}$$

The plasticity equations from Chapter 5 (Equations 5-12a, b and c) give:

$$\dot{\epsilon}_2 = \dot{\epsilon}_y = \lambda(\sigma_2 - \sigma_m) = 0, \quad \text{or} \quad \sigma_2 = \sigma_m \tag{10-7}$$

Per definition, $\sigma_m = (\sigma_1 + \sigma_2 + \sigma_3)/3$ or, with Equation 10-7, $\sigma_m = \sigma_2 = (\sigma_1 + \sigma_3)/2$.

For plane strain, i.e., $\sigma_2 = \sigma_m$, the von Mises rule (Equation 5-7c) gives:

$$3[(\sigma_1 - \sigma_m)^2 + (\sigma_3 - \sigma_m)^2 - 0] = 2\bar{\sigma}^2 \tag{10-8}$$

and, after simplification, the flow rule is:

$$\sigma_1 - \sigma_3 = \sigma_z - \sigma_x = |2\bar{\sigma}/\sqrt{3}| \tag{10-9}$$

Estimation of Stress Distribution

In applying slab analysis to plane-strain upsetting, a slab of infinitesimal thickness is selected perpendicular to the direction of metal flow (Figure 10-2). Assuming a depth of "1" or unit length, a force balance is made on this slab. Thus, a simple differential equation of static equilibrium is obtained, as shown below.[10-2,10-3]

The sum of forces in the x direction is zero, or:

$$\Sigma F_x = \sigma_x h - (\sigma_x + d\sigma_x)h - 2\tau dx = 0$$

or

$$d\sigma_x = -2\tau dx/h$$

Integration gives:

$$\sigma_x = -\frac{2\tau}{h}x + C$$

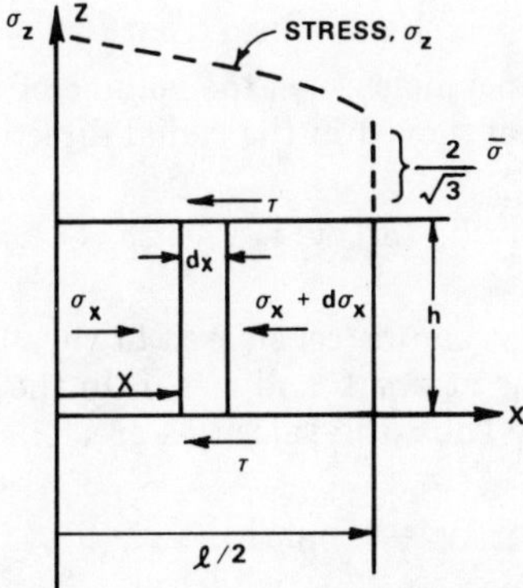

Figure 10-2. Equilibrium of forces in plane-strain homogeneous upsetting.

From the flow rule for plane strain (Equation 10-9), it follows that:

$$\sigma_z = -\frac{2\tau}{h}x + C + \left|\frac{2}{\sqrt{3}}\bar{\sigma}\right| \tag{10-10}$$

The constant C is determined from the boundary condition at $x = l/2$, where $\sigma_x = 0$, and, from Equation 10-9, $\sigma_z = |2\bar{\sigma}/\sqrt{3}|$. Thus:

$$\sigma_z = -\frac{2\tau}{h}\left(\frac{1}{2} - x\right) - \frac{2}{\sqrt{3}}\bar{\sigma} \tag{10-11}$$

Equation 10-11 illustrates that the vertical stress increases linearly from the edge ($x = l/2$) of Figure 10-2 toward the center ($x = 0$). The value of σ_z is negative, because z is considered to be positive acting upward (Figure 10-2) and the upsetting stress is acting downward. Integration of Equation 10-11 gives the upsetting load.

In Equation 10-11, the shear stress, τ, is equal to $m\bar{\sigma}/\sqrt{3}$. Thus, integration of Equation 10-11 over the entire width, l, of the strip of unit depth (Figures 10-1 and 10-2) gives the upsetting load per unit depth:

$$L = \frac{2\bar{\sigma}}{\sqrt{3}}\left(1 + \frac{ml}{4h}\right)l \tag{10-12}$$

APPLICATION OF SLAB METHOD TO AXISYMMETRIC UPSETTING

Figure 10-1 illustrates the notations used in homogeneous axisymmetric upsetting. The analysis procedure is similar to that used in plane-strain upsetting.

Velocity Field

The volume constancy holds; i.e., the volume of material moved in the z direction is equal to that moved in the radial direction, or:

$$\pi r^2 V_D = 2\pi r v_r h, \quad \text{or} \quad v_r = V_D r/2h$$

In the z direction, v_z can be considered to vary linearly while satisfying the boundary conditions at z = 0 and z = h. In the tangential direction, Θ, there is no metal flow. Thus, the velocities are:

$$v_r = V_D r/2h; \quad v_z = -V_D z/h; \quad v_\Theta = 0 \tag{10-13}$$

In obtaining the strain rate in the tangential Θ direction, it is necessary to consider the actual metal flow since $v_\Theta = 0$ and cannot be used for taking a partial derivative. Following Figure 10-3, the increase in strain in the Θ direction, i.e., the length of the arc, is given by:

$$d\epsilon_\Theta = \frac{d\Theta(r + dr) - d\Theta r}{d\Theta r} = dr/r, \quad \text{or the strain rate is}$$

$$\dot{\epsilon}_\Theta = d\epsilon_\Theta/dt = \frac{dr}{dt}\frac{1}{r} = v_r/r = V_D/2h \tag{10-14a}$$

The other strain rates are:

$$\dot{\epsilon}_z = \frac{\partial v_z}{\partial z} = -\frac{V_D}{h} \tag{10-14b}$$

$$\dot{\epsilon}_r = \frac{\partial v_r}{\partial r} = \frac{V_D}{2h} = \dot{\epsilon}_\Theta \tag{10-14c}$$

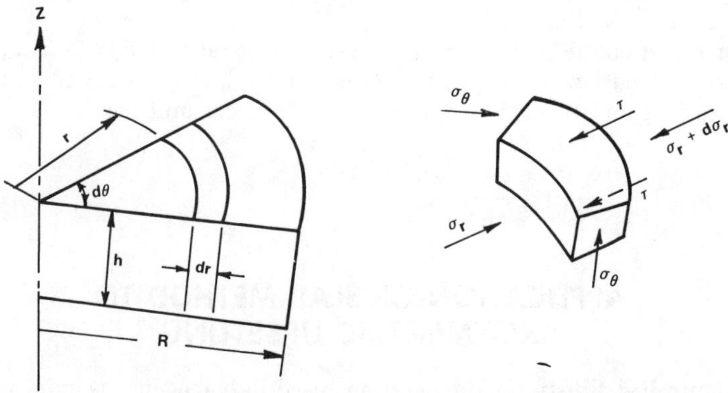

Figure 10-3. Equilibrium of forces in axisymmetric homogeneous upsetting.

$$\dot{\gamma}_{rz} = \frac{1}{2}\left(\frac{\partial v_r}{\partial z} + \frac{\partial v_z}{\partial r}\right) = 0 \qquad (10\text{-}14d)$$

$$\dot{\gamma}_{\Theta z} = \dot{\gamma}_{r\Theta} = 0 \qquad (10\text{-}14e)$$

Using Equation 5-26, the effective strain rate is:

$$\dot{\bar{\epsilon}} = \sqrt{\frac{2}{3}(\dot{\epsilon}_\Theta^2 + \dot{\epsilon}_r^2 + \dot{\epsilon}_z^2)} = |\dot{\epsilon}_z| \qquad (10\text{-}15)$$

The strains can be obtained by integrating the strain rates with respect to time, i.e.:

$$\epsilon_z = \int_{t_0}^{t} \dot{\epsilon}_z dt = -\int_{t_0}^{t} \frac{V_D dt}{h}, \quad \text{or, with} \quad -dh = -V_D dt,$$

$$\epsilon_z = \int_{h_0}^{h} -\frac{dh}{h} = -\ln(h/h_0) \qquad (10\text{-}16a)$$

Similarly, the other strains can be obtained as:

$$\epsilon_\Theta = \epsilon_r = 1/2 \ln(h/h_0) = -\epsilon_z/2 \qquad (10\text{-}16b)$$

In analogy with Equation 10-15, the effective strain is:

$$\bar{\epsilon} = |\epsilon_z| \qquad (10\text{-}17)$$

Flow Rule

The flow rule for axisymmetric deformation is obtained by using a derivation similar to that used in plane-strain deformation. Because $\dot{\epsilon}_r = \dot{\epsilon}_\theta$, the plasticity equations (Equations 5-12a, b and c) give:

$$\sigma_r = \sigma_\theta \quad \text{or} \quad \sigma_2 = \sigma_3$$

Thus, the von Mises flow rule for axisymmetric upsetting is:

$$\sigma_1 - \sigma_2 = |\bar{\sigma}| \quad \text{or} \quad \sigma_z - \sigma_r = |\bar{\sigma}| \qquad (10\text{-}18)$$

Estimation of Stress Distribution

Following Figure 10-3, the equilibrium of forces in the r direction gives:[(10-2,10-3)]

$$\Sigma F_r = \sigma_r(d\theta)rh - (\sigma_r + d\sigma_r)(r + dr)hd\theta$$
$$+ 2\sigma_\theta \sin\frac{d\theta}{2} hdr - 2\tau rd\theta dr = 0 \qquad (10\text{-}19)$$

The angle $d\theta$ is very small. Thus, with $\sin d\theta/2 = d\theta/2$, and after canceling appropriate terms, Equation 10-19 reduces to:

$$-\sigma_r - \frac{d\sigma_r}{dr} r + \sigma_\theta - \frac{2\tau}{h} r = 0 \tag{10-20}$$

Since, in axisymmetric deformation, $\dot{\epsilon}_r = \dot{\epsilon}_\theta$, the plasticity equations (5-12) give:

$$\sigma_r = \sigma_\theta, \quad \text{or} \quad \frac{d\sigma_r}{dr} + \frac{\tau}{h} = 0 \tag{10-21}$$

Integration gives:

$$\sigma_r = -\frac{2\tau}{h} r + C$$

The constant C is determined from the condition that, at the free boundary, r = R in Figure 10-3, and the radial stress $\sigma_r = 0$. Thus, integration of Equation 10-21 gives:

$$\sigma_r = \frac{2\tau}{h}(r - R) \tag{10-22}$$

With the flow rule, Equation 10-18, Equation 10-22 is transformed into:

$$\sigma_z = \frac{2\tau}{h}(r - R) - \bar{\sigma} \tag{10-23}$$

Equation 10-23 illustrates that the stress increases linearly from the edge toward the center. The upsetting load can now be obtained by integrating the stress distribution (Equation 10-23) over the circular surface of the cylindrical upset:

$$L = \int_0^R \sigma_z 2\Pi r dr$$

Considering that τ in Equation 10-23 is equal to $m\bar{\sigma}/\sqrt{3}$, integration gives:

$$L = \bar{\sigma}\pi R^2 \left(1 + \frac{2mR}{3h\sqrt{3}}\right) \tag{10-24}$$

THE UPPER BOUND METHOD AND ITS APPLICATION TO AXISYMMETRIC UPSETTING

Principles of the Method

Among the various methods of analysis, the upper bound method is the most practical technique for simulating metal flow in simple deformation processes. This method can be used to estimate the deformation load and the average forming pressure. For describing metal flow with the upper bound method it is necessary to make the usual assumptions, discussed earlier, and to perform the following steps:

1. Describe a family of admissible velocity fields (use parameters to be determined later); these must satisfy the conditions of:
   - o Incompressibility,
   - o Continuity, and
   - o Velocity boundaries.
2. Calculate the energy rates for deformation, internal shear and friction shear.
3. Calculate the total energy rate, and minimize it with respect to unknown parameters of velocity field formulation.

The load is then obtained by dividing the energy rate by the relative velocity between the die and the deforming material.

The total energy rate, $\dot{E}_T$, is given by $\dot{E}_T$ = load × die velocity, or:[(10-4)]

$$\dot{E}_T = LV_D = \dot{E}_D + \dot{E}_S + \dot{E}_F, \quad \text{or}$$

$$\dot{E}_T = \int_V \bar{\sigma}\dot{\bar{\epsilon}}\, dV + \int_{SS} \tau|\Delta v|ds + \int_{SF} \tau_i v_i ds \tag{10-25}$$

where $\dot{E}_D$, $\dot{E}_S$ and $\dot{E}_F$ are the energy rates for deformation, internal shear and friction, respectively, L is the forming load, V is the volume of deforming material, v is the relative velocity between two zones of material, when the velocity field has internal shear surfaces, S indicates surface (internal or at die-material interface), v_i is the die material interface velocity in the "i" portion of the deforming material, $\tau = \bar{\sigma}/\sqrt{3}$, and $\tau_i = m_i\bar{\sigma}/\sqrt{3}$ = interface shear stress at the "i" portion of the deforming material.

Based on limit theorems,[(10-4)] the load calculated with Equation 10-25 is necessarily higher than the actual load and therefore represents an upper bound to actual forming load. Thus, the lower this upper bound load is, the better the prediction. Often the velocity field considered includes one or more parameters that are determined by minimizing the total energy rate with respect to those parameters. Thus, a somewhat better upper bound velocity field and solution are obtained. In general, with an increasing number of parameters in the velocity field, the solution improves while the computations become more complex. Consequently, in the practical use of the upper bound method, practical compromises are made in selecting an admissible velocity field.

Application to Axisymmetric Homogeneous Upsetting

The velocity field for homogeneous upsetting is given by Equations 10-13, 10-14 and 10-15. Thus, all the velocities and strain rates are known. Assuming a constant flow stress, $\bar{\sigma}$, the deformation energy rate is:

$$\dot{E}_D = \int_V \bar{\sigma}\dot{\bar{\epsilon}}\, dV = h\pi R^2\, \bar{\sigma}\, \frac{V_D}{h} \tag{10-26}$$

$\dot{E}_S$ (internal shear energy rate) = 0, because there are no internal velocity discontinuities in the present homogeneous velocity field.

The friction energy rate is:

$$\dot{E}_F = 2 \int_{SF} \tau_i v_i ds$$

where v_i is the radial velocity, given in Equation 10-13, and $ds = 2\Pi r dr$. $\dot{E}_F$ includes the friction energies on both top and bottom surfaces of the deforming part. Thus,

$$\dot{E}_F = 2 \int_0^R \tau_i \frac{V_D}{2h} r 2\pi r dr = \frac{4\pi\tau_i V_D}{2h} \int_0^R r^2 dr$$

or, with $\tau_i = m\bar{\sigma}/\sqrt{3}$,

$$\dot{E}_F = \frac{2}{3} \pi m \frac{\bar{\sigma}}{\sqrt{3}} \frac{V_D}{h} R^3 \tag{10-27}$$

The total energy rate is:

$$\dot{E}_T = \dot{E}_D + \dot{E}_F, \quad \text{or}$$

$$\dot{E}_T = \pi R^2 \bar{\sigma} V_D + \frac{2}{3} \pi m \frac{\bar{\sigma}}{\sqrt{3}} \frac{V_D}{h} R^3 \tag{10-28}$$

The load is:

$$L = \frac{\dot{E}_T}{V_D} = \pi R^2 \bar{\sigma} \left(1 + \frac{2}{3\sqrt{3}} m \frac{R}{h}\right) \tag{10-29}$$

Comparison of Equations 10-29 and 10-24 indicates that in axisymmetric homogeneous upsetting, the loads calculated by the slab and upper bound methods both give the same end result.

Application to Nonhomogeneous Upsetting

Homogeneous upsetting can only be achieved at low strains and with nearly perfect lubrication. In all practical upsetting operations, the friction at the material-die interface prevents the metal from flowing radially in a uniform fashion. As a result, "bulging" of the free surfaces occurs, and the radial and axial velocities are functions of z as well as of r. In this case, a velocity field may be given by:[(10-5)]

$$v_\theta = 0 \tag{10-30a}$$

$$v_z = -2Az(1 - \beta z^2/3) \tag{10-30b}$$

$$v_r = A(1 - \beta z^2)r \tag{10-30c}$$

where β is a parameter representing the severity of the bulge; and A is determined, from the velocity boundary condition at z = h, to be:

$$A = \frac{V_D}{2h(1 - \beta h^2/3)}$$

The strain rates are:

$$\dot{\epsilon}_r = \frac{v_r}{r} = A(1 - \beta z^2) \quad (10\text{-}31a)$$

$$\dot{\epsilon}_\theta = \frac{v_r}{r} = A(1 - \beta z^2) \quad (10\text{-}31b)$$

$$\dot{\epsilon}_z = \frac{v_z}{z} = -2A(1 - \beta z^2) \quad (10\text{-}31c)$$

$$\dot{\gamma}_{r\theta} = \dot{\gamma}_{\theta z} = 0; \quad \dot{\gamma}_{rz} = \frac{\partial v_r}{\partial z} + \frac{\partial v_z}{\partial r} = -2A\beta zr \quad (10\text{-}31d)$$

The effective strain rate is calculated from a general form of Equation (5-26):

$$\dot{\bar{\epsilon}} = \left[\frac{2}{3}\left(\dot{\epsilon}_r^2 + \dot{\epsilon}_\theta^2 + \dot{\epsilon}_z^2 + \frac{1}{2}\dot{\gamma}_{rz}^2\right)\right]^{1/2}, \quad \text{or}$$

$$\dot{\bar{\epsilon}} = \frac{2A}{\sqrt{3}}[3(1 - \beta z^2)^2 + (\beta rz)^2]^{1/2} \quad (10\text{-}32)$$

The total energy dissipation, $\dot{E}_T$, given by Equation 10-25 can now be calculated analytically or numerically. The exact value of β is determined from the minimization condition, i.e., from:

$$\frac{\partial \dot{E}_T}{\partial \beta} = 0 \quad (10\text{-}33)$$

The value of β, obtained from Equation 10-33, is used to calculate the velocities and strain rates which then give the minimum value for the energy rate, $\dot{E}_{min}$. The upsetting load is then given by:

$$L = \dot{E}_{min}/V_D \quad (10\text{-}34)$$

REFERENCES

10-1. Altan, T., and Lahoti, G. D., "Limitations, Applicability and Usefulness of Different Methods in Analyzing Forming Problems", Annals of CIRP, Vol 28, No. 2, 1979, p 473.

10-2. Thomsen, E. G., Yang, C. T., and Kobayashi, S., *Mechanics of Plastic Deformation in Metal Processing,* Macmillan, New York, 1965.

10-3. Hoffman, O., and Sachs, G., "*Introduction to the Theory of Plasticity for Engineers*", McGraw-Hill, New York, 1953.

10-4. Avitzur, B., *Metal Forming: Processes and Analysis,* McGraw-Hill, New York, 1968.

10-5. Lee, C. H., and Altan, T., "Influence of Flow Stress and Friction Upon Metal Flow in Upset Forging of Rings and Cylinders", ASME Transactions, J. of Engr. for Industry, Aug 1972, p 775.

CHAPTER 11
Impression- and Closed-Die Forging

In impression- or closed-die forging, two or more dies are moved toward each other to form a metal billet, at a suitable temperature, in a shape determined by the die impressions. These processes are capable of producing components of high quality at moderate cost. Forgings offer a high strength-to-weight ratio, toughness, and resistance to impact and fatigue. In terms of tonnage, more than half of the forgings produced are used in automobiles. Approximately one-fourth of the total output of the forging industry is used in producing trucks, tractors and off-highway equipment; the remainder is used in the manufacture of aircraft, railroad and mining equipment and in other general mechanical and energy-related engineering production.[11-1]

FUNDAMENTAL ASPECTS

For understanding the variables of the forging process it is best to consider the process as a system. The different components of such a system are shown in Figure 11-1 and are discussed in detail in Chapter 2. The interactions of most significant variables in forging are shown, in a simplified manner, in Figure 11-2. It can be seen that for a given billet material and part geometry, the ram speed of the forging machine influences strain rate and flow stress. Ram speed, part geometry and die temperature influence the temperature distribution in the forged part. Finally, flow stress, friction and part geometry determine metal flow, forging load and forging energy.

In closed-die forging, a material must satisfy two basic requirements: (a) the material strength (or flow stress) must be low so that die pressures can be kept within the capabilities of practical die materials and constructions, and (b) the capability of the material to deform without failure (forgeability) must be sufficient to allow the desired amount of deformation. By convention, impression- and closed-die forging are considered to be hot working opera-

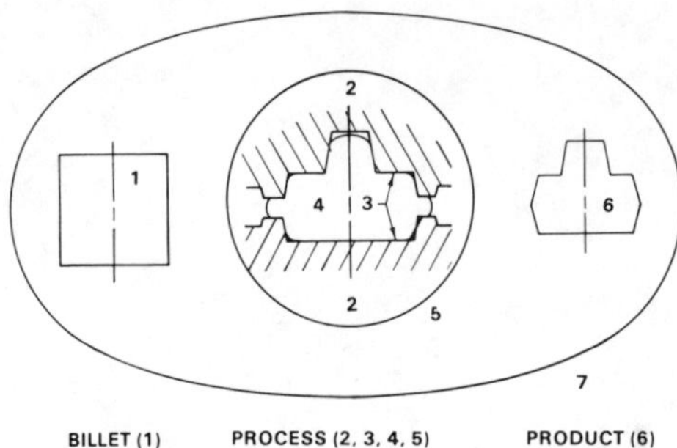

Figure 11-1. One-blow impression-die forging considered as a system: (1) billet, (2) tooling, (3) tool/material interface, (4) deformation zone, (5) forging equipment, (6) product, (7) plant and environment.

tions. In Table 11-1, different metals and alloys are listed in order of their respective forging difficulty.[11-2] The forging material influences the design of the forging itself as well as the details of the entire forging process. For example, Figure 11-3 shows that, owing to difficulties in forging, nickel alloys allow for less shape definition than do aluminum alloys.

In most practical hot forging operations, the temperature of the workpiece material is higher than that of the dies. Metal flow and die filling are largely determined by (a) the forging material's resistance to flow and ability to flow, i.e., its flow stress and forgeability, (b) the friction and cooling effects at the die/material interface and (c) the complexity of the forging shape.

For a given metal, both flow stress and forgeability are influenced by (a)

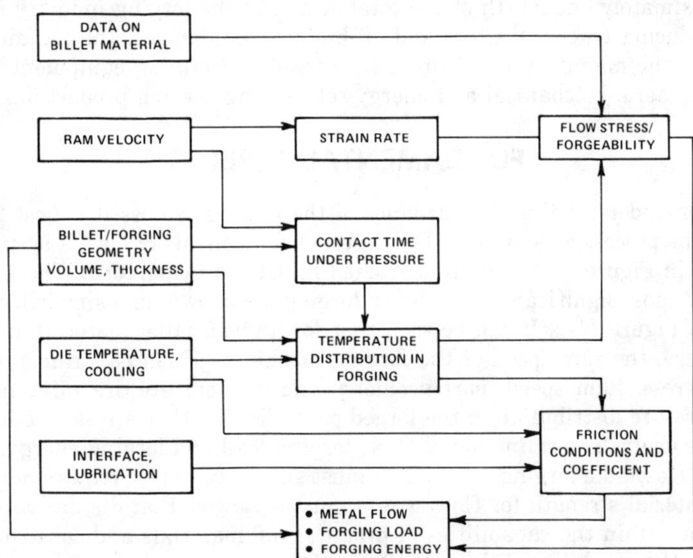

Figure 11-2. Interactions among significant system variables in die forging.

Table 11-1. Classification of metals in order of increasing forging difficulty(11-2)

Metal or alloy	Approximate range of forging temperature, C
Aluminum alloys (least difficult)	400-550
Magnesium alloys	250-350
Copper alloys	600-900
Carbon and low-alloy steels	850-1150
Martensitic stainless steels	1100-1250
Maraging steels	1100-1250
Austenitic stainless steels	1100-1250
Nickel alloys	1000-1150
Semiaustenitic PH stainless steels	1100-1250
Titanium alloys	700-950
Iron-base superalloys	1050-1180
Cobalt-base superalloys	1180-1250
Niobium alloys	950-1150
Tantalum alloys	1050-1350
Molybdenum alloys	1150-1350
Nickel-base superalloys	1050-1200
Tungsten alloys (most difficult)	1200-1300

the metallurgical characteristics of the billet material and (b) the temperatures, strains, strain rates and stresses which occur in the deforming material. Flow stress is discussed in Chapter 4. The concept of forgeability has been used vaguely in the literature to denote a combination of both resistance to deformation and ability to deform without fracture. A diagram illustrating this type of information is presented in Figure 11-4. Since the resistance of a metal to plastic deformation is essentially determined by the flow stress of the material under given temperature and strain-rate conditions, it is more appropriate to define forgeability as the capability of the material to deform without failure, regardless of pressure and load requirements.

In general, the forgeabilities of metals increase with increasing temperature. However, as temperature increases, grain growth occurs, and, in some alloy systems, forgeability decreases with increasing grain size. In other al-

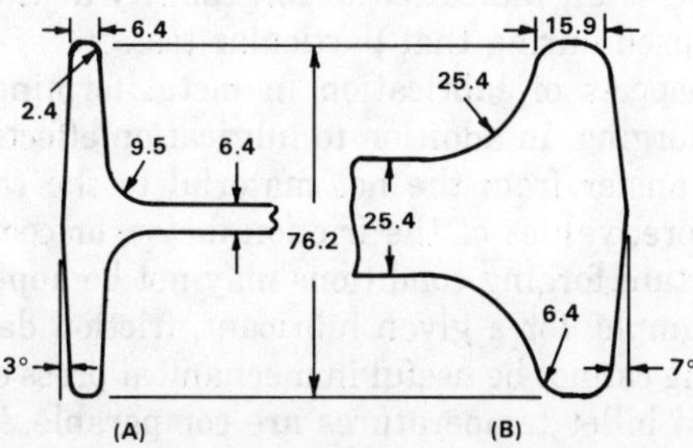

Figure 11-3. Comparison of typical design limits for rib-web structural forgings of (A) aluminum alloys and (B) nickel-base superalloys (all dimensions are in millimetres).(11-2)

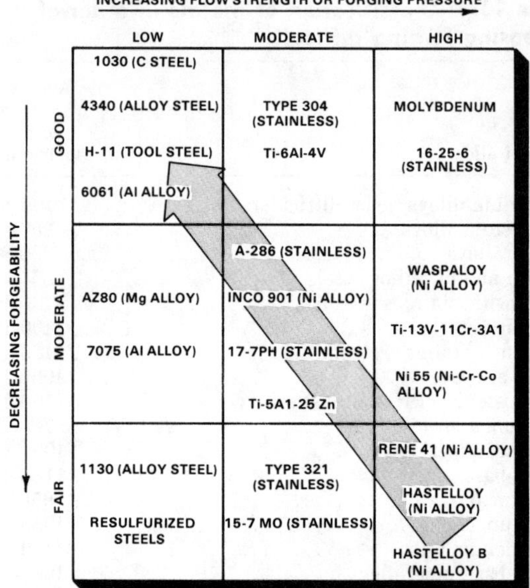

Figure 11-4. Generalized diagram illustrating the influences of forgeability and flow strength on die filling.[11-2]

loys, forgeability is greatly influenced by the characteristics of second-phase compounds. The state of stress in a given deformation process significantly influences forgeability. In upset forging at large reductions, for instance, cracking may occur at the outside fibers of the billet, where excessive barreling occurs and tensile stresses develop. In certain extrusion-type forging operations, axial tensile stresses may be present in the deformation zone and may cause centerburst cracking. As a general and practical rule, it is important to provide compressive support to those portions of a less-forgeable material that are normally exposed to tensile and shear stresses.

The forgeabilities of metals at various deformation rates and temperatures can be evaluated by using various tests such as torsion, tension and compression tests. In all these tests, the amount of deformation prior to failure of the specimen is an indication of forgeability at the temperature and deformation rates used during that particular test.

The general aspects of lubrication in metal forming are discussed in Chapter 6. In hot forging, in addition to lubrication effects, the effects of die chilling or heat transfer from the hot material to the colder dies must be considered. Therefore, values of the friction factor, or coefficient of friction, obtained under certain forging conditions may not be applicable under other conditions. For example, for a given lubricant, friction data obtained in hydraulic press forging cannot be useful in mechanical press or hammer forging, even if the die and billet temperatures are comparable. This point is often ignored in the literature, where data are presented for given lubricants and materials without sufficiently emphasizing the effects of pressing speeds and contact times.

In forging, the lubricant is expected to have the following characteristics and to perform all or some of the following significant functions:[11-3]

- Reduce sliding friction between the dies and the forging in order to reduce pressure requirements, fill the die cavity and control metal flow; it is necessary to note, however, that die cavity filling is promoted by high friction in the flash area.
- Act as a parting agent and prevent local welding and subsequent damage to the die and workpiece surfaces.
- Possess insulating properties so as to reduce heat losses from the workpiece and minimize temperature fluctuations on the die surface.
- Wet the surface uniformly so that local lubricant breakdown and uneven metal flow are prevented.
- Be nonabrasive and noncorrosive so as to prevent erosion of the die surface.
- Be free of residues that would accumulate in deep impressions.
- Develop a balanced gas pressure to assist quick release of the forging from the die cavity; this characteristic is particularly important in hammer forging, where ejectors are not used.
- Be free of polluting or poisonous components and not produce smoke on application to the dies.

No single lubricant can fulfill all the requirements listed above, and no single method of testing lubricants can evaluate all these characteristics simultaneously. Therefore, several methods have been developed for evaluating the characteristics of forging lubricants.[11-3] The method most widely used for evaluating lubricity and for determining the coefficient of friction or friction factor in forging is the ring test. The principles of this test are discussed in Chapter 6.

SHAPE COMPLEXITY IN FORGING

The main objective of forging-process design is to ensure adequate flow of the metal in the dies so that the desired finish part geometry can be obtained without any external or internal defects. Metal flow is greatly influenced by part or die geometry. Often, several operations (preforming or blocking) are needed to achieve gradual flow of the metal from an initially simple shape (cylinder or round-cornered square billet) into the more complex shape of the final forging. In a general sense, spherical and blocklike shapes are the easiest to forge in impression or closed dies. Parts with long, thin sections or projections (webs and ribs) are more difficult to forge because they have more surface area per unit volume. Such variations in shape maximize the effects of friction and temperature changes and, hence, influence the final pressure required to fill the die cavities. There is a direct relationship between the surface-to-volume ratio of a forging and the difficulty of producing that forging.

The ease of forging more complex shapes depends on the relative proportions of vertical and horizontal projections on the part. Figure 11-5 is a schematic representation of the effects of shape on forging difficulties. Parts "C" and "D" would require not only higher forging loads but also at least one

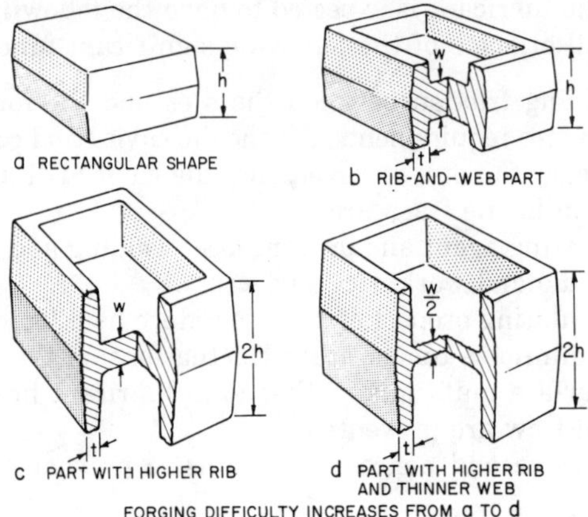

Figure 11-5. Rectangular shape and three modifications showing increasing forging difficulty with increasing rib height and decreasing web thickness.[11-2]

more forging operation than parts "A" and "B" to ensure die filling.

As shown in Figure 11-6, the majority of forgings can be classified into three main groups.[11-4] The first group consists of the so-called "compact shapes", whose three major dimensions (length, l, width, b, and height, h) are approximately equal. The number of parts that fall into this group is rather small. The second group consists of "disk shapes", for which two of the three dimensions (length, l, and width, b) are approximately equal and are larger than the height, h. All round forgings belong to this group, which includes approximately 30% of all commonly used forgings. The third group consists of long shapes which have one major dimension significantly larger than the other two ($l > b \geq h$). These three basic groups are further divided into subgroups depending on the presence and type of elements subsidiary to the basic shape.

This "shape classification" can be useful for practical purposes, such as for estimating costs and for predicting preforming steps. However, this method is not entirely quantitative and requires some subjective evaluation based on past experience.

A quantitative value called the "shape difficulty factor" has been suggested by Teterin *et al* for expressing the geometrical complexities of round forgings (having one axis of rotational symmetry).[11-5] A "longitudinal shape factor", α, is defined as:

$$\alpha = X_f / X_c \qquad (11\text{-}1)$$

with

$$X_f = P^2 / F \qquad (11\text{-}2)$$

and

$$X_C = P_c^2 / F_c \qquad (11\text{-}3)$$

SHAPE CLASS 1 COMPACT SHAPE $l \approx b \approx h$ SPHERICAL AND CUBICAL	SUB-GROUP	101 NO SUBSIDIARY ELEMENTS	102 UNILATERAL SUBSIDIARY ELEMENTS	103 ROTATIONAL SUBSIDIARY ELEMENTS	104 UNILATERAL SUBSIDIARY ELEMENTS

SHAPE CLASS 2 DISC SHAPE $l \approx b > h$ PARTS WITH CIRCULAR, SQUARE AND SIMILAR CONTOURS CROSS PIECE WITH SHORT ARMS UPSET HEADS AND LONG SHAPES (FLANGES, VALVES) ETC	SUB-GROUP / SHAPE GROUP	NO SUBSIDIARY ELEMENTS	WITH HUB	WITH HUB AND HOLE	WITH RIM	WITH RIM AND HUB
	21 DISC SHAPE WITH UNILATERAL ELEMENT	211	212	213	214	215
	22 DISC SHAPE WITH BILATERAL ELEMENT		222	223	224	225

SHAPE CLASS 3 OBLONG SHAPE $l > b \gtrapprox h$ PARTS WITH PRONOUNCED LONGIT. AXIS LENGTH GROUPS: 1 SHORT PARTS $l > 3b$ 2. AV. LENGTH $l = 3 \cdots 8b$ 3. LONG PARTS $l = 8 \cdots 16b$ 4. V LONG PTS $l > 16b$ LENGTH GROUP NUMBERS ADDED BEHIND BAR - e.g.: 334/2	SUB-GROUP / SHAPE GROUP	NO SUBSIDIARY ELEMENTS	SUBSIDIARY ELEMENTS PARALLEL TO AXIS OF PRINCIPAL SHAPE	WITH OPEN OR CLOSED FORK ELEMENT	WITH SUBSIDIARY ELEMENTS ASYMMETRICAL TO AXIS OF PRINCIPAL SHAPE	WITH TWO OR MORE SUBSIDIARY ELEMENTS OF SIMILAR SIZE
	31 PRINCIPAL SHAPE ELEMENT WITH STRAIGHT AXIS	311	312	313	314	315
	32 LONGIT. AXIS OF PRINCIPAL SHAPE ELEMENT CURVED IN ONE PLANE	321	322	323	324	325
	33 LONG. AXIS OF PRINCIPAL SHAPE ELEMENT CURVED IN SEVERAL PLANES	331	332	333	334	335

Figure 11-6. Classification of forging shapes.[11-4]

where P is the perimeter of the axial cross section of the forging, F is the surface area of the axial cross section of the forging (surface that includes the entire axis of symmetry), P_c is the perimeter of the axial cross section of the cylinder which circumscribes the forging and F_c is the surface area of the axial cross section of the cylinder which circumscribes the forging. Since the circumscribing cylinder has the maximum diameter and the maximum height of the forging, the factor α represents a comparison of the shape of the forging with that of the cylinder.

On round forgings, bosses and rims placed farther from the center are increasingly more difficult to forge. Therefore, a "lateral shape factor", β, is defined as:

$$\beta = 2R_g/R_c \tag{11-4}$$

where R_g is the radial distance from the symmetry axis to the center of gravity of half of the cross section and R_c is the maximum radius of the forged piece, which is equal to the radius of the circumscribing cylinder.

A "shape difficulty factor", S, incorporating both the longitudinal and the lateral factors, is defined as:

$$S = \alpha\beta \tag{11-5}$$

The factor S expresses the complexity of a half cross section of a round forging with respect to that of the circumscribing cylinder. In round forgings, during the forging operation, the material is moved laterally (toward the ends of the cylinder) from the center, which is considered to be at the "neutral axis". In a nonsymmetric forging the material is still moved out laterally from a "neutral surface". Thus, once this neutral surface is defined, a "shape difficulty factor" can also be calculated in nonsymmetric forgings.

DESIGN OF BLOCKER (PREFORM) DIES

One of the most important aspects of impression- and closed-die forging is proper design of preforming operations and of blocker dies to achieve adequate metal distribution.[11-6] Thus, in the finish forging operation, defect-free metal flow and complete die filling can be achieved, and metal losses into the flash can be minimized. In preforming, round or round-cornered square stock with constant cross section is deformed in such a manner that a desirable volume distribution is achieved prior to impression-die forging. In blocking, the preform is die forged in a blocker cavity prior to finish forging.

Determination of the preform configuration is a very difficult task and is an art in itself, requiring skills achieved only by years of extensive experience. Although there are several publications in the technical literature on design of finish forgings, very little quantitative information on preform design has been published.

The main objective of preforming is to distribute the metal in the preform in order to:

- Ensure defect-free metal flow and adequate die filling: for example, Figure 11-7 illustrates how a defect can form with insufficient volume distribution in an H-shape cross section.[11-7]
- Minimize the material lost into flash.
- Minimize die wear in the finish forging cavity by reducing metal movement in this operation.
- Achieve desired grain flow and control mechanical properties.

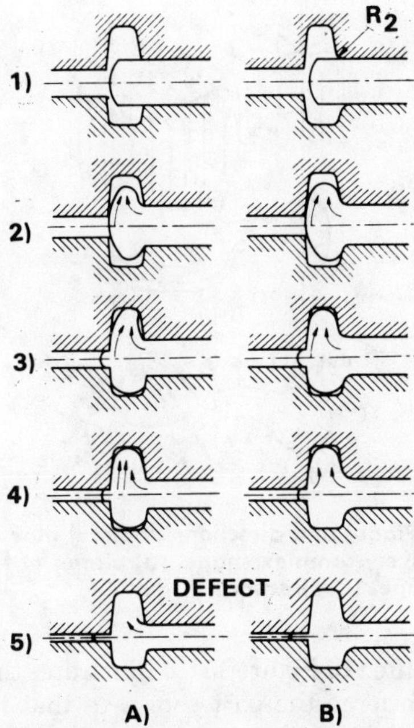

Figure 11-7. Defect formation in forging when fillet radii are too small.[11-7]

Common practice in preform design is to consider planes of metal flow, i.e., selected cross sections of the forging, as shown in Figures 11-8 and 11-9.[11-6]

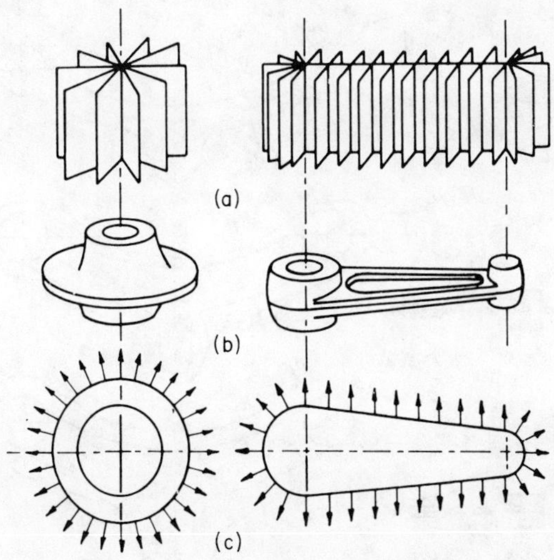

Figure 11-8. Planes and directions of metal flow during forging of two simple shapes: (a) planes of flow, (b) finish forged shapes, (c) directions of flow.[11-6]

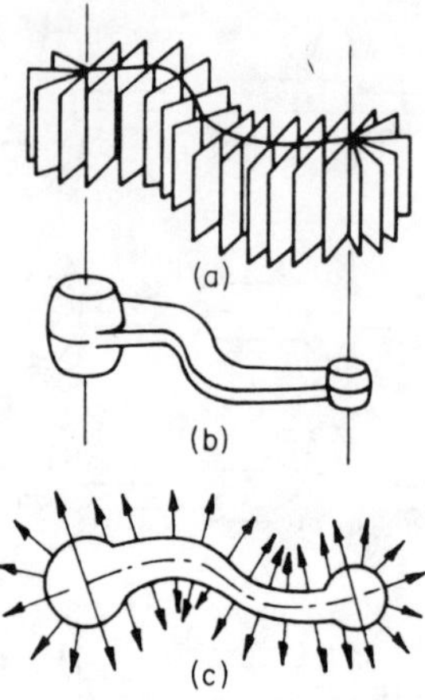

Figure 11-9. Planes and directions of metal flow during forging of a relatively complex shape: (a) planes of flow, (b) finish forged shape, (c) directions of flow.[11-6]

The example presented in Figure 11-10 illustrates the various preforming operations necessary to forge the part shown in that figure.[11-7] The round bar from rolled stock is (a) rolled in a reducer roller for volume distribution,

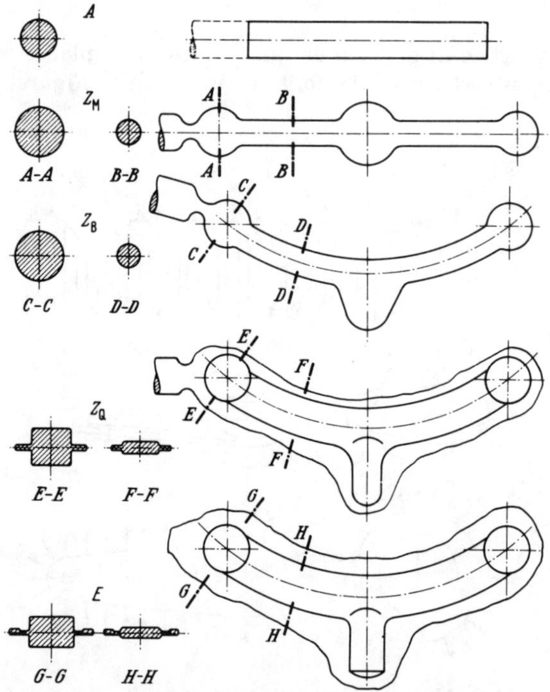

Figure 11-10. Preforming, blocking and finish forging operations for an example forging.[11-7]

(b) bent in a die to provide the appropriate shape, (c) blocked in a blocker die cavity and (d) finish forged. In determining the various forging steps, it is first necessary to obtain the volume of the forging, based on the areas of successive cross sections throughout the forging.

Figure 11-11 shows two examples of obtaining a volume distribution through the following procedure:[11-7,11-8]

1. Lay out a dimensioned drawing of the finish configuration, complete with flash.
2. Construct a baseline for area determination parallel to the centerline of the part.
3. Determine maximum and minimum cross-sectional areas perpendicular to the centerline of the part.
4. Plot these area values at proportional distances from the baseline.
5. Connect these points with a smooth curve (in instances where it is not clear how the curve would best show the changing cross-sectional areas, additional points should be plotted to assist in determining a smooth representative curve).
6. Above this curve, add the approximate area of the flash at each cross section, giving consideration to those sections where the flash should be widest. The flash will generally be of a constant thickness but will be widest at the narrower sections and smallest at the wider sections (the proportional allowance for flash is illustrated by the examples in Figure 11-11).
7. Convert the maximum and minimum area values to rounds or rectangular shapes having the same cross-sectional area.

There are various methods for preforming, i.e., for distributing the metal prior to die forging in a blocker or finisher die.[11-6,11-7,11-9] In designing the cross sections of a blocker (preform) die impression, several basic rules must be followed:[11-9]

- The area of each cross section along the length of the preform must be equal to the area of the finish cross section augmented by the area necessary for flash. Thus, the initial stock distribution is obtained by determining the areas of cross sections along the main axis of the forging.
- All the concave radii (including fillet radii) of the preform should be larger than the radii of the forged part.
- Whenever practical, the dimensions of the preform should be larger than those of the finished part in the forging direction so that metal flow is mostly of the upsetting rather than the extrusion type. During the finishing operation, the material then will be squeezed laterally toward the die cavity without additional shear at the die/material interface. Such conditions minimize friction and forging load and reduce wear along the die surfaces.

The application of these three principles to steel forgings is illustrated in Figure 11-12 for H-shape cross sections of various rib heights and in Figure 11-13 for some solid cross sections.[11-9] The qualitative principles of preform design are well known, but quantitative information is rarely available in the literature. For forging of rib-web-type aluminum- and titanium-alloy parts,

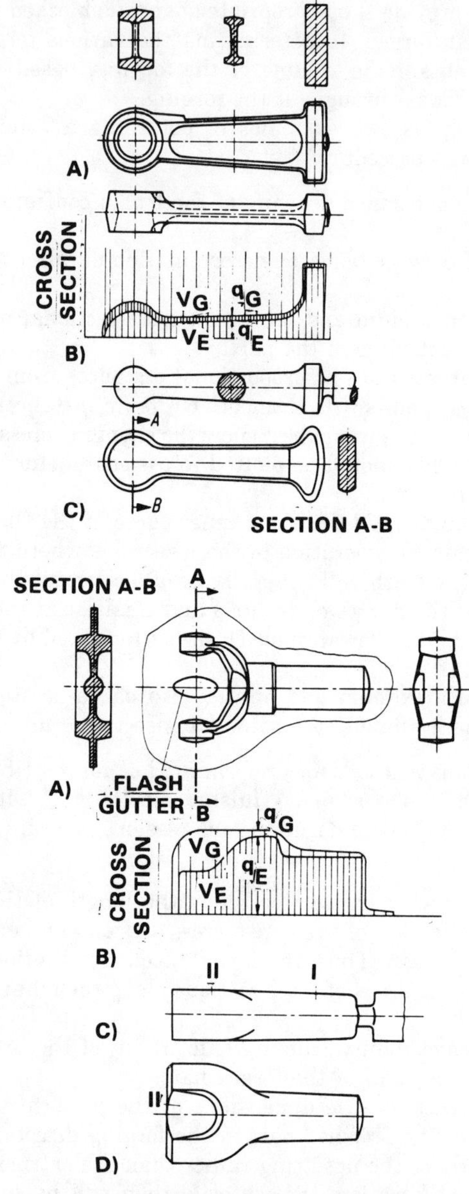

In both examples, A = forging, B = cross-sectional area vs length, C and D = ideal preform, V_E and q_E = volume and cross section of the finish forging, and V_G and q_G = volume and cross section of the flash.

Figure 11-11. Preform designs for two example parts.[11-7]

preform dimensions recommended by various companies fall into the ranges given in Table 11-2.[11-6] More experience in preform design exists for forging of carbon and alloy steels than for forging of titanium and high-temperature

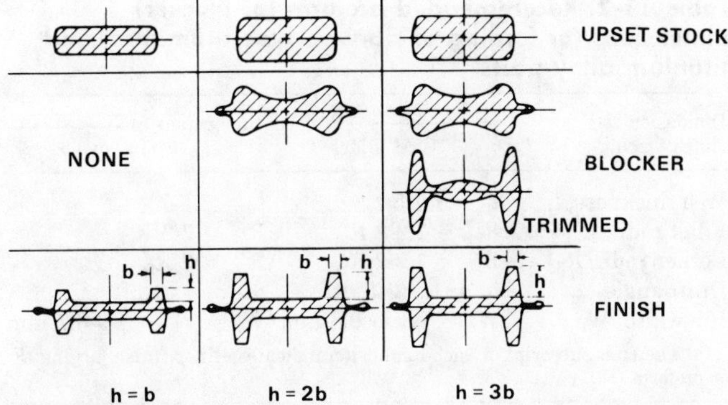

Figure 11-12. Suggested preform cross sections for various H-shape forgings in steel.[11-9]

alloys; however, this information is not published and is usually kept company-confidential by most experienced die designers.

For forging of complex parts, empirical guidelines may not suffice, and trial-and-error procedures may be time-consuming and expensive; a more systematic and well-proven method for developing preform shapes is physical modeling, using a soft material such as lead, plasticine or wax as a model forging material and hard plastic or mild steel dies as tooling. Thus, with relatively low-cost tooling and with some experimentation, preform shapes can be determined.

EMPIRICAL METHODS FOR FLASH DESIGN

The influences of flash thickness and flash-land width on forging pressure are reasonably well understood from a qualitative viewpoint (Figure 11-14). Essentially, forging pressure increases with (a) decreasing flash thickness and (b) increasing flash-land width because of combinations of increasing restriction, increasing frictional forces and decreasing metal temperatures at the flash gap.

A typical load-versus-stroke curve for a closed-die forging is shown in

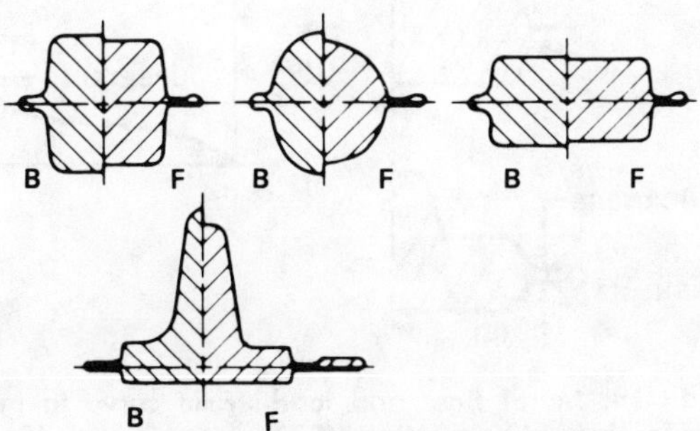

Figure 11-13. Suggested blocker cross sections for various steel forgings (B = blocker, F = finish forging).[11-9]

Table 11-2. Recommended preform (or blocker) dimensions for forging of rib-web-type aluminum and titanium alloy parts[11-6]

Dimension in finish forging	Preform dimensions(a)	
	Al alloys	Ti alloys
Web thickness, t_F	$t_P = 1\text{-}1.5\ t_F$	$t_P = 1.5\text{-}2.2\ t_F$
Fillet radii, R_{FF}	$R_{PF} = 1.2\text{-}2\ R_{FF}$	$R_{PF} = 2\text{-}3\ R_{FF}$
Corner radii, R_{FC}	$R_{PC} = 1.2\text{-}2\ R_{FC}$	$R_{PC} = 2\ R_{FC}$
Draft angle, α_F	$\alpha_P = \alpha_F\ (2\text{-}5°)$	$\alpha_P = \alpha_F\ (3\text{-}5°)$
Rib width, W_F	$W_P = W_F - 0.8$ mm	$W_P = W_F - 1.6\text{-}3.2$ mm

(a) The first subscript of each dimension indicates either finish forging (F) or preform (P).

Figure 11-15. Loads are relatively low until the more difficult details are partly filled and the metal reaches the flash opening (Figure 11-14). This stage corresponds to point P_1 in Figure 11-15. For successful forging, two conditions must be fulfilled when this point is reached: (a) a sufficient volume of metal must be trapped within the confines of the die to fill the remaining cavities and (b) extrusion of metal through the narrowing gap of the flash opening must be more difficult than filling of the more intricate detail in the die.

As the dies continue to close, the load increases sharply to point P_2, the stage at which the die cavity is filled completely. Ideally, at this point, the cavity pressure provided by the flash geometry should be just sufficient to fill the entire cavity, and the forging should be completed. However, P_3 represents the final load reached in normal practice for ensuring that the cavity

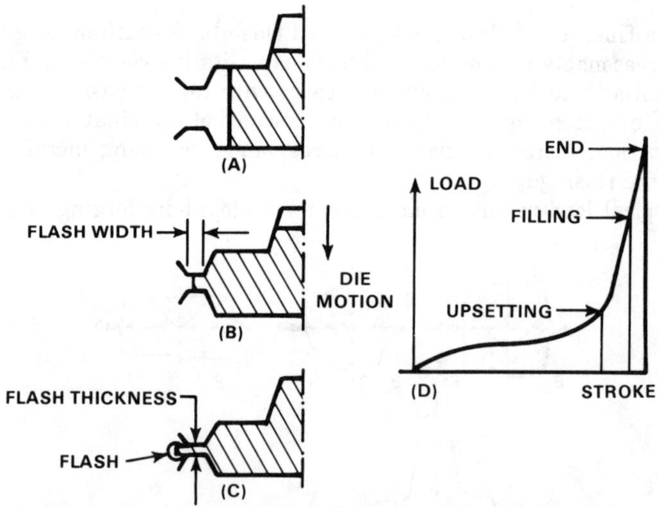

Figure 11-14. Metal flow and load-stroke curve in impression-die forging: (A) upsetting, (B) filling, (C) end, (D) load-stroke curve.

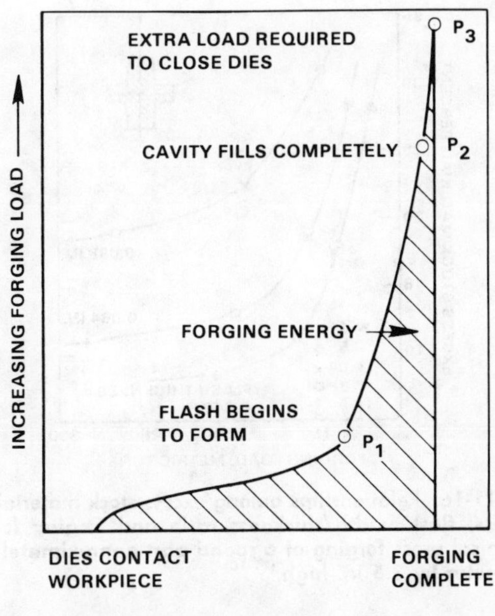

Figure 11-15. Typical load-stroke curve for closed-die forging, showing three distinct stages.(11-6)

is completely filled and that the forging has the proper dimensions. During the stroke from P_2 to P_3, all metal flow occurs near or in the flash gap, which in turn becomes more restrictive as the dies close. In that respect, the detail most difficult to fill determines the minimum load for producing a fully filled forging. Thus, the dimensions of the flash determine the final load required for closing the dies. Formation of the flash, however, is greatly influenced by the amount of excess material available in the cavity, because that amount determines the instantaneous height of the extruded flash and, therefore, the die stresses.

The effect of excess metal volume in flash formation was studied extensively.(11-10) It was found that a cavity can be filled with various flash geometries provided that there is always a sufficient supply of material in the die. Thus, it is possible to fill the same cavity by using a less-restrictive, i.e., thicker, flash and to do this at a lower total forging load if the necessary excess material is available (in this case, the advantages of lower forging load and lower cavity stress are offset by increased scrap loss) or if the workpiece is properly preformed (in which case low stresses and material losses are obtained by extra preforming). These relationships are illustrated in Figures 11-16 and 11-17.

The "shape classification" (Figure 11-6) has been utilized in systematic evaluation of flash dimensions in steel forgings. For this purpose, 1500 forgings from eight different forging companies have been classified into shape groups, as shown in Figure 11-6. By evaluating the flash designs suggested for these forgings, an attempt was made to establish a relationship between

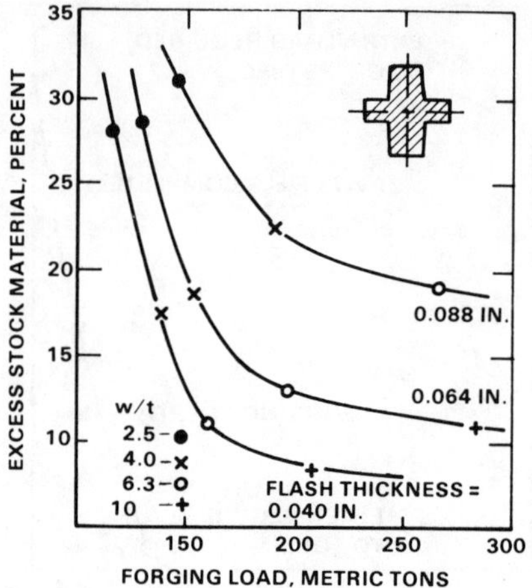

Figure 11-16. Relationships among excess stock material, flash thickness, flash width/thickness ratio and forging load for mechanical press forging of a round part approximately 3 in. in diameter by 3.5 in. high.(11-10)

forging weight and flash dimensions. The results for shape group 224 are presented in Figure 11-18 as an example.(11-6)

In general, the flash thickness is shown to increase with increasing forging weight, while the ratio of flash width to flash thickness (w/t) decreases to a limiting value. In order to investigate the effect of forging shape on flash dimensions, other subgroups were studied and it was concluded that the influence of shape is not as significant as that of forging weight.(11-6)

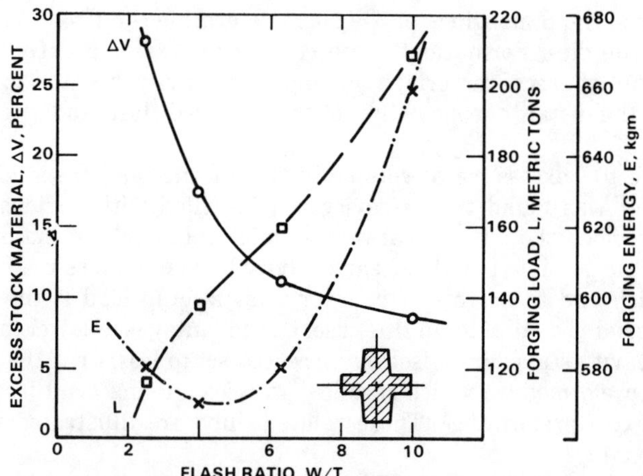

Figure 11-17. Relationships among flash width/thickness ratio, excess stock material, forging load and energy for a constant flash thickness, t, of 0.04 in. (same forging as that shown in Figure 11-16).(11-10)

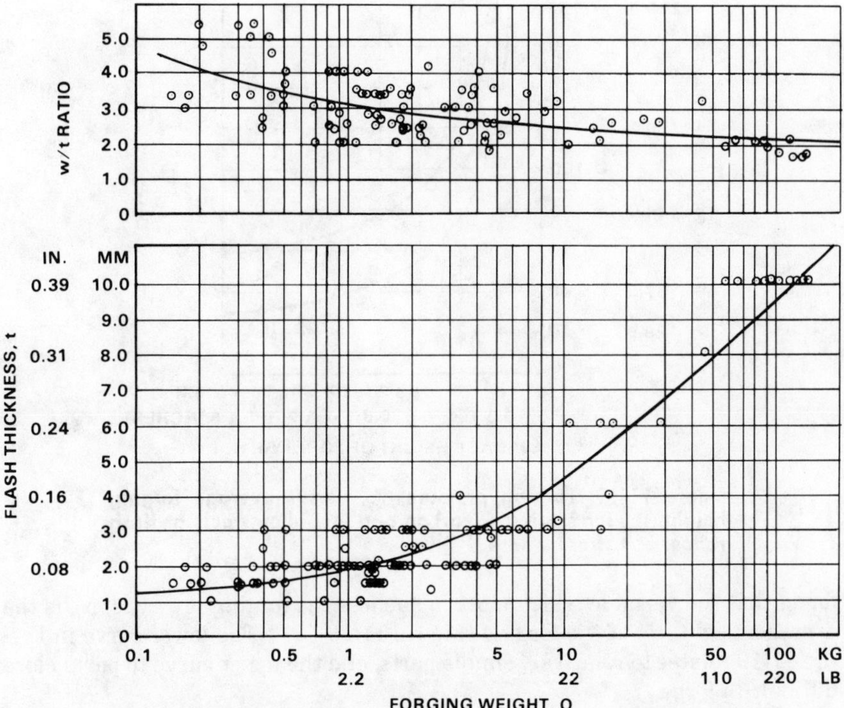

Figure 11-18. Variations in flash-land-to-thickness ratio and in flash thickness, t, with weight, Q, of forgings of group 2.24 (materials: carbon and alloy steels).[11-6]

PREDICTION OF FORGING STRESSES AND LOADS

Prediction of forging load and pressure in closed- and impression-die forging operations is difficult. Most forging operations are of a nonsteady-state type in terms of metal flow, stresses and temperatures — i.e., all these variables vary continuously during the process. In addition, forgings comprise an enormously large number of geometrical shapes and materials which require different, even though similar, techniques of engineering analysis. Because of these difficulties encountered in practice, forging loads are usually estimated on the basis of empirical procedures using empirically developed formulae.

Empirical Methods

In estimating the forging load empirically, the surface area of the forging, including the flash zone, is multiplied by an average forging pressure known from experience. The forging pressures encountered in practice vary from 20 to 70 tons/in.^{2}, depending on the material and the geometry of the part. Neuberger and Pannasch[11-11] conducted forging experiments with various carbon steels (up to 0.6% C) and with low-alloy steels using flash ratios, w/t (where w is flash-land width and t is flash thickness), from 2 to 4. They

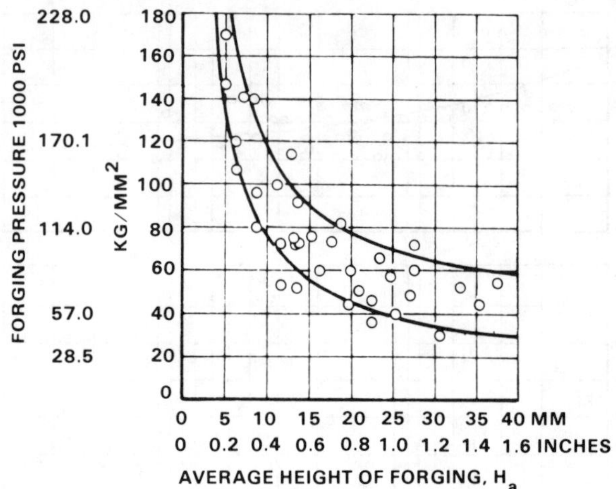

Figure 11-19. Forging pressure, P_a, versus average forging height, h_a, for forging of carbon and low-alloy steels at flash ratios, w/t, from 2 to 4.[11-11]

found that the variable which most influences the forging pressure, p_a, is the average height, h_a, of the forging (Figure 11-19).[11-11] The lower curve in Figure 11-19 relates to relatively simple parts, and the upper curve to parts more difficult to forge.

Most empirical methods, summarized in terms of simple formulae or nomograms, are not sufficiently general to predict forging loads for a variety of parts and materials. Lacking a suitable empirical formula, one may use analytical techniques of varying degrees of complexity for calculating forging load and stresses. Among these techniques, the relatively simple slab method has been proven to be very practical for predicting forging loads.

Simplified Slab Method

The slab method has been successfully used for predicting forging loads and stresses with acceptable engineering accuracy.[11-12] For this purpose, a forging is divided into various plane-strain and axisymmetric sections, and then simplified equations are used to predict the average pressure and load for each section before all these load components are added together.

This method, used in practical prediction of forging loads, is based on the simplified model shown in Figure 11-20. In this analysis, it is assumed that the cavity has a rectangular shape and the flash geometry illustrated in Figure 11-20. In actual practice, where the cavity is not rectangular, the cross section is simplified to conform to this model.

As shown in Figure 11-20, the cavity height is denoted by H, the radius (or half width of the cavity) by r, the flash thickness by t and the flash width by w. The stresses at various locations of the cross section, and hence the load acting on the cross section, can be estimated as follows:

With the flow stress in the flash region denoted by σ_f, and the frictional shear factor (see Chapter 6) by m, the stress at the entrance from the cavity into the flash of an axisymmetric cross section, σ_{ea}, given by:

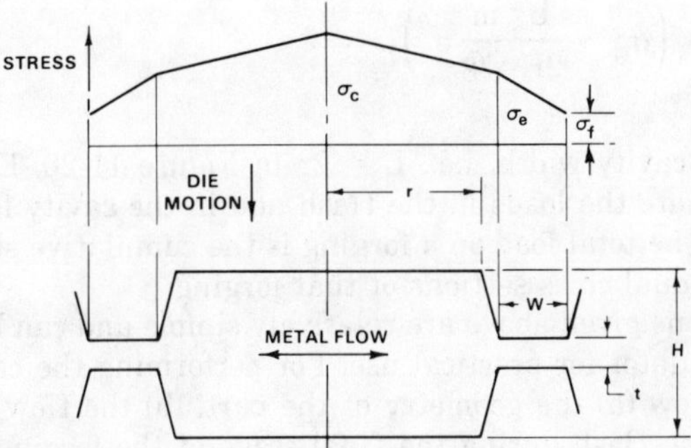

Figure 11-20. Schematic of a simple closed-die forging and its distribution of forging stresses.[11-12]

$$\sigma_{ea} = \left(\frac{2}{\sqrt{3}} m \frac{w}{t} + 1\right)\sigma_f \tag{11-6}$$

By integrating the stress, the forging load acting on the flash region, P_{fa}, is obtained as follows:

$$P_{fa} = 2\pi\sigma_f\left[-\frac{2}{3}\frac{m}{\sqrt{3}}\frac{1}{t}(R^3 - r^3) + \left(1 + 2\frac{m}{\sqrt{3}}\frac{R}{t}\right)\left(\frac{R^2 - r^2}{2}\right)\right] \tag{11-7}$$

where $R = r + w$. Similarly, the load acting on the die cavity, P_{ca}, can be obtained as

$$P_{ca} = 2\pi r^2\left(\frac{m}{\sqrt{3}}\frac{\sigma_c}{3}\frac{r}{H} + \frac{\sigma_{ea}}{2}\right) \tag{11-8}$$

where σ_c is the flow stress in the cavity. Because of rapid chilling and a high deformation rate, the flow stress in the flash region is considered to be different from the flow stress in the cavity. Hence, two different flow stresses are used for the flash and cavity regions. The total load on the cross section, P_{ta}, is:

$$P_{ta} = P_{fa} + P_{ca} \tag{11-9}$$

For the plane-strain cross sections, equations corresponding to Equations 11-6, 11-7 and 11-8 are:

$$\sigma_{ep} = \frac{2}{\sqrt{3}}\sigma_f\left(1 + m\frac{w}{t}\right) \tag{11-10}$$

$$P_{fp} = \frac{2}{\sqrt{3}} w\sigma_f\left(2 + \frac{mw}{t}\right) \tag{11-11}$$

$$P_{cp} = \left(\sigma_{ep} + \frac{L}{2H}\frac{m}{\sqrt{3}}\sigma_c\right)L \tag{11-12}$$

where L is the cavity width, i.e., L = 2r in Figure 11-20. Equations 11-11 and 11-12 estimate the loads in the flash and in the cavity for a unit depth of the forging. The total load on a forging is the cumulative sum of the loads acting on individual cross sections of that forging.

The equations given above are relatively simple and can be programmed for a hand calculator for practical use. For performing the calculations it is necessary to know (a) the geometry of the part, (b) the flow stresses in the cavity and in the flash during the final stage of the forging operation and (c) the friction at the die/forging interface.

In order to understand the details of estimating the appropriate values of flow stress and to predict the forging load, it is useful to carry out a simple calculation.

EXAMPLE: PREDICTION OF LOAD FOR FORGING A CONNECTING ROD

The accuracy and practicality of the simple load calculation method discussed above was evaluated in a study conducted at Battelle-Columbus Laboratories for the Forging Industry Association.[11-12] For this purpose the connecting rod illustrated in Figure 11-21 was selected. The part was forged in a 500-ton mechanical press, and the measured loads were compared with results of computer-aided analysis as well as with results obtained by the present simplified method.

For estimating the forging load, three representative cross sections of the connecting rod were considered (Figure 11-21). All cross sections had the same flash dimensions (blocker: 0.10 in. thick by 0.31 in. wide; finish: 0.06 in. thick by 0.31 in. wide). These dimensions were the dimensions of the flash lands in the dies. The values of flash thickness used in forging load estimations were those actually measured on the forged parts. All cavity cross sections were approximated as rectangles, as shown in Figures 11-20 and 11-21. The dimensions (in inches) of the rectangles used for load estimation were:

Section A-A
- Blocker: r = 0.96, H = 0.32
- Finish: L = 0.2, H = 0.18

Section B-B
- Blocker: L = 0.93, H = 0.32
- Finish: L = 0.95, H = 0.18

Section C-C
- Blocker: r = 0.53, H = 0.64
- Finish: r = 0.55, H = 0.59.

During finish forging, in order to reduce the excessive load resulting from forging a very thin web, the central portion of cross section A-A was relieved.

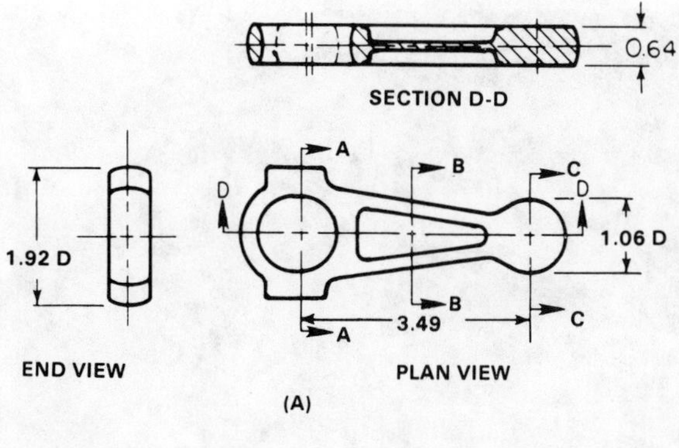

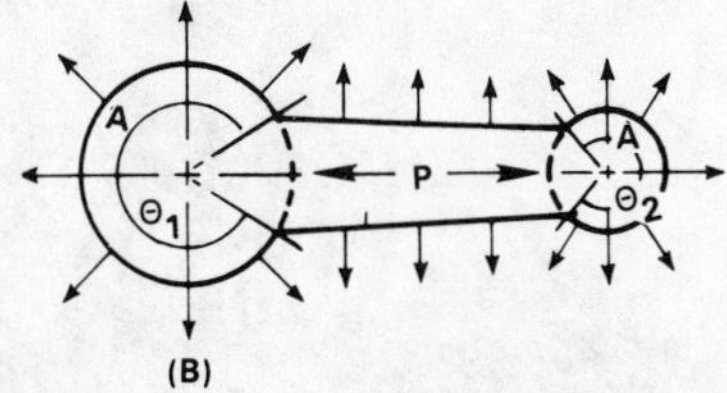

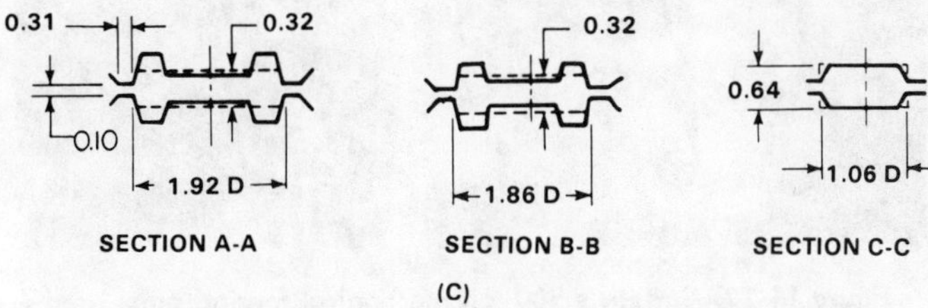

Figure 11-21. Geometry, directions of metal flow and representative cross sections of a connecting rod: (A) cross-sectional views of the connecting rod, (B) directions of metal flow (A = axisymmetric, P = plane strain), (C) representative sections and their simplification.

Hence, to estimate the load in this cross section, only one-half of the section was considered and was treated as a plane-strain cross section of a length equal to the average circumference of the lower boss of the connecting rod.

Estimating Flow Stress

The forging trials were conducted in a mechanical press with a stroke length of 10 in. and a speed of 90 strokes/min (Figure 11-22). The blocker and finish dies were mounted side by side on the press bolster (Figure 11-23). Both dies were heated to about 350 F. AISI type 1016 steel billets were heated to 2100 F prior to blocker forging. The temperature of the billet prior

Figure 11-22. Battelle's 500-ton mechanical forging press used for forging trials.

to finish forging, as measured during trial runs, was about 1950 F. Thus, some cooling occurred during forging in the blocker cavity and transfer into the finisher.

The flow stress is a function of the strain, strain rate and temperature which exist at a given time during the deformation process and can be expressed approximately as:

$$\bar{\sigma} = C \cdot \dot{\bar{\varepsilon}}^{m} \tag{11-13}$$

Equation 11-13 is the same as Equation 4-24 and was discussed earlier (in Chapter 4) in detail. Values of C and m for the material used in the present example are given in Table 11-3. The values of C and m vary significantly with temperature. Hence, in order to estimate the flow stress accurately, the temperature of the deforming material should be known

The temperature of the stock at the end of the forging stroke depends on

Figure 11-23. Blocker and finish forging dies as mounted on the bolster of the mechanical press.

stock temperature, die temperature, speed of deformation and frictional conditions. Further, the temperature varies across the forging due to die chilling and due to heat generation by friction and deformation. However, if the temperature gradient is neglected and the forging is considered to be a thin plate of uniform temperature cooled symmetrically from both sides, the average temperature of the forging in the cavity or in the flash can be expressed, using Equation 7-5, as follows:

$$\theta = \theta_1 + (\theta_s - \theta_1) \exp\left(-\frac{\alpha T}{c\rho t}\right) \tag{11-14}$$

(The symbols in Equation 11-14 are defined in Chapter 7.) Considering, as

Table 11-3. Summary of C (ksi) and m values describing the flow-stress relation, $\bar{\sigma} = C(\dot{\varepsilon}^m)$, for type 1016 steel(a) at various temperatures[11-6]

	Value of C or m at a temperature, F (C), of:							
	1650	(900)	1830	(1000)	2010	(1100)	2190	(1200)
Strain	C	m	C	m	C	m	C	m
0.05	11.8	0.133	10.7	0.124	9.0	0.117	6.4	0.150
0.1	16.5	0.099	13.7	0.099	9.7	0.130	7.1	0.157
0.2	20.8	0.082	16.5	0.090	12.1	0.119	9.1	0.140
0.3	22.8	0.085	18.2	0.088	13.4	0.109	9.5	0.148
0.4	23.0	0.084	18.2	0.098	12.9	0.126	9.1	0.164
0.5	23.9	0.088	18.1	0.109	12.5	0.141	8.2	0.189
0.6	23.3	0.097	16.9	0.127	12.1	0.156	7.8	0.205
0.7	22.8	0.104	17.1	0.127	12.4	0.151	8.1	0.196

(a) AISI type 1016 steel (composition: 0.15 C, 0.12 Si, 0.68 Mn, 0.034 S, 0.025 P) in the hot rolled and annealed condition.

an example, cross section A-A of the blocker dies in Figure 11-21:

- θ_1 (initial die temperature) = 350 F
- θ_s (initial stock temperature) = 2100 F
- α (heat transfer coefficient) = 0.0039 Btu/in.^{2}/F (estimated from values obtained in forging of steel)
- t (average plate thickness) = 0.32 in.
- c (specific heat of the billet material) = 0.108 Btu/lb/F
- ρ (density of the billet material) = 0.285 lb/in.^{3}.

To estimate the duration of contact, the average velocity of the ram during forging should be known. This velocity is half of the velocity of the ram when it touches the billet. In the present case, the billet has round sections with an average diameter of 0.75 in. The average thickness of the blocker is 0.32 in. Hence, the average distance of the ram from the bottom dead center (BDC) position during forging is:

$$w = \frac{0.75 - 0.32}{2} = 0.215 \text{ in.}$$

Thus, the ram velocity with respect to the ram location (w) before BDC is obtained from the kinematics of the crank-slider mechanism (see Chapter 9):

$$V = w\frac{\pi n}{30}\sqrt{\frac{S}{w} - 1} \tag{11-15}$$

The mechanical press used in the forging trials had a stroke, S, of 10 in. and a speed, n, of 90 rpm. Hence.

$$V = \frac{0.215 \times \pi \times 90}{30}\sqrt{\frac{10}{0.215} - 1}$$
$$= 13.67 \text{ in./s}$$

The duration of contact, T, is:

$$T = \frac{\text{(Average billet thickness)} - \text{(Average forging thickness)}}{\text{Average ram velocity}}$$
$$= \frac{0.75 - 0.32}{13.67} = 0.0315 \text{ s}$$

The value of T can also be obtained from a load- and stroke-versus-time recording similar to that shown in Figure 11-24. The instantaneous average forging temperature is:

$$\theta = 350 + (2100 - 350)\exp\left(-\frac{0.0039 \times 0.0315}{0.108 \times 0.285 \times 0.32}\right)$$
$$= 2078.3 \text{ F}$$

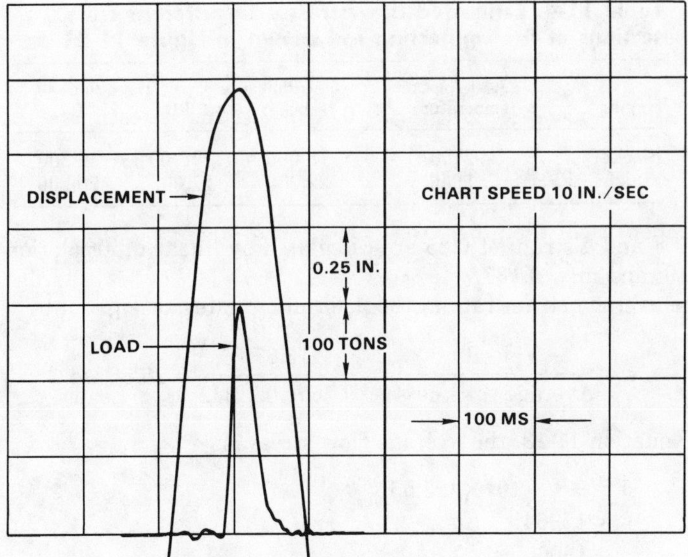

Figure 11-24. Typical visicorder recording of load and displacement curves for a forging operation.

The temperature increase due to deformation is given by:

$$\theta_d = A\bar{\sigma}_a\bar{\epsilon}_a/c\rho$$

where, in addition to the symbols previously defined, θ_d is the temperature increase due to deformation; A is a factor used to convert mechanical energy to heat energy ($A = 1.07 \times 10^{-4}$ Btu/in. · lb); $\bar{\sigma}_a$ is the average flow stress in the material (18,000 psi assumed); and $\bar{\epsilon}_a$ is the average strain, estimated from initial and final thickness (in./in.):

$$\bar{\epsilon}_a = \ln\left(\frac{\text{Initial thickness}}{\text{Final thickness}}\right) = \ln\frac{0.75}{0.32} = 0.85$$

Hence:

$$\theta_d = \frac{1.07 \times 10^{-4} \times 18{,}000 \times 0.85}{0.108 \times 0.285} = 53.2 \text{ F}$$

Ignoring the heat gain due to friction, the average temperature in the cavity of the blocker die is:

$$\theta_{cb} = \theta + \theta_d = 2078.3 + 53.2 = 2131.5 \text{ F}$$

Values of C and m in Equation 11-13 for different materials at various strains and temperatures are given in Reference 11-6. Table 11-3 presents C and m values for AISI type 1016 steel. Using this table, values of C and m

Table 11-4. Estimated flow stresses in different cross sections of the connecting rod shown in Figure 11-21

Forging	Stock/blocker temperature, F	Flow stress, psi, in section: A-A	B-B	C-C
Blocker	2100	18,000	17,000	16,300
Finish	1950	22,000	21,600	20,200

at 2130 F and a strain of 0.85 are calculated by linear interpolation as C = 9.8×10^3 and m = 0.187.

The average strain rate in the deforming material is given by:

$$\dot{\bar{\epsilon}} = \frac{\text{Velocity}}{\text{Average thickness}} = \frac{13.67}{(0.75 + 0.32)/2} = 25.55 \text{ l/s}$$

Using Equation 11-13, the average flow stress is:

$$\begin{aligned} \bar{\sigma} &= 9.8 \times 10^3 \times (25.55)^{0.187} \\ &= 17964 \\ &\cong 18000 \text{ psi} \end{aligned}$$

This is the value of the flow stress in the cavity of Section A-A in blocker shape. Similarly, the corresponding $\bar{\sigma}$ values estimated for other sections of the blocker and finish forgings are given in Table 11-4.

Estimation of Friction Factor

The frictional shear stress is given by $\tau = m\bar{\sigma}/\sqrt{3}$. The value of m varies between 0.25 and 0.4 for most steel forging operations. The simplified model, shown in Figure 11-20, assumes that metal flow occurs by sliding along the entire die/material interface. In reality, however, metal deforms by sliding along the web surfaces but internal shearing is inevitable in the rib regions. Hence, to assume a nominal average m value of 0.4, which is usual for sliding surfaces in forging, would be unrealistic. In the present case, the length of the rib regions is almost equal to that of the web regions in cross sections A-A and B-B. Hence, considering a weighted average, the values for m are chosen to be 0.7 for Sections A-A and B-B, and 0.4 for Section C-C, of both blocker and finish forgings.

Estimation of Forging Load

The average length of plane-strain cross section B-B for both blocker and finish forgings is 2.0 in. Substituting the appropriate values in Equations 11-6 to 11-12 and using a programmable hand calculator, the loads were estimated for the cross sections, as shown in Table 11-5.

Table 11-5. Estimated loads in different cross sections of the connecting rod shown in Figure 11-21

Forging	Load, lb, in section: A-A	B-B	C-C	Total lb	Total tons
Blocker	337,214	196,998	89,285	623,497	311.7
Finish	407,234	285,509	123,947	816,690	408.3

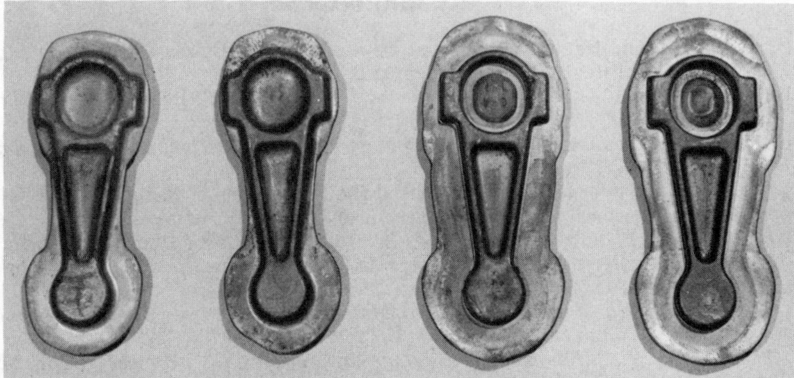

Figure 11-25. Parts that were blocker and finish forged in forging trials.

Comparison of Predictions With Data From Actual Forging Trials

To evaluate the accuracy of the simplified forging load estimation procedure, forging trials were conducted in the Metalworking Laboratory of Battelle Columbus. The 500-ton Erie scotch-yoke-type mechanical press, shown in Figure 11-22, was used for this purpose. Both the blocker and finish dies were mounted side by side on the press bolster, as shown in Figure 11-23. The dies were lubricated, by spraying, with Acheson's Delta-forge 105. The billets were heated in an induction coil to 2100 F. The dies were heated to 350 F by infrared gas-fired burners. A typical load and displacement recording is shown in Figure 11-24. Example forgings are shown in Figure 11-25.

The forging loads, measured in experiments and predicted by the simplified slab method, are compared in Table 11-6. The experimental values represent averages of several measurements. It can be seen that the results of the simplified analysis are within practical engineering accuracy. For simple to moderately complex forgings, this analysis can be used effectively for die material selection and for press selection. However, it should be noted that the accuracy of the final results depends largely on proper estimation of flow stress and of the frictional shear factor. Some experience and knowledge of forging analyses are necessary to make these estimates with acceptable accuracy. If the capabilities of a large high-speed computer are available, then detailed calculations of flow stress, forging stress and forging load can be made more accurately and with less effort than is possible with a programmable calculator.

Table 11-6. Summary and comparison of forging loads (tons)

	Simple analysis	Experimental results
Blocker	311.7	320.67
Finish	408.3	425.00

REFERENCES

11-1. Altan, T., and Nagpal, V., "Recent Developments in Closed Die Forging", Int. Metallurgical Reviews, Dec 1976, p 322.
11-2. Sabroff, A. M., *et al*, "*Forging Materials and Practices*", Reinhold, New York, 1968.
11-3. Schey, J. A. (editor), "*Metal Deformation Processes: Friction and Lubrication*", Marcel Dekker, New York, 1970.
11-4. Spies, K., "Preforming in Forging and the Preparation of Reducer Rolling" (in German), Doctoral Dissertation, Technical University Hannover, 1959.
11-5. Teterin, G. P., and Tarnovskij, I. J., "Calculation of Plastic Dimensions in Forging Axisymmetric Parts in Hammers" (in Russian), Kuznechno-Stampovochnoe Proizvodstvo, 1968 (5), p 6.
11-6. Altan, T., *et al*, "*Forging Equipment, Materials and Practices*", MCIC Handbook 3, Battelle-Columbus Laboratories, Columbus, OH, 1973.
11-7. Haller, H. W., "*Handbook of Forging*" (in German), Carl Hanser Verlag, Munich, 1971.
11-8. Drabing, G., "Guide to Die Making for Multiple Impression and Closed-Die Drop Forging", Chambersburg, PA.
11-9. Lange, K., and Meyer-Nolkemper, H., "*Close-Die Forging*" (in German), Springer-Verlag, Berlin, 1977.
11-10. Vieregge, K., "Contribution to Flash Design in Closed Die Forging" (in German), Doctoral Dissertation, Technical University Hannover, 1968.
11-11. Neuberger, F., and Pannasch, S., "Material Consumption in Die Forging of Steel" (in German), Fertigungstechnik and Betrieb, Vol 12, 1962, pp 775-779.
11-12. Subramanian, T. L., and Altan, T., "Practical Method for Estimating Forging Loads with the Use of a Programmable Calculator", Journal of Applied Metalworking, ASM, Vol 1, No. 2, Jan 1980, p 60.

CHAPTER 12
Computer-Aided Design and Manufacturing (CAD/CAM) Applications in Impression-Die Forging

The conventional methods of designing forging dies are based on empirical guidelines, experience and intuition. However, recently developed computer-aided methods may be used to (a) predict forging loads and stresses, (b) design the preforming dies and (c) manufacture the dies by NC (Numerical Control) machining.

The practical design of a forging process involves:

- Conversion of the available machined part geometry into a forging geometry by using guidelines associated with design of forgings and limitations of the forging process.
- Design of finisher dies, including determination of flash dimensions, forging stresses and forging load. In some cases it may even be appropriate to calculate die stresses and modify the die geometry in critically stressed areas of the die to reduce the probability of premature die failure.
- Design of blocker or preblocker dies; this includes calculation of forging volume, including flash allowance and the estimation of blocker and preblocker die geometry (including web thicknesses, rib heights, and fillet and corner radii).
- Design of the preform and estimation of stock size; this includes prediction of desired metal distribution in the stock (by preforming or busting operations) prior to forging in the blocker die.

Traditionally, the above process and die-design steps are carried out using empirical guidelines, experience and intuition. Once the die-design steps have been concluded, the forging dies are conventionally manufactured by (a) directly machining from a die block, (b) making a solid model and copy milling, or (c) making a graphite electrode and electrodischarge machining (EDM) the dies. The graphite electrodes, in turn, can be manufactured by (a) copy milling, (b) abrading using a special abrading machine, or (c) numerical control (NC) machining.

STATUS OF CAD/CAM APPLICATIONS IN FORGING

During the last decade, computers have been used to an increasing extent for forging applications. The initial developments were concentrated on NC machining of forging dies and of models for copy milling.[12-1,12-2] In the mid-1970's, computer-aided drafting and NC machining were also introduced for structural forgings and for forging steam turbine blades. During the early 1980's, several companies started to use stand-alone CAD/CAM systems — normally used for mechanical designs, drafting and NC machining — for design and manufacture of forging dies.[12-3] Software for forging process analysis and metal flow simulation is also being developed in various research laboratories around the world.[12-4 to 12-6] Some of this software is utilized together with the drafting and NC capabilities of a stand-alone CAD/CAM system.[12-7 to 12-9]

These recent applications and developments of new methods for simulating forging operations indicate that CAD/CAM can significantly augment productivity and the skill of the die designer. This is accomplished primarily by computerizing area and volume calculations, by predicting the stresses and forging loads for a given die geometry, and, in some relatively simple cases, by simulating metal flow during forging.[12-10]

HOT FORGING AS A SYSTEM

In application of CAD/CAM in hot forging, each forging operation (such as finish or blocker forging) should be considered as a "system", as illustrated in Figure 11-1. For the purpose of die design and manufacture, the major interactions among the variables of the system must be known. These interactions are illustrated schematically in Figure 11-2. Ideally, use of CAD/CAM should make it possible to simulate the forging process in terms of metal flow (kinematics), stresses and temperatures. Temperature and the details of metal flow influence the microstructure or properties of the forging and the force/energy requirements. In addition, the simulation of metal flow allows it to be ascertained whether or not the initial billet or blocker geometry is adequate for filling the die cavity, i.e., for producing the desired forging, without any forging defects. As shown in Figure 11-2, to simulate metal flow and to predict forging load and energy it is necessary to know:

- The flow stress and the forgeability of the forged material under processing conditions.
- The conditions of friction and heat transfer at the tool/material interface and the frictional shear factor (or the coefficient of friction).
- The geometry of the product or of the die cavity under consideration.

If the finisher die is being investigated, its geometry is known from the forging drawing. If a blocker or a preblocker die is being designed, its geometry is initially estimated using empirical rules and is later modified based on the results of metal flow simulation. The value of the friction factor is obtained in a ring test or some other appropriate test, as discussed in Chapter 6. Flow stress data are determined most commonly by conducting a uniform compression test or a torsion test.[12-11] Details of these tests are discussed in Chapter 4.

PRINCIPLES OF CAD/CAM APPLICATION IN FORGING

A brief outline of an integrated CAD/CAM approach to hot forging is shown in Figure 12-1. This approach is general in nature and can be applied to most forgings. The most critical information necessary for forging die design is the geometry of the forging to be produced. The forging geometry, in turn, is obtained from the machined part drawing by modifying this part geometry to facilitate forging. In the process of conversion, the necessary forging envelope, corner and fillet radii, and appropriate draft angles are added to the machined part geometry. Further, difficult-to-forge deep recesses and holes are eliminated and thin, tall ribs are thickened.

This geometric manipulation is best done on a stand-alone CAD/CAM system. Such systems are commercially available and have the necessary software for computer-aided drafting and NC machining.[12-7] A typical CAD/CAM system consists of a minicomputer, a graphics display terminal, a keyboard, a digitizer with menu for data entry, an automatic drafting machine, and hardware for information storage and NC tape punching or floppy disk preparation. Such stand-alone CAD/CAM systems are expensive — on the order of $100,000 to $300,000 in the United States. However, they can increase productivity in mechanical drafting by 2 to 5 times, depending on the specific application. Such CAD/CAM systems also allow, at various levels of automation, three-dimensional representation of the forging and the possibility of zooming and rotating the forging geometry display on the graphics terminal screen for the purpose of visual inspection. Ideally, these systems should

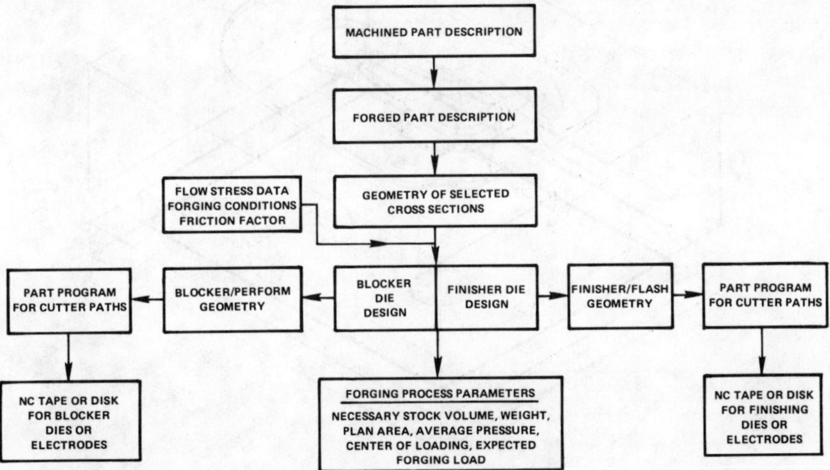

Figure 12-1. Outline of an integrated CAD/CAM approach for hot forging.

also allow sectioning of a given forging, i.e., the description, drawing and display of desired forging cross sections for the purpose of die stress and metal flow analyses. An example of a three-dimensional representation of a connecting rod forging die is shown in Figure 12-2.[12-12] In this figure, hidden lines (behind the displayed viewing surfaces) are not removed. There are CAD/CAM systems and color graphics terminals which allow hidden line removal or display of lines on various surfaces in different colors.

In designing the finisher and blocker dies for hot forging it is best to consider critical cross sections of a forging, where metal flow is plane strain or axisymmetric. Such sectioning is illustrated schematically in Figure 11-9,[12-7] and this procedure is exactly the same as the methods used in today's design practice. Cross sectioning approximates, in two dimensions, the complex three-dimensional geometry of and metal flow in a practical forging, and thus stresses and pressures can be calculated and the blocker and preform sections can be designed for each section. Using an interactive graphics terminal, the results can be displayed for easy interaction between the designer and the computer system. Thus, modifications on die design can be made easily and alternatives can be explored.

DESIGN OF FINISHER DIES

In a typical multiple die forging setup, the stresses and the load are higher in the finisher die than in blocker and preblocker dies. Therefore, it is necessary to predict these stresses and the forging load so that the appropriate forging machine can be selected and so that dies can be designed to avoid breakage. In addition, the dimensions of the flash should be optimized. The

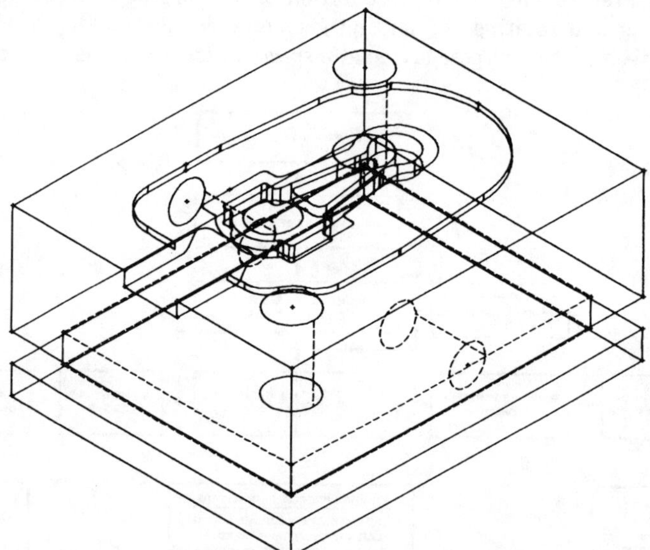

Figure 12-2. Three-dimensional display of a connecting rod forging die, prepared on a computervision CAD/CAM system.[12-12]

flash geometry is selected such that the flash is encouraged to restrict metal flow into the flash gutter. This results in an increase in the forging stresses. Therefore, the designer must make a compromise: on the one hand, it is desirable to increase the die stresses by restricting the flash dimensions (thinner and wider flash on the dies); but, on the other hand, the designer does not want the forging pressure to reach a certain value which may cause die breakage due to mechanical fatigue.

To analyze stresses, the computerized "slab method of analysis" has been found to be most practical.[12-5 to 12-7] This method, discussed in Chapter 10, can be used to estimate forging stresses for plane-strain as well as axisymmetric metal flow sections. In applying this technique, selected sections of a forging are considered, as shown in Figures 11-9 and 12-3.[12-7] A section is considered as an assembly of several connected components, or deformation units, each having a characteristic metal flow behavior. The boundaries of these deformation units, within a particular region, may consist of the die cavity surface or of surfaces within the material along which internal shearing occurs, as illustrated in Figure 12-4.[12-7]

Toward the end of the forging stroke, material does not flow along the die surface at all points as the dies come together. In areas under tall ribs, the material in the rib stays stationary once the rib is filled. Below the rib,

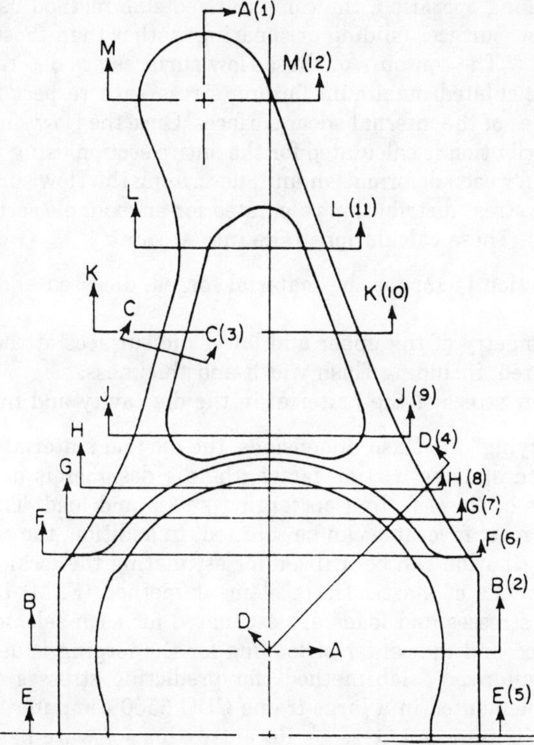

Figure 12-3. Plan view of a titanium alloy connecting link and the sections analyzed in a previous study.[12-7]

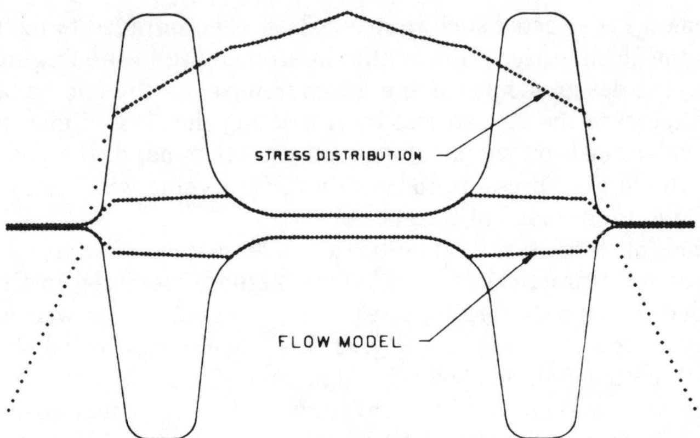

Figure 12-4. Stress distribution on cross section J-J of the connecting link in Figure 12-3 for an assumed flow stress of 1000 psi, calculated by new CV software (section width, including flash, = 7.6 in.).(12-7)

material continues to flow, but by shearing within itself rather than by sliding across the die surface (Figure 12-4). To predict the forging stresses at the end of the forging operation, the computerized slab method uses the geometries of the flow surfaces (sliding or shearing) rather than those of the actual die surfaces.[12-5] The contours of these flow surfaces are determined by minimizing the calculated maximum forging stress with respect to the heights and taper angles of the internal shear surfaces. Once the flow surface is known, the stress distribution is calculated for the entire section using modular equations, derived for each deformation unit, describing the flow surface. The flow model and the stress distribution calculated for an example section are shown in Figure 12-4. These calculations take into account:

- The friction factor for the material forged, die used and lubricant applied.
- The geometry of the upper and lower die surfaces at the cross section considered, including flash width and thickness.
- The flow stress of the material in the die cavity and in the flash.

By "modifying" the flash dimensions, the die and material temperatures, the press speed and the friction factor, the die designer is able to evaluate the influences of these factors on forging stress and load. Thus, conditions which appear most favorable can be selected. In addition, the calculated forging stress distribution can be utilized for estimating the local die stresses in the dies by means of elastic finite element method (FEM) analysis. After these forging stresses and loads are estimated for each selected section, the loads are added and the center of loading for the forging is determined.

The computerized "slab method" for predicting stresses and loads was originally implemented in a large-frame CDC 6500 computer[12-13] as well as in a PDP 11/40 minicomputer.[12-6] Recently, this software has also been developed for a Computervision (CV) stand-alone CAD/CAM system.[12-7] Thus, the CV system can now be used for (a) preparing forging and die drawings,

(b) generating forging cross sections and (c) calculating forging loads and stresses. As an example, Figure 12-4 shows the flow model and the stress distribution obtained with this new CV software.[12-7]

DESIGN OF BLOCKER DIES

Design of blocker and preform geometries is the most critical part of forging die design. The blocker operation has the purpose of distributing the metal adequately within the blocker (or preform) to achieve the following objectives:

- Fill the finisher cavity without any forging defects.
- Reduce the amount of material lost as forging flash.
- Reduce die wear by minimizing metal movement in the finisher die.
- Provide the required amounts of deformation and grain flow so that desired forging properties are obtained.

Traditionally, blocker dies and preforms are designed by experienced die designers and are modified and refined by die tryouts. The initial blocker design is based on several empirical guidelines. These guidelines depend on the material used and on the forging machine utilized. They can be summarized, in a general sense, as follows:

- In plan view, the blocker is slightly narrower than the finisher, about 0.5 to 1 mm on each side, so that it can fit into the finisher die.
- The blocker usually has larger fillet and corner radii, to enhance metal distribution.
- The areas of blocker cross sections are slightly larger (1 to 3%) than those of finisher cross sections.
- For forging high ribs in the finisher, it is at times necessary to have lower ribs in the blocker. At the same time, the web thickness in the blocker is larger than that in the finisher.
- In forging, in order to enhance metal flow toward the ribs, it is useful to provide an opening taper from the center of the web toward the ribs.
- In steel forgings, whenever possible, the ribs in the blocker sections should be narrower but slightly higher than those in the finisher sections. This reduces die wear.

At present, computer-aided design (CAD) of blocker cross sections can be carried out using interactive graphics. However, this method still employs the same empirical relationships listed above, but stored in a quantitative manner in the computer memory. At present, the main advantages of computer-aided design of blocker dies are:

- Cross-sectional areas and volumes can be calculated rapidly and accurately.
- The designer can easily modify geometric parameters such as fillet and corner radii, web thickness, rib height and width, etc, and can immediately review the alternative design on the screen of the computer graphics terminal, as shown in Figure 12-5.[12-13]
- The designer can zoom in to investigate a given portion of the forging (see Figure 12-6) and can perform sectional area calculations for a given

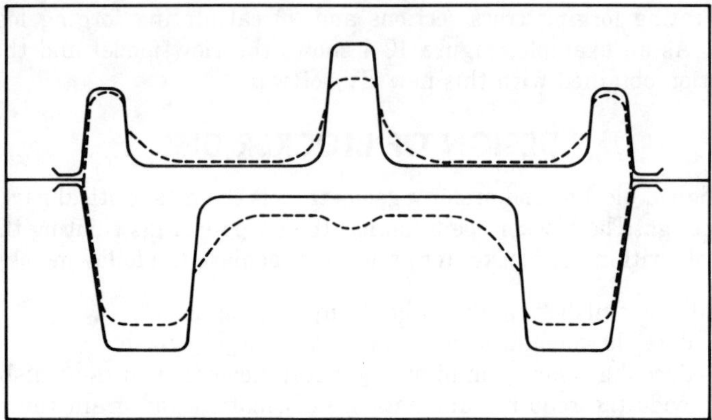

Figure 12-5. A typical forging cross section and a possible blocker design displayed on a computer graphics terminal.[12-13]

portion of the forging, where the metal flow is expected to be localized, i.e., where the metal would not flow into neighboring regions.

- If necessary, the designer may review the blocker positions in the finisher dies at various opening positions to study the initial die blocker contact point during finish forging, as shown in Figure 12-7.

These geometric manipulations and drawings are basically no different from what is being done manually today, but with the aid of computers they can be done much faster and much more accurately.

EXPERIMENTAL VERIFICATION OF CAD/CAM TECHNIQUE

Computer programs, developed earlier for designing blocker and finisher dies, were evaluated by using the example forging shown in Figure 12-8.[12-14] As shown in this figure, the forging was divided into a large number of cross sections, 66 in all. Axisymmetric metal flow was assumed at the ends.

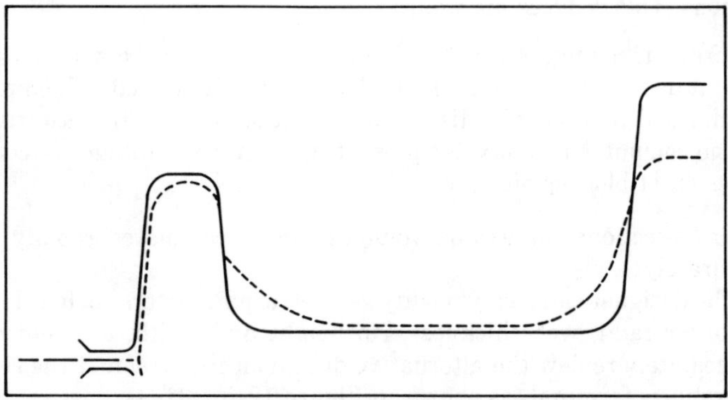

Figure 12-6. Use of "zooming" to examine a small portion of the blocker/finisher cross sections in a computer-aided design.

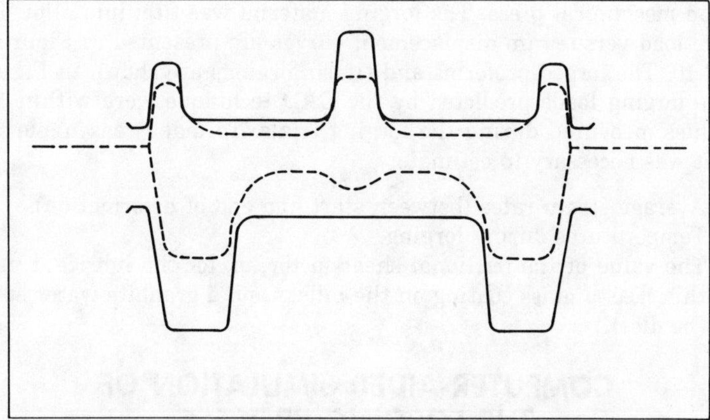

Figure 12-7. Computer-designed blocker, shown with finisher dies in separated position.

The rectangular end was represented by a different cross section every 5°, because of its complexity. However, only one cross section was used to represent the 180° at the round end. In a practical application, it would suffice to use a much smaller number of cross sections.

The finisher and blocker forging dies for the part shown in Figure 12-8 were designed by the CAD method and manufactured by NC machining. The forging experiments were conducted in a 2500-ton hydraulic press and in a

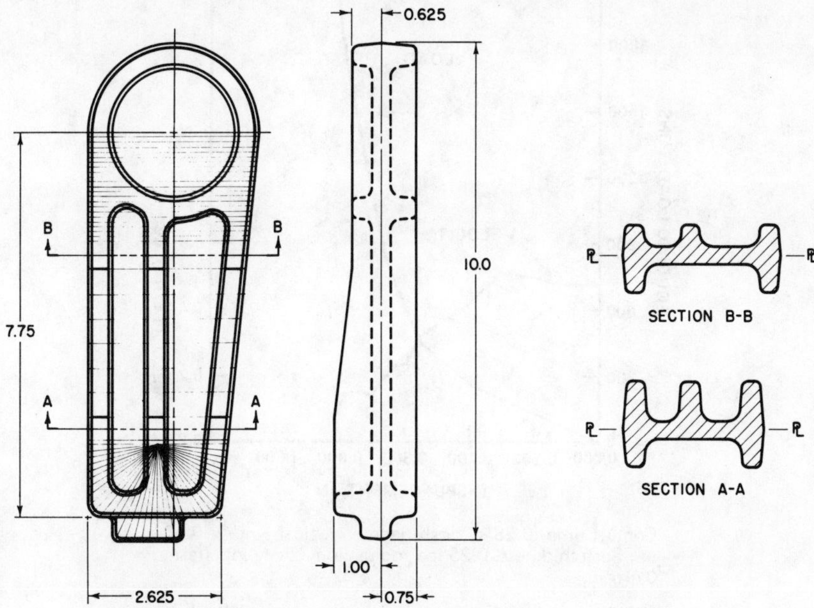

Figure 12-8. Experimental part forged by use of dies produced by CAD/CAM.[12-14]

1300-ton mechanical press. The forging material was titanium alloy Ti-6Al-4V. The load versus ram displacement curves are presented in Figures 12-9 and 12-10. The forged preforms and finish forgings are shown in Figure 12-11. The forging loads predicted by the CAD technique were within 10% of the values measured during the forging trials. To make reasonable predictions, it was necessary to estimate:

- Average strain rates (between start and end of deformation).
- Temperatures during forging.
- The value of the frictional shear factor, m, for the lubricant used (in this case, a glass coating on the billets and a graphite-water spray on the dies).

COMPUTER-AIDED SIMULATION OF THE FORGING PROCESS

The ultimate advantage of computer-aided design in forging is achieved when reasonably accurate and inexpensive computer software is available for simulating metal flow throughout a forging operation. Thus, forging "experiments" can be run on a computer by simulating the finish forging that would result from an "assumed" or "selected" blocker design. The results can be displayed on a graphics terminal. If the simulation indicates that the selected blocker design would not fill the finisher die or that too much material would be wasted, then another blocker design can be selected and the computer sim-

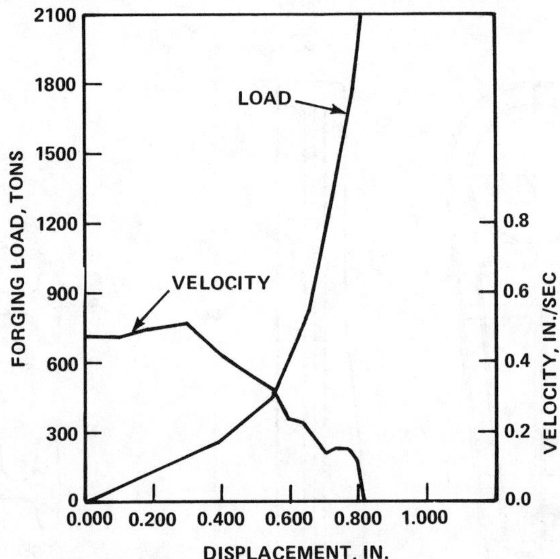

Contact time, 0.28 s. Flash geometry: flash width, 0.60 in.; flash thickness, 0.25 in.; radius from cavity into flash, 3/16 in.

Figure 12-9. Forging load and velocity versus displacement during finish forging of titanium alloy Ti-6Al-4V in a 2500-ton hydraulic press.

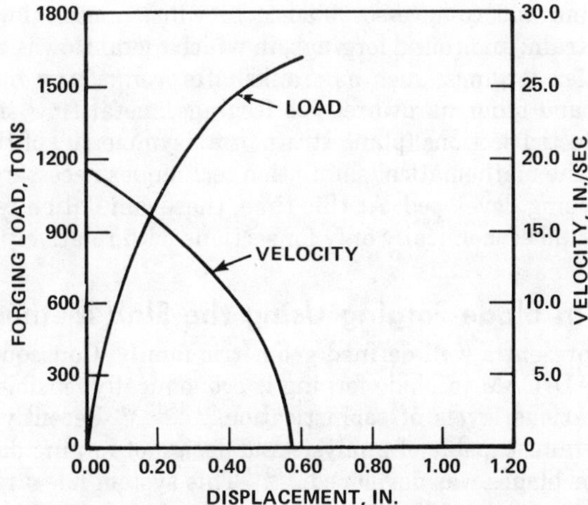

Contact time, 0.06 s. Flash geometry: flash width, 0.40 in.; flash thickness, 0.20 in.; radius from cavity into flash, 3/16 in.

Figure 12-10. Forging load and velocity versus displacement during finish forging of titanium alloy Ti-6Al-4V in a 1300-ton mechanical press.

ulation, or the "experiment", can be repeated. This computer-aided simulation will reduce the required number of expensive die tryouts.

The plastic deformation phenomenon in hot forging is very complex and involves: (a) nonsteady-state flow, (b) nonuniform distribution of strains, strain rates and temperatures in the deforming metal, (c) difficulties in estimating the flow stresses in various parts of the forging during deformation and (d) difficulties in estimating the friction factor. Consequently, only a limited amount of progress has been made so far in simulating an entire forging operation. At this time, computer codes are available for two well-defined part

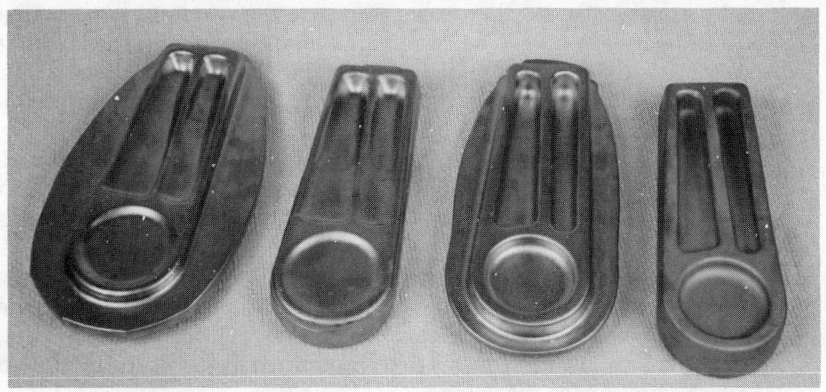

Figure 12-11. Titanium alloy (Ti-6Al-4V) forging (right) and its blocker (left), with flash and as trimmed.

families: turbine and compressor blades, in which metal flow is predominantly plane strain; and round forgings, in which metal flow is axisymmetric. In more complex forgings, such as crankshafts, connecting rods, structural aircraft parts and other hardware-type forgings, metal flow simulation can be done for selected sections (plane strain or axisymmetric) of the given forging. However, the mathematical simulation techniques necessary for this purpose are still being developed. At this time, these simulation techniques can be used easily and economically only for sections with relatively simple geometries.

Simulation in Blade Forging Using the Slab Method

Blades represent a well-defined geometric family. Consequently, the application of CAD/CAM in blade forging is economically feasible and is being practiced to various levels of sophistication.[12-15,12-16] Recently, a system of computer programs capable of analysis and design of forging dies for turbine and compressor blades was developed.[12-17] This system has a modular structure based on the various functions it is required to perform and thus is capable of being extended into an integrated CAD/CAM system.

The major functions performed by this system may be summarized as:

- Read in and preprocess the blade geometry. Check for errors in the input data and convert into internal standard form (canonical form). Calculate the cross-sectional area.
- Determine the flow stress under the forging conditions (lubrication, temperature, equipment characteristics), based on available data. An average flow stress is calculated on the basis of an average temperature in the cavity and in the flash.
- Determine the forging plane based on minimum side loading of the dies during forging. The turbine blade is rotated around its stacking axis in small increments until the position with minimum resultant horizontal force is determined. Load calculations are based on the "slab method" and on deformation elements, as illustrated in Figure 12-12. The stress distribution, the expected vertical and horizontal loads, and the center of loading are calculated. The summations of the horizontal and vertical loads on all cross sections give the resultant loads acting on the two die halves. The "optimum" forging plane position is that position where the horizontal forces on the dies are minimized. This, in turn, minimizes die shift during forging, resulting in improved tolerances on the product.
- Modify leading edge flash geometry so as to bring all neutral surfaces to the same line. Thus, more uniform metal flow, with uniform flash losses, will result. (The neutral surface is the plane where the stress distribution is at its peak, as can be seen in Figure 12-12.)
- Perform a simulation of the forging process, as illustrated in Figure 12-13, in order to determine the best position of the preform in the die cavity. This position not only ensures die cavity filling during forging, but also may allow flash losses to be minimized by use of the minimum preform dimensions indicated.
- Summarize the results. Provide a printout of all results obtained in a concise format in engineering terms.

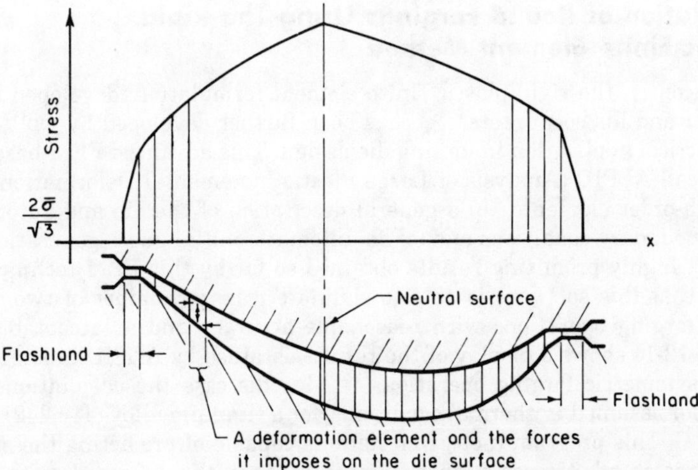

Figure 12-12. An airfoil die cross section. Its deformation elements and the expected stress distribution at die closure.

- Provide a 3-D display of the die surfaces together with the flash land as designed by the computer programs. The user can rotate the blade in space and view the blade in perspective or orthographic projection and modify the calculated forge-plane position, if deemed necessary.

After the user is satisfied with the design, the die cavity geometry together with the boundary stress state can be made available to specialized finite element elastic deflection analysis routines. These consist, in principle, of two major modules: the first one prepares the grid system and the second one performs the actual finite element deflection analysis. Where necessary, the local elastic deflections may be superimposed on the gross deflection of the particular press bed. Using these routines, the die surface coordinates can be corrected for the deflection expected during forging and can be stored in a special format. These data can then be used for NC machining of the upper and lower die surfaces.

This CAD/CAM procedure, although it still needs some further development, has been found to be very valuable in the establishment of an integrated production system for forged blades.

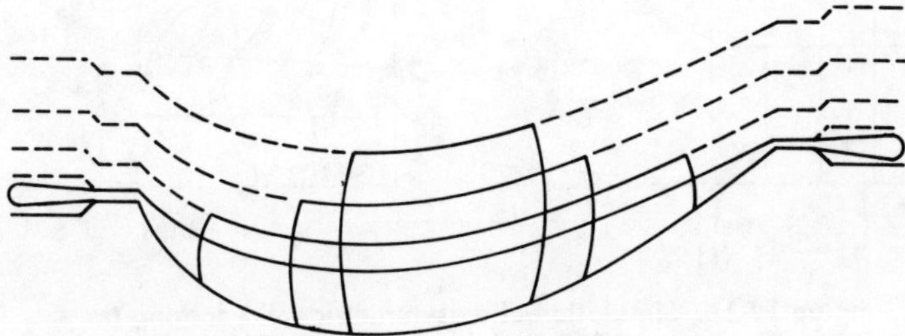

Figure 12-13. Metal flow and die filling in blade forging, as simulated by a computer program.

Simulation of Round Forgings Using The Rigid Plastic Finite Element Method

Recently, the rigid plastic finite element formulation, developed by Kobayashi and his co-workers,[12-18] has been further developed by Oh[12-19,12-20] for practical application in forging die design. This advanced FEM-based program, call ALPID (Analysis of Large Plastic Incremental Deformation), uses (a) high-order elements, (b) a general description of the die and automation of the boundary conditions and (c) an automatic initial guess generation. Initial but highly promising results obtained so far by this FEM technique indicate that this software is able to simulate a large number of two-dimensional forging operations with reasonable accuracy and at acceptable cost. Figure 12-14 shows a display of the results obtained by ALPID in simulating an axisymmetric forging operation.[12-19] In this case the calculations were made, for assumed isothermal conditions, for a titanium alloy (Ti-6242) forged at 950 C. This program (not given here) is capable of predicting the strains, strain rates and stresses at specific grid points in the deformed material. In fact, by use of special plotting software, these results can be displayed on a graphics terminal and plotted on paper in the form of contour plots.

Another example of simulation is presented in Figure 12-15, this time for a backward extrusion operation.[12-20] In this case, the initial billet was

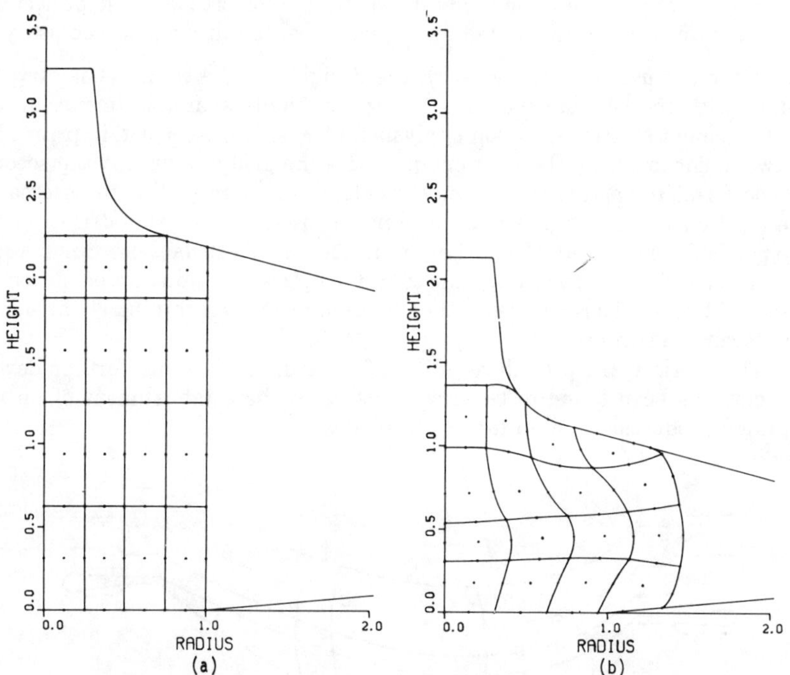

Figure 12-14. Simulation of axisymmetric spike forging (m = 0.3; temperature, 1750 F): (a) undeformed FEM grid; (b) deformation at a die stroke of $0.5H_0$, where H_0 is the initial billet height.[12-19]

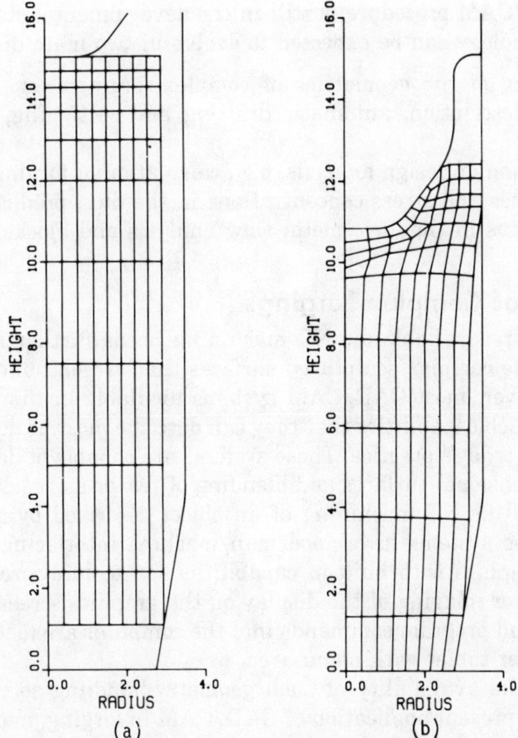

Figure 12-15. Simulation of a backward extrusion operation: (a) undeformed FEM grid; (b) deformation at a die stroke of 0.30 $2H_0$.[12-20]

149 mm in diameter and 345 mm in "height". The material was type 1045 steel forged at 1100 C.

FUTURE OUTLOOK

CAD/CAM is being applied to an increasing extent in forging technology. Using the three-dimensional description of a machined part, which may have been computer designed, it is possible to generate the geometry of the associated forging. For this purpose, it is best to use a stand-alone CAD/CAM system with software for geometry handling, drafting, dimensioning and NC machining. Thus, the forging sections can be obtained from a common data base. Using well-proven analyses based on slab-method or FEM techniques, forging loads and stresses can be obtained and flash dimensions can be selected for each section, where metal flow is approximated as two dimensional (plane strain or axisymmetric). In some relatively simple section geometries, a computer simulation can be conducted to evaluate initial guesses on blocker or preform sections. Once the blocker and finisher sections are obtained to the designer's satisfaction, this geometric data base can be utilized to write NC part programs to obtain NC tapes or disks.

This CAD/CAM procedure is still in the developmental stage. In the future, this technology can be expected to evolve in two main directions:

1. Handling of the geometries of complex forgings, e.g., three-dimensional description, automatic drafting and sectioning, and NC machining.
2. Utilization of design analysis, e.g., calculation of forging stresses and of stresses and stress concentrations in the dies, prediction of elastic deflections in the dies, metal flow analysis and blocker/preform design.

Geometries of Complex Forgings

The software available for NC machining needs further improvements for handling the complex sculptured surfaces that are encountered in many forgings. However, most CAD/CAM systems available in the market today have reached such capabilities that they can describe most, if not all, forgings encountered in today's practice. These systems are capable of describing complex three-dimensional surfaces and blending of two or more adjacent surface patches, as well as NC machining of an object described by such surfaces. Several of these systems have good man/machine interfacing, using interactive color graphics with built-in capabilities for zooming, rotating, translating and mirror imaging of the display on the graphics screen. In addition, entry of data and program commands into the computer are facilitated by the use of a digitizer tablet with menu area.

Based on the availability of such geometry-handling software, we can expect that the present application of CAD/CAM in forging, mainly for drafting and NC machining of forging dies (electrodes or models), will continue to increase at a rapid rate. The principal barriers to widespread acceptance of such application appear to be (a) the apparent high cost of introducing CAD/CAM, (b) management inertia and (c) lack of trained personnel. However, the worldwide forging industry is under considerable pressure to modernize and to increase the productivity of skilled diemakers, who are becoming increasingly scarce. In addition, computer-aided systems for drafting and NC machining are becoming relatively inexpensive. Consequently, we can expect to see, in the next decade a very significant increase in the number of forge and die shops in which CAD/CAM is used.

Design Analysis

At this time, it is possible to estimate forging stresses, average pressure, total forging load and the center of loading, as described in this chapter. The technology that requires additional research and development is that of metal flow simulation for optimum blocker/preform design. Some significant advances have been made in this direction through the use of plastic FEM analysis. However, a considerable number of questions still need to be answered before such analysis can become a practical and cost-effective design tool.

For two-dimensional metal flow simulation, it is necessary to develop procedures/techniques for:

- Automatic generation of forging cross sections (plane strain or axisymmetric)

- Selection of initial FEM mesh and distribution of the mesh size.
- Remeshing, and deciding when, after a certain amount of deformation is simulated, remeshing is necessary
- Assembly of blocker sections, obtained from analysis by metal flow simulation.

At this time, there are no methods available for describing and/or simulating three-dimensional metal flow encountered in practical forging operations. Considerable effort is necessary for development of these techniques.

In summary, it can be expected that application of CAD/CAM in forging will continue to increase. Initially, CAD/CAM will be used for drafting and NC machining. Next, the geometric capabilities of available CAD/CAM systems will be augmented by analysis software to (a) calculate forging stresses and load and (b) design blocker shapes for relatively simple forgings, using metal flow simulation. At a later date, we can expect that three-dimensional metal flow simulation and design of practical complex forging shapes will also be possible. As a result, the need for expensive die tryout trials cn the forge shop floor will be reduced. In addition, material utilization will be improved by optimizing the geometries of blockers and preforms through computer-aided simulation and by optimizing flash design.

REFERENCES

12-1. Wood N. F., "Three-Pronged Attack on Die Sinking Problems", Machine and Tool Blue Book, Nov 1973, p 87.

12-2. Post, C. T., "The Strong Link That Ties CAD to CAM", Iron Age, Aug 22, 1977, p 29.

12-3. Dawson, K. G., "Meeting the Diesinker's Challenge of the Future", Precision Metal, Feb 1980, p 17.

12-4. Akgerman, N., "Design and Manufacture of Forging Dies: Computer Aided Methods", SME Technical Paper MF 72-531, 1972.

12-5. Akgerman, N., and Altan, T., "Modular Analysis of Geometry and Stresses in Closed-Die Forging: Application to a Structural Part", ASME Trans., J. Engr. for Industry, Nov 1972, p 1025.

12-6. Altan, T., Billhardt, C. F., and Akgerman, N., "CAD/CAM for Closed-Die Forging of Track Shoes and Links", SME Paper MS 76-739, 1976.

12-7. Badawy, A., Billhardt, C. F., and Altan, T., "Implementation of Forging Load and Stress Analysis on a Computervision CADDS-3 System", Proceedings of the Third Annual Computervision Users Conference, Dallas, TX, Sept 1981.

12-8. Chan, Y. K., and Knight, W. A., "Computer Aided Design and Manufacture of Dies for Long Hot Forgings", Proceedings of the 6th NAMRC, Gainesville, FL, 1978, p 455.

12-9. Chan, Y. K., and Knight, W. A., "Computer Aided Manufacture of Forging Dies by Volume Building", Journal of Mechanical Workings Technology, Vol 3, 1979, p 167.

12-10. Altan, T., and Lahoti, G. D., "Limitations, Applicability and Usefulness of Different Methods in Analyzing Forming Problems", Keynote Paper, Annals of CIRP, Vol 28 (2), 1979, p 473.

12-11. Douglas, J. R., and Altan, T., "Flow Stress Determination for Metals at Forging Rates and Temperatures", ASME Trans., J. Engr. for Industry, Feb 1975, p 66.

12-12. Semiatin, S. L., and Lahoti, G. D., "Forging of Metals", Scientific American, Aug 1981, p 82.

12-13. Subramanian, T. L., and Altan, T., "Application of Computer Aided Techniques to Precision Closed Die Forging", Annals of CIRP, Vol 27 (1), 1978, p 123.

12-14. Akgerman, N., and Altan, T., "Computer-Aided Design and Manufacturing of Forging Dies for Structural Parts", presented at the North American Metalworking Research Conference, May 14-15, 1973, Hamilton, Ontario, Canada, published in the Proceedings.
12-15. Voigtlander, O., "The Manufacturing of Blades for Turbines and Compressors: Precision Forging of the Airfoil" (in German), Industrie-Anzeiger, Vol 91, No. 40, May 13, 1969, p 908.
12-16. Winship, J. T., "Third Screw Press for Blades", American Machinist, Oct 1976, p 133.
12-17. Akgerman, N., and Altan, T., "Application of CAD/CAM in Forging Turbine and Compressor Blades", ASME Paper 75-GT-42, published in ASME Trans., J. Engr. for Power, Vol 98, Series A, No. 2, April 1976, p 290.
12-18. Lee, C. H., and Kobayashi, S., "New Solutions to Rigid-Plastic Deformation Problems Using a Matrix Method", ASME Trans., J. Engr. for Industry, Vol 95, 1973, p 865.
12-19. Oh, S. I., "Finite Element Analysis of Metal Forming Problems with Arbitrarily Shaped Dies", Int. Journal of Mech. Sciencs, Vol 24, No. 4, p 479.
12-20. Oh, S. I., Lahoti, G. D., and Altan, T., "ALPID – A General Purpose FEM Program for Metal Forming", Proceedings of NAMRC IX, May 1981, State College, PA, p 83.

CHAPTER 13

Hot Extrusion of Rods, Tubes and Shapes

Extrusion is the process of forcing a heated billet to flow through a die opening of desired shape. This process is used to produce long, straight, semifinished metal products of constant cross section, such as bars, solid and hollow sections, tubes, wires and strips. There are basically three variations of extrusion, depending on the lubrication technique used. In the nonlubricated extrusion process (Figure 13-1 left), a "flat-face" die is used, and the material flows by internal shear and causes a "dead-metal zone" to form in front of the extrusion die. In lubricated extrusion, (Figure 13-1 middle), a suitable lubricant is present between the extruded billet and the extrusion tooling, i.e., the container and the die. The third and most recently developed technique is hydrostatic extrusion (Figure 13-1 right), in which a fluid film between the billet and the tooling exerts pressure on the deforming billet. Hydrostatic extrusion is used only in unusual applications for extruding special alloys, composites or clad materials, where adequate lubrication cannot be easily provided by conventional lubrication techniques. For all practical purposes, hydrostatic extrusion can be considered to be a special advanced version of the lubricated extrusion process.

The significant differences between nonlubricated and lubricated extrusion processes are summarized in Table 13-1.

NONLUBRICATED HOT EXTRUSION

In nonlubricated hot extrusion, lubrication is not used and the entire operation appears rather straightforward once conditions have been defined. In this process, however, a vast number of metallurgical and processing factors interact and affect the mechanical properties, surface finish and corrosion resistance of the final extruded shape. This extrusion method, which uses no lubrication between the billet, container and die, is able to produce very com-

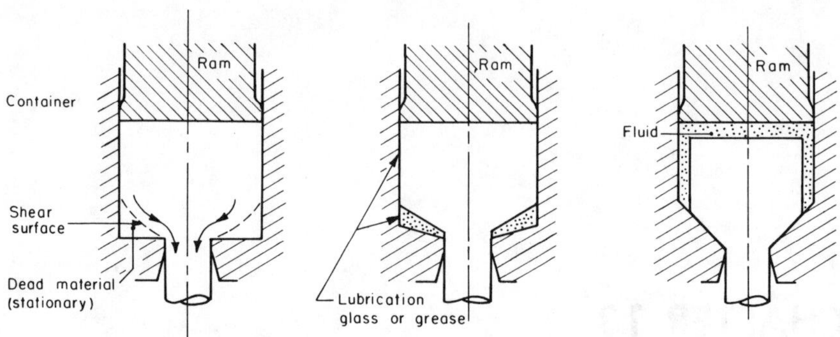

Figure 13-1. Schematic illustrations of the nonlubricated (left), lubricated (middle) and hydrostatic (right) extrusion processes.

plex sections, with "mirror" surface finishes and close dimensional tolerances, that are considered net extrusions. With this extrusion technique, a flat-face (shear-face) die is utilized.

There are basically two methods of hot extruding materials without lubrication: (a) direct or forward extrusion and (b) indirect or backward extrusion. In direct extrusion, as shown in Figure 13-2(a), the ram travels in the same direction as the extruded section, and there is relative movement between the billet and the container.[13-1] In indirect extrusion (Figure 13-2b), the billet does not move relative to the container, and the die is pushed against the billet by means of a hollow stem.

Direct Extrusion

A typical sequence of operations for direct extrusion of a solid section (see Figure 13-3) is as follows:[13-1]

Table 13-1. Significant characteristics of the nonlubricated and lubricated extrusion processes

Characteristic	Nonlubricated extrusion	Lubricated extrusion
Materials	Alloys of aluminum, copper, magnesium, zinc	Steels, titanium alloys, nickel alloys, copper alloys
Die design/manufacture	Relatively simple, flat	Smooth entry, more complex
Die wear	Not excessive	Very significant
Product geometry	Thinner and more intricate sections, closer tolerances	Shapes not very intricate due to complexity of the die and difficulty of extruding these alloys
Product surface finish	Shiny, very good	Not very smooth
Extrusion pressure	Relatively high due to friction and internal shear	Relatively low because of low friction
Extrusion speed	High in extruding soft Al alloys, low for hard Al alloys because of internal heat generation	Independent of the alloy

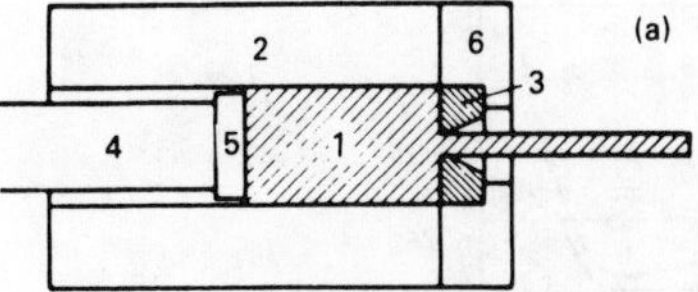

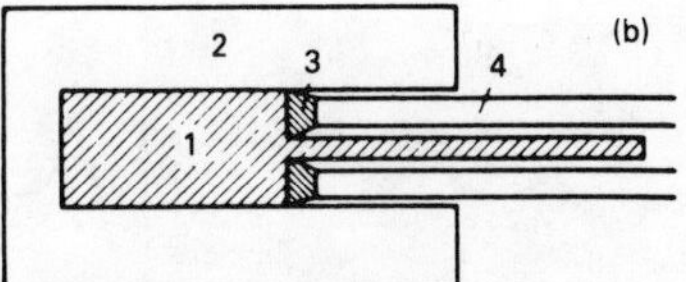

Figure 13-2. Basic methods of extrusion: (a) direct extrusion, (b) indirect extrusion.[13-1]

1. The heated billet and the dummy block are loaded into the container.
2. The billet is extruded by the force of the ram being pushed against it. This first upsets the billet and then forces the metal to flow through the die. During extrusion, a thin shell of material may be left on the container walls. Extrusion is stopped so as to leave a thin disk of material (butt) in the container.
3. The container is separated from the die, the extruded section with the butt, and the dummy block.
4. The discard (butt) is sheared off.
5. The shear, the container and the ram are returned to their initial (loading) positions.

Typical load versus ram displacement curves for direct and indirect extrusion are presented in Figure 13-4.[13-1] It can be seen that the load in direct extrusion initially increases very rapidly as the billet upsets to fill the container. There is then a further increase in pressure, and extrusion commences. A somewhat cone-shape deformation zone then develops in front of the die aperture. After the maximum load has been reached, the extrusion pressure falls as the billet length decreases until a minimum is reached, and then rapidly increases again. This last pressure increase occurs because only a disk of the billet remains and the metal has to flow radially toward the die aperture. Resistance to deformation increases considerably with decreasing thickness.

Indirect Extrusion

In indirect extrusion (Figure 13-2b), the die is pushed by the hollow stem and moves relative to the container, but there is no relative displacement

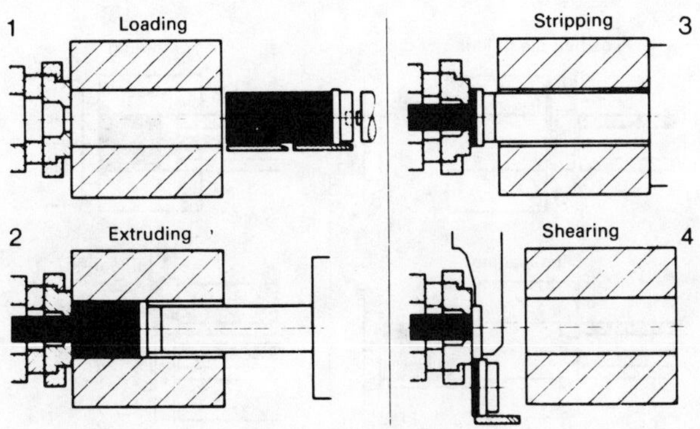

Figure 13-3. Sequence of operations in direct extrusion.[13-1]

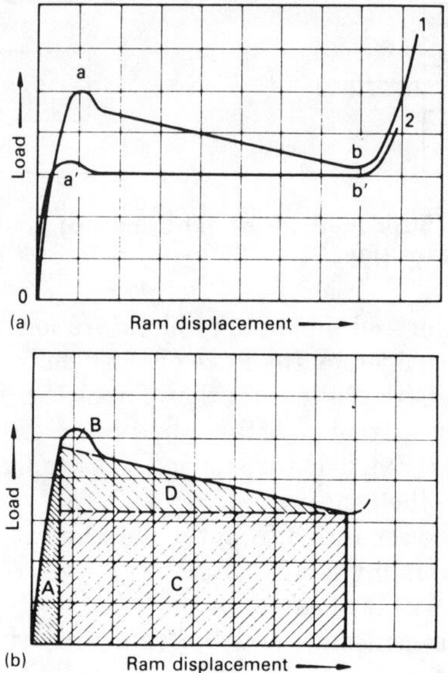

(a) Dependence of extrusion load on ram displacement: a-b, direct extrusion; a'-b', indirect extrusion. (b) Division of the work of deformation: A, work of upsetting; B, work needed to initiate deformation; C, work of deformation; D, work needed to overcome friction and shearing in direct extrusion.

Figure 13-4. Typical load versus ram displacement curves for nonlubricated extrusion processes.[13-1]

between the billet and the container.[13-1] As a result, there is no frictional stress at the billet/container interface, and therefore the extrusion load and the temperature generated by deformation and friction are reduced, as can be seen in Figure 13-4.

The sequence of operations for indirect extrusion of a solid section, shown in Figure 13-5,[13-1] is as follows:

1. The dummy block and the die are inserted into the press.
2. The billet is loaded into the container.

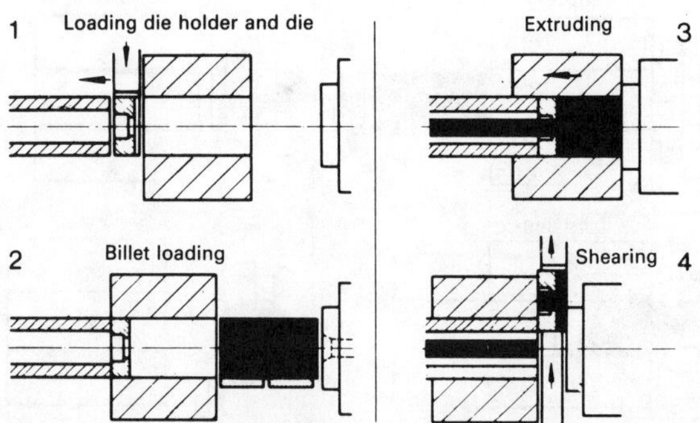

Figure 13-5. Sequence of operations for indirect extrusion.[13-1]

3. The billet is extruded, leaving a butt.
4. The dummy block with the die and the butt are separated from the section.

Indirect extrusion offers a number of advantages, which can be summarized as follows:

- A 25 to 30% reduction in maximum load can be realized relative to direct extrusion.
- Extrusion pressure is not a function of billet length, because there is no relative displacement between the billet and the container. Billet length is therefore not limited by the load required for this displacement but only by the length and stability of the hollow stem needed for a given container length.
- No heat is produced by friction between the billet and the container, and consequently no temperature increase occurs at the billet surface toward the end of extrusion, as is typical in direct extrusion of aluminum alloys. Therefore, there is a lesser tendency for the surfaces and edges to crack in the indirect process, and significantly higher extrusion speeds can be used.
- The service life of the tooling is increased, especially that of the inner liner, because of reduced friction and temperatures.

The disadvantage of indirect extrusion is that impurities or defects on the billet surface affect the surface of the extrusion and are not automatically retained as a shell or discard in the container. Therefore, machined billets have to be used in many cases. In addition, the cross-sectional area of the extrusion is limited by the size of the hollow stem.

Extrusion of Tubes and Hollow Sections

Both direct and indirect techniques can be used for extruding tubular products.[13-1,13-2] To produce a hollow section, the metal must flow through an annular gap formed by the die and a mandrel. There are basically two methods for extruding tubular products.

The first method uses a billet with an internal bore machined or pierced in the press. In this case, the mandrel is guided to provide concentricity. During extrusion, the mandrel either remains stationary (Figure 13-6) or moves with the ram (Figure 13-7).[13-1]

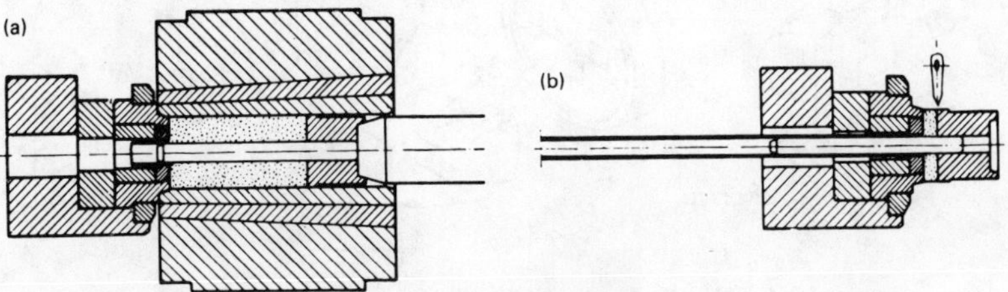

Figure 13-6. Extrusion with a floating mandrel: (a) beginning of extrusion, (b) final position before shearing of the discard.[13-1]

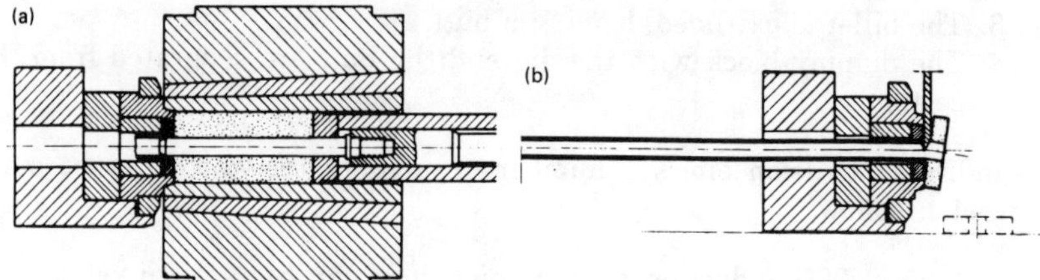

Figure 13-7. Extrusion with independent mandrel movement: (a) beginning of extrusion, (b) final position before shearing of the discard.(13-1)

For extrusion of hollow sections, special multihole dies can be used, provided that the material can weld under pressure. The multihole die designs shown in Figure 13-8 have openings in the top face of the die from which material is extruded into two or more segments and then, beneath the surface of the die, welded and forced through the final shape configuration to form a part.(13-1) The tubular portion of the extruded shape is formed by a mandrel attached to the lower side of the top die segment. This provides a fixed support for the mandrel and a continuous hole in the extrusion. Section type H through N in Figure 13-9 comprise typical complex parts that can be made from aluminum through the use of multihole-type tooling.(13-3)

Higher extrusion pressures are required with multihole dies, compared with flat-face dies with mandrels, in extruding the same section. The material has to shear in order to flow through various segments and form a sound weld before extruding out. Therefore, this process is limited to materials such as aluminum alloys, which have low shear strengths at extrusion tempera-

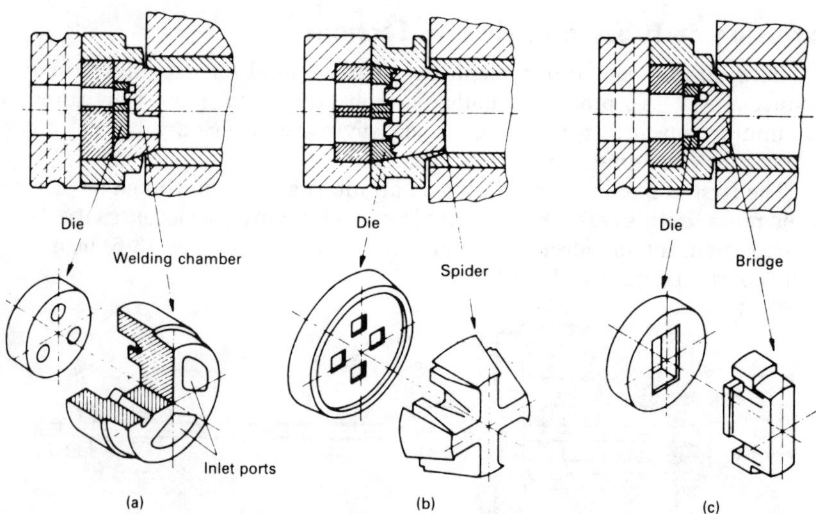

Figure 13-8. Multihole dies used for extrusion of aluminum: (a) multihole porthole die, (b) multihole spider die, (c) bridge die (recessed bridge).(13-1)

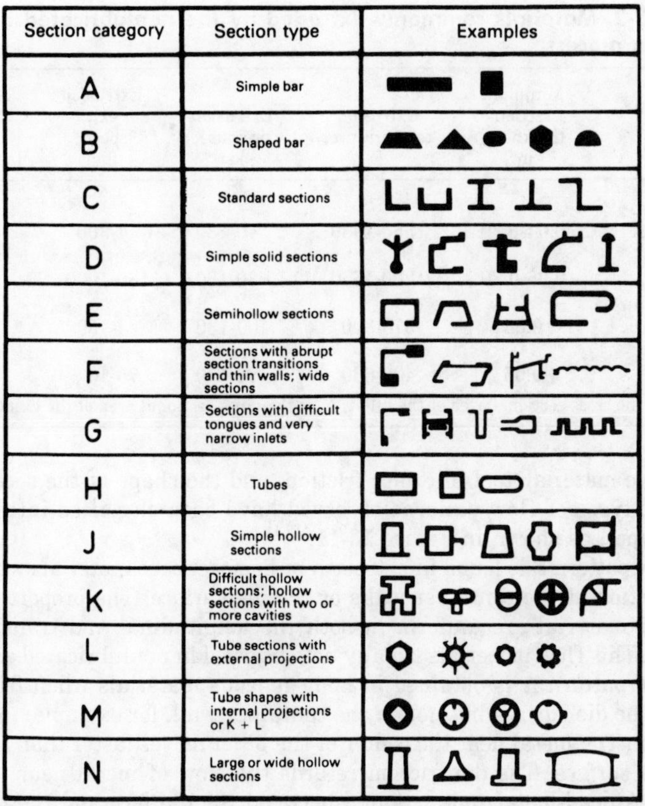

Section category	Section type	Examples
A	Simple bar	
B	Shaped bar	
C	Standard sections	
D	Simple solid sections	
E	Semihollow sections	
F	Sections with abrupt section transitions and thin walls; wide sections	
G	Sections with difficult tongues and very narrow inlets	
H	Tubes	
J	Simple hollow sections	
K	Difficult hollow sections; hollow sections with two or more cavities	
L	Tube sections with external projections	
M	Tube shapes with internal projections or K + L	
N	Large or wide hollow sections	

Figure 13-9. Classification of extruded aluminum sections according to the degree of difficulty of extrusion.[13-3]

tures. Copper alloys, for example, are not generally extruded using multihole dies.

Materials and Metal Flow

The flow stress at extrusion temperature and the workability are the main characteristics which determine the extrudability of a given material without lubrication. Materials most commonly processed by nonlubricated extrusion are given in Table 13-2. Most copper alloys are first extruded and then cold drawn to obtain sections with sharper corners. Examples of extruded copper and copper alloy sections are shown in Figure 13-10.[13-1] Various aluminum alloys (1000 to 7000 series) are extruded for a large number of commercial and military applications. Examples of extruded aluminum alloy sections are given in Figure 13-9. Among all available alloys, the high-strength aluminum alloys (2000 and 7000 series) are most widely used for aircraft applications. Other alloys, such as 1100, 3003, 6061, 6062, 6063 and X6463, are used for manufacturing goods for a variety of applications, such as construction, household appliances and transportation.

Metal flow during extrusion varies considerably, depending on the ma-

Table 13-2. Materials commonly extruded by the nonlubricated hot extrusion process

Materials	Minimum section thickness, in.	Extrusion temperature, F	Extrusion pressure, ksi	Extrusion exit speed, fpm	Extrusion ratio $\ln(A_0/A_1)$(a)
Aluminum alloys	0.04-0.30	550-1050	40-130	4-300	4-7
Copper alloys	0.05-0.30	1200-1650	30-130	80-1000	5-6.5
Magnesium alloys	0.04	570-800	100-130	4-100	4-5.3
Zinc alloys	0.06	400-660	90-110	75-10	4-5

(a) A_0 is the cross-sectional area of the billet; A_1 is the cross-sectional area of the extruded shape.

terial, the material/tool interface friction, and the shape of the section. The different types of flow patterns observed have been classified into four different types, as shown in Figure 13-11.[13-1]

Flow pattern S is found in extrusion of homogeneous materials when there is no friction at the container walls or the die surface. The properties of the extruded material are uniform in both the longitudinal and transverse directions. This flow pattern is usually not observed in nonlubricated extrusion.

Flow pattern A is obtained in homogeneous materials when friction occurs on the die surface but not on the container wall, for example, in indirect extrusion. The metal near the center of the billet moves faster than the metal near the surface. The die friction retards the flow of metal near the billet surface. A dead-metal zone is found between the die face and the container wall. The material in this zone does not move during extrusion. The material

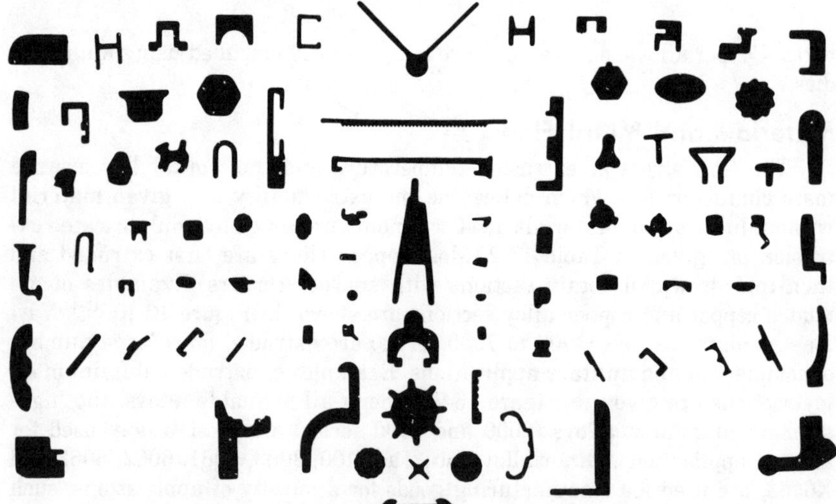

Figure 13-10. Extruded copper and copper alloy sections.[13-1]

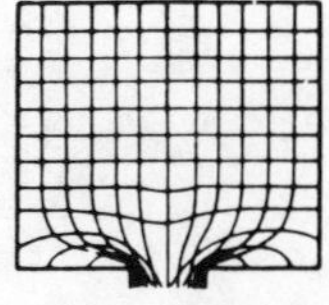

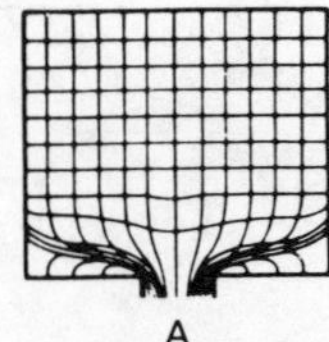

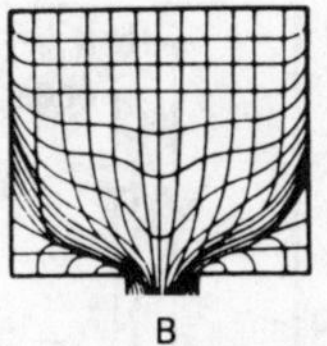

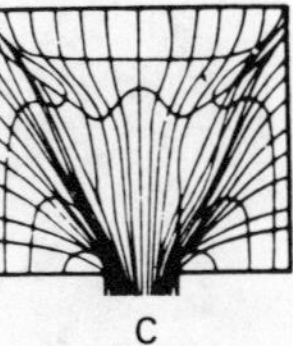

Figure 13-11. Four types of flow patterns observed in extrusion of metals.[13-1]

near the surface is deformed more than the material near the center.

Flow pattern B is obtained in homogeneous materials when friction is present on both the container wall and the die surface. A dead-metal zone larger than that in flow pattern A is formed. Due to the shearing caused by friction, the surface is deformed more than the center. The resulting product has nonuniform properties across the cross section.

Flow pattern C is obtained with billets having inhomogeneous material properties or with uneven distribution of temperature over the billet cross section. The flow stress of the material is much greater near the surface of the container than near the center. The angle of the dead-metal zone is relatively large.

Extrusion Speeds and Temperatures

Temperatures developed during extrusion greatly influence the speed at which the process can be carried out. This is especially true in extrusion of hard aluminum alloys (2000 and 7000 series). A complex thermal situation exists as soon as the heated billet is loaded into the preheated container and extrusion begins. As discussed in Chapter 7, the temperatures are influenced by:

- Heat generation due to plastic deformation.
- Heat generation due to internal shear and friction between the deforming material and the tooling.
- Heat transfer within the billet.
- Heat transfer between the billet and the tooling.
- Heat transported with the extruded product.

All of the above-cited phenomena take place simultaneously and result in a complex relationship among the process variables, i.e., billet material and temperature, friction, tool material and temperature, extrusion speed, shape of the extruded section and reduction in area.

In order to increase the production rate, it is desirable to increase the extrusion ratio (cross-sectional area of billet/cross-sectional area of product) and the extrusion speed while maintaining the extrusion pressure at an acceptable level. For this purpose, the flow stress of the extruded material must be kept relatively low, e.g., the billet preheating temperature must be increased. The combination of high billet temperature, large reduction in area and high extrusion speed causes a considerable rise in temperature in the extruded material, especially near the section surface, because most of the plastic deformation and frictional energy are transformed into heat. This can cause surface defects or hot shortness, especially with difficult-to-extrude hard

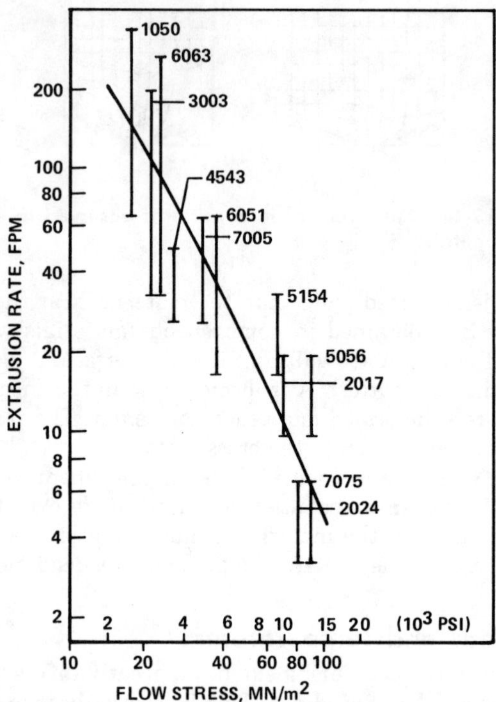

Figure 13-12. Relation between extrusion rate and flow stress for various aluminum alloys.[(13-4)]

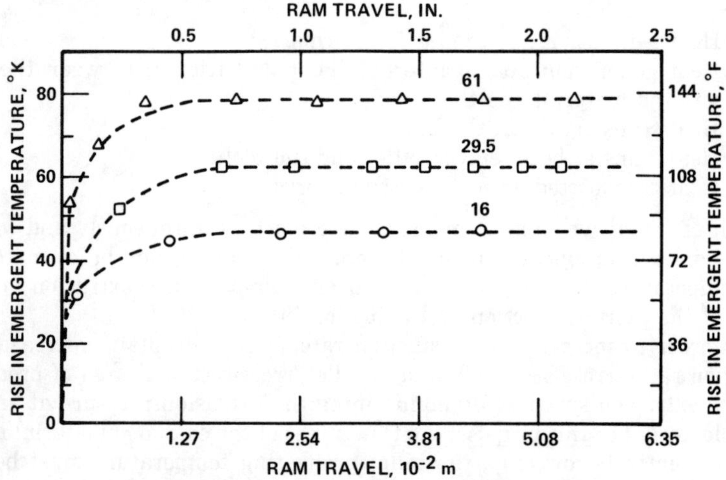

Billet diameter, 0.05 m (2.0 in.); billet length, 0.064 m (2.5 in.); ram speed, 0.001 m/s (3 in./min); starting temperature, 293 K (68 F); extrusion ratios indicated on curves.

Figure 13-13. Effect of extrusion ratio on rise in emergent temperature in extrusion of lead.[(13-5)]

aluminum alloys of the 2000 and 7000 series. With a typical extrusion ratio of 40:1, exit speeds in extruding these alloys would be on the order of 2 to 4 ft/min. Figure 13-12 shows the range of exit speeds encountered in extrusion of various aluminum alloys.[13-4] It can be seen that the extrusion rate is very much dependent on the flow stress of the alloy under the process conditions, i.e., extrusion temperature and strain rate. While exit speeds for soft alloys, i.e., 6000 and 5000 series, are relatively high, those for harder alloys, e.g., 7075 and 2024, are quite low.

Temperature rise and temperature distribution during extrusion have been investigated by many researchers.[13-5 to 13-10] Singer and Coakham[13-5] measured the emergent temperatures of aluminum, tin and lead extruded at ram speeds varying from 1 to 30 m/min. The effects of extrusion ratio and ram speed on the temperature rise are shown in Figures 13-13 and 13-14. Singer and Al-Samarrai[13-9] carried out a simple theoretical analysis to investigate

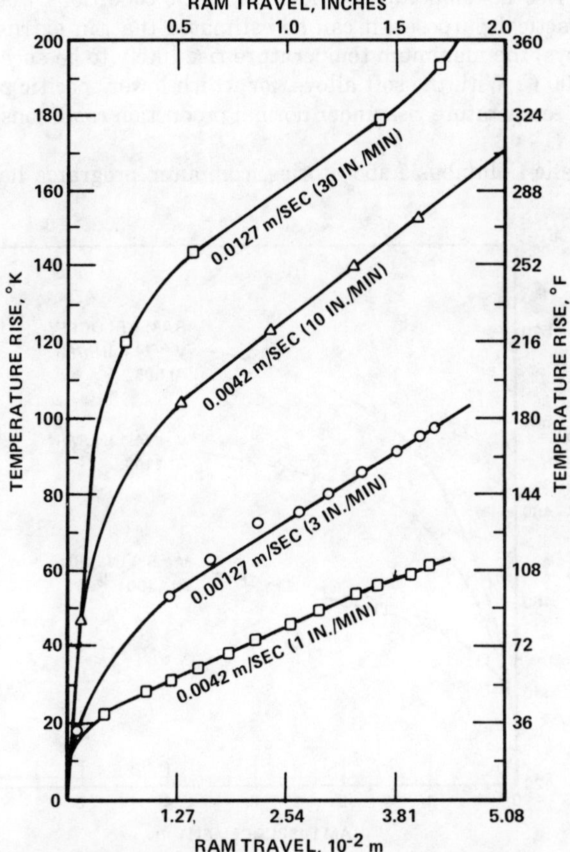

Billet diameter, 0.038 m (1.5 in.); billet length, 0.051 m (2.0 in.); extrusion ratio, 16; starting temperature, 293 K (68 F); ram speeds indicated on curves.

Figure 13-14. Effect of ram speed on rise in emergent temperature in extrusion of superpure aluminum.[13-5]

the effect of ram speed on temperature rise. They assumed a billet of infinite length, neglected container friction, and assumed the interior of the container to be at the same temperature as the billet. The temperature of the billet varied along its length, but was assumed to be constant at any cross section. The model predicted a sigmoidal relationship between the logarithm of ram speed and the temperature rise. Based on this model, a ram speed program that would give a constant emergent temperature was devised. Experimental evaluation of this speed program resulted in maintenance of constant temperatures within ±3 K (6 F) for lead and ±6 K (11 F) for aluminum. The drop in extrusion pressure with programmed ram speed was less than that with constant ram speed.

Akeret[13-10] conducted theoretical and practical studies of temperature distributions in extrusion of aluminum alloys under conditions at which the container and tools were initially below, equal to or above the initial billet temperature. He deduced that, for the particular experimental conditions examined, the rise in temperature under adiabatic conditions would be about 95 C. For practical purposes, it can be estimated that, in extrusion of high-strength alloys, the maximum temperature rise likely to be encountered will not exceed 100 C. With the soft alloys, for which lower specific pressures are required, the temperature rise under normal production conditions is not likely to exceed 50 C.

At Battelle-Columbus Laboratories, computer programs have been de-

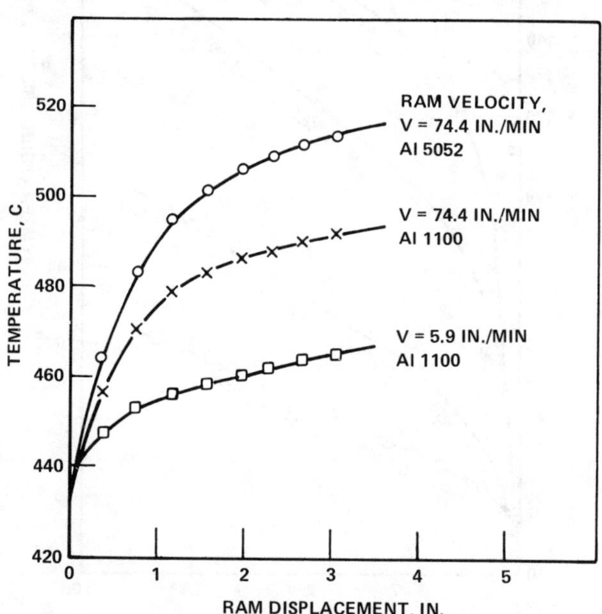

Reduction ratio, 5:1; billet diameter, 2.8 in.; billet length, 5.6 in.; initial billet and tooling temperature, 440 C.

Figure 13-15. Surface temperatures of the extruded product at the exit from the die.[13-7]

veloped for predicting temperatures in extrusion of rods and tubes in various materials.[13-7,13-8] As shown in Figure 13-15, based on theoretical predictions as well as on experimental evidence, the product temperature increases as extrusion proceeds. The temperature at the product surface is higher than the temperature at the product center. This is illustrated in Figure 13-16 for given extrusion conditions. Thus, it can be seen that the surface temperature of the product may approach the critical temperature at which hot shortness may occur, only toward the end of the extrusion cycle. The temperature of the extruded product as it emerges from the die is one of the essential factors influencing product quality. Therefore, an ideal procedure for establishing the maximum speed of extrusion at all times would be to measure this temperature and to use it for controlling the ram speed. This procedure has been proposed by many researchers, but the problem of obtaining accurate and continuous measurement of the temperature of the extruded product remains unsolved. Methods of measuring product temperature by using various types of contact thermocouples, or by radiation pyrometry, have not been proven to be practical.

Laue[13-11] proposed a system for isothermal extrusion in which the variation in ram speed necessary for maintaining the product temperature within the required limits was programmed. In presses designed to operate on this principle, the working stroke is divided into zones, each having a preset speed. In a press used for extrusion of high-strength alloys, a time savings of 60%

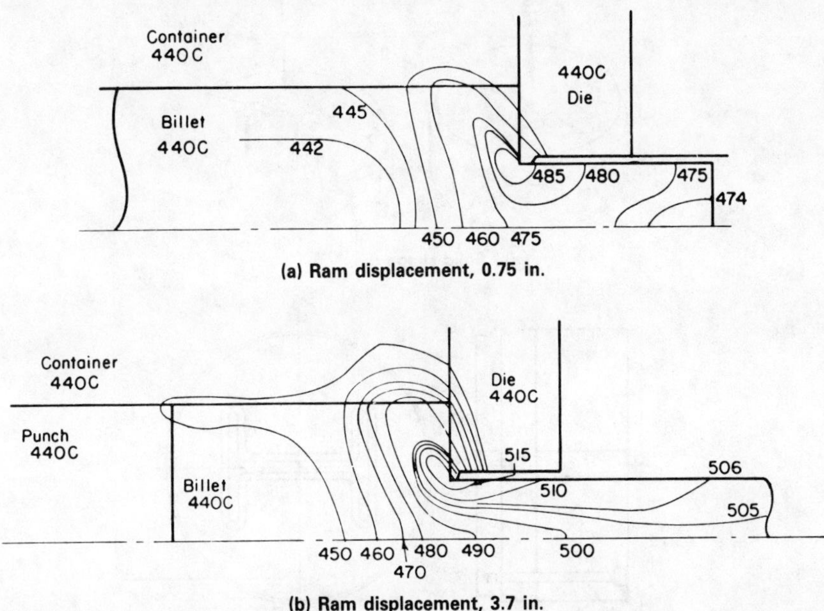

(a) Ram displacement, 0.75 in.

(b) Ram displacement, 3.7 in.

Reduction ratio, 5:1; ram speed, 74.4 in./min; billet diameter, 2.8 in.; billet length, 5.6 in.; initial billet and tooling temperature, 440 C.

Figure 13-16. Temperature distributions in extrusion of aluminum alloy 5052 rod through a flat die.[13-7]

was claimed. This savings would certainly be less for alloys that are more easily extruded.

In extrusion of aluminum alloys, temperature variations in the emerging product can be reduced by imposing a temperature gradient in the billet.[13-12] The billet is inserted into the container such that the hot end is extruded first while the temperature of the cooler end increases during extrusion. This practice is not entirely satisfactory because of the relatively high thermal conductivities of aluminum alloys, so that if any delays occur in the extrusion sequence, the temperatures in the billet tend to become uniform throughout the billet length. A better method is to water quench the feed table to the container. Another approach that has been used to increase extrusion speed is to cool the die with water or nitrogen.

For controlling and predicting variations in ram speed during extrusion, it may be useful to use computer simulations to predict the temperature rise during the process.[13-7,13-8] The purpose of such computer-aided speed control is to attain maximum extrusion speeds with minimum variations in temperature in the extruded product.

Tooling for Nonlubricated Extrusion

As can be seen in Figure 13-2, the major tooling components in extrusion are:

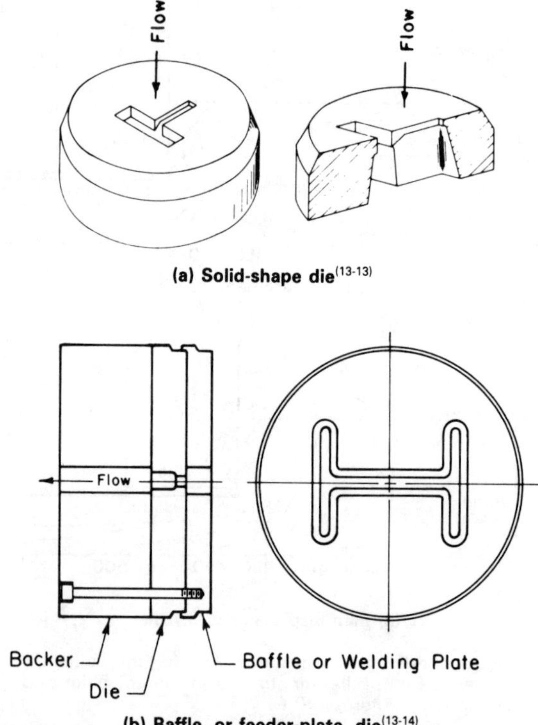

(a) Solid-shape die[13-13]

(b) Baffle, or feeder-plate, die[13-14]

Figure 13-17. Extrusion dies for aluminum alloys.

- Extrusion stem (and mandrel for hollow extrusions).
- Container.
- Die and die holder or die support.

The designs of the extrusion stem and the container are the same regardless of whether solid or hollow products are to be extruded. Bridge and porthole dies (Figure 13-8) are used primarily for aluminum alloys, whereas solid-shape or feeder-plate dies (Figure 13-17) are used for extrusion of solids in aluminum or copper alloys.[13-13,13-14] The feeder-plate design provides smooth feeding of the metal into the die opening. This controls metal flow and assists in obtaining complete filling of the die opening and the desired geometry of the extruded section.

In extrusion of shapes, nonuniform metal flow is present in the deformation zone. This may result, depending on the complexity of the extruded section, in twisting or bending of the product as it emerges from the die. To prevent this, the flow rate of the extruded metal is controlled through proper design of the die land (at the exit side of the die) and by proper positioning of the die opening with respect to the billet axis.[13-15,13-16]

Practical design of die lands for extrusion of shapes is still an art. The land is varied in length according to section width, in order to obtain uniformity of flow. As shown in Figure 13-18, the thinner section is provided with less land than the thicker section.[13-17] An empirical guideline is to keep the land length between 1 and 2 times the section thickness.[13-16] Analytically, die land design has not been investigated extensively. Systematic, theoretical and experimental studies are needed to provide a scientific basis for die land and extrusion die design.

In die design, the position of the die opening with respect to the billet axis is affected by two main considerations:

1. The metal near the extrusion axis tends to flow faster than the metal located near the die and container walls, due to friction at these surfaces. Thus, in design of the die, thinner portions of the shape, with

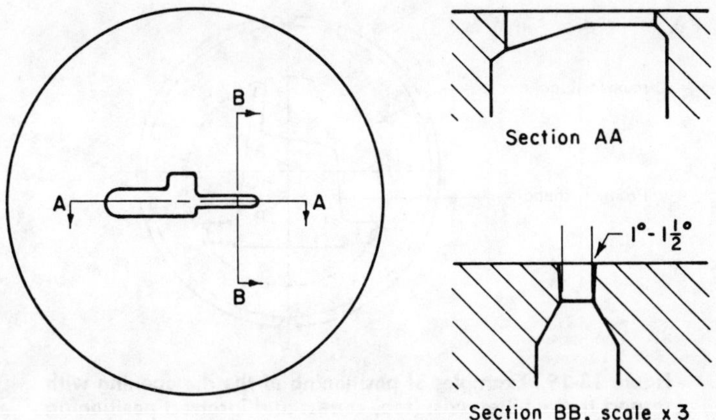

Figure 13-18. Variation of die land length with section thickness.[13-17]

larger perimeter-to-area ratios, are usually moved toward the center. Figure 13-19(top) shows the correct positioning of a die opening with respect to the billet center.[13-18]

2. The rate of metal flow in any segment of the extruded profile can be reduced by "starving" that portion, or can be increased by "feeding" more material to that portion. "Starving" is done by placing the die opening such that less billet material flows into the "starved" portion of the die opening. The opposite is done for "feeding".

Perlin[13-18] suggested an empirical approach for positioning the die opening with respect to the billet axis, R. According to this approach, the center of gravity of the cross section of the extruded profile, P, and the center, Q, of its circumscribing circle are determined, as shown in Figure 13-19(bottom). If points P and Q coincide, or are very close to each other, then one of these points is made to coincide with the center of the billet, R. If P and Q are at a large distance from each other, then the center of the circumscribing circle, Q, is displaced from the center of the billet, R, in a direction toward the center of gravity, P. By this approach, the portion of the profile with the smaller

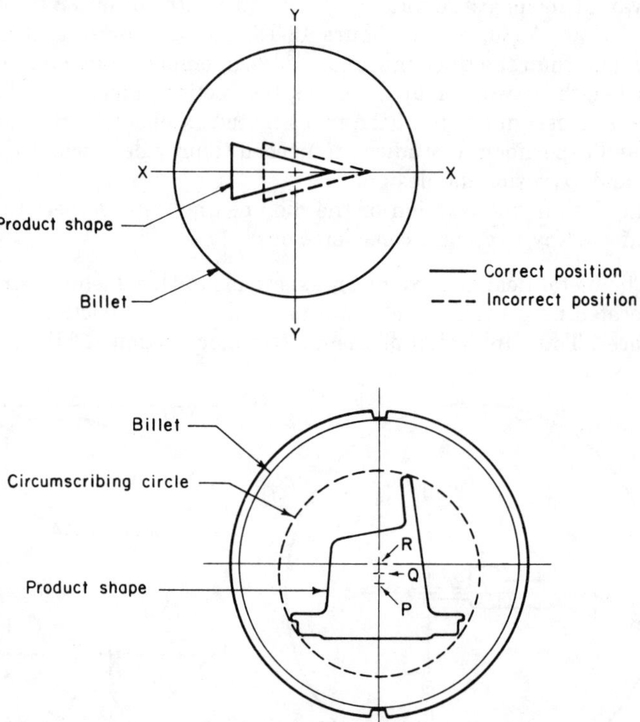

Figure 13-19. Examples of positioning of the die opening with respect to the billet axis: (top) correct and incorrect positioning of the die opening; (bottom) relative positioning of the center of gravity of the shape (P), the center of the circumscribing circle (Q), and the center of the billet (R).[13-18]

cross-sectional area will be opposite the portion of the billet with the larger cross-sectional area, and vice versa.

The unique ability of the aluminum extrusion process to manufacture thin, complex shapes with sharp corner radii immediately poses problems in the design and fabrication of an extrusion die which will have a sufficient practical life. Such an extrusion die must withstand heat, prolonged stresses, thermal shock, and, of course, frictional wear. In general, the 5% chromium hot work tool steels (H-11, H-12, H-13) find their most widespread use as extrusion die materials, because they combine good thoughness and strength with wear and heat resistance. Longer-life tooling (such as backers, bolsters and containers) is most frequently made from lower-alloy steels such as AISI 4140 and 4340. Because these tools still undergo high pressures but do not experience extreme temperatures, somewhat lower-strength materials can be used.

In general, however, today's die-manufacturing techniques do not vary greatly from those employed in the industry over the past several decades. Considerable hand work must be done in the manufacture of a new die, and even more hand grinding and polishing are required in reconditioning used dies in order to enhance their useful life. Thus, the "artistic" factor remains an important part of present die manufacture for extrusion of aluminum. Recently, CAD/CAM techniques have been developed for extrusion design and manufacture. These will be discussed in Chapter 14.

LUBRICATED HOT EXTRUSION

In extrusion, lubrication reduces load and energy requirements, die wear, and temperature increases due to friction and internal shear. In addition, lubrication improves the uniformity of mechanical properties of the extruded product.

Lubricated Extrusion of Aluminum Alloys

Lubricated extrusion of aluminum alloys is not a commonly used practical production process. Some laboratory experiments have indicated that, with adequate lubrication, uniform metal flow (similar to the conditions encountered in cold extrusion) can be obtained. However, inadequate lubrication may easily result in surface defects. While some studies have indicated the impracticality of extruding aluminum alloys with lubrication,[13-19] others have reported promising laboratory experiments. Studies conducted with alloy 2024, a hard aluminum alloy, showed that rounds and L-sections could be extruded at exit speeds over 100 ft/min without surface cracking at a billet temperature of only 550 F.[13-20] It should be noted that these exit speeds are approximately 5 to 10 times the exit speeds encountered in conventional extrusion. This study showed that surface finish improved with increasing extrusion ratio and with increasing extrusion speed. In general, however, the quality of the extruded rods and L-sections was comparable to that of conventionally extruded material.

Despite various published reports on the success of using lubrication in hot extrusion of aluminum alloys, this practice is not widely accepted except when these alloys are extruded using conical (rather than flat-face) dies at or near room temperature, where lubrication at the material/tool interface can be reasonably reproducible and reliable.

Extrusion of High-Strength Materials

Titanium alloys, alloy steels, stainless steels and tool steels are extruded on a commercial basis, using a variety of graphite and glass-base lubricants. Commercial grease mixtures containing solid-film lubricants, such as graphite, often provide little or no thermal protection to the die; therefore, die wear in conventional extrusion of steels and titanium alloys is very significant.[13-21]

The process most commonly used for extrusion of steels and titanium alloys is the Sejournet process.[13-21] In this process, the heated billet is commonly rolled over a bed of ground glass, or sprinkled with glass powder, which supplies a layer of low-melting glass to the billet surface. Prior to insertion of the billet into the hot extrusion container, a suitable die glass lubricating system is positioned immediately ahead of the die. This may consist of a compacted glass pad or glass wool, or both. The prelubricated billet is quickly inserted into the container followed by appropriate followers or a dummy block, and the extrusion cycle is started, as shown in Figure 13-20.

The unique features of glass as a lubricant are its ability to soften selectively during contact with the hot billet and, at the same time, to insulate the hot billet material from the tooling, which is usually maintained at a temperature considerably lower than that of the billet. In extrusion of titanium and steel, billet temperature is usually 1800 to 2300 F, whereas the maximum temperature which tooling can withstand is 900 to 1000 F. Thus, the only way to obtain compatibility between the very hot billet and the considerably cooler tooling is to use appropriate lubricants, insulative die coatings and ceramic die inserts, and to design dies so as to minimize tool wear. To date, glass lubrication has worked successfully on a production basis in extrusion of long lengths.

The actual ram speed attainable during extrusion of steels and titanium varies with alloy composition, extrusion temperature and extrusion ratio, but is usually in the range from 200 to 300 in./min. High extrusion speeds are preferred regardless of whether grease or glass is used as the lubricant. Be-

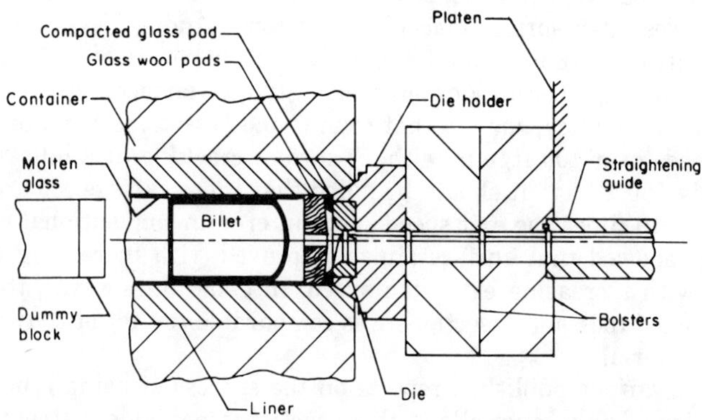

Figure 13-20. Hot extrusion setup using glass lubrication.

cause grease lubricants offer little protection from high extrusion temperatures, the hot billet should be in contact with the die for as short a time as possible. The basic principle of glass lubrication, i.e., glass in a state of incipient fusion flowing continuously from a reservoir, requires high extrusion speeds. With low speeds, the glass reservoir may be depleted before the extrusion stroke is completed, because the melting rate of the glass is a function of time.

Basically, two types of dies are used for extruding steel and titanium: (a) flat-face dies, or modified flat-face dies with radiused entries, and (b) conical-entry dies. It seems that flat-face dies, or modified flat-face dies, are used with glass lubrication provided by a glass pad that forms the die contour at the entrance. The conical-entry die is mostly used with grease lubrication, although in some cases conical-contour dies are also used with glass lubrication.

CHARACTERIZATION OF EXTRUDED SHAPES

Extruded shapes in aluminum alloys are generally characterized according to geometric complexity. This characterization is useful also in classifying shapes extruded from other alloys.

Size of an Extruded Shape

The size of an extruded shape is measured by the diameter of the circle circumscribing the cross section of that shape, as shown in Figure 13-21. This dimension is commonly referred to as the Circumscribing Circle Diameter, or CCD.

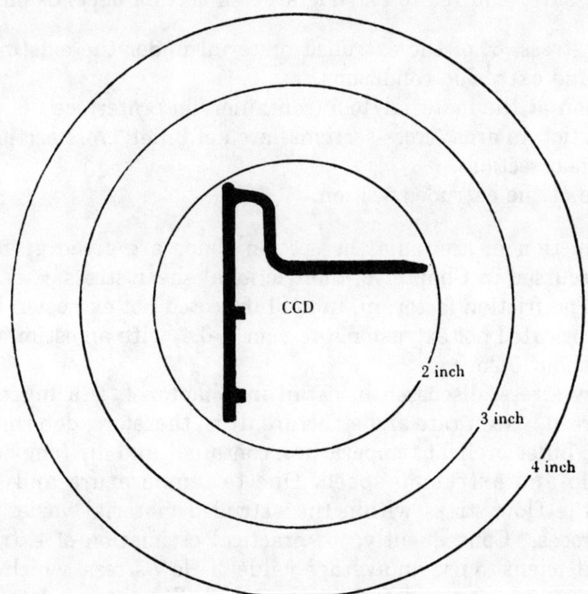

Figure 13-21. Definition of size by circumscribing circle diameter (CCD).

In extrusion, metal tends to flow more slowly at die locations which are far away from the axis of the billet. Therefore, the larger the CCD, the more control is required to maintain the dimensions of the extruded shape. Special care is needed in extruding large and thin shapes, especially those with thin portions near the periphery of the die. Thus, size is one of the factors that describes the complexity of a shape.

Complexity of an Extruded Shape

There are two accepted methods for defining the complexity of an extruded shape. One method is by the use of the shape factor, defined as follows:

$$\text{Shape factor} = \frac{\text{Perimeter, in inches}}{\text{Weight, in pounds per foot}}$$

This factor is a measure of the amount of surface that is generated per pound of metal extruded. The shape factor affects the production rate and the cost of manufacturing and maintaining the dies. It is used by many extruders as a basis for pricing and gives the designer a means of comparing the relative complexities of alternate designs.

The other measure of shape complexity is the classification of extruded shapes into different groups, based on difficulty of extrusion (see Figure 13-9).

PREDICTION OF EXTRUSION PRESSURE

The pressure required to extrude a given section depends on:

- Flow stress, $\bar{\sigma}$, of the extruded material under the existing temperature and extrusion conditions.
- Friction at the material/tool (container/die) interface.
- Reduction in area (cross-sectional area of billet/cross-sectional area of extruded section).
- Shape of the extruded section.

The reduction in area and the section shape are given geometric variables. As discussed in Chapter 6, the frictional shear stress, τ, is given by: $\tau = m\bar{\sigma}/\sqrt{3}$. The friction factor, m, in nonlubricated hot extrusion is given by: $m = 1$. In lubricated hot extrusion, $0.1 \leq m \leq 0.4$, with an estimated average m value of about 0.25.

The flow stress, discussed in detail in Chapter 4, is a function of temperature, strain, strain rate and structure. It is, therefore, determined by billet material, billet preheat temperature, container and die temperatures, extrusion ratio and extrusion speed. Due to temperature and strain-rate variations, the flow stress within the extruded material varies during the extrusion process. Consequently, for practical estimation of extrusion pressure, it is sufficient to use an average value of flow stress, which is assumed to be valid throughout the deforming material. Flow stress data for various alloys are given in Chapter 4.

A simple but practical method of estimating average flow stresses in extrusion studies is back-calculation of flow stress values from measured values of extrusion pressure. For this purpose, an analytical relationship for predicting extrusion pressure can be used. Thus, the calculated flow stress value can then be used for estimating the extrusion pressures for other extrusion ratios and shapes.

A review of theoretical methods and experimental studies reveals that the extrusion pressure, p, near the end of the extrusion stroke (i.e., without container friction) is a nearly linear function of the homogeneous extrusion strain, or:

$$p = a\ln(A_B/A_S) + b \tag{13-1}$$

where p is the extrusion pressure, A_B is the cross-sectional area of the billet, A_S is the cross-sectional area of the extruded section, and a and b are empirical constants which depend on material, press speed, temperatures and section geometry.

Extrusion pressures as functions of the homogeneous strain, $\ln(A_B/A_S)$, are given in Figure 13-22 for various alloys.[13-22] As indicated in Equation 13-1, pressure increases nearly linearly with strain. Values of parameters a and b are available in the literature[13-1] for some extrusion conditions.

USE OF SLAB METHOD FOR PREDICTION OF LOAD IN AXISYMMETRIC EXTRUSION

Considering average values of strain, $\bar{\epsilon}$, strain rate, $\dot{\bar{\epsilon}}$, and flow stress, $\bar{\sigma}$, the extrusion load, P, is given by:

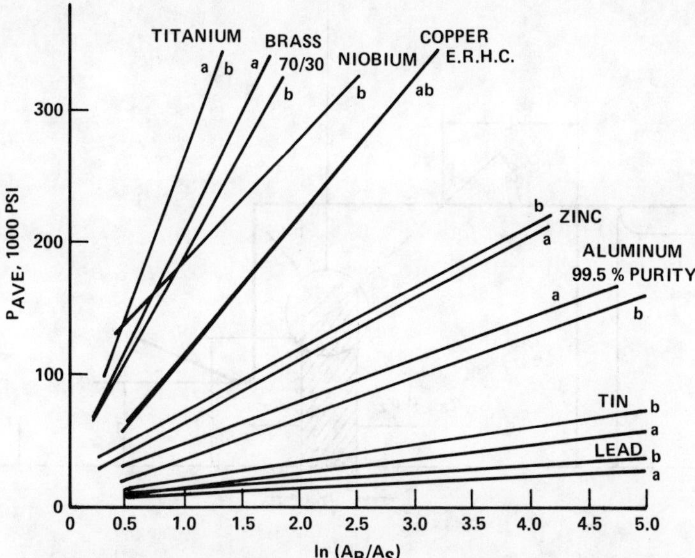

Figure 13-22. Maximum pressures required for extrusion of rods over a range of reductions in different metals: (a) relatively low ram speeds ranging from 0.4 to 5.5 in./min, (b) high ram speeds ranging from 1.3 to 15.7 in/s.[13-22]

$$P = P_{fd} + P_{fc} + P_{dh} + P_{ds} \tag{13-2}$$

where P_{fd} and P_{fc} are the loads necessary to overcome die and container frictions, respectively, and P_{dh} and P_{ds} are the loads necessary to carry out the homogeneous and shear deformations, respectively.

Container Friction

In the cylindrical portion of the deforming material, i.e., over length "L" in Figure 13-23, the load necessary to overcome the container friction is calculated by considering the frictional shear stress, τ, and the surface area over which τ acts. Thus:

$$P_{fc} = 2\Pi r_0 L \tau_c \tag{13-3}$$

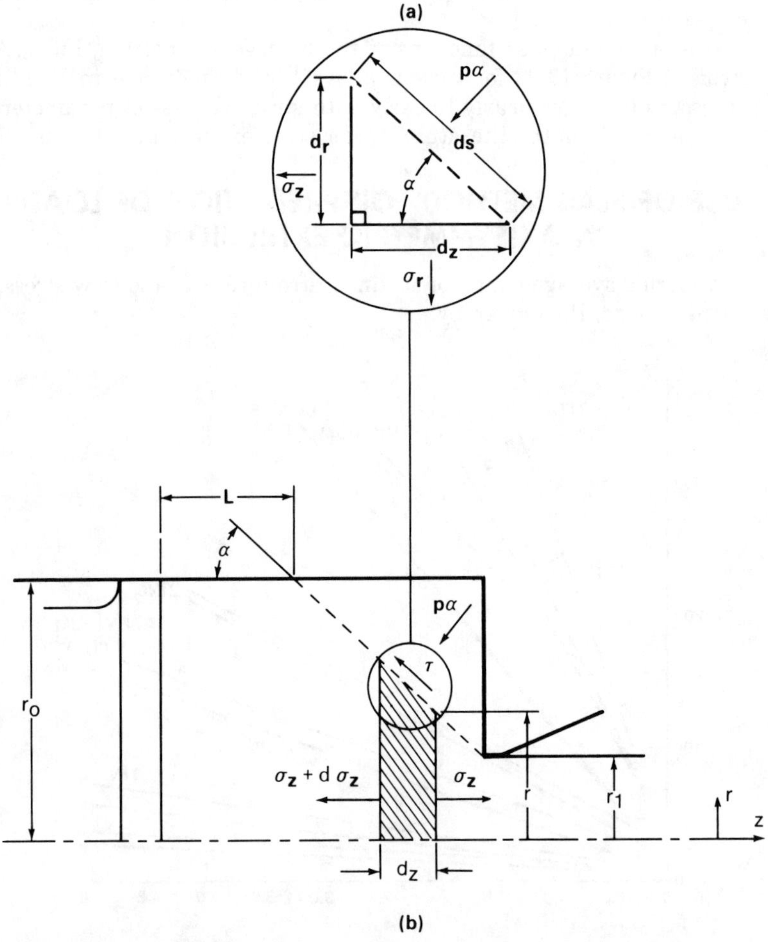

Figure 13-23. Schematic of stresses in extrusion of a round section from a round billet: (a) radial and axial stresses and normal pressure at interface, (b) stresses acting on a "slab".

where r_0 is the radius of the container, L is the length of the cylindrical portion of the deforming material and τ_c is the frictional shear stress at the container surface ($\tau_c = m_c\bar{\sigma}/\sqrt{3}$).

Force Equilibrium in the Conical Deformation Zone

Following Figure 13-23, the equilibrium of forces in a slab of infinitesimal thickness, dz, in the axial z direction gives:

$$(\sigma_z + d\sigma_z)(r + dr)^2\Pi - \Pi r^2\sigma_z + p_\alpha 2\Pi r\, ds \sin\alpha$$
$$+ \tau 2\Pi r\, ds \cos\alpha = 0 \tag{13-4}$$

where σ_z and $d\sigma_z$ are the axial stress and the incremental change in axial stress, respectively; r and dr are the radius and the incremental change in radius, respectively; p_α is the normal pressure at the "die" surface; and $ds = dr/\sin\alpha = dz/\cos\alpha$.

Following Figure 13-23(a), the radial force balance at the "die" surface of the slab under consideration gives:

$$p_\alpha\, ds \cos\alpha + \sigma_r dz = \tau\, ds \sin\alpha, \quad \text{or}$$
$$p_\alpha = \tau \tan\alpha - \sigma_r \tag{13-5}$$

With the von Mises flow rule, $\sigma_z - \sigma_r = \bar{\sigma}$, Equation 13-5 gives:

$$p_\alpha = \tau \tan\alpha + \bar{\sigma} - \sigma_z \tag{13-6}$$

By expansion and simplification, Equation 13-4 is transformed into:

$$2r\, dr\, \sigma_z + r^2 d\sigma_z + 2p_\alpha r\, dr + 2r\, dr\, \tau/\tan\alpha = 0 \tag{13-7}$$

Equations 13-6 and 13-7 result in:

$$r^2 d\sigma_z + 2(\tau \tan\alpha + \bar{\sigma})r\, dr + 2r\, dr\, \tau/\tan\alpha = 0 \tag{13-8}$$

Further simplification and integration give:

$$-\sigma_z = 2(\tau \tan\alpha + \bar{\sigma} + \tau/\tan\alpha)(\ln r) + C \tag{13-9}$$

The following boundary conditions must be satisfied:

- At $r = r_1$, i.e., at the exit from the "die":

$$\sigma_z = 0$$

or, from Equation 13-9:

$$C = -2\left(\tau \tan\alpha + \bar{\sigma} + \frac{\tau}{\tan\alpha}\right)\ln r_1$$

○ At $r = r_0$, i.e., at the entrance into the "die":

$$\sigma_{z0} = -\ln (A_0/A_1)\left(\tau \tan \alpha + \bar{\sigma} + \frac{\tau}{\tan \alpha}\right) \tag{13-10}$$

where $\ln (A_0/A_1) = 2 \ln (r_0/r_1)$ and where A_0 and A_1 are the cross-sectional areas of the billet and the extrusion, respectively.

Equation 13-10 can also be written in the form:

$$-\sigma_{z0} = \bar{\sigma} \ln (A_0/A_1) + \frac{\tau \ln (A_0/A_1)}{\sin \alpha \cos \alpha} \tag{13-11}$$

In Equation 13-11, the first term is the homogeneous deformation and the second term is the "die" friction, i.e., using the expressions of Equations 13-1:

$$P_{dh} = \bar{\sigma} \ln (A_0/A_1)\Pi r_0^2 \tag{13-12}$$

and

$$P_{fd} = \frac{\tau_d \ln (A_0/A_1)}{\sin \alpha \cos \alpha} \Pi r_0^2 \tag{13-13}$$

where τ_d is the frictional shear stress at the "die" surface.

Shear Deformation

At the entrance into and the exit from the conical "die" zone, the material undergoes nonhomogeneous shear deformation. The energy and load necessary to perform this deformation can be estimated. For this purpose, it is useful to approximate this shear deformation as occurring suddenly at the assumed discontinuity surfaces, as shown in Figure 13-24. At the entrance boundary, the component of the material velocity normal to the boundary surface is continuous. The velocity discontinuity, ΔV, parallel to this surface is:

$$\Delta V = V_0 \sin \theta \tag{13-14}$$

where V_0 is the billet or ram velocity.

The shear energy rate at a given point on this surface of discontinuity at the entrance is:

$$d\dot{W}_E = \tau \Delta V \, dA \tag{13-15}$$

where τ is the shear stress ($\tau = m\bar{\sigma}/\sqrt{3}$, with $m = 1$), ΔV is the velocity discontinuity, from Equation 13-14, and dA is the surface element (parallel to the velocity discontinuity, ΔV) where shear occurs. With the symbols and geometry given in Figure 13-24:

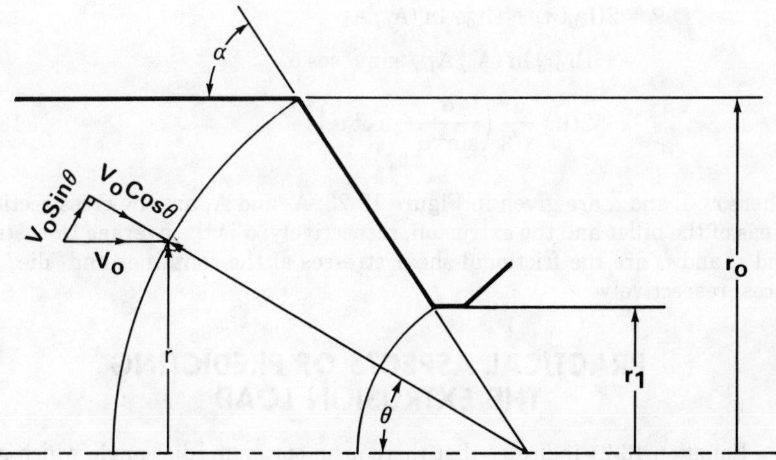

Figure 13-24. Schematic illustration of velocity discontinuity at entrance into deformation zone.

$$R = r_0/\sin\alpha \tag{13-16}$$

$$r = R\sin\theta;\quad dr = R\cos\theta\, d\theta \tag{13-17}$$

$$dA = 2\Pi r(dr/\cos\theta) = 2\Pi R^2\sin\theta\, d\theta \tag{13-18}$$

Thus, Equations 13-14, 13-15 and 13-18 give:

$$\dot{W}_E = \frac{\bar{\sigma}}{\sqrt{3}} V_0 2\Pi R^2 \int_0^\alpha \sin^2\theta\, d\theta$$

$$= V_0 \Pi R^2 \frac{\bar{\sigma}}{\sqrt{3}}[\alpha - (\sin\alpha)\cos\alpha]$$

with Equation 13-16

$$= V_0 \Pi r_0^2 \frac{\bar{\sigma}}{\sqrt{3}}\left(\frac{\alpha}{\sin^2\alpha} - \cot\alpha\right) \tag{13-19}$$

Shear occurs at the entrance into and the exit from the "die" zone; therefore, the total shear energy rate is $\dot{W}_T = 2\dot{W}_E$. Thus, the portion of the extrusion load necessary to overcome the shear energy is:

$$P_{ds} = \dot{W}_T/V_0 = 2\Pi r_0^2 \frac{\bar{\sigma}}{\sqrt{3}}\left(\frac{\alpha}{\sin^2\alpha} - \cot\alpha\right) \tag{13-20}$$

Equations 13-3, 13-12, 13-13 and 13-20 give the expressions for various components of the extrusion load. Thus, the total extrusion load, given by Equation 13-2 is:

$$P = 2\Pi r_0 L \tau_c + \Pi r_0^2 \bar{\sigma} \ln (A_0/A_1) + \Pi r_0^2 \tau_d \ln (A_0/A_1)/(\sin \alpha \cos \alpha) + 2\Pi r_0^2 \frac{\bar{\sigma}}{\sqrt{3}} \left(\frac{\alpha}{\sin^2 \alpha} - \cot \alpha \right) \quad (13\text{-}21)$$

where r_0, L and α are given in Figure 13-23; A_0 and A_1 are the cross-sectional areas of the billet and the extrusion, respectively; $\bar{\sigma}$ is the average flow stress; and τ_c and τ_d are the frictional shear stresses at the container and "die" surfaces, respectively.

PRACTICAL ASPECTS OF PREDICTING THE EXTRUSION LOAD

Equation 13-21 indicates that there is an optimum "die" angle which gives the lowest extrusion load. This angle can be obtained by minimizing this expression, or by solving the equality:

$$\partial P/\partial \alpha = 0 \quad (13\text{-}22)$$

However, for practical hot extrusion applications, it is sufficient to assume that $\alpha = 45°$, since the "die" angle is formed by metal flow itself and is not a well-defined angle (as it is in cold extrusion, for example).

Equations derived by methods other than the slab method can also be used for predicting the extrusion load. A good example is the expression, given by Avitzur,[13-23] derived by using the upper-bound method of analysis. This expression is slightly more complicated than Equation 13-21 and has been shown to be reasonably accurate. The application of upper-bound-base formulas for calculating extrusion loads is also summarized in Reference 13-24.

In most production applications, the extrusion container is cylindrical but the extruded section is not. It is also the usual practice to provide several openings in the die to decrease the extrusion ratio and to increase the production rate. In the case of multihole dies, it is necessary to approximate all the die openings as one single die opening with a cross-sectional area equal to the sum of the cross-sectional areas of all the openings. Studies conducted on the influence of extrusion shape on extrusion load showed that, for the same extrusion ratio, nonsymmetric sections may require loads 1.2 to 2.5 times larger than those required by equivalent round sections.[13-1] This is illustrated in Figure 13-25. The round extrusion, with a 90° "die" angle and a 6-mm die land, required a load 2.1 times smaller than that required by the nonsymmetric section shown in this figure. Both sections had the same cross-sectional area.

A practical method of estimating extrusion pressures for shapes is to consider a shape factor, i.e.:

$$P = P_0 C$$

where P is the extrusion load for the shape under consideration, P_0 is the extrusion load for a round bar of equivalent cross-sectional area, and C is a

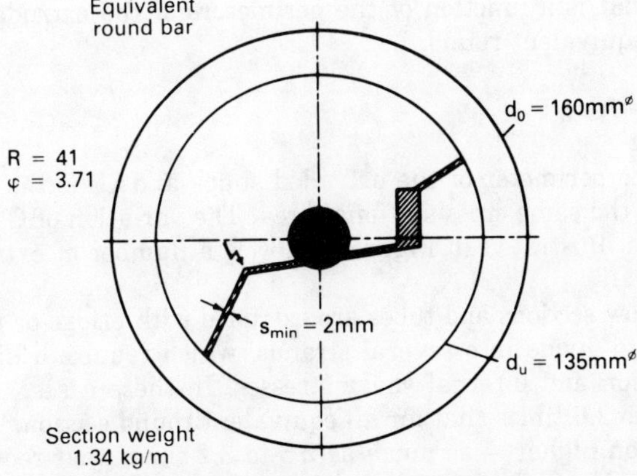

Reduction ratio, 41; homogeneous strain, 3.71. d_0 is container diameter; d_u is circumscribing circle diameter; S_{min} is minimum wall thickness.

Figure 13-25. Comparison of an open section (weight, 1.34 kg/m) with an equivalent round bar (25-mm diam).[13-1]

	Material	Symbol	Load	Lubricant	φ
Ref 69	Lead	—·—	$P_{max.}$	None	2.15
		—··—	$P_{min.}$		
	Al99.5	——	P_A	Oil-graphite	
	AlMgSi1	----			
Ref 74	Al alloy	△	$P_{min.}$	None	4.3
Ref 75	Al99.5	◊	$P_{max.}$		3.7
			$P_{min.}$		
Ref 76	Pure lead	□	$P_{min.}$	Not stated	1.4
Ref 12	Tin	○	$P_{max.}$	None	
			$P_{min.}$		

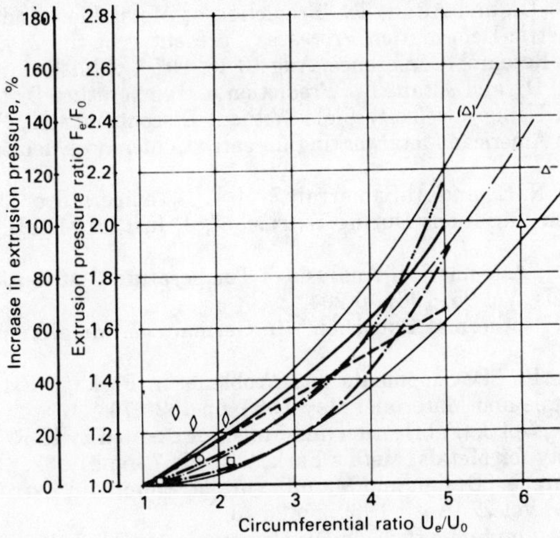

Figure 13-26. Increase in extrusion load as a function of the perimeter ratio, U_e/U_0, in direct extrusion of sections.[13-1]

shape factor that is a function of the perimeters of the extruded shape and of that of an equivalent round, i.e.:

$$C = f(U_e/U_0)$$

where U_e is the perimeter of the extruded shape and U_0 is the perimeter of a round bar of the same cross-sectional area. The variation of C with various U_e/U_0 ratios is illustrated in Figure 13-26 for a number of extrusion conditions.

When hollow sections and tubes are extruded with bridge or porthole dies, the billet has to divide into several strands, which require a higher load to overcome friction and internal shear stresses. In these cases, the extrusion load can be 2 to 2.6 times that for an equivalent round section. The required load can be even higher — as much as 2.5 to 3.2 times that required for the equivalent round section — in the case of multihole dies.

REFERENCES

13-1. Laue, K., and Stenger, H., *"Extrusion: Processes, Machinery, Tooling"*, American Society for Metals, Metals Park, OH, 1981.

13-2. Byrer, T. G., *et al,* "Design Guide for Use of Structural Shapes in Aircraft Applications", Battelle-Columbus Laboratories, Columbus, OH, Technical Report AFML-TR-73-211, Sept 1973.

13-3. Laue, K., "Possibilities of Materal Related Design of Light Alloy Sections" (in German), Z. F. Metallkunde, Vol 54, 1963, p 667.

13-4. Akeret, R., and Stratman, P. M., "Unconventional Extrusion Processes for the Harder Aluminum Alloys", Parts I and II, Light Metal Age, April 1973, p 6-10; and June 1973, pp 15-18.

13-5. Singer, A. R. E., and Coakham, J. W., "Temperature Changes Occurring During the Extrusion of Aluminum, Tin and Lead", J. Inst. of Metals, Vol 89, 1961-62, p 177.

13-6. Akeret, R., "A Numerical Analysis of Temperature Distribution in Extrusion", J. Inst. Metals, Vol 95, 1967, p 204.

13-7. Lahoti, G. D., and Altan, T., "Prediction of Metal Flow and Temperatures in Axisymmetric Deformation Processes", presented at the 21st Sagamore Army Materials Research Conference, Aug 13-16, 1974, published in the Proceedings.

13-8. Lahoti, G. D., and Altan, T., "Prediction of Temperature Distributions in Tube Extrusion Using a Velocity Field Without Discontinuities", Proceedings of the 2nd North American Metalworking Research Conference, Madison, WI, May 1974, pp 209-224.

13-9. Singer, A. R. E., and Al-Samarrai, S. H. K., "Temperature Changes Associated with Speed Variations During Extrusion", J. Inst. of Metals, Vol 89, 1960-61, p 225.

13-10. Akeret, R., "A Numerical Analysis of Temperature Distribution in Extrusion", J. of Metals, Vol 95, 1967, p 204.

13-11. Laue, K., "Isothermal Extrusion" (in German), Z. Metallkunde, Vol 51, 1960, pp 491.

13-12. Chadwick, R., "Developments and Problems in Package Extrusion Press Design", Metals and Materials, May 1969, pp 162-170.

13-13. *Aluminum,* Vol 3, (Fabrication and Finishing), edited by K. R. Van Horn, American Society for Metals, Metals Park, OH, 1967, pp 81-132.

13-14. Carl DeBuigne, "Design and Manufacture of Aluminum Extrusion Dics", Light Metal Age, Vol 27, April 1969, pp 28-33.

13-15. Bello, L., *Aluminum Extrusion Die Correction,* 1st Ed., Fellom Publications, San Francisco.

13-16. Mockli, P., and Locher, M., "State of the Art in Making Extrusion Dies", Aluminum (in German), 1965, p 629.
13-17. Chadwick, R., "The Hot Extrusion of Nonferrous Metals", Metallurgical Reviews, Vol 4, No. 15, 1959, pp 189-255.
13-18. Perlin, I. L., *Theory of Metal Extrusion,* published by "Metallurgiya", Moscow, 1964 (English translation FTD-HT-23-616-67).
13-19. Akeret, R., "Research in the Nonferrous Metal Product Industry, Part XX, Effects of Lubricating the Container on the Extrusion of Aluminum and Aluminum Alloys" (in German), Z. Metallkunde, Vol 55, No. 10, 1964, pp 570-573.
13-20. Nichols, D. E., Byrer, T. G., and Sabroff, A. M., "Lubricated Extrusion of 2024 Aluminum Alloy Using Conical and Conical-Flat Dies", Summary Report to Battelle Development Corporation, Battelle-Columbus Laboratories, Columbus, OH, Jan 23, 1970.
13-21. Sejournet, J., and Delcroix, J., "Glass Lubricant in the Extrusion of Steel", Lubrication Engineering, Vol 11, 1955, p 389.
13-22. Thomsen, E. G., Yang, C. T., and Kobayashi, S., "Mechanics of Plastic Deformation in Metal Processing", The Macmillan Co., New York, 1965.
13-23. Avitzur, B., "Metal Forming: Process and Analysis", McGraw-Hill Book Co., New York, 1968.
13-24. Nagpal, V., Billhardt, C. F., Gagne, R., and Altan, T., "Automated Design of Extrusion Dies by Computer", paper submitted to International Aluminum Extrusion Technology Seminar, Atlanta, Nov 15-17, 1977.

CHAPTER 14
CAD/CAM Applications in Hot Extrusion

Structural shapes with uniform cross sections, such as T-, L-, Z-, H- and U-shape sections (and others), are usually manufactured by direct or indirect extrusion methods, as discussed in Chapter 13. In hot extrusion of aluminum and copper alloys, container lubrication is not used and the dies are of the "flat-face" type, with the die opening imparting the desired section geometry to the extrusion. In extrusion of steels, titanium alloys and other high-temperature materials, glass- or graphite-base lubricants are used. The dies have some sort of "smooth entry" design to provide for easy metal flow and to avoid severe internal shear, or a dead-metal zone, during extrusion. "Smooth entry" dies are also used successfully for extruding composite materials. In these applications, internal shear, which occurs in extrusion with flat dies, must be avoided in order to maintain the integrity and the uniformity of the composite structure.

In today's industrial practice, the design of extrusion dies, whether of the "flat-face" or the "smooth entry" type, is still an art rather than a science. Die design for a new extrusion is developed from previous experience and through costly experimentation and in-plant trials. Thus, process and die development may require relatively long periods of time and may tie up extrusion presses that should be used preferably for actual production. To reduce the costs of designing and manufacturing extrusion dies, automated design systems have been developed for both nonlubricated and lubricated extrusion processes.[14-1 to 14-4]

Many years of experience lie behind the production of extrusion dies with increasing complexity of shape, thinness of section and quality of surface. Some of this experience is rationalized in empirical design rules, but much die design is still dependent on personal judgment, intuition and experience. The dies are proven out through production of trial extrusions. Invariably, the die orifice is corrected to achieve the required control of cross-sectional dimensions, straightness and surface quality.

The objectives of applying computer-aided design techniques to extrusion are:

- To provide a scientific basis and rationalize the die-design procedure as much as possible.
- To improve productivity by reducing the trials and corrections needed to prove out the dies.
- To optimize die design so as to achieve optimum material yield and maximum productivity.
- To reduce the lead time required for designing and manufacturing the die.
- To reduce die manufacturing costs by using cost-effective numerical control (NC) machining techniques whenever appropriate.

COMPUTER-AIDED DESIGN OF FLAT-FACE DIES

Flat-face dies are primarily used for extrusion of aluminum alloys and basically consist of flat disks of tool steel containing one or more shaped orifices.[14-5] The hot metal is forced (extruded) through these orifices to produce the desired sections, as shown in Figure 14-1. The detailed design of the die involves determination of the following:

- Optimum number of shaped orifices in the die.
- Location of the orifices relative to the billet axis for uniform metal flow through each orifice.
- Orientation of the orifices.
- Modification of the shape of the orifices to correct for thermal shrinkage and die deflection under load.
- Determination of bearing lengths for balancing metal flow.

The details of a computer-aided design (CAD) technique for flat-face dies are given in References 14-3 and 14-5, where the capabilities and application of an interactive CAD program, called ALEXTR, are described. An overview

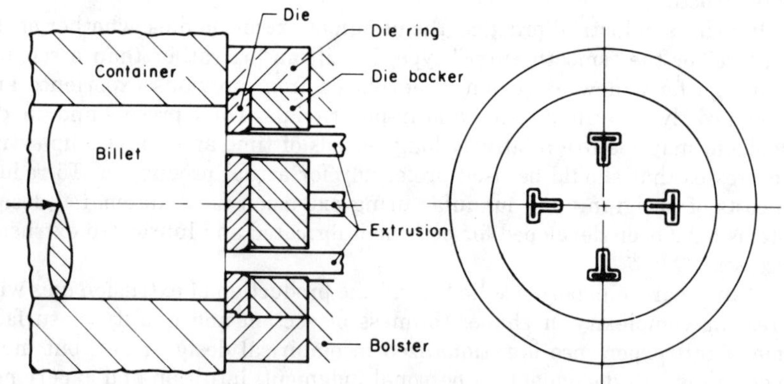

Figure 14-1. Schematic illustration of a flat-face die for extrusion of "T" sections.[14-3]

of the operation of this program is presented in Figure 14-2. The first input into the program is the cross section of the extrusion, expressed in terms of x,y coordinates and the associated fillet or corner radii. These data are used to calculate geometric parameters such as cross-sectional area, perimeter, shape factor (perimeter/weight/length), location of centroid, and size and location of the circumscribing circle. The extrusion shape and the circumscribing circle are displayed on the graphics terminal with the calculated geometric variables.

Next, ALEXTR determines the number of extrusion orifices in the die.[14-3] For this purpose, the user is asked to enter the specific press number (among several available), the alloy to be used and the extrusion temperature. For each available press, characteristics such as press capacity, container diameter, maximum billet length, runout length, etc., are stored in a data table. By use of this information, load and yield calculations are made. The yield Y, in percent, is defined as:

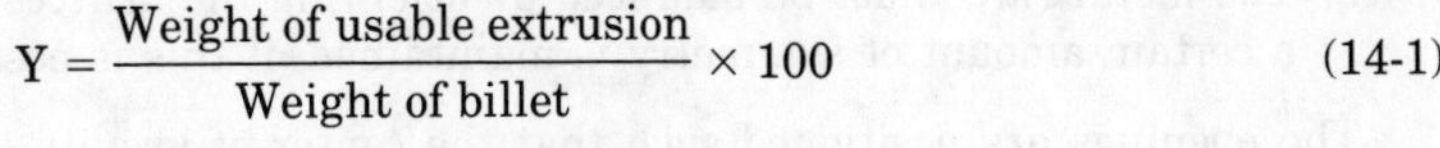

$$Y = \frac{\text{Weight of usable extrusion}}{\text{Weight of billet}} \times 100 \quad (14\text{-}1)$$

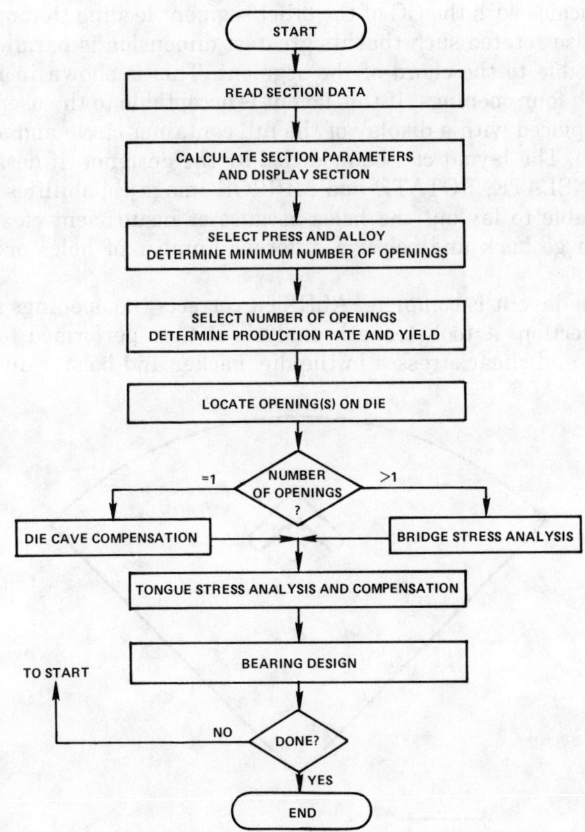

Figure 14-2. General operation of ALEXTR.[14-3]

Because the load decreases as the number of openings increases, the program makes the first load calculation based on a single opening. If the result exceeds the press capacity, the calculation is repeated until the expected load is less than the press capacity or until the number of openings required is greater than the number allowed by the defined press characteristics. The number of openings is selected on the basis of (a) operator specifications, (b) maximum extrusion length or (c) maximum material yield. The program also determines the optimum billet size for the number of openings to be used.

The next step in the design process is layout of the extrusion orifices. This step considers that:

1. Certain minimum clearances have to be maintained (a) between the die openings, so that the die and the backup tooling have the strength to withstand the extrusion pressure, and (b) between the die opening and the cylinder wall, to avoid flow of metal from the outside surface of the billet into the product.
2. The metal flow must be balanced by orienting the orifices such that a certain amount of symmetry is maintained, if this is possible.

The openings are positioned such that the center of gravity (CG) of an opening coincides with the CG of the billet segment feeding that opening. The opening is also rotated such that its greatest dimension is parallel to and as close as possible to the chord of the segment. This is shown in Figure 14-3 for a die with four openings. If this layout is acceptable to the user, the single display is replaced with a display of the full container circle and all openings (Figure 14-4). The layout can be modified by the designer, if desired, by use of the TRANSLATE, ROTATE and MIRROR image capabilities of the program. If unable to lay out the holes because of insufficient clearances, the designer can go back and select a different number of holes or a different press.

After the layout is complete, ALEXTR corrects the openings for die cave and die deflection. A tool-strength analysis is then performed to determine the bending and shear stresses in the die, backer and bolster due to the ex-

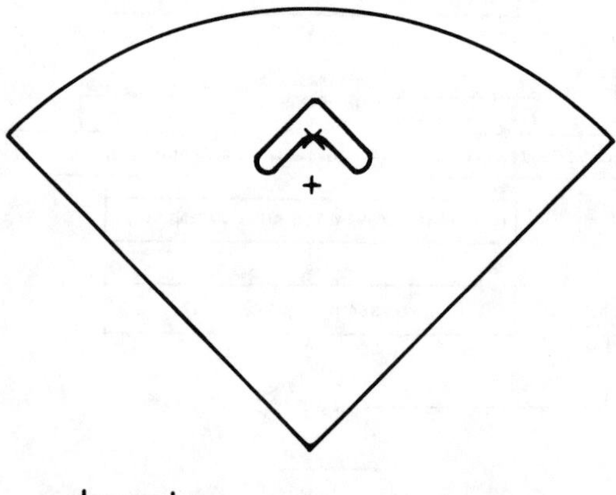

Figure 14-3. Extrusion section placed in one quadrant of die.

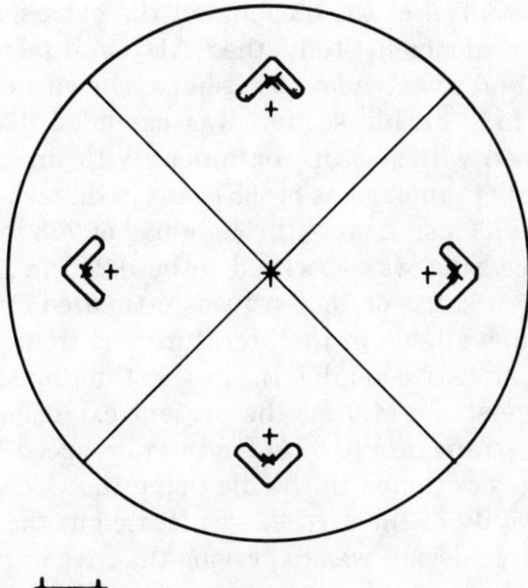

Figure 14-4. Arrangement of entire die by repeating layout of segment shown in Figure 14-3.

trusion pressure. The need for conforming tools to support the die is also determined by the tool-strength analysis. These calculations allow the user to evaluate the need for support tooling. Die deflection analysis also includes estimation of the "bending" of the die at various locations. This information is helpful in predicting the dimensional changes in the die orifices under load, during extrusion. Thus, the dimensions of the die orifices can be modified to correct for these dimensional changes in order to obtain the desired tolerances in the extruded shape.

The next step in the design process is determination of die-bearing lengths. The die bearing at any position is dependent on the section thickness at that position and on its distance from the die center. The designer indicates, with the light pen on the screen of the graphics terminal, the applicable thicknesses at various points on the extrusion perimeter. These dimensions are used by the computer program to calculate the die-bearing lengths.

COMPUTER-AIDED MANUFACTURE AND EVALUATION OF FLAT-FACE DIES

After die design has been completed, the geometric design information can be used to manufacture the dies via numerical control (NC) techniques.

For manufacturing extrusion dies, either conventional Electro Discharge Machining (EDM) or wire EDM is used. In the first case, two EDM electrodes are machined via NC; one electrode is used for EDM'ing the die opening(s) from the billet entry side, and the other is used for EDM'ing the die bearings from the exit side of the die. In wire EDM'ing, a wire electrode can be used for machining of the die opening. However, the backside of the die, i.e., the bearing areas, still must be machined conventionally by milling or by conventional EDM. NC programs are also used for preparing the templates for dimensional quality control of the dies and of the extrusion.

In an example development study, the CAD/CAM technique was used to make flat-face dies and to extrude a "T" shape, shown in Figure 14-5, from aluminum alloy 7075.[14-3] This section was extruded using a 700-ton hydraulic press equipped with a 3-in. container. With an average bearing of 0.187 in., starting billet dimensions of 2.875 in. in diameter and 6.0 in. long, and a flow stress of 7500 psi, a breakthrough load of 263 tons was calculated. When the average bearing was specified to be 0.250 in., the expected load was 273 tons. The flow stress of 7500 psi was estimated for the present billet of Al 7075 from data available in the literature and from preliminary extrusion tests with a round extrusion die. In these estimations, calculations were made for the average strain (4.0 for the present extrusion ratio of approximately 15 to 1) and strain rate (0.37/s for the ram speed of 16 in./min).

The opening was positioned in the die using the CAD-generated layout, i.e., the center of gravity of the section was located at the center of the container. The next step in design was to provide the cave or dish compensation. This was applied to the long side of the base of the "T". Points H and A were indicated as the cave axis end points and then a new point, J, was added. The cave compensation rate was 0.004 in./in. The stress on the tongues was then determined. The tongues were defined by points BCD and EFG in Figure 14-5.

The final step in the die design process was to indicate the section thicknesses and bearing transition points. The die design data were then saved on a disk file for subsequent access by NC programs. Thus, this geometry was used for NC machining of the EDM electrodes and the die bearings. The die opening, in H-13 die steel with a hardness of HRC 42 to 46, was EDM'ed through the die from the front. The die bearings were machined by NC from the back. Figure 14-6 shows a model of the die. This model was made of aluminum, but was machined in the same way as the steel die. It was sectioned as shown, to illustrate the bearing contours.

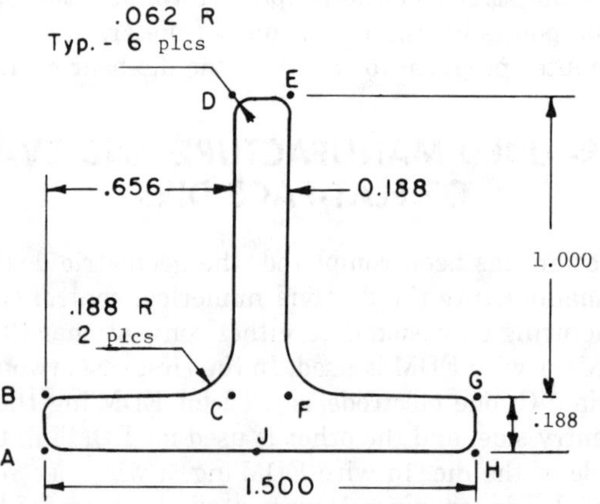

Figure 14-5. "T" shape used to test a CAD/CAM system.[14-3]

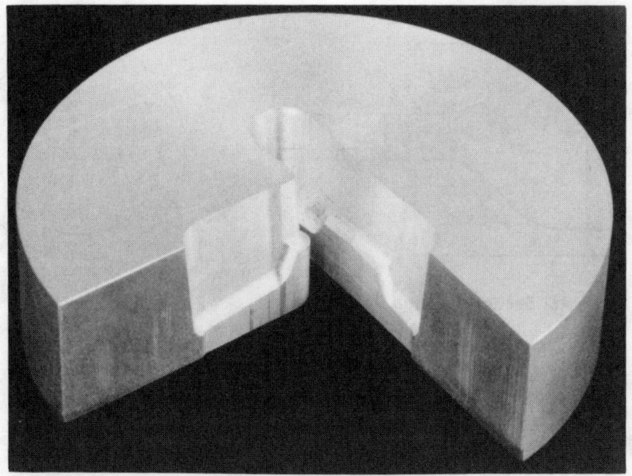

Figure 14-6. Sectioned model of CAD/CAM-made flat-face extrusion die, showing contours of bearings.

COMPUTER-AIDED DESIGN OF LUBRICATED EXTRUSION DIES

Lubrication in extrusion reduces load and energy requirements, reduces tool wear, improves surface finish, and provides a product with nearly uniform properties. This technique is commonly used in extruding shapes from steels, titanium alloys and nickel alloys. Proper die design is critical in lubricated extrusion, especially when noncircular shapes are extruded. An effective die design must ensure smooth metal flow with consistent lubrication. It is desirable to use "streamlined" dies, which provide a smooth transition for the billet from the round or rectangular container to the shaped-die exit.

Recently, computer-aided design (CAD) techniques were developed for design of dies for lubricated extrusion.[14-4,14-6] For example, the design of a "streamlined" die for extruding a "T" shape from a round billet is illustrated schematically in Figure 14-7. The geometry of this die should be optimized to (a) give a defect-free extrusion requiring minimum post-extrusion treatment (twisting and straightening), (b) minimize load and energy requirements, and (c) yield maximum throughput at minimum cost. The design procedure for determining the optimal shape of the die involves the following three steps:

1. Define the die geometry in a general manner.
2. Calculate the extrusion load as a function of the die geometry.
3. Optimize and determine the die shape which requires the minimum extrusion load.

To define the die geometry for a "T" extrusion, first the position of the die opening with respect to the container axis is determined. As shown in

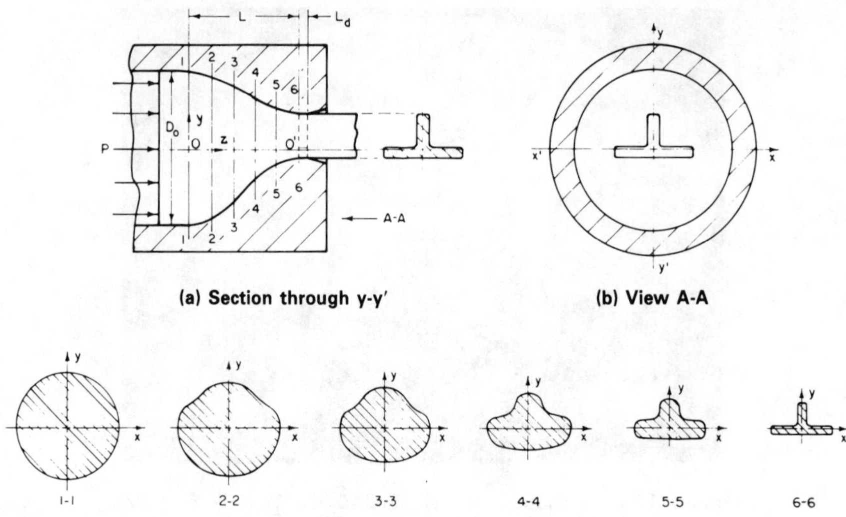

(a) Section through y-y′

(b) View A-A

(c) Cross sections of the billet during extrusion

Figure 14-7. Schematic illustration of a streamlined die for extrusion of a "T" shape.[14-6]

Figure 14-8, the symmetry line, x′-x, of the die opening coincides with one of the symmetry lines of the round container. The position of point 0′ in this figure is such that the ratio of area 5′0′1′ to area 50′1 is equal to the overall extrusion area reduction, i.e., the ratio of the cross-sectional area of the billet to the cross-sectional area of the extruded "T" shape.

The initially circular cross section of the billet is then divided into a number of sectors, as shown in Figure 14-8. Starting from a plane of symmetry, the final cross section is divided into the same number of segments. This is done while keeping the extrusion ratios (ratio of the area of a sector in the

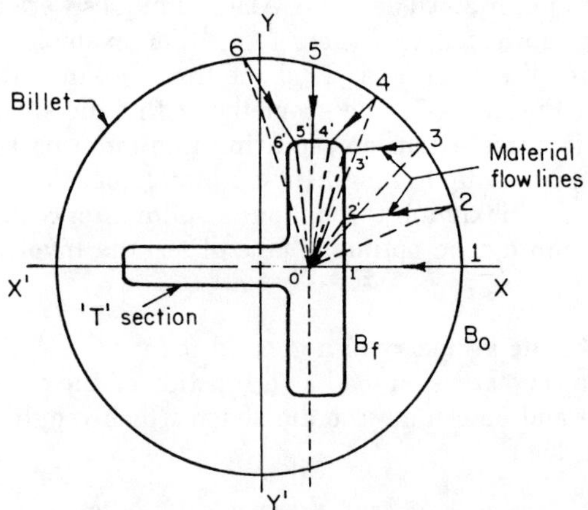

Figure 14-8. Construction of a streamlined die surface in extrusion of a "T" section (see also Figures 14-9 and 14-10).[14-6]

billet to the area of the corresponding segment in the product) equal to the over-all extrusion ratio. Thus:

$$\frac{\text{Area } 012}{\text{Area } 01'2'} = \frac{\text{Area } 023}{\text{Area } 02'3'} \cdots = \frac{\text{Area } 056}{\text{Area } 05'6'} = \frac{A_0}{A_f} \qquad (14\text{-}2)$$

According to this construction, the material points at positions 1, 2, 3, 4, 5 and 6 on boundary B_0 of the initial cross section move during extrusion to positions 1′, 2′, 3′, 4′, 5′ and 6′, respectively, on boundary B_f of the final cross section. Thus, the initial and final positions of the material flow lines along the die surface are determined. The path followed by any material point between the initial and final positions is determined by calculating and optimizing the extrusion pressure.[14-6]

COMPUTER-AIDED MANUFACTURE AND EVALUATION OF LUBRICATED EXTRUSION DIES

The surface of a "streamlined" die is defined as an array of points. The pratical method of manufacturing this die is to NC machine a carbon electrode and then to EDM the die. For this purpose, the cutter paths for machining the electrode surface must be determined. In using a ball-end mill, the position of the center of the spherical portion of the mill, with respect to any given point on the surface, can be determined by constructing a vector normal to the surface at that given point. In the present case, the normal vector is calculated from the cross product of two vectors: one tangent to the surface along the material path line, and the other tangent to the cross-sectional boundary. For a tool of given radius, the coordinates of the cutter paths are determined as the tool moves, in a predetermined manner, over the array of points defining the die surface. The computer programs developed for calculating the cutter paths contain special routines to check for undercutting and gouging. The calculated cutter center points are plotted on the screen of a graphics terminal as shown in Figure 14-9. The model of the EDM electrode, machined by NC, is shown in Figure 14-10.

The CAD/CAM technique was used to design and manufacture stream-

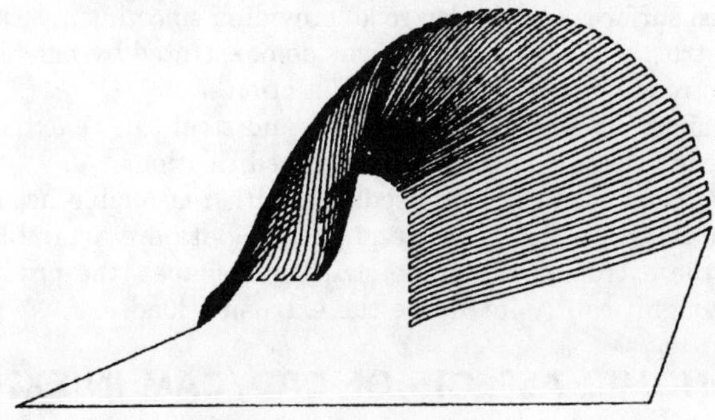

Figure 14-9. Cutter path for NC machining of the EDM electrode for the streamlined "T"-shape die.[14-6]

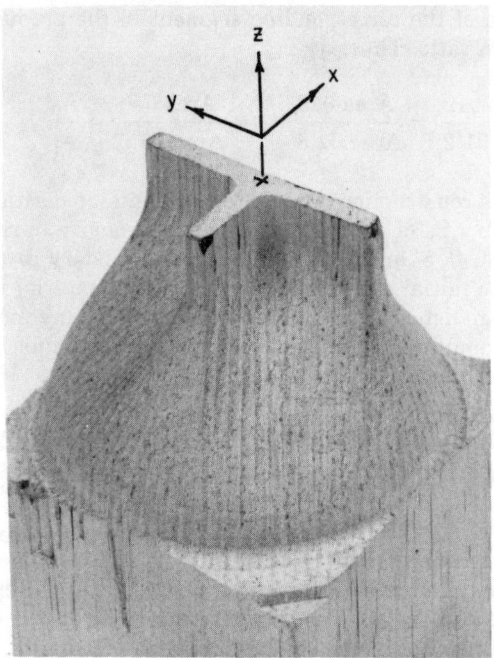

Figure 14-10. NC-machined wood model of the EDM electrode used in manufacturing the "T"-shape die.

lined dies for a "T" shape with a 2-in.-wide web and a 1-in.-high rib. Billets 3 in. in diameter, from aluminum alloy 7075, type 4340 steel and alloy Ti-6Al-4V, were extruded in a 700-ton hydraulic extrusion press. Comparison of experimental results with computer-aided predictions showed that:

- Streamlined dies for lubricated extrusion of simple structural shapes in titanium and steel can be designed and manufactured using computer-aided techniques.
- NC programs are adequate for machining three-dimensional streamlined surfaces (die or electrode) providing smooth transitions from round to structural sections. This was demonstrated by machining the EDM electrode for a streamlined "T" section.
- Straight "T" sections of titanium and steel can be extruded through a streamlined die without any die modification.
- Extrusion loads can be predicted with reasonable accuracy, provided that accurate flow stress and friction data are available.
- In the extrusion of simple structural shapes, the product shape does not significantly influence the extrusion load.

ECONOMIC ASPECTS OF CAD/CAM IN EXTRUSION

The application of CAD/CAM in extrusion continues to increase. Already several extrusion companies are using computer-aided techniques for diemaking and process optimization.[14-1,14-7] The implementation of CAD/CAM in extrusion provides, in addition to cost reductions, the following potential benefits:

- More precise estimation, and reductions in estimation costs.
- Reduction in delivery schedules.
- Less dependence on skilled diemakers.
- Reductions in the number of die failures and in die-design and manufacturing costs.
- Improved utilization of existing press capacity by reducing die trials.
- Continuous improvement of die and process technology.
- Increases in material yield and press productivity.

REFERENCES

14-1. Purnell, C., and Males, D., "Extrusion Die Design by Computer", Light Metal Age, April 1980, p 12.
14-2. Post, C. T., "The Strong Link That Ties CAD to CAM", Iron Age, Aug 22, 1977, p 29.
14-3. Billhardt, C. F., Nagpal, V., and Altan, T., "A Computer Graphics System for CAD/CAM of Aluminum Extrusion Dies", SME Paper MS78-957, May 1978.
14-4. Nagpal, V., and Altan, T., "Design and Manufacturing of Dies for Lubricated Extrusion of Shapes", published in J. of Mechanical Working Technology, Vol 1, No. 2, Nov 1977, p 183.
14-5. Nagpal, V., Billhardt, C. F., Gagne, R., and Altan, T., "Automated Design of Extrusion Dies by Computer", paper submitted to International Aluminum Extrusion Technology Seminar, Altanta, Nov 15-17, 1977.
14-6. Nagpal, V., Billhardt, C. F., and Altan, T., "Lubricated Extrusion of 'T' Sections from Aluminum, Titanium and Steel Using Computer-Aided Techniques", ASME Trans., J. Engr. Industry, Aug 1979, Vol 101, p 319.
14-7. Fielding, R. A. P., "Computer Aided Design and Manufacture of Extrusion Dies", Light Metal Age, April 1979, p 22.

CHAPTER 15
Cold Forging (Cold Extrusion)

Cold extrusion is a special type of forging process wherein cold metal is forced to flow plastically under compressive force into a variety of shapes. These shapes are usually axisymmetric with relatively small nonsymmetrical features, and, unlike impression die forging (see Chapter 11), the process does not generate flash. The terms "cold forging" and "cold extrusion" are often used interchangeably and refer to well-known forming operations such as extrusion, upsetting or heading, coining, ironing and swaging.[15-1 to 15-4] These operations are usually performed in mechanical or hydraulic presses, which are discusssed in Chapter 9. Several forming steps are used to produce a final part of relatively complex geometry, starting with a slug or billet of simple shape, as shown in Figure 15-1.[15-5] Some basic techniques of cold forging are illustrated in Figure 15-2.[15-6] Through combination of these techniques, a very large number of parts can be produced, as illustrated schematically in Figures 15-3 and 15-4.[15-6]

In warm forging, the billet is heated to temperatures below the recrystallization temperature, for example, up to 700 to 800 C for steels, in order to lower the flow stress and the forging pressures. In cold forging, the billet or the slug is at room temperature when deformation starts.

Cold and warm forging are extremely important and economical processes, especially for producing round or nearly round parts in large quantities. Some of the advantages provided by this process are: (a) high production rates, (b) excellent dimensional tolerances and surface finish of forged parts, (c) significant savings in material and machining, (d) higher tensile strengths in the forged part than in the original material, because of strain hardening, and (e) favorable grain flow to improve strength. By far the largest area of application of cold and warm forging is the automobile industry. However, cold forged parts are also used in manufacturing bicycles, motorcycles, farm machinery, off-highway equipment, and nuts and bolts.

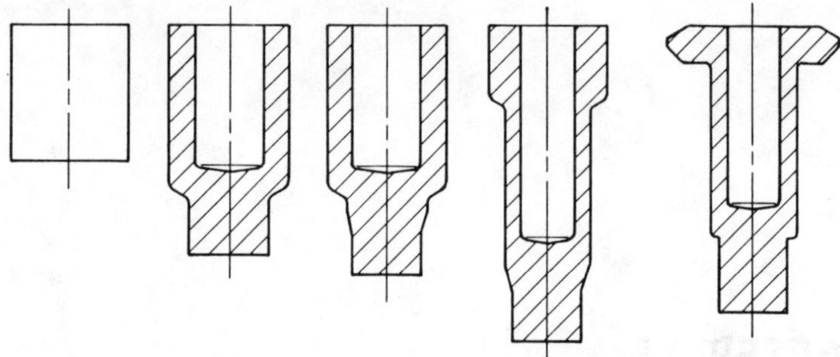

Left to right: sheared blank, simultaneous forward rod and backward cup extrusion, forward extrusion, backward cup extrusion, simultaneous upsetting of flange and coining of shoulder.

Figure 15-1. Schematic illustration of forming sequences in cold forging of a gear blank.[15-5]

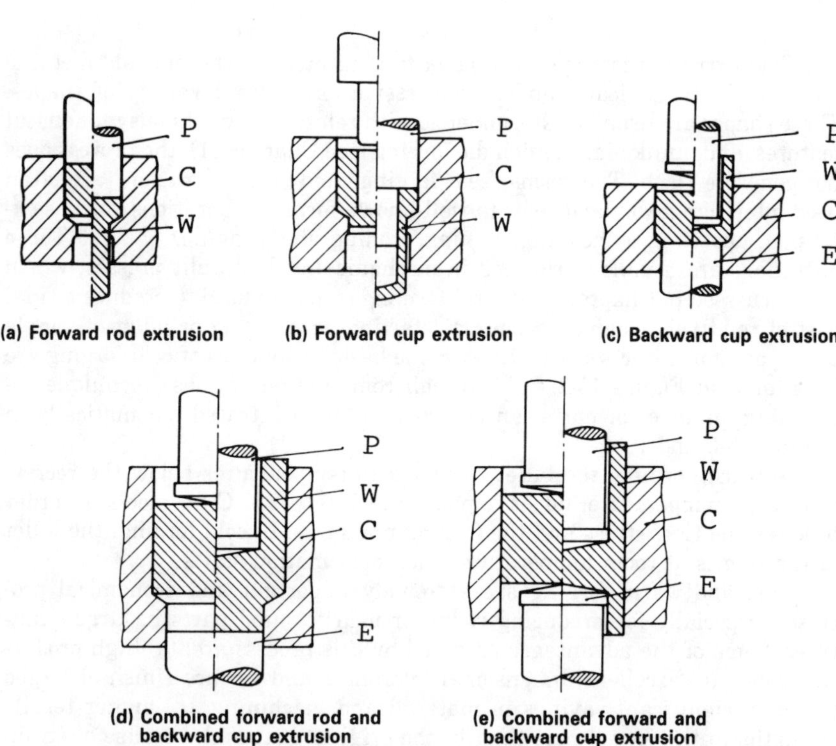

(a) Forward rod extrusion **(b) Forward cup extrusion** **(c) Backward cup extrusion**

(d) Combined forward rod and backward cup extrusion **(e) Combined forward and backward cup extrusion**

Figure 15-2. Various types of cold forging (extrusion) techniques (P = punch, C = container, W = workpiece, E = ejector).[15-6]

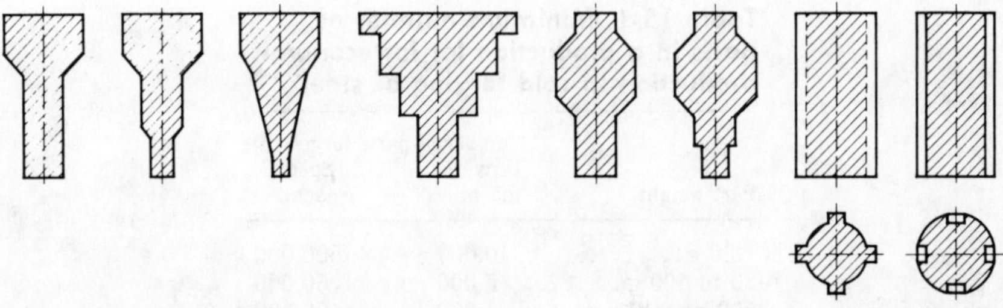

Figure 15-3. Examples of cold forged solid parts.[15-6]

In cold forging, process development and die costs are relatively high. Therefore, cold forging is, in general, a high production volume process. The weights of parts produced by cold forging range from five grams to fifty kilograms. As a general rule, the economic minimum production volume depends on part weight, as given in Table 15-1.[15-6]

MATERIALS FOR COLD FORGING

All metals that exhibit ductility at room temperature can be cold forged. This group consists primarily of steels and aluminum alloys. However, alloys of copper, zinc, tin, titanium, beryllium and nickel are also cold forged for special applications.[15-7] Examples of steels that are used extensively for producing cold extruded parts are:

- Case hardening steels: unalloyed – 1010, 1015; alloyed – 5115, 5120, 3115.
- Heat treatable steels: unalloyed – 1020, 1035, 1045; alloyed – 5140, 4130, 4140, 8620.
- Stainless steels: pearlitic – 410, 430, 431; austenitic – 302, 304, 316, 321.

Examples of commonly cold forged aluminum alloys are:

- Pure or nearly pure aluminum alloys: 1285, 1070, 1050, 1100.
- Nonhardenable aluminum alloys: 3003, 5152, 5052.
- Hardenable aluminum alloys: 6063, 6053, 6066, 2017, 2024, 7075.

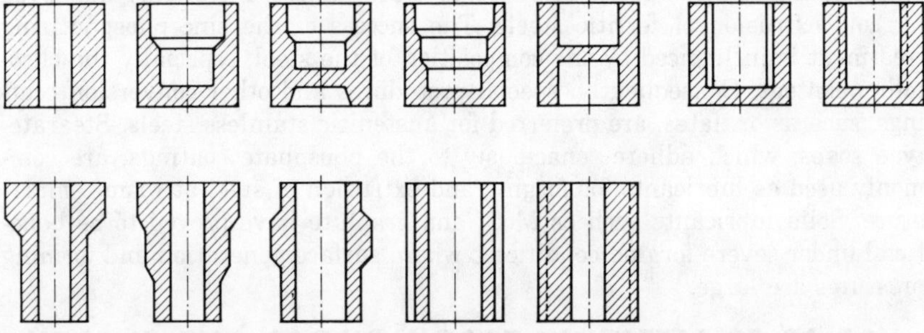

Figure 15-4. Examples of cold forged tubular or cup-shape parts.[15-6]

Table 15-1. Minimum number of parts in a production lot for economic production in cold forging of steel[15-6]

Part weight	Number of parts forged in: Universal machines	Special machines
<20 g	10,000	500,000
20 to 500 g	5,000	50,000
500 g to 10 kg	1,000	20,000
10 to 50 kg	1,000	10,000

Materials for cold forging are supplied as rolled or drawn rod or wire as well as in the form of sheared or sawed-off billets. The dimensions, weight and surface finish of the sheared (or sawed) billet or preform must be closely controlled in order to maintain dimensional tolerances in the cold forged part and to avoid excessive loading of the forging press and tooling.

BILLET PREPARATION AND LUBRICATION IN COLD FORGING OF STEEL

By far the largest area of application for cold forging is the production of steel parts. Cold forging plants usually receive small-diameter material in coils and large-diameter stock in bars. In very large volume production, horizontal mechanical presses, called headers or upsetters, are used. The coil, coated with lubricant, is fed into the machine, where it is sheared and forged in several steps. In forging of relatively small production lots, vertical presses are used and individual billets (after being lubricated) are fed into the first die station. Billet volume or weight is closely controlled, and it is desirable to obtain square billet faces during shearing or sawing.[15-8]

In cold forging, the lubricant is required to withstand high pressures, on the order of 280 ksi in extrusion of steel, so as to avoid metal-to-metal contact between the tool and the extruded material. In cold forging of low-carbon and low-alloy steels it is accepted practice to coat the surface of the billet or coil with a lubricant carrier. This zinc phosphate coating provides a good substrate for lubricants that withstand high forming pressures. The phosphating and lubricating steps given in Table 15-2 are almost universally employed for cold extrusion of ferritic steels. The success of the zinc phosphatizing treatment is influenced by the composition of the steel, especially the chromium content. Consequently, special procedures and other conversion coatings, such as oxalates, are preferred for austenitic stainless steels. Stearate-type soaps, which adhere tenaciously to the phosphate coatings, are commonly used as lubricants for forging and extrusion of steel at room temperature. Solid lubricants such as MoS_2 and graphite have proved to be beneficial under severe forging conditions, where surface generation and forming pressures are large.[15-9]

VARIABLES AFFECTING FORGING LOAD AND ENERGY

In predicting loads and stresses in cold upsetting or coining-type operations, the methods described in Chapters 10 and 11 for upset forging are ap-

Table 15-2. Typical procedure for phosphating and lubricating billets of carbon and low-alloy steels for cold extrusion

1. Degrease and clean slugs in a hot alkaline solution for 1 to 5 min at 66 to 95 C.
2. Rinse in cold water.
3. Remove scale, usually by pickling.
4. Rinse in cold water.
5. Rinse in neutralizing solution if a pickling process was used.
6. Dip in a zinc phosphate solution (usually of a proprietary type) for approximately 5 min at 82 to 95 C, to develop a uniform coating of appropriate thickness.
7. Rinse in cold water; neutralize if necessary.
8. Lubricate the slugs, usually with a stearate soap, but sometimes with other types of lubricants.
9. Air dry the slugs to obtain a thin, adherent coating of lubricant adsorbed on the zinc phosphate coating.

plicable also in cold forging. The two most commonly used extrusion processes, forward rod extrusion and backward cup extrusion, are illustrated in Figure 15-5. The qualitative variations of the punch load versus punch displacement curves are shown in Figure 15-6. The areas under these curves represent energy and can be easily calculated: (a) when the extrusion load in backward extrusion, which is constant, is estimated; or (b) when, in forward rod extrusion, both the peak load at the beginning of the stroke and the end load at the end of the stroke are known.

In cold extrusion, material at various locations in the deformation zone

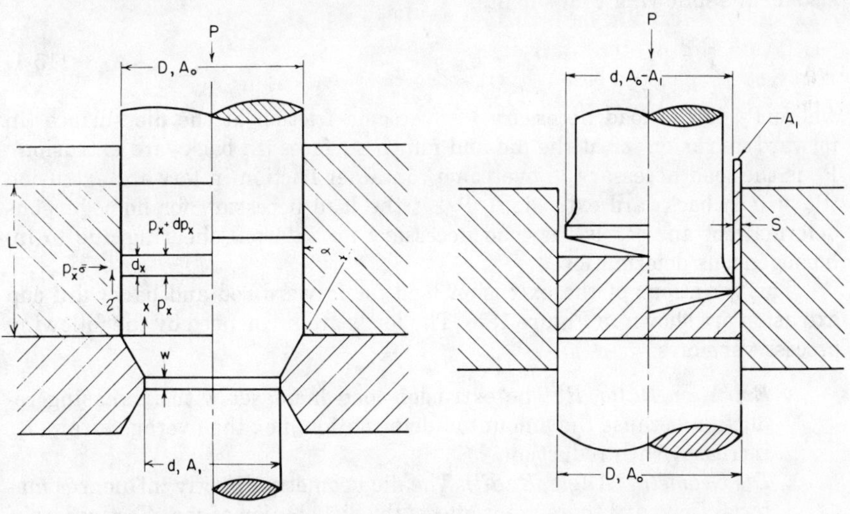

Figure 15-5. Schematic illustration of forward rod (a) and backward cup (b) extrusion processes.

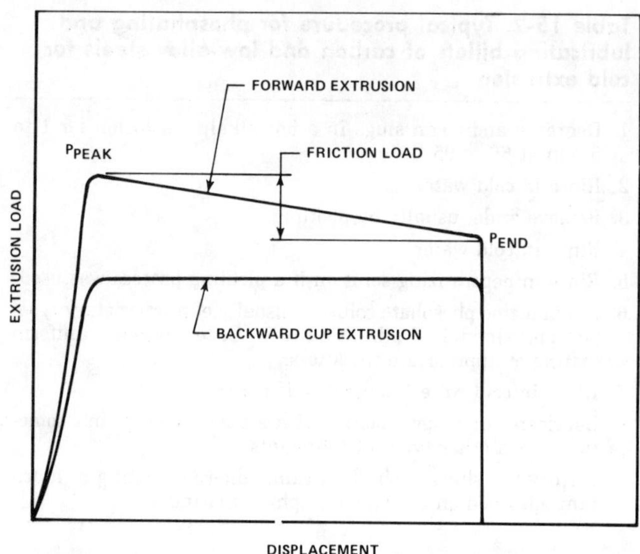

Figure 15-6. Schematic illustration of punch load versus punch displacement curves in forward rod and backward cup extrusion processes.

is subject to different amounts of deformation. The value of strain, $\bar{\epsilon}$, and corresponding flow stress, $\bar{\sigma}$, vary within the deformation zone. It is therefore necessary to use average values of flow stress, $\bar{\sigma}$, and effective strain, $\bar{\epsilon}$, to characterize the total deformation of the material. The total forging load consists of the following components:

$$P = P_{fd} + P_{fc} + P_{dh} + P_{ds} \tag{15-1}$$

where P_{fd} is the load necessary to overcome friction at the die surface (in forward extrusion) or at the die and punch surfaces (in backward extrusion), P_{fc} is the load necessary to overcome container friction in forward extrusion (P_{fc} = 0 in backward extrusion), P_{dh} is the load necessary for homogeneous deformation, and P_{ds} is the load necessary for internal shearing due to inhomogeneous deformation.

The variations of the extrusion load for forward rod and backward cup extrusion are shown in Figure 15-6. The loads are influenced by the following process variables:

- *Extrusion Ratio, R*. The extrusion load increases with increasing reduction because the amount of deformation, i.e., the average strain, $\bar{\epsilon}_a$, increases with reduction.
- *Die Geometry (Angle, Radii)*. The die geometry directly influences material flow, and therefore it affects the distribution of the effective strain and flow stress in the deformation zone. In forward extrusion, for a given reduction, a larger die angle increases the volume of metal undergoing shear deformation and results in an increase in shear de-

formation load, P_{ds}. On the other hand, the length of the die decreases, which results in a decrease in die friction load, P_{fd}. Consequently, for a given reduction and given friction conditions there is an optimum die angle which minimizes the extrusion load.

- *Extrusion Velocity.* With increasing velocity, both the strain rate and the temperature generated in the deforming material increase. These effects counteract each other, and consequently the load in cold extrusion is not affected significantly by the extrusion velocity.
- *Lubrication.* Improved lubrication lowers the container friction force, P_{fc}, and the die friction force, P_{fd}, of Equation 15-1, resulting in lower extrusion loads.
- *Workpiece Material.* The flow stress of the billet material directly influences the loads P_{dh} and P_{ds} of Equation 15-1. The prior heat treatment and/or any prior work hardening also affect the flow stress of a material. Therefore, flow stress values depend not only on the chemical composition of the material but also on its prior processing history. The temperature of the workpiece material infuences the flow stress, $\bar{\sigma}$. This will be discussed later.
- *Billet Dimensions.* In forward extrusion, an increase in billet length results in an increase in container friction load, P_{fc}. In backward extrusion, the billet length has little effect on the extrusion load. This is illustrated in Figure 15-6.

ESTIMATION OF FRICTION AND FLOW STRESS

There are a number of formulas for predicting the pressures in forward and backward extrusion.[15-1,15-2,15-7] These formulas are derived either through approximate methods of plasticity theory or empirically from a series of experiments. In both cases, in addition to the approximation inherent in a given formula, estimation of the material flow stress and of the friction factor for a specific process also introduces inaccuracies into the predictions.

Friction is discussed in detail in Chapters 2 and 7. The value of the friction factor, f (used in expressing the frictional shear stress $\tau = f\bar{\sigma} = m\bar{\sigma}/\sqrt{3}$), is on the order of 0.03 to 0.08 in cold extrusion. This value is approximately the same as the value of μ (used in expressing $\tau = \sigma_n\mu$, with σ_n = normal stress) used in some literature references.

In the deformation zone, the strain and, consequently, the flow stress, $\bar{\sigma}$, vary with location. Due to inhomogeneous deformation and internal shearing, the volume of the material near the die surface is subject to more severe deformation. Near the interface, therefore, the local strains and flow stresses are higher. Since the flow stress varies over the deformation zone, most formulas use a so-called "average" or "mean" flow stress, $\bar{\sigma}_a$, which is difficult to determine accurately. A reasonable approximation of the average flow stress, $\bar{\sigma}_a$, can be obtained from the curve for flow stress, $\bar{\sigma}$, versus effective strain, $\bar{\epsilon}$, as follows:

$$\bar{\sigma}_a = \frac{1}{\ln R}\int_0^{\ln R} \bar{\sigma}\, d\bar{\epsilon} = \frac{a}{\ln R} \quad (15\text{-}2)$$

where R is the ratio of the initial cross-sectional area, A_o, to the final cross-sectional area, A_1, i.e., $R = A_0/A_1$

$$a = \int_0^{\ln R} \bar{\sigma} d\bar{\epsilon} \tag{15-3}$$

The value "a" of the integral is the surface area under the effective stress – effective strain curve and corresponds to the specific energy for homogeneous deformation up to the strain $\bar{\epsilon}_i = \ln R$. If the flow stress can be expressed in the exponential form, then:

$$\bar{\sigma} = K\bar{\epsilon}^n \tag{15-4}$$

and

$$\bar{\sigma}_a = \frac{1}{\ln R} \int_0^{\ln R} K\bar{\epsilon}^n d\bar{\epsilon} = \frac{K(\ln R)^n}{n + 1} \tag{15-5}$$

where n is the strain-hardening exponent, and K is the flow stress at effective strain $\bar{\epsilon} = 1$, as discussed in Chapter 4.

Since the material flow is influenced by tool geometry and by interface lubrication conditions, the strain distribution, and consequently the average strain, $\bar{\epsilon}$, and the average flow stress, $\bar{\sigma}_a$, are also influenced by tool geometry and lubrication. This fact, however, is not reflected in the approximate estimation of the average flow stress, $\bar{\sigma}_a$, described above.

VARIATIONS IN EXTRUSION LOAD UNDER PRODUCTION CONDITIONS

Precise predictions of extrusion pressures cannot be expected from the numerous formulas available in the literature. To be useful, however, approximations should be within the fluctuations observed in measured extrusion pressures under production conditions. Although large amounts of experimental data have been generated under laboratory conditions, very little information has been obtained under production conditions. The Forming Institute of the Stuttgart Technical University conducted extrusion load and energy measurements under production conditions in various cold forging plants.[15-10] Approximately 900 samples of four shapes, one tube and three rods, were forward extruded during each run. All parts were extruded from carbon steel grades used in cold forging and were lubricated according to the usual practice at each plant (phosphate coating and soap lubricant). In tube extrusion, starting with cold tooling, the extrusion pressures showed a slight decrease (about 5%) in time with increasing number of samples until a steady-state temperature condition was established. This condition was reached after 400 samples had been forged. In the least favorable cases, the measured extrusion pressures showed a fluctuation range (between maximum and minimum measured values) of about 17% of the measured average pressure. This means that the choice of cold forging equipment and the design of tooling should be such that a 15 to 20% difference in maximum forging load should not result in tool or equipment damage. These data also indicate that prediction of cold extrusion loads to within 15 to 20% can be considered to be of practical value.

PREDICTION OF EXTRUSION LOADS FROM SELECTED FORMULAS

Various formulas for forward and backward extrusion were evaluated in predicting forming loads for 35 different material values (17 different steels with various heat treatments). Values of container friction were included in predictions of pressures in forward extrusion.[15-11] The formulas that gave the best results are summarized in Tables 15-3 and 15-4. The symbols used in these formulas are explained in text above, in this section or in Figure 15-5.

The flow stress data were obtained, in the form $\bar{\sigma} = K\bar{\epsilon}^n$, from tensile tests. Whenever necessary, the average flow stress, $\bar{\sigma}_a$, used in the formulas was determined from Equation 15-5. In some formulas, values of tensile strength, σ_u, yield stress, $\bar{\sigma}_o$, or hardness were used. The properties of the billet materials considered in this study are given in Table 15-5. A friction factor, f, or a coefficient of friction $\mu = 0.04$ was used in evaluating all formulas. The value $\mu = 0.04$ was selected on the basis of previous studies which indicated that, in cold forging (zinc phosphate coating + Bonderlube 235 lubricant), μ can be estimated to be between 0.03 and 0.08. As expected, the

Table 15-3. Formulas for calculation of load in forward rod extrusion

Source	Formula	Remarks
Siebel[13]; also Feldmann[1]	$P = A_0 \cdot \bar{\sigma}_a \ln R + \frac{2}{3} \alpha A_0 \bar{\sigma}_a + \frac{A_0 \bar{\sigma}_a \ln R\mu}{\cos\alpha \sin\alpha} + \pi D \cdot L \bar{\sigma}_0 \mu$	P includes loads due to homogeneous deformation, shearing, die friction, container friction.
P.E.R.A.[12]	$P = A_0 \bar{\sigma}_0 (3.45 \ln R + 1.15)$	For 0.1 to 0.3% C steels.
Billigmann[3]	$P = \bar{\sigma}_a \cdot A_0 (\ln R + 0.6) \cdot \left(1.25 + 2\mu \sqrt{\frac{\pi L}{A_0}}\right)$	
Pugh et al[14]	$P = 8.2 A_0 \sigma_u^{0.78} (\ln R)^{0.73}$	Originally derived for steels with zinc phosphate + MoS_2.
	$= 2.7 A_0 H^{0.78} (\ln R)^{0.73}$	H = hardness of billet before extrusion, kg/mm^2. σ_u in $tons/in.^2$, 1 ton = 2240 lb, P in tons.
James-Kottcamp[15]	$P = 0.5 A_0 (\bar{\sigma}_0 + \sigma_u \cdot F_n) \bar{\epsilon}_a \exp \frac{4\mu L}{D}$	Based on average strain, ϵ_a, determined in model test with lead and with $\alpha = 27°$.
	$F_n = \left(\frac{e\bar{\epsilon}_a}{n}\right)^n$	
	$\bar{\epsilon}_a = 1.24 \ln R + 0.53$	e = 2.71828.

Table 15-4. Formulas for calculation of forming load in backward cup extrusion

Source	Formula	Remarks
P.E.R.A.[12]	$P = A_0 \cdot \sigma_0 \left(3.45 \ln \frac{A_0}{A_1} + 1.15\right)$	For 0.1 to 0.3% C steel.
Pugh, et al[14]	$P = A_0 6.0 \sigma_u^{0.8} (\ln R)^{0.72}$	Steels with zinc phosphate + Bonderlube 235.
	$= A_0 2.8 H^{0.72} (\ln R)^{0.72}$	H, hardness in kg/mm^2 σ_u in tons/in.^{2}, 1 ton = 2240 lb, p in tons.
James-Kottcamp[15]	$P = A_0 \left(\frac{\bar{\sigma}_0 + \sigma_u F_n}{2.4}\right) \bar{\epsilon}_a$	Based on average strain, $\bar{\epsilon}_a$, determined in model test with lead and with 5% cone-nosed punch.
	$\bar{\epsilon}_a = 2.36 \ln R + 0.28$	
	$F_n = \left(\frac{e\bar{\epsilon}_a}{n}\right)^n$	e = 2.71828.
Schoffmann[16]	$P = A_0 K_c \sigma_u \ln \frac{A_0}{A_1}$	K_c = 2.5 to 3 for low-carbon steel, used K_c = 3.

predicted extrusion pressures would vary considerably with the value of the friction factor.

The formulas which gave the best predictions for punch loads in forward extrusion are given in Table 15-3. The experimental results were obtained by extruding various steel billets 1 in. in diameter and 1.5 to 3.5 in. in length, with zinc-phosphate-stearate lubrication, at different reductions through a die with a 60° die half angle and a 1/8-in. die land.

The predicted extrusion pressures obtained by use of the formulas in Table 15-3 are compared with experimental data in Table 15-6. The predicted pressure values correspond to breakthrough pressures, i.e., they include the container friction. It can be seen in Table 15-3 that the simplest formulas, suggested by P.E.R.A.[15-12] and by Pugh,[15-14] give predictions approximately as good as those given by the other formulas in Table 15-3.

The formulas which gave the best predicted values of punch loads, or pressures, in backward cup extrusion are given in Table 15-4. The predicted and measured punch pressures are compared in Table 15-7 for five steels. The

Table 15-5. Mechanical properties of forward and backward extruded steels

Steel	K, 10^3 psi	n	σ_0, 10^3 psi	σ_u, 10^3 psi	Hardness, HRB
1005, hot rolled	86	0.250	35	47	50
1018, hot rolled	117	0.224	45	68	70
12L14, annealed	115	0.312	43	59	60
1038, annealed	134	0.255	44	70	71
8620, subcritical annealed	120	0.173	55	74	82

Table 15-6. Comparison of measured and predicted breakthrough punch pressures in forward extrusion of various steels

Steel	Reduction, %	Measured pressure, ksi	Pressure, ksi, predicted using formula (Table 15-3) from: Siebel[15-13]	P.E.R.A.[15-12]	Billigmann[15-3]	Pugh[15-14]	James and Kottcamp[15-15]
1005, hot rolled	20	68	84	70	64	60	84
	50	120	132	128	127	132	137
	60	144	153	154	155	161	153
	70	161	184	189	194	195	181
1018, hot rolled	20	111	118	92	93	80	115
	50	186	183	166	178	176	187
	60	205	212	201	216	214	208
12L14, annealed	20	96	99	87	75	72	111
	50	172	165	158	159	158	185
	60	187	194	191	197	192	209
1038, annealed	20	103	124	87	99	82	121
	50	190	200	161	197	181	198
	60	210	234	195	241	220	221
8620, subcritical annealed	20	98	137	112	106	86	124
	50	178	202	202	194	188	195
	60	205	230	245	232	230	216

Table 15-7. Comparison of measured and predicted punch pressures in backward cup extrusion of various steels

Steel	Reduction, %	Measured pressure, ksi	Pressure, ksi, predicted using formula (Table 15-4) from: P.E.R.A.[15-12]	Pugh[15-14]	James and Kottcamp[15-15]	Schoffmann[15-14]
1005, hot rolled	50	223	245	236	214	194
	60	228	248	240	237	213
	70	249	260	249	270	240
8620, subcritical annealed	50	305	389	340	300	307
	60	309	393	345	326	337
	70	341	412	359	366	377
1038, annealed	50	304	309	325	309	290
	60	313	312	331	343	319
	70	327	327	344	392	357
1018, hot rolled	50	286	320	317	290	281
	60	293	323	322	319	308
	70	313	338	335	362	345
12L14	50	274	303	284	293	245
	60	282	306	288	329	269
	70	316	321	300	380	301

backward extruded billets were 1 in. in diameter and 1.0 in. long. The lubrication was the same as in forward extrusion, i.e., zinc-phosphate-stearate lubrication. The mechanical properties of backward extruded steels are given in Table 15-5.

None of the formulas given in Table 15-4 takes into account the tool geometry (punch angles, radii, die angles). The experimental results are obtained, in most backward extrusion trials, for two punch designs (with 0.090-in. and 0.005-in. punch edge radii). For comparing the predicted and measured punch pressures, an average of the pressures obtained with both punches was used whenever experimental data were available for both cases.

PREDICTION OF EXTRUSION LOADS FROM MODEL TEST

Except where exaggerated inhomogeneities are present in the deforming material, metal flow in extrusion is influenced mainly by tool geometry and lubrication conditions. The effects of material properties on metal flow are relatively insignificant.[15-16,15-17]

If a strain-hardening material is considered and the friction at the tool/material interfaces of the deformation zone is neglected, the external mechanical energy is equal to the internal deformation energy,[15-16] i.e.:

$$p_a A_0 v \Delta t = \int_V \bar{\sigma} d\bar{\epsilon} dV \tag{15-6}$$

or

$$p_a V = V \int_0^{\bar{\epsilon}_h} \bar{\sigma} d\bar{\epsilon} \tag{15-7}$$

where, in addition to the symbols previously defined, p_a is average punch pressure, V is volume of deforming material, v is punch velocity, and Δt is time increment. The left side of Equation 15-6 represents the amount of mechanical energy necessary for deformation. This energy is introduced by the punch which moves at a velocity (v) during the time, Δt, necessary to extrude the volume of material equal to the volume of the deformation zone ($V = A_0 v \Delta t$). The right side of Equation 15-6 represents the total deformation energy obtained by adding the deformation energies consumed within each volume element in the deformation zone. This total deformation energy can be calculated only if the flow stress, $\bar{\sigma}$, and effective strain, $\bar{\epsilon}$, at each volume element are known. Since this information is not usually available, the following averaging method can be used.

Assuming that every volume element in the deformation zone has the same average strain, $\bar{\epsilon}_a$, and the same average flow stress, $\bar{\sigma}_a$, then Equation 15-7 can be written as

$$p_a V = \sigma_a \cdot \bar{\epsilon}_a \cdot V \tag{15-8}$$

and, with $\bar{\sigma} = K\bar{\epsilon}^n$, Equation 15-8 gives

$$p_a = K\bar{\epsilon}_a^{n+1} \quad (15\text{-}9)$$

or

$$\bar{\epsilon}_a = \left(\frac{p_a}{K}\right)^{1/n+1} \quad (15\text{-}10)$$

Equations 15-9 and 15-10 can be used for predicting extrusion pressures from a model test. First, a model material (plasticine, aluminum or mild steel) is extruded using a certain tool geometry, and the extrusion pressure, p_a, is measured. By use of Equation 15-10 and the known K and n values of the model material, the average strain ϵ_a is calculated. Then, the calculated value of ϵ_a, and the K and n values of the real material, are used with Equation 15-9 to estimate the real extrusion pressure.

Using 1005 hot rolled steel ($\bar{\sigma} = 86{,}000 \times \bar{\epsilon}^{0.25}$ psi) as the model material, the model test method described above was applied in order to predict punch pressures in forward extrusion for a series of the other steels. A comparison of the experimental and predicted values is given in Table 15-8. It can be seen that the largest difference between the two values does not exceed 20%, while predictions are within 10% for most extrusions. It should be noted that the extrusion pressure, p_a, in Equation 15-9 is the same as the ejector pressure. The punch pressure is obtained from the extrusion ratio. For instance, for R = 80%, punch pressure = $p_a/0.80$.

In forward extrusion, only the deformation pressure, i.e., the end pressure, can be predicted from a model test. In order to predict the maximum

Table 15-8. Comparison of measured and predicted (model method) punch pressures in backward extrusion of various steels (model material, hot rolled 1005 steel; $\bar{\sigma} = 86{,}000 \times \bar{\epsilon}^{0.25}$ psi)

Steel	K, ksi	n	Reduction, %	Pressure, ksi: Measured	Pressure, ksi: Predicted
8620, subcritical annealed	120	0.173	50	305	304
			60	309	308
			70	341	334
1038, annealed	134	0.255	50	304	347
			60	313	357
			70	327	387
1018, hot rolled	117	0.224	50	286	300
			60	293	305
			70	313	335
12L14, annealed	115	0.312	50	274	302
			60	282	315
			70	316	343

load, the friction in the extrusion container must be considered. With the symbols illustrated in Figure 15-5(a), the equilibrium of forces in the axial direction gives:

$$dp_x \left(\frac{\pi D^2}{4}\right) = dx \tau_f \pi D \tag{15-11}$$

Assuming a constant frictional shear stress, τ_f, at the tool/material interface:

$$\tau_f = f \cdot \bar{\sigma}_0$$

Equation 15-11 transforms into

$$\frac{dp_x}{dx} = \frac{4f\bar{\sigma}_0}{D} \tag{15-12}$$

by integrating, Equation 15-12 gives

$$p_x = \frac{4f\bar{\sigma}_0}{D} x + C \tag{15-13}$$

The integration constant C is determined from the condition: for $x = 0$, $p_x = p_a$ in Equation 15-9, or, in forward extrusion,

$$p_p = p_e + \frac{4f\bar{\sigma}_0}{D} L \tag{15-14}$$

Equation 15-14 illustrates that the peak pressure, p_p, in forward rod extrusion is equal to the sum of the end pressure, p_e, necessary for deformation and the additional pressure, $p_{fc} = 4f\bar{\sigma}_0 L$, necessary to overcome the container friction.

The shear friction, f, is to be determined from Equation 15-14 for a given billet length, L, and for the known yield stress, $\bar{\sigma}_0$, of the model material — in this case, 1005 HR steel. It is reasonable to assume that the friction factor, f, would not significantly change from one steel to another. The average strain, $\bar{\epsilon}_a$, is determined from Equation 15-10, using the data for 1005 HR steel. The end pressure, p_e, is then determined from Equation 15-9. Finally the peak pressures, p_p, are calculated for different steels using Equation 15-14. The results are compared with experimental values in Table 15-9. The agreement between prediction and experiment is, in most cases, within 10 to 15% and can be considered acceptable for practical purposes.

WARM FORGING OF STEELS

In cold forging of parts with relatively complex geometries from high-carbon and alloy steels, forging pressures are extremely high and the ductilities of the materials are low. As a result, short tool life and defects formed during forging limit the economic use of the cold forging processes. Consequently, in many cases, warm forging — i.e., forging at temperatures of 200 to 800 C — is commonly used. The advantages of warm forging are:

Table 15-9. Comparison of measured and predicted (model method) peak punch pressures in forward extrusion of various steels

Steel	K, ksi	n	Reduction, %	Pressure, ksi: Measured	Pressure, ksi: Predicted
1018, hot rolled	117	0.224	20	111	95
			50	186	165
			60	205	190
12L14, annealed	115	0.312	20	86	90
			50	172	158
			60	187	192
8620, subcritical annealed	120	0.173	20	98	100
			50	178	182
			60	205	220
1038, annealed	134	0.255	20	103	100
			50	190	180
			60	210	220
4340, annealed	167	0.193	20	122	132
			50	228	232
			60	251	275

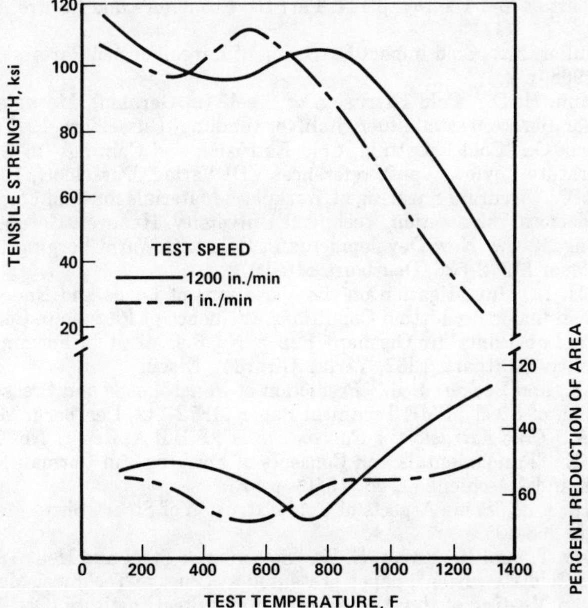

Figure 15-7. Effects of test temperature and test speed (strain rate) on tensile strength and reduction of area of hot rolled type 1045 steel.(15-18)

- A reduction in flow stress. This is applicable in particular to high-alloy steels. As a result, tool stresses and forging loads are reduced.
- Greater ductility of the forged part. This allows more complex shapes to be forged.
- A reduction in strain hardening. This may reduce the number of forming and annealing operations.
- Greater toughness of the forged part.

As an example, variations of tensile stress and ductility (as expressed by reduction of area) with temperature are shown in Figure 15-7 for 1045 steel.[15-18] It can be seen that the tensile stress does not decrease continuously with temperature. There is a temperature range, in this case around 400 to 800 F, wherein forging would not be recommended.

Warm forging requires determination of (a) the optimum forging temperature and (b) the suitable lubricant. Selection of warm forging lubricants has proved to be especially difficult. Nevertheless, there are many examples of warm forging operations being used successfully in production.[15-19 to 15-21]

REFERENCES

15-1. Feldmann, H. D., "Cold Forging of Steel", Hutchinson and Company, Ltd., London, 1961.

15-2. Wick, C. H., "Chipless Machining", Industrial Press, New York, 1961.

15-3. Billigmann, J., and Feldmann, H. D., "Upsetting and Pressing" (in German), Carl Hansen Verlag, Munich, 1973.

15-4. Watkins, M. T., "Cold Forming and Extrusion of Steel", Review 176, International Metallurgical Review, Vol 18, 1973 (Part I: Basic Principles, p 123; Part II: Properties and Tooling, p 147; Part III: Economics and Future Applications, p 162).

15-5. Sagemuller, Fr., "Cold Impact Extrusion of Large Formed Parts", Wire, No. 95, June 1968, p 2.

15-6. Feldmann, H. D., "Cold Extrusion of Steel" (in German), Merkblatt 201, prepared for Beratungsstelle fuer Stahlverwendung, Dusseldorf, 1977.

15-7. Gentzsch, G., "Cold Upsetting, Cold Extrusion and Coining" (in German), Vol 1, Literature Review, Vol 2; references VDI Verlag, Dusseldorf, 1967.

15-8. Herbst, V., "Accurate Shearing of Workpiece Materials for Cold Forging (in German), doctoral dissertation, Technical University, Hanover, Germany, 1967.

15-9. Doehring, R. C., "New Developments in Cold and Warm Forging", SME Technical Paper MF72-526, Dearborn, MI, 1972.

15-10. Witte, H. D., "Investigation on the Variations of Loads and Energies in Cold Extrusion under Production Conditions, Influence of Phosphate Coating Thickness and Lubricants" (in German), Report No. 6, Institut for Forming, Technical University, Stuttgart, 1967, Verlag Girardet, Essen.

15-11. Altan, T., and Becker, J. R., "Prediction of Punch Loads and Pressures in Cold Extrusion of Steel", SME Technical Paper MF72-142, Dearborn, MI, 1972.

15-12. P.E.R.A., "*Cold Extrusion of Carbon Steels*", P.E.R.A. Report No. 69.

15-13. Siebel, E., "Fundamentals and Concepts of Forming" (in German), Werkstattstechnik and Maschienbau, *40* (1950), p 373.

15-14. Pugh, H., *et al*, "Some Aspects of Cold Extrusion of Steel", Sheet Metal Ind., *43,* 1966, pp 268-305.

15-15. James, C. T., and Kottcamp, E. H., "Selection of Steel and Heat Treatment for Ease of Cold Extrusion", paper presented at Chicago Technical Meeting of the American Meeting of the American Iron and Steel Institute (Oct 20, 1965).

15-16. Altan, T., *et al,* "The Use of Model Materials in Predicting Forming Loads in Metalworking", Transactions ASME, May 1970, p 444.

15-17. Sashar, L. J., "Prediction of Extrusion Pressures in the Cold Forging of Steel", Trans. Metall. Society AIME, *239,* 1967, pp 1461-1468.
15-18. "Warm Forging of Steel: How to Predict Ductilities and Press Loads", Technical Report by Bethlehem Steel Corporation, Bethlehem, PA.
15-19. Chepko, F. K., "Preheating Improves Properties and Processing of Cold Formed Parts", Material Engineering, May 1971, p 22.
15-20. Wilms, H. D., "Precoining Aids Cold Forming", American Machinist, Oct 19, 1970, p 102.
15-21. McClymonds, N. L., "Forming of Stainless Bar and Wire", Metals Engineering Quarterly, Feb 1968, p 27.

CHAPTER 16
Rolling of Strip, Plate and Shapes

Most engineering metals, such as aluminum alloys, copper alloys and steels, are first cast into ingots and are then further processed by hot rolling into "blooms", "slabs" and "billets". These are known as semifinished products because they are subsequently rolled into other products such as plate, sheet, tube, rod, bar and structural shapes. The definitions of these terms are rather loose and are based on the traditional terminology used in the primary metal industry.[16-1] For example, a bloom has a nearly square cross section with an area larger than 32 in.^{2}; the minimum cross section of a billet is about 1.5 × 1.5 in., and a slab is a hot rolled ingot with a cross-sectional area greater than 16 in.^{2} and a section width of at least twice the section thickness. Plates are generally thicker than 0.25 in., whereas sheets are thinner-gage materials with very large width-to-thickness ratios. Sheet material with a thickness of a few thousandths of an inch is referred to as foil. Rolling of blooms, slabs, billets, plates and structural shapes is usually done at temperatures above the recrystallization temperature, i.e., in the hot forming range, where large reductions in height or thickness are possible with moderate forming pressures. Sheet and foil are usually rolled cold at room temperature, in order to maintain close thickness tolerances.

A rolling mill consists of one or several stands. A rolling mill stand contains a cast steel frame or housing that holds the roll bearings and sustains the roll separating force imposed on the bearings (Figure 16-1). The rolls are driven by an electric motor via a mechanical gear box. As illustrated in Figure 16-2(A) and (B), there are rolling mill stands with two rolls (two-high mills) that roll the material in one direction only (pull-over) or in both directions (reversing).[16-1] A three-high mill (Figure 16-2C) consists of upper and lower driven rolls and a middle roll that rotates by friction. By use of small-diameter work rolls, it is possible to roll very thin sheet and to decrease the power required for rolling. In this case, backup rolls are needed to over-

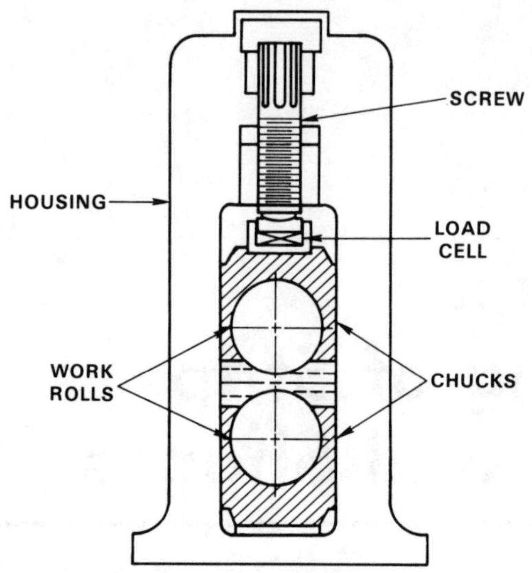

Figure 16-1. Schematic illustration of a two-high roll stand.

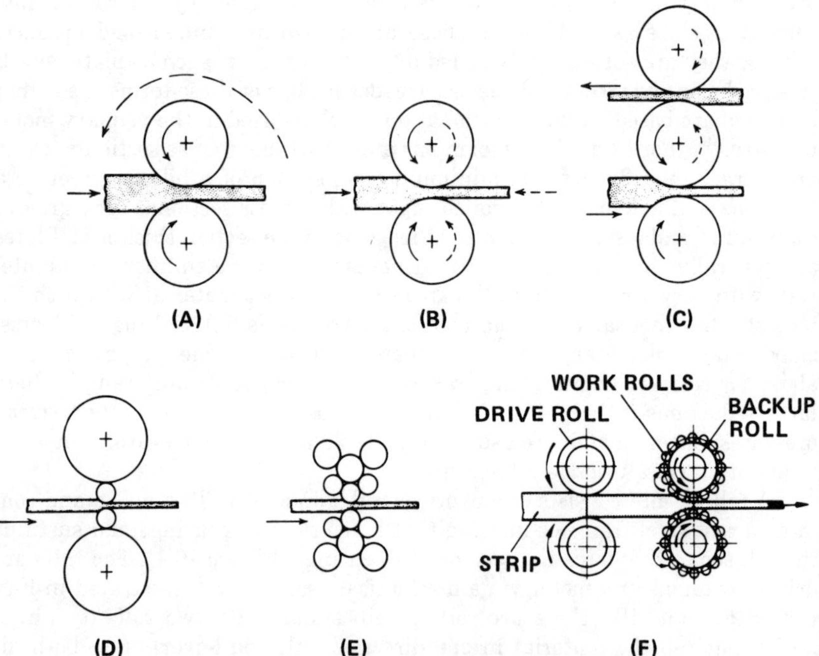

Figure 16-2. Schematic illustration of roll stand types for rolling mills: (A) two-high, pull-over; (B) two-high, reversing; (C) three-high; (D) four-high; (E) cluster; (F) planetary.[16-1]

come the elastic deflection of the work rolls (Figure 16-2D, E and F). For high-volume production it is common to set up several roll stands one after another. Thus, the metal is rolled continuously; a different reduction is taken at each stand, and the rolling speed increases gradually with decreasing metal cross section. A certain amount of tension is maintained between the rolls in order to control the process and to prevent the material from coiling up between the stands.

The primary objectives of the rolling process are to reduce the cross section of the incoming material while improving its properties and to obtain the desired section at the exit from the rolls. The process can be carried out hot, warm or cold, depending on the application and the material involved. The technical literature on rolling technology, equipment and theory is very extensive because of the significance of the process.[16-1 to 16-5] Many industrial investigators prefer to divide rolling into cold and hot rolling processes. However, from a fundamental point of view, it is more appropriate to classify rolling processes on the bases of the complexity of metal flow during the process and the geometry of the rolled product. Thus, rolling of solid sections can be divided into the following categories, as illustrated in Figure 16-3:

(a) *Uniform Reduction in Thickness With No Change in Width.* This is the case in strip, sheet or foil rolling where the deformation is in plane strain, i.e., in the directions of rolling and sheet thickness. This type of metal flow exists when the width of the deformation zone is at least 20 times the length of that zone.

(b) *Uniform Reduction in Thickness With an Increase in Width.* This type of deformation occurs in rolling of blooms, slabs and thick plates. The material is elongated in the rolling (longitudinal) direction, is spread in the width (transverse) direction and is compressed uniformly in the thickness direction (Figure 16-3B).

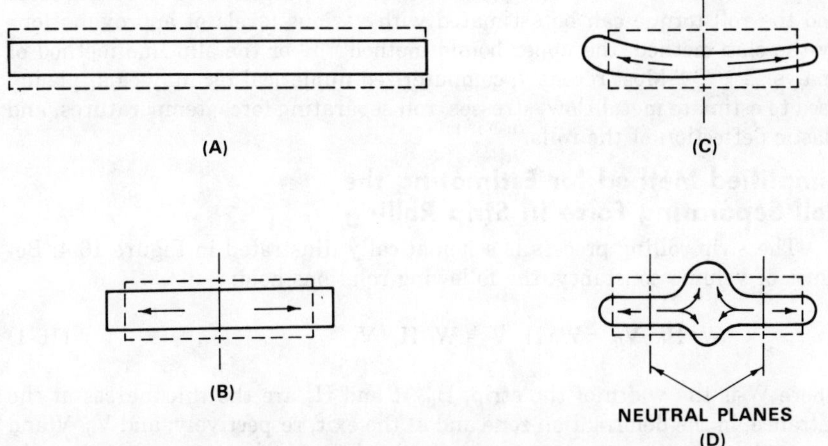

Figure 16-3. Four types of metal flow in rolling: (A) strip, (B) plate, (C) simple shape, (D) complex shape (broken and solid lines illustrate the sections before and after deformation, respectively).

(c) *Moderately Nonuniform Reduction in Cross Section.* In this case the reduction in the thickness direction is not uniform. The metal is elongated in the rolling direction, is spread in the width direction and is reduced nonuniformly in the thickness direction. Along the width, metal flow occurs only toward the edges of the section. Rolling of an oval section in rod rolling, or rolling of an airfoil section (Figure 16-3C), would be considered to be in this category.

(d) *Highly Nonuniform Reduction in Cross Section.* In this type of deformation, the reduction is highly nonuniform in the thickness direction. A portion of the rolled section is reduced in thickness while other portions may be extruded or increased in thickness (Figure 16-3D). As a result, in the width (lateral) direction metal flow may be toward the center. Of course, in addition, metal flows in the thickness direction as well as in the rolling (longitudinal) direction.

The above discussion illustrates that, except in strip rolling (Figure 16-3A), the metal flow in rolling is in three dimensions, i.e., in the thickness, width and rolling directions. Determinations of metal flow and rolling stresses in 3-D rolling, i.e., shape rolling, are very important in designing rolling mills and in setting up efficient production operations. However, the theoretical prediction of metal flow in such complex cases is nearly impossible at this time. Numerical techniques are being developed in an attempt to simulate metal flow in such complex rolling operations.

ROLLING OF STRIP

Very large numbers of books and papers have been published on the subject of strip rolling. The most rigorous analysis was performed by Orowan[16-6] and has been applied and computerized by various investigators.[16-7 to 16-12] More recent studies consider elastic flattening of the rolls and temperature conditions that exist in rolling.[16-9,16-13] The roll separating force and the roll torque can be estimated with various levels of approximations by the slab method, the upper bound method[16-10] or the slip line method of analysis.[16-2,16-4] Most recently, computerized numerical techniques are being used to estimate metal flow, stresses, roll separating force, temperatures, and elastic deflection of the rolls.[16-9,16-13]

Simplified Method for Estimating the Roll Separating Force in Strip Rolling

The strip rolling process is schematically illustrated in Figure 16-4. Because of volume constancy, the following relations hold:

$$W \cdot H_0 \cdot V_0 = W \cdot H \cdot V = W \cdot H_1 \cdot V_1 \tag{16-1}$$

where W is the width of the strip; H_0, H and H_1 are the thicknesses at the entrance, in the deformation zone and at the exit, respectively; and V_0, V and V_1 are the velocities at the entrance, in the deformation zone and at the exit, respectively. In order to satisfy Equation 16-1, the exit velocity V_1 must be larger than the entrance velocity V_0. Therefore, the velocity of the deforming material in the x or rolling direction must steadily increase from entrance to exit. At only one point along the roll/strip interface the surface velocity of

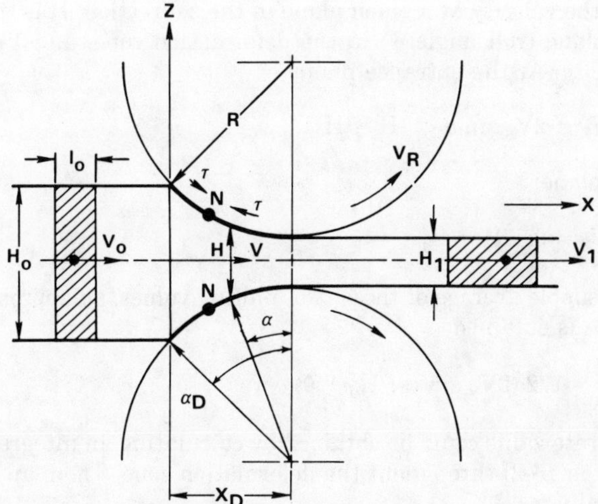

Figure 16-4. Schematic representation of strip rolling (strip has constant width, w, in y or width direction).

the roll, V_R, is equal to the velocity of the strip. This point is called the neutral point or neutral plane, indicated by N in Figure 16-4.

The interface frictional stresses are directed from the entrance and exit planes toward the neutral plane because the relative velocity between the roll surface and the strip changes its direction at the neutral plane. This will be considered later in estimating rolling stresses.

An approximate value for the roll separating force can be obtained by approximating the deformation zone, shown in Figure 16-4, with the homogeneous plane-strain upsetting process. Thus, Equation 10-12 would be valid, i.e., the load per unit width of the strip is:

$$L = \frac{2\bar{\sigma}}{\sqrt{3}}\left(1 + \frac{ml}{4h}\right) l \qquad (10\text{-}12)$$

However, in this case the following approximations must be made:

- Average strip height, $h = 0.5(H_0 + H_1)$.
- Average length of the deforming strip, $l = R\alpha_D$, with $\cos \alpha_D = 1 - (H_0 - H_1)2R$. In the literature, it is often recommended that the value of the projection of strip length X_D (Figure 16-4) be used for l; however, considering the effect of friction on the roll/strip interface length, $R\alpha_D$, it is more appropriate to use $l = R\alpha_D$.

To estimate the average value of the flow stress, $\bar{\sigma}$ ($\bar{\epsilon}$, $\dot{\bar{\epsilon}}$, θ), at a given rolling temperature θ, the average strain ε is obtained from the thickness reduction, i.e., $\bar{\epsilon} = \ln(H_0/H_1)$. The strain rate $\dot{\bar{\epsilon}}_\alpha$ is given by:

$$\dot{\bar{\epsilon}}_\alpha = V_Z/H = 2V_R \sin \alpha/H$$

$$= 2V_R \sin \alpha|[H_1 + 2R(1 - \cos \alpha)] \qquad (16\text{-}2)$$

where V_Z is the velocity at a given plane in the z direction, H is the thickness at a given plane (roll angle α) in the deformation zone, and V_R is the roll surface velocity. At the entrance plane:

$$V_Z = 2V_R \sin \alpha_D; \quad H = H_0$$

At the exit plane:

$$V_Z = 0; \quad H = H_1$$

By taking a simple average of these two limiting values, an approximate value of strain rate is obtained:

$$\dot{\bar{\epsilon}} = 1/2\,(2V_R \sin \alpha_D/H_0 + 0) \tag{16-3}$$

A more accurate value could be obtained by calculating an integrated average of $\dot{\bar{\epsilon}}_\alpha$ (Equation 16-2) throughout the deformation zone. Then, an average approximate value is:[16-1]

$$\dot{\bar{\epsilon}} = \frac{V_R}{H_0}\left[\frac{2(H_0 - H_1)}{R}\right]^{1/2} \tag{16-4}$$

Stress Distribution in Strip Rolling

The stress distribution in rolling is schematically illustrated in Figure 16-5. The maximum stress is at the neutral plane N. These stresses increase with increasing friction and length of the deformation zone, X_D. Tensile stresses applied to the strip at entrance or exit have the effects of reducing the maximum stress (by an amount approximately equal to $\Delta\sigma_z$ in Figure 16-5b) and shifting the position of the neutral plane. The analogy to plane-strain upsetting (Chapter 10) is illustrated in Figure 16-5(a).

The stress distribution can be calculated by using the equations derived in most textbooks[16-1 to 16-5] or by following the theory presented by Orowan.[16-6] However, these calculations are quite complex and require numerical techniques in order to avoid an excessive number of simplifying assumptions.

A computerized solution, with all necessary details and the listing of the FORTRAN computer program, is also given by Alexander.[16-8] Consequently, it is not useful to repeat in this chapter the classical derivations for calculating the stress distribution.

For a computerized calculation of rolling stresses, the deformation zone can be divided into an arbitrary number of elements with flat inclined surfaces (Figure 16-6). The element, illustrated in this figure, is located between the neutral and exit planes because the frictional stress τ is acting against the direction of metal flow. When this element is located between the entrance and neutral planes, τ acts in the direction of metal flow. The stress distribution within this element can be obtained by use of the slab method, as applied to plain-strain upsetting:[16-14]

$$\sigma_Z = \frac{K_2}{K_1} \ln\left(\frac{h_1}{h_0 + K_1 X}\right) + \sigma_{Z1} \tag{16-5}$$

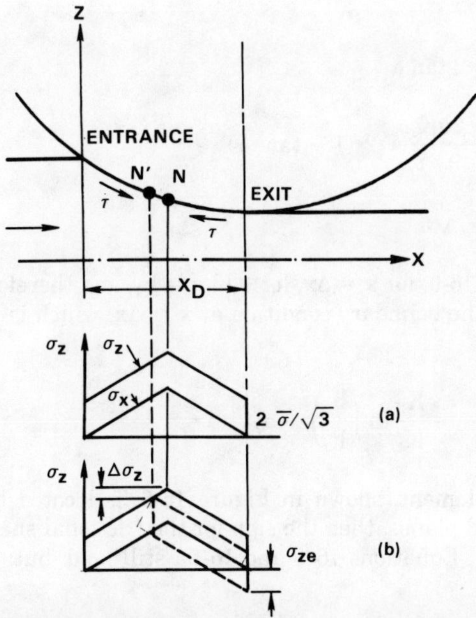

Figure 16-5. Schematic representation of stress distribution in rolling (a) without any tensile stresses at entry or exit and (b) with tensile stress σ_{ze} at exit.

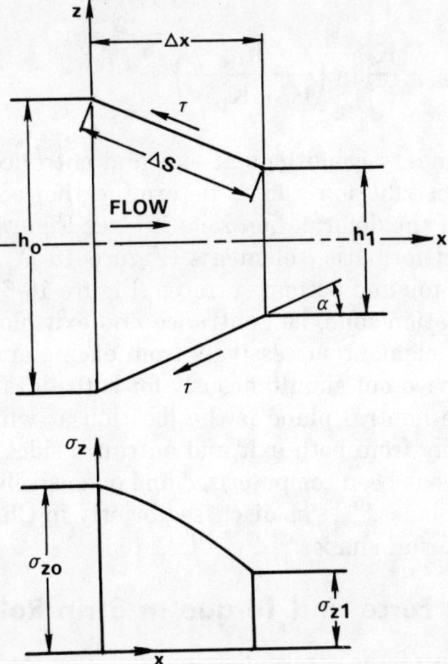

Figure 16-6. Schematic representation of stresses in deformation element.

where

$$K_1 = -2 \tan \alpha \tag{16-5a}$$

$$K_2 = -\frac{2\bar{\sigma}K_1}{\sqrt{3}} + 2\tau(1 + \tan^2 \alpha) \tag{16-5b}$$

$$\tau = m\bar{\sigma}/\sqrt{3}$$

Following Figure 16-6, for $x = \Delta x$, $h_0 + K_1 x = h_1$, and therefore Equation 16-5 gives $\sigma_z = \sigma_{z1}$, the boundary condition at $x = \Delta x$, which is known. For $x = 0$:

$$\sigma_Z = \sigma_{Z0} = \frac{K_2}{K_1} \ln\left(\frac{h_1}{h_0}\right) + \sigma_{Z1}$$

In case the element, shown in Figure 16-6, is located between the entrance and neutral planes, then the sign for the frictional shear stress τ must be reversed. Thus, Equations 16-5 and 16-5a still hold, but:

$$K_2 = -\frac{2\bar{\sigma}}{\sqrt{3}} K_1 - 2\tau(1 + \tan^2 \alpha) \tag{16-5c}$$

In this case, the value of the boundary condition at $x = 0$, i.e., σ_{Z0}, is known, and σ_{Z1} can be determined from Equation 16-5 to be:

$$\sigma_{Z1} = \sigma_{Z0} - \frac{K_2}{K_1} \ln\left(\frac{h_1}{h_0 + K_1 \Delta x}\right) \tag{16-6}$$

The stress boundary conditions at exit and entrance are known. To calculate the stress distribution and to determine the location of the neutral plane, the length of the deformation zone X_D (see Figures 16-4 and 16-5) can be divided into n deformation elements (Figure 16-7). Each element is approximated by flat top and bottom surfaces (Figure 16-6). Starting from both ends of the deformation zone, i.e., entrance and exit planes, the stresses are calculated for each element successively from each element to the next. The calculations are carried out simultaneously for both sides of the neutral plane. The location of the neutral plane is the location at which the stresses, calculated progressively from both exit and entrance sides, are equal.

This procedure has been computerized and extensively used in plane-strain forging of turbine blades,[16-15] as discussed briefly in Chapter 12, and in rolling of plates and airfoil shapes.[16-16,16-17]

Roll Separating Force and Torque in Strip Rolling

The integration of the stress distribution over the length of the deformation zone gives the total roll separating force per unit width.

The total torque is given by:

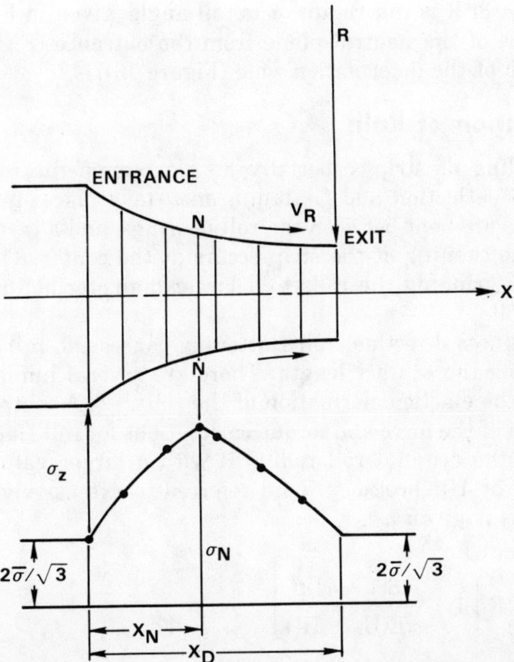

Figure 16-7. Calculation of stress distribution by dividing the deformation zone into a number of tapered elements (in this case, tensile stresses in strip are zero at both entrance and exit).

$$T = \int_0^{X_D} R\, dF \tag{16-7}$$

where X_D is the length of the deformation zone (Figure 16-7), R is roll radius, and F is the tangential force acting on the roll.

Assuming that all energy is transmitted from the roll to the workpiece by frictional force:

$$dF = \tau dS$$

In Figure 16-6, it can be seen that:

$$dS = dx/\cos\alpha = \sqrt{1 + \tan^2\alpha}\, dx \tag{16-8}$$

In the deformation zone, the frictional force is in the rolling direction between entry and neutral planes. It changes direction between the neutral and exit planes. Thus, the total roll torque per unit width is:

$$T = R\tau \left[\int_0^{X_N} (1 + \tan^2\alpha)dx - \int_{X_N}^{X_D} (1 + \tan^2\alpha)dx \right] \tag{16-9}$$

where $\tau = m\bar{\sigma}/\sqrt{3}$; R is roll radius; α is roll angle, given in Figure 16-4; X_N is the x distance of the neutral plane from the entrance (Figure 16-7); and X_D is the length of the deformation zone (Figure 16-7).

Elastic Deflection of Rolls

During rolling of strip, especially at room temperature, considerable amounts of roll deflection and flattening may take place. In the width direction, the rolls are bent between the roll bearings, and a certain amount of "crowning" or thickening of the strip occurs at the center. This can be corrected either by grinding the rolls to a larger diameter at the center or by using backup rolls.

In the thickness direction, roll flattening causes the roll radius to "enlarge", increasing the contact length. There are several numerical methods for calculating the elastic deformation of the rolls.(16-9) A method for approximate correction of the force and torque calculations for roll flattening entails replacement of the original roll radius R with a larger value R′. A value R′ is suggested by Hitchcock(16-18) and referred to extensively in the literature.(16-2,16-4) This is given as:

$$R' = R\left[1 + \frac{16(1 - \nu^2)p}{\pi E(H_0 - H_1)}\right] \tag{16-10}$$

where ν is the Poisson's ratio of the roll material, p is average roll pressure, and E is the E modulus of the roll material.

It is obvious that R′ and p influence each other. Therefore, a computerized iteration procedure is necessary for consideration of roll flattening in calculating rolling force or pressure. Thus, the value of p is calculated for the nominal roll radius R. Then R′ is calculated from Equation 16-10. If $R'/R \neq 1$, then the calculation of p is repeated with the new R′ value and so on until R′/R has approximately the value of 1.

ROLLING OF PLATE

In rolling of thick plates, metal flow occurs in three dimensions, as can be seen in Figure 16-3(B). The rolled material is elongated in the rolling direction as well as spread in the lateral or width direction. Spread in rolling is usually defined as the increase in width of a plate or slab as a percentage of its original width. The spread increases with increasing reduction and interface friction, decreasing plate width-to-thickness ratio, and increasing roll-diameter-to-plate-thickness ratio. In addition, the free edges tend to bulge with increasing reduction and interface friction. The three-dimensional metal flow that occurs in plate rolling is difficult to analyze. Therefore, most studies of this process have been experimental in nature, and several empirical formulae have been established for estimating spread.(16-19 to 16-21) Recently, attempts were also made to predict elongation or spread theoretically.(16-22 to 16-24) Once the spread has been estimated, the elongation can be determined from the volume constancy, or vice versa.

An Empirical Method for Estimating Spread in Plate Rolling

Among the various formulae available for predicting spread, Wusatowski's formula[16-20] is used most extensively and is given as:

$$W_1/W_0 = abcd(H_0/H_1)^P \qquad (16\text{-}11)$$

where W_1 and W_0 are final and initial widths of the plate, respectively; H_1 and H_0 are final and initial thicknesses of the plate, respectively; $P = 10^{(-1.269)}(W_0/H_0)(H_0/D)^{0.556}$; D is effective roll diameter; and a, b, c and d are constants that allow for variations in steel composition, rolling temperature, rolling speed and roll material, respectively. These constants vary slightly from unity, and their values can be obtained from the literature.[16-16,16-20,16-24]

An empirical formula for predicting spread, such as Equation 16-11, gives reasonable results within the range of conditions for the experiments from which the formula was developed. There is no formula that would make accurate predictions for all the conditions that exist in rolling. Thus, it is often necessary to attempt to estimate spread or elongation by theoretical means.

A Theoretical Method for Estimating Spread

The theoretical prediction of spread involves rather complex analysis and requires the use of computerized techniques.[16-16,16-22,16-23] A modular upper bound method has been recently used to predict metal flow, spread, elongation and roll torque.[16-16] The principles of this method are described below. Figure 16-8 illustrates the coordinate system, the division of the deformation zone into elements, and the notations used. The spread profile is defined in terms of a third-order polynomial, w(x), with two unknown coefficients, a_1 and a_2. The location of the neutral plane, x_n, is another unknown quantity. The following kinematically admissible velocity field, initially suggested by Hill,[16-25] was used:

$$V_x = 1/[w(x)h(x)] \qquad (16\text{-}12a)$$

$$V_y = \frac{1}{h(x)}\frac{d}{dx}\left[\frac{1}{w(x)}\right] \qquad (16\text{-}12b)$$

$$V_z = \frac{1}{w(x)}\frac{d}{dx}\left[\frac{1}{h(x)}\right] \qquad (16\text{-}12c)$$

Using Equations 16-12a, b and c, which contain two unknown parameters, a_1 and a_2, the following steps of the upper bound method were carried out:

1. Derive the expressions for strain-rate components $\dot{\epsilon}_x$, $\dot{\epsilon}_y$, $\dot{\epsilon}_z$ and $\dot{\gamma}_{xz}$. For this purpose, the formulae discussed in Chapter 3 are used.
2. Derive an expression for the effective strain rate $\dot{\bar{\epsilon}}$.
3. Calculate the total energy rate for plastic deformation:

$$\dot{E}_p = \int_v \bar{\sigma}\dot{\bar{\epsilon}}\, dV \qquad (16\text{-}13)$$

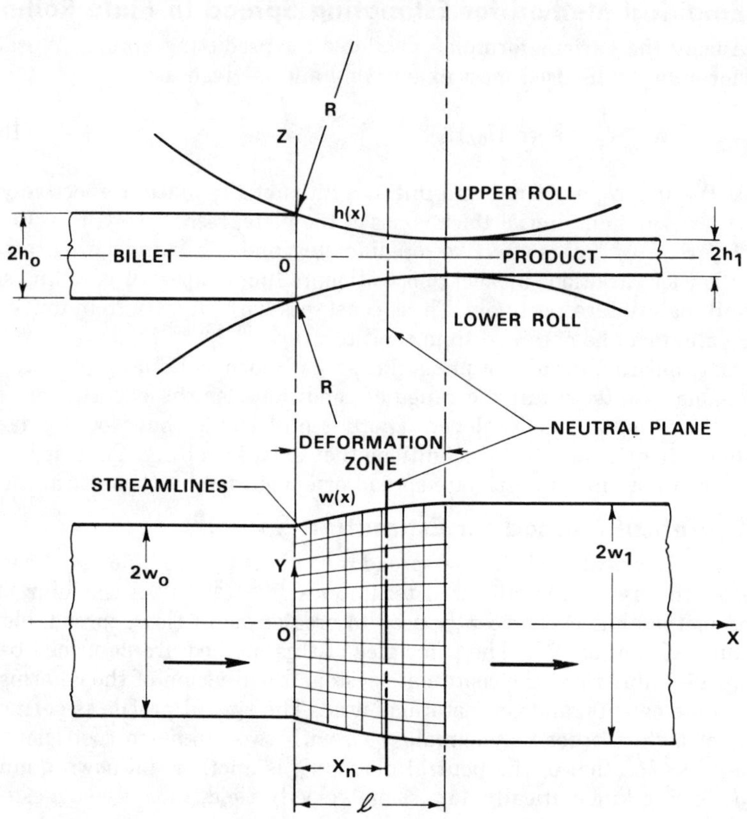

Figure 16-8. Configuration of deformation, and the grid system used in analysis of rolling thick plates.[16-16]

4. Calculate the rate of energy dissipated in overcoming friction at the roll/plate interface, $\dot{E}_f$. If ΔU is the velocity differential at the roll/material interface with surface area S, $\dot{E}_f$ is given as:

$$\dot{E}_f = \tau \int_s |\Delta U| dS \tag{16-14}$$

The frictional shear stress, $\tau = mk = m\bar{\sigma}/\sqrt{3}$, is considered to be constant and to act against the direction of relative slip between the rolls and the deformed plate. At this time the position of the neutral surface, described by the coordinate x_n in Figure 16-8, is an unknown.

5. Calculate the energy rate $\dot{E}_d$ due to shearing along the boundaries of velocity discontinuities. Such a boundary, for example, exists at the plane of entrance into the deformation zone at $x = 0$ in Figure 16-8. The energy rate due to a velocity discontinuity along a section of cross-sectional area A is given as:

$$\dot{E}_d = (\bar{\sigma}/\sqrt{3}) \int_A |\Delta V| dS \tag{16-15}$$

where ΔV is the magnitude of the velocity discontinuity across the boundary with area A.

6. Calculate the total energy dissipation rate, $\dot{E}_t$:

$$\dot{E}_t = \dot{E}_p + \dot{E}_f + \dot{E}_d \tag{16-16}$$

7. Minimize the total energy rate $\dot{E}_t$ with respect to the three unknown parameters (a_1, a_2 and x_n). Thus, determine the values of these parameters and the configuration of the spread, as given by the polynomial w(x).
8. Compute the value of the torque from the known spread profile, w(x), and the location of the neutral plane, x_n.

Steps 3 through 8 are carried out numerically using a computer program called SHPROL. The strains and strain rates are calculable numerically at any point in the deformation zone. Therefore, the flow stress of the deforming material, $\bar{\sigma}$, is considered to be a function of strain under cold rolling conditions and to be a function of strain, strain rate and temperature under hot rolling conditions.

Prediction of Stresses and Roll Separating Force in Plate Rolling

Once the spread (i.e., the boundaries of the deformation zone) has been calculated, this information can be used to predict the stresses and the roll separating force. The computerized procedure used here is in principle the same as the method discussed earlier for predicting the stresses in strip rolling.[16-16]

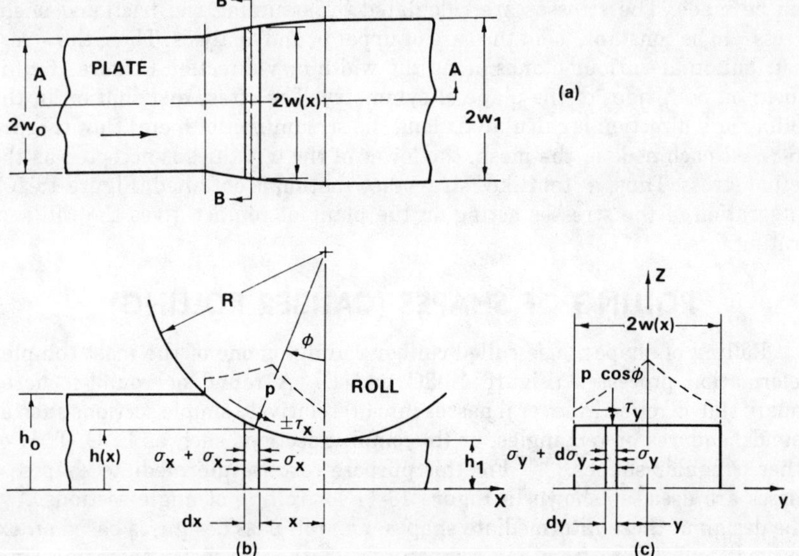

Figure 16-9. Schematic of the stress analysis in rolling of plates: (a) top view of the rolled plate, (b) stresses in the rolling direction, (c) stresses in the transverse direction.[16-16]

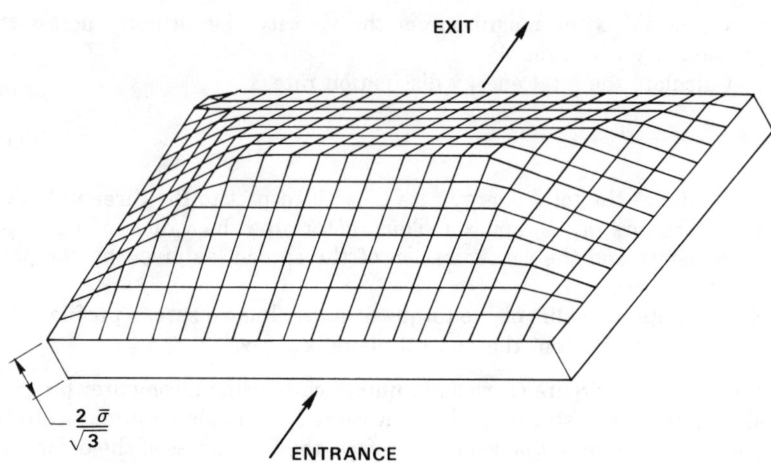

Figure 16-10. Three-dimensional schematic representation of the calculated stress (σ_z) distribution in plate rolling.[16-16]

The deformation zone under the rolls is divided into trapezoidal slabs, by planes normal to the rolling direction and along the stream tubes, as illustrated in Figures 16-6 and 16-9. The stresses acting on "strips" in the rolling and transverse directions are illustrated in Figure 16-9(b) and 16-9(c), respectively. As expected from the slab analysis, the stress distributions are very similar to those illustrated for strip rolling in Figures 16-5 to 16-7. By use of a numerical approach similar to that discussed for strip rolling, detailed predictions of stresses, in both the longitudinal and lateral directions, can be made. The stresses are calculated by assuming the frictional shear stress τ to be constant, as in the case of upper bound analysis. Thus, the stress distribution at various planes along the width or y direction (Figure 16-9) is linear on both sides of the plane of symmetry. The stress distribution in the rolling or x direction is calculated along the streamlines of metal flow (Figure 16-8). At each node of the mesh, the lower of the σ_z values is accepted as the actual stress. Thus, a "tentlike" stress distribution is obtained (Figure 16-10). Integration of the stresses acting on the plane of contact gives the roll separating force.

ROLLING OF SHAPES (CALIBER ROLLING)

Rolling of shapes, also called caliber rolling, is one of the most complex deformation processes (Figure 16-3C and D). A round or round-cornered square slab is rolled in several passes into (a) relatively simple sections such as rounds, squares or rectangles, or (b) complex sections such as L, U, T, H or other irregular shapes.[16-26] For this purpose certain intermediate shapes or passes are used, as shown in Figure 16-11 for rolling of angle sections.[16-27] The design of these intermediate shapes, i.e., roll pass design, is based on experience and differs from one company to another, even for the same final rolled section geometry. Relatively few quantitative data on roll pass design are available in the literature. Good summaries of references on this subject

Figure 16-11. Schematic illustration of five different roll-pass designs for a steel angle section.[16-27]

are given in several books[16-24,16-26,16-28 to 16-31] and in a few recent articles.[16-32,16-33]

There are basically two methods of rolling shapes or sections. The first method is "universal rolling", shown in Figure 16-12.[16-34] The second method is "caliber rolling", illustrated in Figures 16-11[16-27] and 16-13.[16-35] In universal rolling, the mill and stand constructions are more complex. However, in rolling of I-beams or other similar sections, this method allows more flexibility than does caliber rolling and requires smaller numbers of passes. This

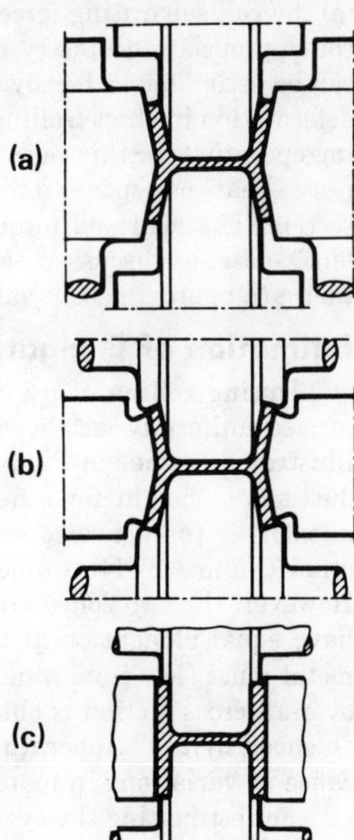

Figure 16-12. Universal rolling of flange beams: (a) universal rolling stand, (b) edging stand, (c) finishing stand.[16-34]

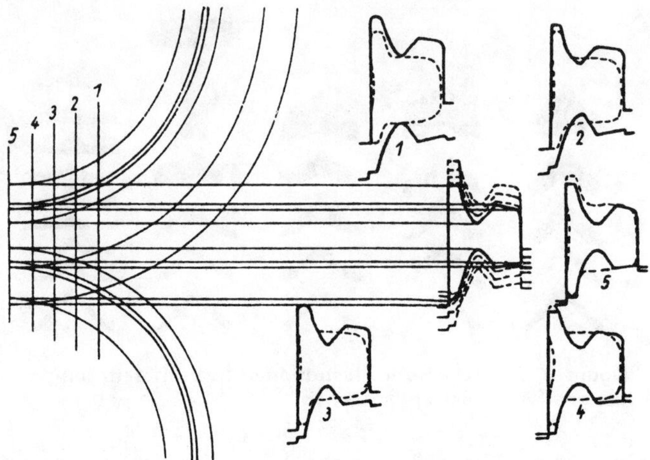

Figure 16-13. Analysis of a roll pass used in caliber rolling of rails (sketches 1 through 5 illustrate the stock in broken lines and the roll in full lines, at various positions in the deformation zone).[16-35]

is achieved because this method provides appropriate amounts of reductions, separately in webs and flanges.

For successful rolling of shapes, it is necessary to estimate for each stand (a) the roll separating force and torque, (b) the spread and elongation and (c) the appropriate geometry of the roll cavity or caliber. The force and torque can be estimated either by using empirical formulae or by approximating the deformation in shape rolling with that occurring in an "equivalent" plate rolling operation. In this case, the "equivalent" plate has initial and final thicknesses that correspond to the average initial and final thicknesses of the rolled section. The load and torque calculations can be performed for the "equivalent" plate, as discussed earlier in this chapter for plate rolling. The results then are approximately valid for the rolled shape considered.

Estimation of Elongation in Shape Rolling

During rolling of a given shape or section, the cross section is not deformed uniformly, as shown clearly by the example in Figure 16-13. This is illustrated further in Figure 16-14 for a relatively simple shape.[16-24] The reductions in height for zones A and B are not equal (Figure 16-14a). Consequently, if these two zones, A and B, were completely independent of each other (Figure 16-14b), zone B would be much more elongated than zone A. However, the two zones are connected and, as part of the rolled shape, must have equal elongation at the exit from the rolls. Therefore, during rolling, metal must flow from zone B into zone A so that a uniform elongation of the over-all cross section is obtained (Figure 16-14c). This lateral flow is also influenced by the temperature differences which exist in the cross section because of variations in material thickness and heat flow.

For estimating the over-all elongation, it is necessary to divide the initial section into a number of "equivalent" plates (A, B, C, etc.), as shown in Figure

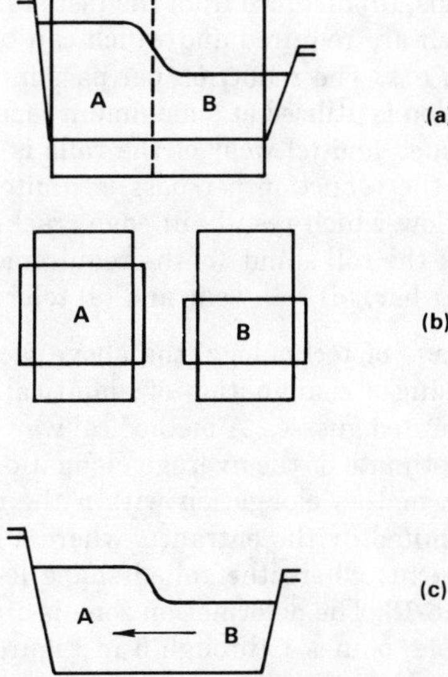

Figure 16-14. Nonuniform deformation in rolling of a shape: (a) initial and final sections, (b) two zones of the section considered as separate plates, (c) direction of lateral metal flow.[16-24]

16-14. The elongation or spread for an individual section, without the combined influence of other portions of the section, can be estimated by using the plate rolling analogy and by using the techniques discussed earlier in this chapter. The combined effect can be calculated by taking a "weighted average" of the individual elongations. For example, if the original section is to be divided into an equivalent system consisting of two plate sections, A and B in Figure 16-14, with individual cross-sectional areas A_a and A_b, then the following weighted-average formula can be used:

$$\lambda_m = \frac{A_0}{A_1} = \frac{A_{a0} + A_{b0}}{A_{a1} + A_{b1}} = \frac{A_{a1}\lambda_a + A_{b1}\lambda_b}{A_{a1} + A_{b1}} \tag{16-17}$$

where λ is elongation coefficient (i.e., cross-sectional area at entrance/cross-sectional area at exit); A is cross-sectional area; m is a subscript denoting average; a and b are subscripts denoting section portions A and B, respectively; and 0 and 1 are subscripts denoting entrance and exit values, respectively.

Computer-Aided Roll Pass Design in Caliber Rolling

Estimation of the number of passes and of the roll geometry for each pass is the most difficult aspect of shape rolling. Ideally, for this purpose the following factors must be considered:

1. *The Characteristics of the Available Installation:* These include: (a) diameters and lengths of the rolls, (b) bar dimensions, (c) distance be-

tween roll stands, (d) distance from the last stand to the shear and (e) tolerances which are required and which can be maintained.

2. *Reduction per Pass:* The reduction per pass must be adjusted so that (a) the installation is utilized at a maximum capacity, (b) the roll stands are not overloaded and (c) wear of the rolls is minimized. The maximum value of the reduction per pass is limited by (a) the excessive lateral metal flow which results in edge cracking, (b) the power and load capacity of the roll stand, (c) the requirement for the rolls to bite in the incoming bar, (d) roll wear and (e) tolerance requirements.

At the present stage of technology, the above factors are considered in roll pass design by using a combination of empirical knowledge, some calculations and some educated guesses. A methodical way of designing roll passes requires not only an estimate of the average elongation, as discussed earlier, but also the variation of this elongation within the deformation zone. The deformation zone is limited by the entrance, where a prerolled shape enters the rolls, and by the exit, where the rolled shape leaves the rolls. This is illustrated in Figure 16-13. The deformation zone is cross sectioned with several planes (for example, planes 1 through 5 in Figure 16-13; 1 is at the entrance, 5 is at the exit). The roll position and the deformation of the incoming billet are investigated at each of these planes. Thus, a more detailed analysis of metal flow and an improved method for designing the configuration of the rolls are possible. It is evident that this technique can be drastically improved and made extremely efficient by use of computer-aided techniques.

In recent years, most companies that produce shapes have computerized their roll pass design procedures for rolling rounds[16-33,16-36 to 16-40] or structural shapes.[16-36,16-40 to 16-43] In most of these applications, the elongation per pass and the distribution of the elongation within the deformation zone for each pass are predicted by using an empirical formula. If the elongation per pass is known, it is then possible, by use of computer graphics, to calculate the cross-sectional area of a section for a given pass, i.e., reduction and roll geometry. The roll geometry can be expressed parametrically, i.e., in terms of angles, radii, etc. These geometric parameters can then be varied to "optimize" the area reduction per pass and to obtain an acceptable degree of "fill" of the roll caliber used for that pass.

Computer-Aided Roll Pass Design of Airfoil Sections

For analyzing metal flow and predicting force and torque in rolling of airfoils, two computer programs have been developed in a recent study.[16-17] The first of these programs is called "SHPROL" and uses upper-bound analysis in a numerical form to predict spread and roll torque. SHPROL is based on the following simplifying assumptions:

1. The initial contact between the rolls and the entrance section can be approximated as a straight line. (This is only correct if the upper and lower surfaces of the initial section already have the shape of the rolls.)
2. An airfoil shape can be considered as an aggregate of slabs, as shown in Figure 16-15.
3. Plane sections perpendicular to the rolling direction remain plane during rolling. Thus, the axial velocity (i.e, velocity in the rolling or x

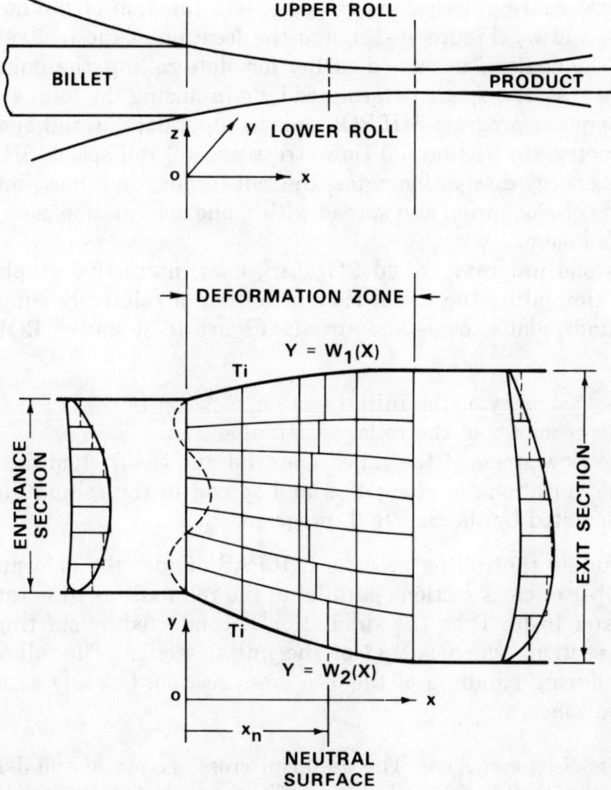

Figure 16-15. Configuration of deformation zone in application of numerical upper bound analysis to rolling of airfoil shapes.[16-17]

direction) at any section perpendicular to the rolling direction is uniform over the entire cross section.

4. The velocity components in the transverse or y direction and in the thickness or z direction are functions of x and linear in the y and z coordinates, respectively.

In Figure 16-15 each element is considered as a plate for which it is possible to derive a kinematically admissible velocity field. The total energy dissipation rate of the process, $\dot{E}_T$, is:

$$\dot{E}_T = \dot{E}_P + \dot{E}_D + \dot{E}_F \qquad (16\text{-}18)$$

where $\dot{E}_P$ is the energy rate of plastic deformation and is calculated for each element by integrating the product of flow stress and the strain rate over the element volume, $\dot{E}_D$ represents the energy rates associated with velocity discontinuities and is due to internal shear between the elements, and $\dot{E}_F$ is the energy rate due to friction between the rolls and the deforming material.

The total energy dissipation rate, $\dot{E}_T$, is a function of unknown spread profiles, w_1 and w_2 (Figure 16-15), and the location of the neutral plane x_n. Similar to the analysis discussed earlier for plate rolling, the unknown coefficients of w_1, w_2 and x_n are determined by minimizing the total energy rate.

The computer program SHPROL uses as input data (a) roll and incoming shape geometry, (b) friction, (c) flow stress and (d) roll speed. SHPROL can predict the energy dissipation rates, the roll torque, and, most importantly, the amounts of elongation and spread within one deformation zone, in rolling of any airfoil shape.

The second program, called ROLPAS, uses interactive graphics and is capable of simulating the metal flow in rolling of relatively simple shapes, such as rounds, plates, ovals and airfoils (Figure 16-3b and c). ROLPAS uses as input:

(a) The geometry of the initial section.
(b) The geometry of the rolls, i.e., final section.
(c) The flow stress of the rolled material and the friction factor.
(d) The variations in elongation and spread in the rolling direction, as calculated by the SHPROL program.

To simulate the rolling process, ROLPAS divides the deformation zone into a number of cross sections parallel to the roll axis, as illustrated in Figures 16-8 and 16-16. Then the simulation is conducted by starting with the first cross section, which is that of the initial section. The following steps take place during handling of the J'th cross section, i.e., any section in the deformation zone:

1. *Cross-Sectional Area.* The material cross section at the J-1st section is input to the J'th roll section (first section has the area of the incoming shape). The variation of spread or elongation, estimated earlier by the SHPROL program, allows calculation of the area at each cross section, J, in Figure 16-16. Due to elongation, the area of the J'th cross section is smaller than that of the J-1st section, as estimated by the spread calculations made by SHPROL.
2. *Stress Analysis and Determination of Boundaries at Each Cross Section.* From step 1, the cross-sectional area at each section is known. In order to determine the metal flow during deformation from the J-1st section to the J'th section, a stress analysis is performed. For this purpose the well-known slab method is used in a numerical form, as discussed earlier for rolling of strips and plates. As can be seen in Figure 16-17, the stress distribution on the J-1st section allows determination of the neutral surface(s). The material flows away from the neutral surface(s), at which deformation is only in the height or z direction. The position of the neutral surface at section J-1, and the known cross-sectional area at section J, allow determination of the material boundaries at section J, as can be seen in Figure 16-16.
3. *Roll Separating Force and Torque.* In step 2 the stress distribution and the metal flow are calculated on the sections in the lateral direction (Figure 16-17). Thus, the ROLPAS program determines the geometry of the actual zone of contact between the material and the rolls, a plan

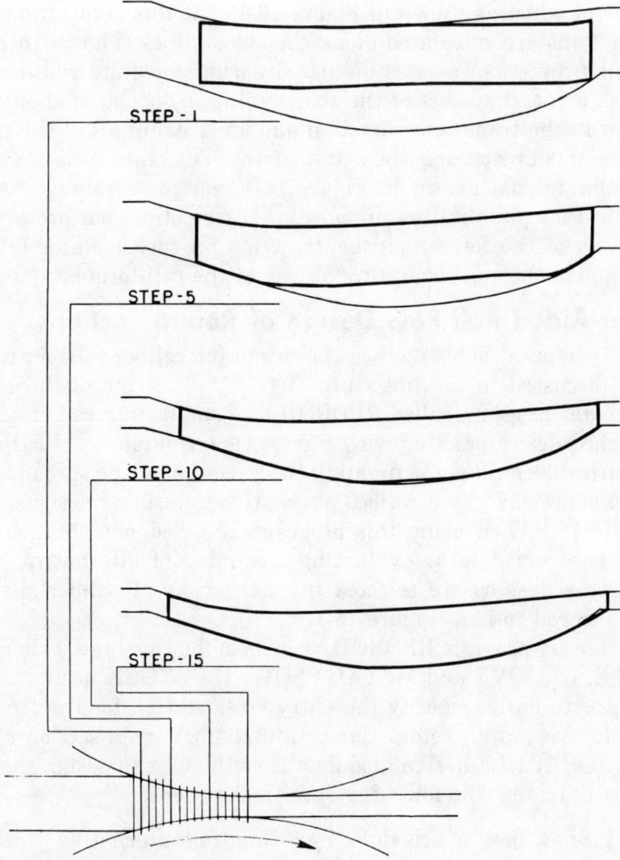

Figure 16-16. Selected simulation steps as displayed by ROLPAS for a test airfoil shape (cold rolling of steel from rectangular stock).

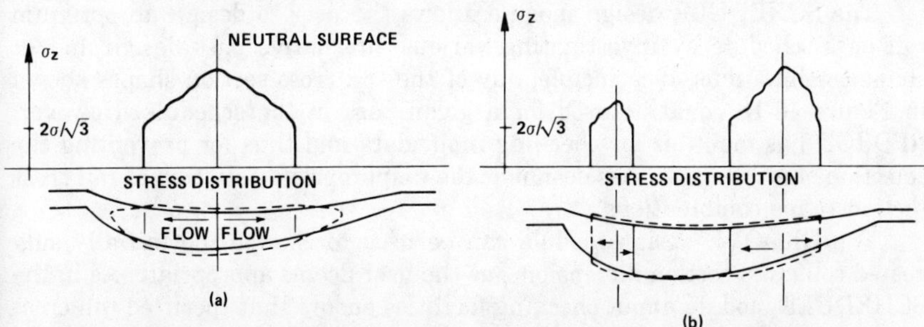

Figure 16-17. Representative stress distributions and metal flow directions for single and dual deformation zones: (a) single deformation zone, one neutral surface; (b) two deformation zones, two neutral surfaces.[16-17]

view of which is shown in Figure 16-15. At this point, the stress distributions are calculated along the streamlines (Figure 16-15) in the rolling direction, as was discussed earlier for plate rolling. At each mesh point, the lower of the stress values σ_Z (calculated on cross sections in the transverse direction and on streamlines in the rolling direction) is accepted as the actual stress. The result is a stress surface similar to that shown in Figure 16-10 for plate rolling. As was described for plate rolling, integration of the stress surface and consideration of the force components acting on each nodular roll surface area give the roll separating force and the roll torque.

Computer-Aided Roll Pass Design of Round Sections

Several computer-aided methods for designing caliber rolls for rod rolling have been discussed in the literature.[16-33,16-36 to 16-40] One of these methods was a computer program called RPDROD for establishing roll cross sections and pass schedules interacting with a graphics terminal.[16-33] RPDROD uses (a) an empirical formula for estimating the variation of the spread in the roll bite and (b) parametrically described alternative roll caliber designs, as shown in Figure 16-18. When using this program, the designer obtains an "optimum" roll pass schedule by evaluating a number of alternatives in which individual pass designs are selected from a variety of caliber shapes commonly used in rod rolling (Figure 16-18).

The computer program RPDROD consists of four modules, called STOCK, SCHEDULE, GROOVE and METAL FLOW. The STOCK design module allows the user to design/specify the entry cross section for the first pass in the schedule. A square, rectangular or round stock cross section can be defined. The SCHEDULE design module allows the user to design the roll pass schedule by providing the following specific functions:

1. Add a new pass to schedule, by estimating alternative roll cross section dimensions from design data provided by spread/elongation calculations.
2. Delete pass design data from the schedule in order to investigate alternative pass designs.
3. Review and/or provide hard copy of existing pass design data.

The SCHEDULE design module allows the user to design an optimum roll pass schedule by investigating various alternative pass design and/or shape combinations. In principle, any of the roll cross section shapes shown in Figure 16-18 could be used for a given pass in the schedule. However, RPDROD has facilities for checking input data and thus for preventing the selection of an illogical pass design or the inappropriate selection of roll cross section shape combinations.

The GROOVE design module can be used to change the initially suggested roll cross section dimensions, as the user deems appropriate. As in the SCHEDULE module, input checking facilities ensure that specified roll cross section dimensions are consistent with the chosen roll cross section shape and bar entry cross section.

The METAL FLOW design module provides the user with details of metal

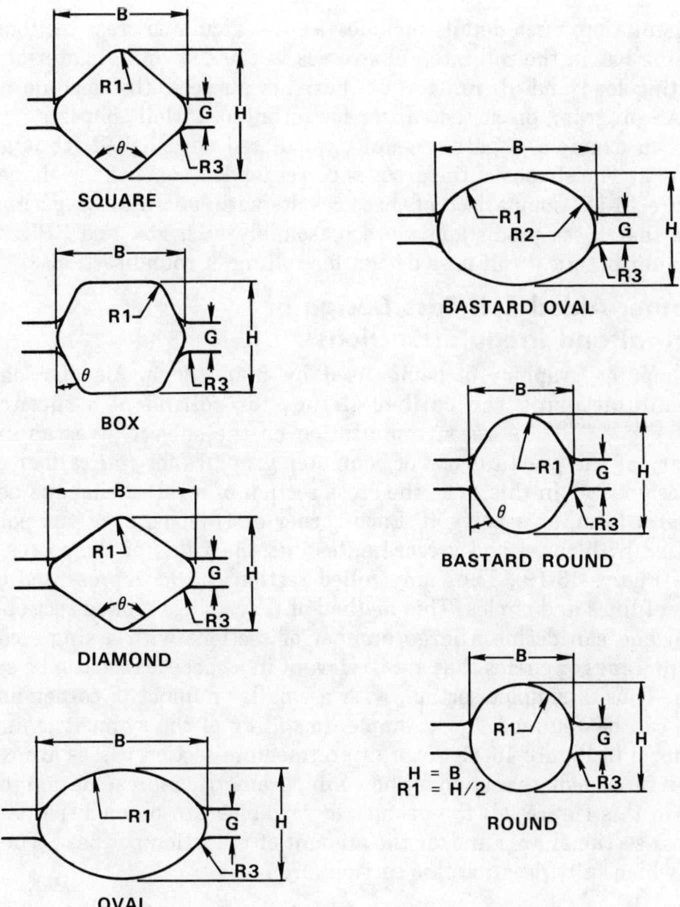

Figure 16-18. Various groove (caliber) shapes considered by the RPDROD program.[16-33]

Table 16-1. Summary of pass schedule information for the laboratory experiments as simulated by the program RPDROD

Pass number	Groove shape	Rotation angle, degrees	Exit area, in.^{2}	Exit speed, fpm	Reduction in area, %	Area fill, %	Roll force, tons	Horse-power	Roll speed, rpm
Stock	Square	0.0	1.559	60.0					
1	Square	45.0	1.394	55.6	10.6	93.2	5.3	1.3	30.0
2	Square	90.0	1.171	57.5	16.0	96.1	16.3	6.3	30.0
3	Square	90.0	1.042	57.7	11.0	95.7	8.7	2.5	30.0
4	Oval	45.0	0.873	59.4	16.2	98.8	14.1	6.2	30.0
5	Round	90.0	0.780	58.1	10.6	99.3	5.9	1.9	30.0
6	Oval	90.0	0.675	58.3	13.5	101.1	9.1	2.9	30.0
7	Round	90.0	0.595	59.1	11.8	98.9	4.8	1.4	30.0

flow simulation. Such details include: (a) the calculated cross sections of the deforming bar in the roll bite, (b) stresses in the deforming material, (c) roll separating load and (d) roll torque. For this purpose, this module uses the ROLPAS program, discussed earlier for rolling of airfoil shapes.

As an example, a pass schedule, calculated with RPDROD, is given in Table 16-1. The shapes of the grooves correspond to some of the shapes given in Figure 16-18. Comparison of these results with laboratory experiments indicated that these predictions were reasonably accurate, and RPDROD can be used for practical roll pass design for rolling of round sections.[16-33]

Computer-Aided Roll Pass Design of Structural and Irregular Sections

Computer graphics is being used by many companies for designing and manufacturing the caliber shapes for rolling of structural sections.[16-36,16-40 to 16-43] A recent publication on the subject gives an excellent summary of the practical use of computer graphics for roll caliber and roll pass design.[16-43] In this case, the cross section of a rolled shape is described in general form, as a polygon. Each corner or fillet point of the polygon is identified with the x and y coordinates and the value of the corresponding radius (Figure 16-19). Thus, any rolled section can be represented by a sequence of lines and circles. This method of describing a rolled section is very general and can define a large number of sections with a single computer program. Lines or circles that are irrelevant in a specific case can be set equal to zero. Thus, a simpler section, with a smaller number of corner and fillet points, can be obtained. For example, in rolling of the symmetric angle section shown in Figure 16-11, several intermediate section passes are required. Such an intermediate section is shown in parametric representation in Figure 16-20. In this figure, all the geometric variables can be modified to change the cross-sectional area and/or the amount of reduction per pass. These variables, which fully describe this section, are:

SELA = length (of one leg) at centerline.
BETAG = angle at top corner.
RK = radius at top corner.
AL = length of straight portion at top.
RD = radius of leg at top.

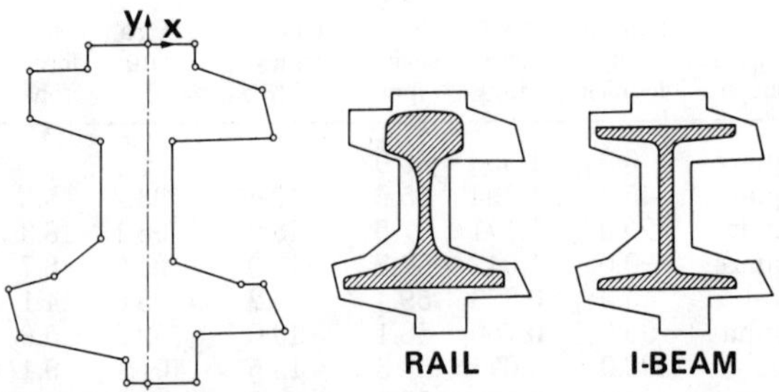

Figure 16-19. Geometric representation of a rolled section as a polygon.[16-43]

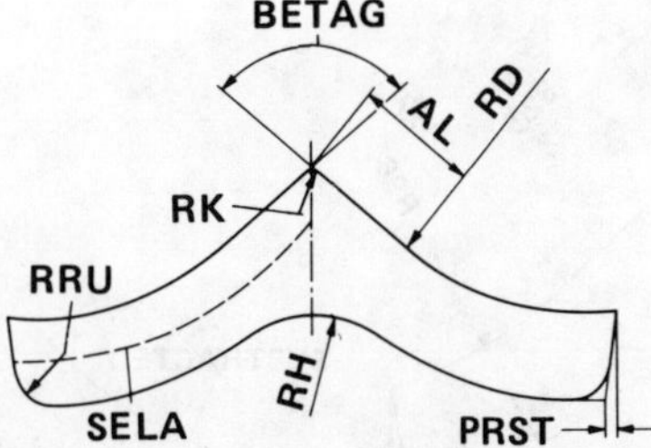

Figure 16-20. Parametric representation of an intermediate caliber pass for a symmetric angle section.[16-43]

PRST = projection of draft angle.
RRU = radius at lower tip of leg.
RH = radius at bottom corner.

In establishing the final section geometry, the designer assigns desired values to the variables listed above and, in addition, inputs the desired cross-sectional area and the degree of caliber fill, e.g., desired ratio of rolled section area versus section area on the caliber rolls. Thus, there is only one geometric variable that is calculated by the computer program, and that is the thickness of the leg of the angle section. In the example shown in Figure 16-21, where all dimensions are in millimetres, the leg thickness is calculated to be 18.2 mm. The designer compares this section geometry, given in Figure 16-21, with the caliber geometry of the next pass that has been generated in a similar way. Let us assume that the section shown in Figure 16-21 appears to be too long, i.e., SELA is 67.5 mm, and should be reduced to 65 mm without modifying the other variables. The interactive program is rerun with the new value of SELA. The modified section, shown in Figure 16-22, is slightly thicker than the original section in order to maintain the same cross-sectional area.

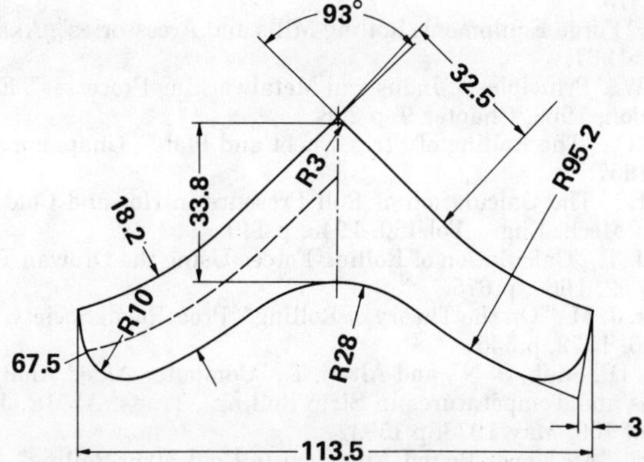

Figure 16-21. Alternative design for an intermediate angle pass, obtained by assigning values to the parameters of Figure 16-20 (cross-sectional area, 2522 mm^2; fill, 100%).[16-43]

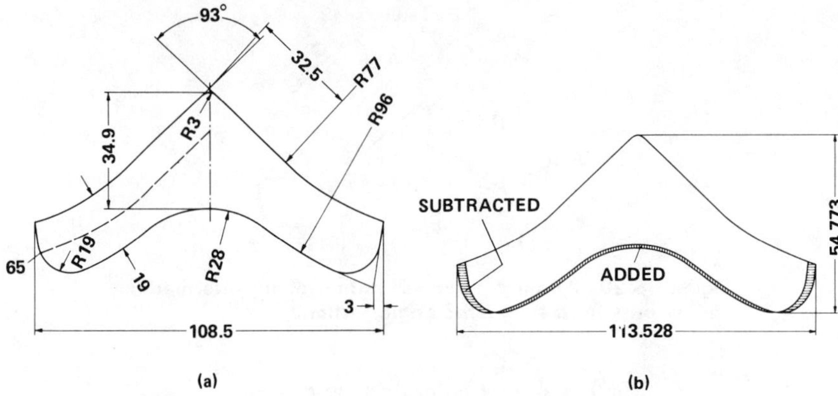

Figure 16-22. Modified design of the intermediate angle pass shown in Figure 16-21: (a) new dimensions, (b) added and subtracted areas (cross-sectional area, 2523 mm²; fill, 100%).[16-43]

This interactive graphics program does not involve any analysis of metal flow or stresses. Nevertheless, it is extremely useful to the designer for (a) modifying section geometries quickly and accurately, (b) calculating cross-sectional areas and (c) cataloging all this geometrical information systematically. The program also prepares automatically (a) engineering drawings of the sections and of the templates for quality control and (b) NC tapes for milling the templates and the graphite EDM electrodes used in manufacturing the cutting tools necessary for machining of the rolls.[16-43]

REFERENCES

16-1. Dieter, G. E., "Mechanical Metallurgy", McGraw-Hill Book Company, Inc., New York, 1961, Chapter 19, p 488.

16-2. Thomsen, E. G., Yang, C. T., and Kobayashi, S., "Mechanics of Plastic Deformation in Metal Processing", The Macmillan Company, New York, 1965, Chapter 18, p 373.

16-3. Geleji, A., "Forge Equipment, Rolling Mills and Accessories", Akademiai Kiado, Budapest, 1967.

16-4. Rowe, G. W., "Principles of Industrial Metalworking Processes", Edward Arnold, Ltd., London, 1968, Chapter 9, p 208.

16-5. Larke, E. C., "The Rolling of Strip, Sheet and Plate", Chapman and Hall, Ltd., London, 1957.

16-6. Orowan, E., "The Calculation of Roll Pressure in Hot and Cold Flat Rolling", Proc. Inst. Mech. Engr., Vol 150, 1943, p 140.

16-7. Hockett, J. T., "Calculation of Rolling Forces Using the Orowan Theory", Trans. ASM, Vol 52, 1960, p 675.

16-8. Alexander, J. M., "On the Theory of Rolling", Proc. Royal Society London, Series A, Vol 326, 1972, p 535.

16-9. Lahoti, G. D., Shah, S. N., and Altan, T., "Computer Aided Analysis of the Deformations and Temperatures in Strip Rolling", Trans. ASME, J. Engr. for Industry, Vol 100, May 1978, p 159.

16-10. Avitzur, B., "An Upper-Bound Approach to Cold Strip Rolling", Trans. ASME, J. Engr. for Industry, Feb 1964, p 31.

16-11. Sims, R. B., "The Calculation of Roll Force and Torque in Hot Rolling Mills", Proc. Inst. Mech. Engr., Vol 168, 1954, p 191.

16-12. Ford, H., and Alexander, J. M., "Simplified Hot-Rolling Calculations", J. Inst. Metals, Vol 92, 1963-64, p 397.
16-13. McPherson, D. J., "Contributions to the Theory and Practice of Cold Rolling", Metallurgical Trans., Vol 5, Dec 1974, p 2479.
16-14. Altan, T., and Fiorentino, R. J., "Prediction of Loads and Stresses in Closed-Die Forging", Trans. ASME, J. Engr. for Industry, May 1971, p 477.
16-15. Akgerman, N., and Altan, T., "Application of CAD/CAM in Forging Turbine and Compressor Blades", Trans. ASME, J. Engr. Power, Vol 98, Series A, No. 2, April 1976, p 290.
16-16. Lahoti, G. D., *et al,* "Computer Aided Analysis of Metal Flow and Stresses in Plate Rolling", J. Mech. Work. Tech., Vol 4, 1980, p 105.
16-17. Akgerman, N., Lahoti, G. D., and Altan, T., "Computer Aided Roll Pass Design in Rolling of Airfoil Shapes", J. Applied Metalworking, Vol 1, 1980, p 30.
16-18. Hitchcock, J. H., "Roll Neck Bearings", Report to ASME Research Committee, 1935, cited in "The Rolling of Metals", by L. R. Underwood, Vol I, pp 15-16, John Wiley and Sons, Inc., New York, 1950.
16-19. Ekelund, S., in H. Neumann, "Roll Pass Design" (in German), VEB Deutscher Verlag, Leibzig, 1963, p 48.
16-20. Wusatowski, Z., "Hot Rolling: A Study of Draught, Spread and Elongation", Iron and Steel, London, Vol 28, 1955, p 69.
16-21. Sparling, L. G. M., "Formula for Spread in Hot Rolling", Proc. Inst. Mech. Engr., 175 (1961), p 604.
16-22. Oh, S. I., and Kobayashi, S., "An Approximate Method for Three-Dimensional Analysis of Rolling", Int. J. Mech. Sci., Vol 17, 1975, p 293.
16-23. Kummerling, R., and Lipmann, H., "On Spread on Rolling", Mech. Research Communications, Vol 2, 1975, p 113.
16-24. Neumann, H., "Design of Rolls in Shape Rolling" (in German), VEB Deutscher Verlag, Leibzig, 1969.
16-25. Hill, R., "A General Method of Analysis for Metalworking Processes", Inst. J. Mech. Sci., Vol 16, 1974, p 521.
16-26. Beynon, R. E., "Roll Design and Mill Layout", Association of Iron and Steel Engineers, Pittsburgh, 1956.
16-27. Schutza, A., "Comparison of Roll Pass Designs Used for Rolling Angle Sections" (in German), Stahl und Eisen, Vol 90, 1970, p 796.
16-28. British Steel Corporation, "Roll Pass Design", Sheffield, England, 1979.
16-29. Trinks, W., Roll-Pass Design, Vol I and II, The Penton Publishing Company, 1941.
16-30. Wusatowski, Z., "Fundamentals of Rolling", Pergamon Press, New York, 1969.
16-31. Hoff, E. H., and Dahl, T., Rolling and Roll-Shape Design (in German), Verlag Stahleisen, Düsseldorf, 1956.
16-32. El-Nikhaily, A. E. G., "Metal Flow Models for Shape Rolling" (in German), Doctoral Dissertation, Technical University of Aachen, 1979.
16-33. Kennedy, K. F., Lahoti, G. D., and Altan, T., "Computer Aided Analysis of Metal Flow, Stresses and Roll Pass Design in Rolling of Rods", paper submitted to AISE Journal, Sept 1982.
16-34. Bollmann, K., and Kuchenbuch, G., "Development of Methods for Manufacturing of Wide- and Parallel-Flanged V-beams" (in German), Stahl und Eisen, Vol 80, 1960, p 1501.
16-35. Kruger, C. M., "Characteristics for the Theory and Practice of Roll Pass Design" (in German), Stahl und Eisen, Vol 81, 1961, p 858.
16-36. Raghupathi, P. S., and Altan, T., "Roll Pass Design in Shape Rolling", unpublished review of German literature, 1980, Battelle-Columbus Laboratories, Columbus, OH.
16-37. Neumann, H., and Schulze, R., "Programmed Roll Pass Design for Blocks" (in German), Neue Hütte, Vol 19, 1974, p 460.
16-38. Gedin, H., "Programmed Roll Pass Design for Quality Steels" (in German), Der Kalibreur, Vol 11, 1969, p 41.
16-39. Suppo, U., Izzo, A., and Diana, P., "Electronic Computer Used in Roll Design Work for Rounds", Der Kalibreur, Vol 19, Sept 1973, p 3.

16-40. Private Communication with A. G. Schloeman-Siemag, Düsseldorf, W. Germany, Sept 1979.

16-41. Spyra, J., and Ludyga, J., "Mechanization of Roll Engineering Calculations Using Modern Electronic Computers", Der Kalibreur, Vol 28, 1978, p 3.

16-42. Metzdorf, J., "Computer Aided Roll Pass Design–Possibilities of Application" (in German and French), Der Kalibreur, No. 34, 1981, p 29.

16-43. Schmeling, F., "Computer Aided Roll Pass Design and Roll Manufacturing" (in German), Stahl und Eisen, Vol 102, 1982, p 771.

CHAPTER 17
Drawing of Rod, Wire, Shapes and Tubes

Drawing is one of the oldest metal forming operations and has major industrial significance. This process allows excellent surface finishes and closely controlled dimensions to be obtained in long products that have constant cross sections. In drawing, a previously rolled, extruded or fabricated product with a solid or hollow cross section is pulled through a die at a relatively high speed.[17-1,17-2] In drawing of steel or aluminum wire, for example, exit speeds of several thousand feet per minute are very common. The die geometry determines the final dimensions, the cross-sectional area of the drawn product, and the reduction in area. Drawing is usually conducted at room temperature using a number of passes or reductions through consecutively located dies. At times, annealing may be necessary after a number of drawing passes before the drawing operation is continued. The deformation is accomplished by a combination of tensile and compressive stresses that are created by the pulling force at the exit from the die, by the back-pull tensile force that is present between consecutive passes, and by the die configuration. The principles of drawing solid and hollow sections were illustrated in Chapter 2 (Figures 2-29, 2-31 and 2-32).

In wire or rod drawing (Figures 2-29), the section is usually round but could also be a shape. Figure 17-1 illustrates a few examples of drawn shapes.[17-2] In cold drawing of shapes, the basic contour of the incoming shape is established by cold rolling passes that are usually preceded by annealing. After rolling, the section shape is refined and reduced to close tolerances by cold drawing, as shown in Figure 17-2.[17-3] Here again, a number of annealing steps may be necessary to eliminate the effects of strain hardening, i.e., to reduce the flow stress and increase the ductility.

In tube drawing without a mandrel, also called tube sinking, the tube is initially pointed to facilitate feeding through the die; it is then reduced in outside diameter while the wall thickness and the tube length are increased

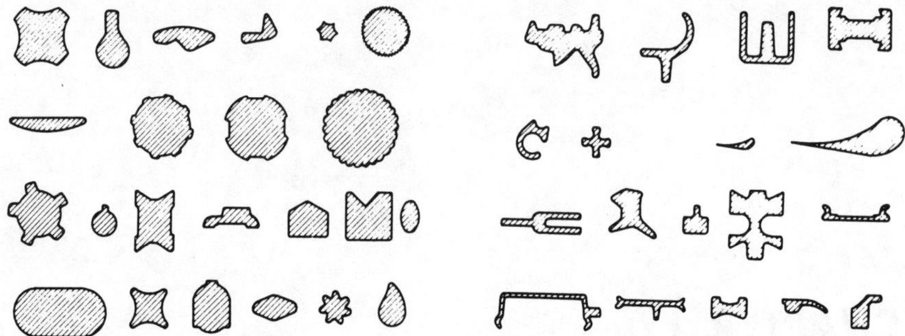

Figure 17-1. Example of cold drawn steel shapes (left) drawn from round or square sections and (right) drawn from pre-rolled sections.[17-2]

(Figure 2-32). The magnitudes of thickness increase and tube elongation depend on the flow stress of the drawn part, die geometry and interface friction.

Drawing with a fixed plug (Figure 17-3) is widely known and used for drawing of large-to-medium-diameter straight tubes. The plug, when pushed into the deformation zone, is pulled forward by the frictional force created by the sliding movement of the deforming tube. Thus, it is necessary to hold the plug in the correct position with a plug bar. In drawing of long and small-diameter tubes, the plug bar may stretch and even break. In such cases it is advantageous to use a floating plug (Figure 17-4). This process can be used to draw any length of tubing by coiling the drawn tube at high speeds up to 2000 ft/min. In drawing with a moving mandrel, the mandrel travels at the speed at which the section exits from the die (Figure 2-31). This process, also called ironing, is widely used for thinning of the walls of drawn cups or shells, for example, in the production of beverage cans or artillery shells.

DRAWING OF WIRE AND ROD

Wire and rod drawing are very similar in principle. Normally, both are cold forming processes that produce excellent surface finishes and close diameter tolerances. Both start with hot rolled bar or rod. This material is first freed from scale and dirt by pickling; it is then lubricated by coating with lime. Lime acts as a lubricant carrier and neutralizes any acid remaining from pickling.[17-1] Rods that cannot be coiled are drawn in draw benches, at draw speeds of up to 500 ft/min. Wire can be coiled, and therefore it is drawn through successive dies and rolled on bull blocks between drawing passes.

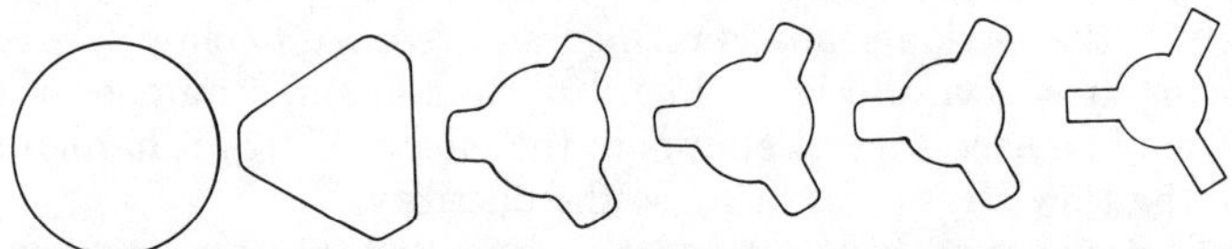

Figure 17-2. Cold rolled (round to triangle) and cold drawn shape, requiring numerous annealing steps.[17-3]

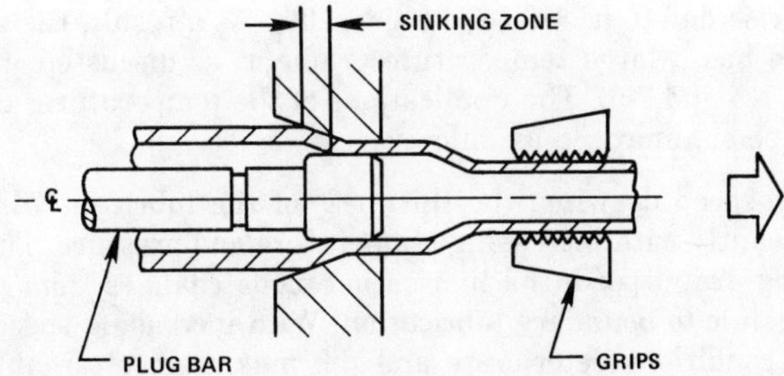

Figure 17-3. Schematic illustration of drawing with a fixed plug.

Reduction per pass varies from 10 to 50% in cross-sectional area. The larger reductions are used for larger-diameter wire and in the initial passes of a multipass drawing operation. The smaller reductions are used for small-diameter wire or in the very last pass of a multipass drawing operation. In the latter case, the small reduction allows an increase in die life. At times, dies are rotated to ensure uniform wear and a circular cross section at the exit. Die wear in wiredrawing is particularly important in the last pass, because this pass helps to size the wire. Draw speeds vary from a few hundred feet per minute in bar drawing to 10,000 ft/min or more in drawing of fine wire.

To increase die life, drawing dies are usually made of carbide or diamond, especially in drawing of small-diameter wire at high speed. The die geometry is basically conical with a bell-shape entry to promote die lubrication. Half die angles range from 2 to 10°.

In drawing, lubrication can be wet or dry. In wet lubrication, the wire is immersed in liquid lubricant (oil or emulsions of soap with additives) or is fed into a die by passing it through a container of the liquid lubricant. In dry lubrication, a soap-type lubricant, in flake or powder form, is placed in a box in front of the draw die. The wire passes through the box and carries solid soap particles into the deformation zone.[17-2]

As discussed in Chapter 7, a considerable amount of heat is generated during wiredrawing. Most of this heat is due to friction at the die/material interface. Especially in drawing of small-diameter wire, where the surface/volume ratio is relatively large and the draw speeds are relatively high, the

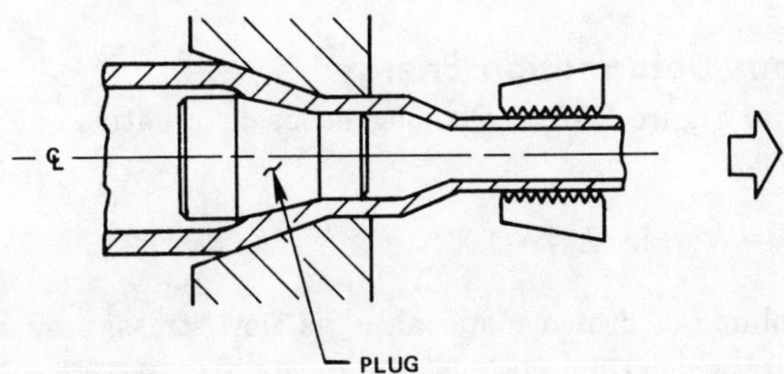

Figure 17-4. Schematic illustration of drawing with a floating plug.

temperature rise due to friction is considerable. As a result, the wire coming out of the die has a large temperature gradient, as discussed in Chapter 7 (Figures 7-2, 7-5 and 7-6). The implications of the temperatures developed in drawing can be summarized as follows:

- In high-speed drawing, the thickness of the lubricant film decreases significantly with increasing temperature and pressure. Thus, with increasing draw speed, the lubrication mode changes from initially hydrodynamic to boundary lubrication. With increasing speed, the lubrication conditions deteriorate and the maximum attainable speed for drawing without a surface defect is reached.
- The highest temperatures in drawing are at the interface, and the maximum temperature is at the exit, where maximum die wear usually occurs.
- Cooling of the wire is essential for improving lubrication conditions. However, cooling through the lubricant film or through external cooling of the die block is not very efficient. The best way is to cool the surface of the wire between two reductions. In multiple reductions, it is preferable to cool the wire more effectively at the last few reductions.

ENERGY AND STRESS IN DRAWING OF BAR AND WIRE

Estimation of the draw stress applied to the drawn section at the die exit is significant from a very practical point of view. If the magnitude of this stress exceeds the yield strength of the drawing material, then the drawn wire or rod breaks or necks, resulting in an unusable product. In addition, the draw force must be known for optimum design of wire and rod drawing machinery. For estimating draw stress it is helpful to consider the various components of the energy consumed in the process. As in all deformation processes, the total energy used in drawing is the sum of the energies required for homogeneous deformation, internal shear and die friction. Among the various methods available for estimating draw force and stress, the upper bound and slab methods have been found to be the easiest to use. Application of the upper bound method to drawing has been extensively discussed by Avitzur.[17-4] The slab method will be considered here in terms of the total volume of drawn material:[17-2,17-5] that is, for a product with cross-sectional area "A" drawn to length "L", the energy required is a function of the volume $V = A \cdot L$.

Homogeneous Deformation Energy

Referring to Figure 17-5, the homogeneous deformation energy, E_{dh}, can be expressed as:

$$E_{dh} = V \bar{\sigma}_a \ln (A_0/A_1) \qquad (17\text{-}1)$$

where V is volume of drawn material; $\bar{\sigma}_a$ is flow stress, assumed to be an average within the deformation zone; and A_0 and A_1 are cross-sectional areas at the entrance to and the exit from the die, respectively.

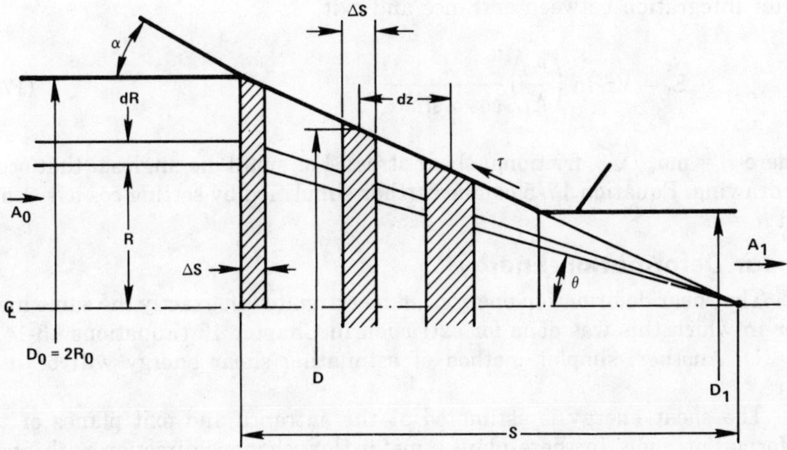

Figure 17-5. Schematic illustration of volume elements used for estimating energies necessary for internal shear and interface friction.

During deformation at room temperature, the material strain hardens; therefore, the values of $\bar{\sigma}$ at entrance and exit are different. A first approximation of the value $\bar{\sigma}_a$ can be obtained from:

$$\bar{\sigma}_a = (\bar{\sigma}_0 + \bar{\sigma}_1)/2 \tag{17-2}$$

where $\bar{\sigma}_0$ and $\bar{\sigma}_1$ are flow stress values at entrance and exit, respectively. A more realistic value of $\bar{\sigma}_a$ can be obtained by integration, as discussed in Chapter 15 (Equations 15-2 to 15-5) for cold extrusion.

Frictional Energy

Estimation of frictional energy is based on (a) the surface area of contact between die and material, (b) flow stress and (c) friction factor.[17-2] In Figure 17-5, a volume element in the deformation zone is considered. This element has diameter D, thickness ΔS and friction surface $\pi D\Delta S|\cos\alpha$. For a displacement dz, in the drawing direction, the infinitesimal frictional energy for this element is:

$$dE_f = (\tau_f \pi D \Delta S\, dz)/(\cos\alpha)^2 \tag{17-3}$$

From the geometry of Figure 17-5, it can be seen that dA = surface over which sliding occurs = $\pi D\, dz \tan\alpha$, and that ΔS = volume of element/cross-sectional area of element = ΔV/A. With these substitutions, Equation 17-3 gives:

$$dE_f = \tau_f \frac{\Delta V}{A} dA \frac{1}{\cos\alpha \sin\alpha} \tag{17-4}$$

After integration between entrance and exit,

$$E_f = V\tau_f \ln\left(\frac{A_0}{A_1}\right)\frac{1}{\cos\alpha\sin\alpha} \tag{17-5}$$

where $\tau_f = m\bar{\sigma}_a/\sqrt{3}$, frictional shear stress. For small die angles α that occur in drawing, Equation 17-5 can be further simplified by setting $\cos\alpha = 1$ and $\sin\alpha = \alpha$.

Shear Deformation Energy

The shear deformation energy can be estimated in exactly the same manner in which this was done for extrusion in Chapter 13 (Equations 13-14 to 13-21). Another, simpler method of estimating shear energy will be used here.[17-2]

The shear energy is estimated at the entrance and exit planes of the deformation zone. In these planes, metal flow changes direction with angle θ, as indicated in Figure 17-5. The shear energy for a volume element dV at the entrance plane is:

$$dE_{s0} = \tan\theta \, dV \, \tau_0 \tag{17-6}$$

where τ_0 = maximum shear stress at entrance = $\bar{\sigma}_0/\sqrt{3}$, and dV = volume element subject to shear = $2\pi R \, dR \, \Delta S$.

In wiredrawing, the angles α and θ are small, less than 15°. Therefore, it is justifiable to consider the approximations: $\tan\theta = \theta = R/S$ (R and S are given in Figure 17-5), and $\tan\alpha = \alpha = R_0/S = D_0/2S$. Thus, Equation 17-6 can be transformed into:

$$\Delta E_{s0} = \int_0^{R_0} \tau_0 R 2\pi R \Delta S \, dR/S \tag{17-7a}$$

$$= 2\pi\Delta S\tau_0 R_0^3/(3S) \tag{17-7b}$$

$$= 2\Delta V\alpha\,\tau_0/3 \tag{17-7c}$$

with $\alpha = R_0/S$, and ΔV = volume of distorted element at entrance = $\pi R_0^2 \Delta S$. For a volume element ΔV, the shear energy at the exit can be obtained by means of an equation similar to Equation 17-7c:

$$\Delta E_{s1} = 2\Delta V\alpha\,\tau_1/3 \tag{17-8}$$

where τ_1 is the maximum shear stress at the exit, $\tau_1 = \bar{\sigma}_1/\sqrt{3}$.

The total shear energy for a volume of drawn material V will then be obtained by multiplying V by the sum of the entrance and exit shear energies per volume element, i.e., from Equations 17-7c and 17-8:

$$E_s = \frac{2}{3}\Delta V\alpha(\tau_0 + \tau_1)\frac{V}{\Delta V} \tag{17-9a}$$

$$= \frac{2}{3} V\alpha(\tau_0 + \tau_1) \tag{17-9b}$$

If an average value $\bar{\sigma}_a$ is used for both shear stresses (at entrance and exit) then:

$$E_s = \frac{2}{3} V\alpha \left(\frac{2\bar{\sigma}_a}{\sqrt{3}}\right) \tag{17-10}$$

Total Draw Energy and Stress

The draw stress is obtained by dividing the sum of the energies consumed during the process by the volume of the material drawn, i.e.:

$$\sigma_D = (E_{dh} + E_f + E_s)/V \tag{17-11}$$

The energies E_{dh}, E_f and E_s are given by Equations 17-1, 17-5 and 17-9b (or 17-10), respectively. As discussed earlier, the value of the flow stress increases from the entrance toward the exit of the deformation zone. As a result, estimation of the average flow stress value and the values of the maximum shear stresses τ_0 and τ_1 (at entrance and exit) will influence the accuracy of the results. The value of the frictional shear factor m is also difficult to estimate. Realistic values of m in wiredrawing have been found to range from 0.02 to 0.06.

Optimum Die Angle

The optimum die angle is often defined as the angle which gives the minimum draw stress. The draw stress (Equation 17-11) contains components of energies used for friction, homogeneous deformation, and internal shear or redundant work. The energy due to homogeneous deformation (Equation 17-1) is independent of the die angle. For a given friction factor, the frictional energy (Equation 17-5) decreases with increasing die half angle α. The shear energy (Equation 17-10) increases with increasing die angle. These relationships are illustrated qualitatively in Figure 17-6. The total draw energy is at a minimum for a certain value of the die half angle α, the so-called optimum die angle. The optimum angle increases with increasing reduction and friction. The effect of reduction on optimum die angle is illustrated in Figure 17-7, where the ratio of draw stress to average flow stress is given, as a function of the die angle, for various reductions. The data given in this figure were obtained from actual drawing experiments conducted on copper wire.[17-6,17-7]

Effect of Back Tension

In practical multipass drawing there is always a certain amount of tension in the wire between any two drawing dies. As a result, the state of stress in the deformation zone changes. The draw stress at the exit from the die becomes larger — about the amount of the back tension stress that is present at the entrance side. The radial stress acting on the die surface, however, is reduced. As a result, the elastic deformation of the die, the energy losses due to friction and the temperature rise due to friction are also reduced. Thus,

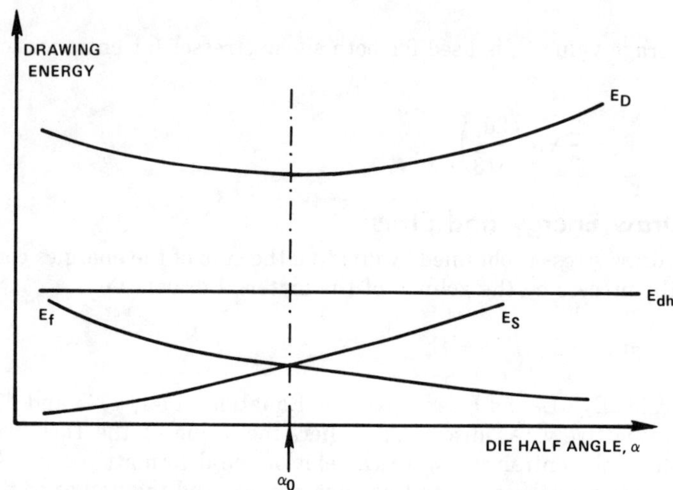

Figure 17-6. Qualitative variation of energy components in drawing with die half angle α (E_D is total drawing energy; E_{dh}, E_s and E_f are energies for homogeneous deformation, shear and friction, respectively; α_0 is optimum die half angle).

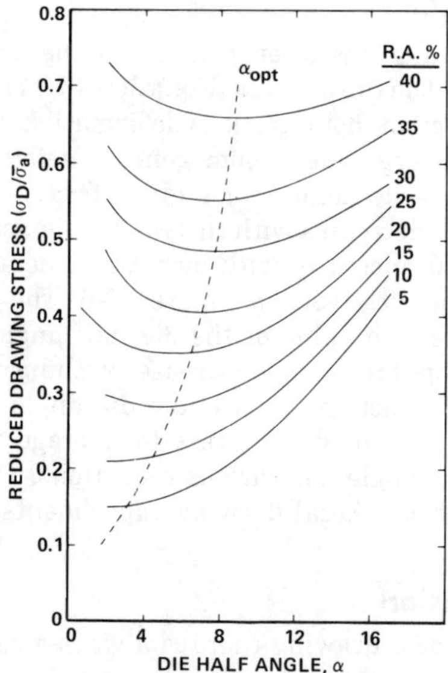

Figure 17-7. Variation of optimum die angle α_{opt} with percent reduction in area (data are from drawing experiments on high-conductivity copper).[17-6,17-7]

die life may increase and improved tolerances may be obtained on the drawn wire or rod.

STRESSES IN TUBE DRAWING

Schematic illustrations of tube drawing processes are given in Figure 2-32 for drawing without a mandrel or for tube sinking, in Figure 17-3 for drawing with a fixed plug, in Figure 17-4 for drawing with a floating plug and in Figure 2-31 for ironing. In most plug drawing operations, there is a "sinking" zone that precedes the actual drawing and sizing zones, as shown in Figure 17-8.

Draw Stress in Tube Sinking

Within the "sinking" zone, some thickening of the tube wall occurs. Most of the deformation, however, is due to "bending" at the entrance to and exit from the die. Using the symbols given in Figure 17-9, the draw stress σ_{x1} at the exit from the sinking zone is given by:[17-8,17-9]

$$\sigma_{x1} = D_2 \bar{\sigma}^* + D_1 \sigma_{x0} \tag{17-12}$$

where σ_{x0} is back-pull stress at entrance to sinking zone; $\sigma^* = 2\,\bar{\sigma}_a/\sqrt{3}$, be-

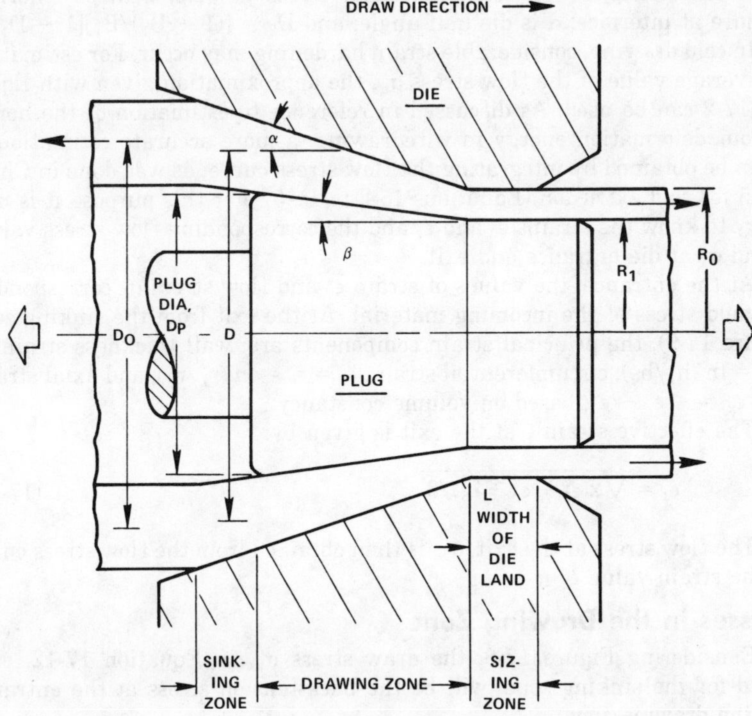

Figure 17-8. Schematic illustration of a plug drawing operation.

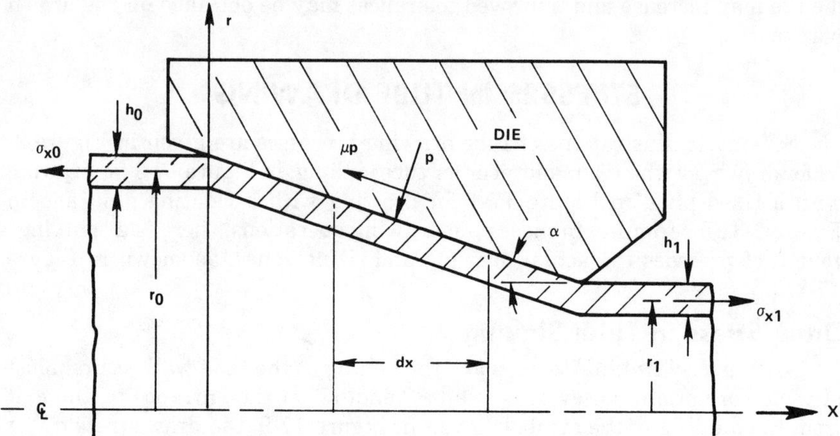

Figure 17-9. Schematic illustration of tube sinking (or sinking zone in Figure 17-8).

cause of plane-strain conditions; $D_1 = (r_0/r_1)^{B_1}$; r_0 and r_1 are mean radii of tube at entrance and exit of sinking zone, respectively; $B_1 = \mu/\tan\alpha$; μ is coefficient of friction, for frictional shear stress $\tau = \mu p$, with p = normal pressure at interface; α is die half angle; and $D_2 = [(1 + B_1)/B_1][1 - D_1]$.

In cold drawing, considerable strain hardening may occur. For estimating the average value of the flow stress $\bar{\sigma}_a$, the approximation given with Equation 17-2 can be used. As discussed in reference to estimation of the homogeneous deformation energy in wiredrawing, a more accurate estimation of $\bar{\sigma}_a$ can be obtained by integrating the flow stress curve, as was done in Chapter 15 for cold extrusion (Equations 15-2 to 15-5). For this purpose it is necessary to know the strains ϵ_0 and ϵ_1 and the corresponding flow stress values σ_0 and σ_1 at die entrance and exit.

At the entrance, the values of strain ϵ_0 and flow stress σ_0 correspond to the yield stress of the incoming material. At the exit from the sinking zone (Figure 17-9), the principal strain components are: wall thickness strain, $\epsilon_1 = \epsilon_r = \ln(h_1/h_0)$; circumferential strain, $\epsilon_2 = \epsilon_\theta = \ln(r_1/r_0)$; and axial strain, $\epsilon_3 = \epsilon_x = -\epsilon_r - \epsilon_\theta$, based on volume constancy.

The effective strain $\bar{\epsilon}$ at the exit is given by:

$$\bar{\epsilon}_1 = \sqrt{2(\epsilon_1^2 + \epsilon_2^2 + \epsilon_3^2)/3} \tag{17-13}$$

The flow stress at the exit, $\bar{\sigma}_1$, is then obtained from the flow stress curve for the strain value $\bar{\epsilon}_1$.

Stresses in the Drawing Zone

Considering Figure 17-8, the draw stress σ_{x1} in Equation 17-12, estimated for the sinking zone, will be the back-tension stress at the entrance into the drawing zone.

The draw stress σ_{x1} at the exit from the drawing zone (Figure 17-10) is given by:[17-8,17-9]

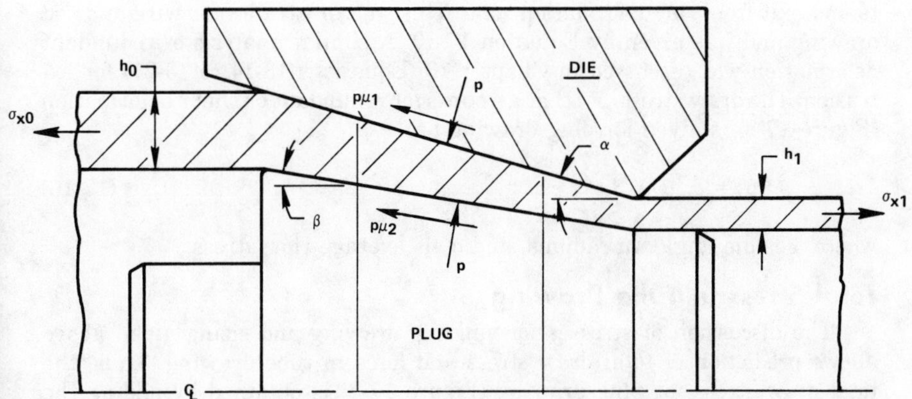

Figure 17-10. Schematic representation of the drawing zone.

$$\sigma_{x1} = C_2\bar{\sigma}^* + C_1\sigma_{x0} \tag{17-14}$$

where σ_{x0} is back-pull stress at entrance to drawing zone (if "sinking" precedes "drawing," this stress is equal to σ_{x1} in Equation 17-2); $C_1 = (h_1/h_0)^{B_2}$; h_1 and h_0 are wall thicknesses at exit and entrance of drawing zone, respectively; $B_2 = (\mu_1 + \mu_2)/(\tan\alpha - \tan\beta)$; μ_1 and μ_2 are coefficients of friction at die and plug surfaces, respectively; α and β are die and plug half angles, respectively; $C_2 = [(1 + B_2)/B_2](1 - C_1)$; and $\bar{\sigma}^* = 2\bar{\sigma}_a/\sqrt{3}$.

Here again, it is necessary to consider variations in strains in order to estimate $\bar{\sigma}$ at the exit. The strain at the exit, $\bar{\epsilon}_1$, is calculated in the same manner as was done for the sinking zone.

Stresses in the Sizing Zone

In the sizing zone, only a small amount of plastic deformation takes place (Figure 17-8). The draw stress, σ_{x1}, at the exit from the sizing zone is:

$$\sigma_{x1} = \sigma^* - (\bar{\sigma}^* - \sigma_{x0})\exp^{(-CL)} \tag{17-15}$$

where $\bar{\sigma}^* = 2\bar{\sigma}_a\sqrt{3}$; σ_{x0} is back-pull stress at entrance to sizing zone (or draw stress σ_{x1}, calculated for drawing zone); $C = 2(\mu_1 R_i + \mu_2 R_0)/(R_0^2 - R_i^2)$; L is length of die land; and R_i and R_0 are radii of tube in sizing zone.

Because, during sizing, plastic deformation is rather small, additional strain hardening can be neglected and $\bar{\sigma}_a$ can be considered to be equal to $\bar{\sigma}_1$ at the exit from the drawing zone.

Draw Stress To Account for Redundant Work

Similar to deformation in wiredrawing, the total deformation energy consumed in tube drawing contains elements of homogeneous, frictional, and shear or redundant deformation energies. The homogeneous deformation and friction components of drawing are considered in Equations 17-12, 17-14 and 17-15 for the sinking, drawing and sizing zones. The draw stress due to redundant work can be estimated by considering the internal shear at the entrance to and exit from the deformation zone. This was illustrated for wire and rod drawing and was given by Equation 17-10. A similar analysis of redundant deformation was discussed in Chapter 13 (Equations 13-14 to 13-21) for extrusion. The draw stress, σ_s, that accounts for redundant or shear deformation (Figure 17-8) is given for plug drawing as:

$$\sigma_s = \bar{\sigma}_a \, \widehat{\alpha}/\sqrt{3} \tag{17-16}$$

where $\widehat{\alpha}$ is die angle, in radians, and $\bar{\sigma}_a$ is average flow stress.

Total Stress in Tube Drawing

The discussion of stresses for sinking, drawing and sizing given above allows prediction of total draw stress and force in tube drawing. Thus, the total draw stress for plug drawing (Figure 17-8) is obtained by adding the stresses for sinking (Equation 17-12), drawing (Equation 17-14), sizing (Equation 17-15) and redundant work (Equation 17-16). It should be noted that the exit draw stress from one zone is to be considered as back-tension stress for the next zone. In cases where only sinking is considered, the stress components due to drawing and sizing (Equations 17-14 and 17-15) can be neglected but the stress that accounts for redundant work (Equation 17-16) must still be considered.

Drawing of Tubes and Cups With a Moving Mandrel (Ironing)

The principle of drawing with a moving mandrel is illustrated in Figure 2-31 for a single-die draw. The process can be conducted hot or cold, to manufacture a variety of discrete hollow cuplike components such as artillery shells, shock absorber sleeves, beverage cans and gas cylinders. Tube drawing with a moving mandrel is often called ironing and is carried out by use of several drawing dies located in tandem (Figure 17-11).

In a typical application, first a relatively thick-wall cup is produced by extrusion or deep drawing. The wall thickness of this cup is then reduced by tandem ironing with a cylindrical punch, while the internal diameter remains unchanged. Both hot and cold ironing produce parts with good dimensional accuracy while maintaining or improving concentricity. A very common application of tandem drawing is the production of beverage cans from steel or aluminum. The principle of a can ironing press is illustrated in Figure 17-12.[17-10] The press is horizontal, and the ram has a relatively long stroke and is guided by the hydrostatic bushing "A". The front seal "B" prevents mixing of the ironing lubricant with the hydrostatic bushing oil. With the ram in the retracted position, the drawn cup is automatically fed into the press, between the redraw die "D" and the redraw sleeve "C". The redraw die centers the cup for drawing and applies controlled pressure while the cup is drawn through the first die "D". As the ram proceeds, the redrawn cup is ironed by passing through the carbide dies "E", which gradually reduce the wall thickness. The ironed can is pressed against the doming punch "I", which forms the bottom shape of the can. When the ram starts its return motion, the mechanical stripper "G", assisted by the air stripper "F", removes the can from the ironing punch "H". The punch is made of carbide or cold forging tool

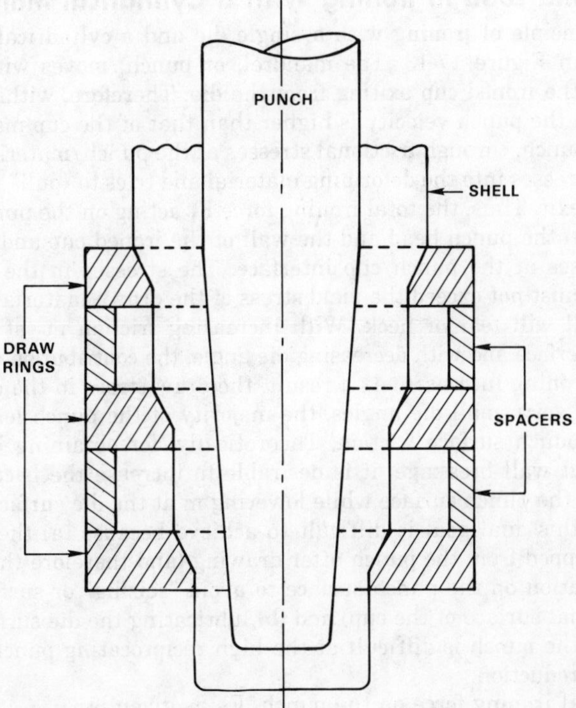

Figure 17-11. Multipass ironing with tapered punch and dies in tandem.

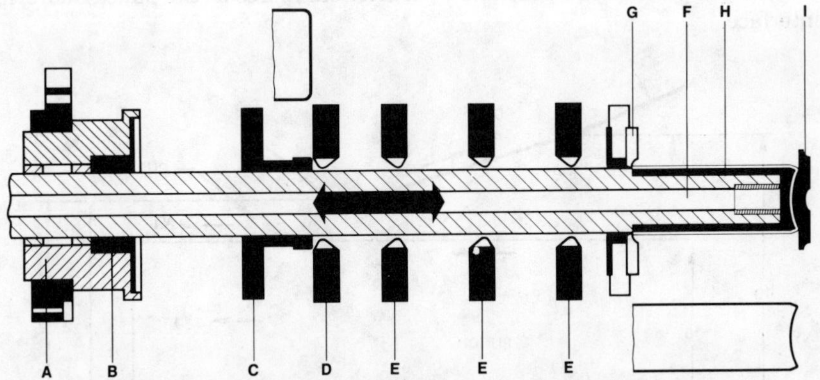

Figure 17-12. Schematic illustration of multiple-die ironing operation for manufacturing beverage cans.(17-10)

steel. The stripped can is automatically transported to the next machine for trimming of the top edge of the can wall to a uniform height.

Stresses and Load in Ironing With a Cylindrical Mandrel

The principle of ironing with a single die and a cylindrical mandrel is illustrated in Figure 17-13. The mandrel, or punch, moves with the same velocity as the ironed cup exiting from the die. Therefore, within the deformation zone the punch velocity is higher than that of the cup material. As a result, the punch, through frictional stresses at the punch/material interface, transmits stresses into the deforming material and tries to "pull" the material toward the exit. Thus, the total ironing force F_T acting on the punch is transmitted by (a) the punch head and the wall of the ironed cup and (b) the frictional stresses at the punch/cup interface. The stresses in the wall of the drawn cup must not exceed the yield stress of the drawn material: otherwise, the cup wall will tear or neck. With increasing friction m_2 at the punch/material interface and with decreasing die angle, the contribution of the punch friction to ironing increases. As a result, the draw stress in the cup wall decreases. For very small die angles, the majority of the punch load would be created by punch surface friction. Theoretically, for obtaining large reductions without wall breakage, it is desirable to increase the frictional shear factor m_2 at the punch surface while lowering m at the die surface. However, in practice this dual goal is difficult to achieve because (a) the drawn cup must be stripped from the punch after drawing (and therefore there must be some lubrication on the punch surface to avoid "seizing" or surface welding at the internal surface of the cup) and (b) lubricating the die surface without lubricating the punch is difficult at the high reciprocating punch speeds required for production.

The total ironing force on the punch, F_T, is given by:

$$F_T = F_H + F_F \tag{17-17}$$

where F_H is punch-head force and F_F is frictional force at the punch/material interface.

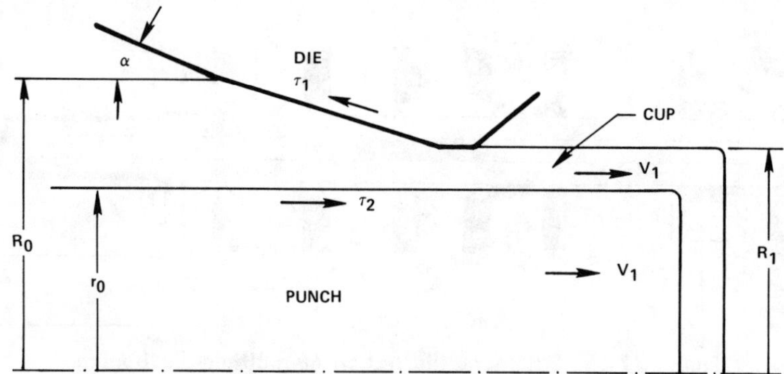

Figure 17-13. Schematic illustration of ironing with a single die and a cylindrical punch ($\tau_1 = m_1\sigma_a/\sqrt{3} = f_1\sigma_a$; $\tau_2 = m_2\sigma_a/\sqrt{3} = f_2\sigma_a$).

For plane-strain deformation, i.e., ironing of thin-wall cups (diameter greater than 10 times wall thickness), a simple formulation can be obtained for these components, using energy considerations. With the symbols of Figure 17-13, the punch-head force, or the draw force in the cup wall (cup sectional area × draw stress) can be expressed as:

$$F_H = A_1\bar{\sigma}_a\left[\ln\left(\frac{A_0}{A_1}\right)\left(1+\frac{f_1}{\sin\alpha\cos\alpha}\right)+\frac{\hat{\alpha}}{\sqrt{3}}\right] \tag{17-18}$$

The punch frictional force F_F equals frictional stress × punch surface subject to interface friction:

$$F_F = (\bar{\sigma}_a f_2)[2\pi r_0(R_0 - R_1)/\tan\alpha] \tag{17-19}$$

where A_1 is cross-sectional area of ironed tube $= \pi(R_1^2 - r_0^2)$; $\bar{\sigma}_a$ is average flow stress; A_0 is cross-sectional area of undeformed tube $= \pi(R_0^2 - r_0^2)$; f_1 is friction factor on die surface $= m_1/\sqrt{3}$; f_2 is friction factor on punch surface $= m_2/\sqrt{3}$; R_0 is initial outside tube radius; R_1 is final outside tube radius; r_0 is punch radius; and $\hat{\alpha}$ is die half angle, in radians.

In Equation 17-18, the first term inside the brackets corresponds to the homogeneous deformation, the second term corresponds to friction and the last term represents the redundant deformation.

To determine the value of $\bar{\sigma}_a$, it is again necessary to know $\bar{\sigma}_0$ and $\bar{\sigma}_1$. The first is known for the incoming material; the second corresponds to the strain $\bar{\epsilon}_1 = \ln(A_0/A_1)$.

Multipass Drawing of a Cup with a Tapered Punch

In certain cup or shell drawing operations — for example, in drawing of thick-wall artillery shells, a tapered punch may be used.[17-11] The principle of this type of deformation is shown in Figure 17-14, where the die is stationary and the punch moves to the right. In this type of drawing or ironing the axial draw stress is given by:

$$\sigma_z = \bar{\sigma}_a^* \ln\left(\frac{R_0^2 - R_i^2}{r_0^2 - r_i^2}\right) + \bar{\sigma}_a^* \frac{(z_2 - z_1)}{(r_0^2 - r_i^2)} \cdot \left[\frac{m_1}{\sqrt{3}}(r_0 + R_0) - \frac{m_2}{\sqrt{3}}(n + R_i)\right] + \bar{\sigma}_a^* \frac{\hat{\alpha}}{\sqrt{3}} \tag{17-20}$$

where, in addition to the symbols shown in Figure 17-14: $\bar{\sigma}_a^* = 2\bar{\sigma}_a/\sqrt{3}$ = average flow stress in plane strain (when tube diameter is greater than about 10 times the tube wall thickness) = $\bar{\sigma}_a$ = average flow stress in axisymmetric deformation (when diameter is less than about 10 times the wall thickness); and where m_1 and m_2 are frictional shear factors at the die/material and punch/material interfaces, respectively.

In hot drawing, it is necessary to estimate the strains, strain rates and temperatures in order to obtain an average value of flow stress.[17-11] In a recent study,[17-11] Equation 17-20 was used to develop a system of computer

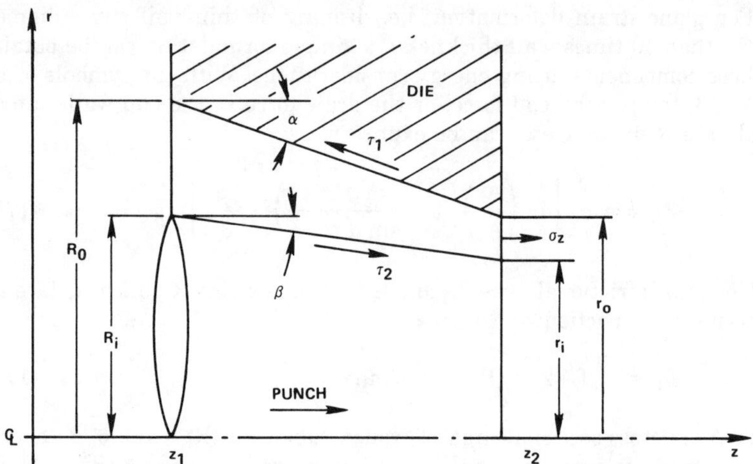

Figure 17-14. Schematic representation of stresses and the symbols used in drawing (ironing) with a tapered punch ($\tau_1 = m_1\sigma_a/\sqrt{3}$; $\tau_2 = m_2\sigma_a/\sqrt{3}$).[17-11]

programs called DRAWNG. These programs can simulate cold, warm and hot ironing operations for cups and shells through multiple dies arranged in tandem, using a tapered punch (Figure 17-11). Inputs to DRAWNG include a set of process variables; material data; and die, billet and punch geometries. The die and punch geometries can be read directly from the keyboard for simple cases or from a prestored data file for multiple sets of data or complex geometries. The material data are stored in the DRAWNG programs in tabular form and are addressed by material code numbers.

For a given set of input data, DRAWNG simulates the tandem die ironing operation on a real-time basis, and the step-by-step results are displayed on the graphics display terminal. On the screen, first the title is printed, and then the dies are drawn, showing specified spacings between them, and the billet and punch are positioned for the beginning of the simulation. Once the simulation begins, the step-by-step movements of the punch and the billet are shown. At the same time, the total ram load versus punch displacement and wall stress versus punch displacement are displayed. During the simulation, the computer programs calculate the correct flow stress in the deformation zone corresponding to local strain, strain rate, and temperature, and utilize appropriate equations for stresses, depending on whether the element is free, is within a die, or is between two dies. In addition, the tensile strength of the product is plotted on the wall-stress-versus-displacement diagram to show whether punch-through is predicted at any stage of the drawing operation.[17-11]

Thus, the computer program DRAWNG is capable of predicting (a) the load/stroke curves, (b) the failure due to punch-through and (c) the effects of process variables on the total ram load and punch-head load.

The load/displacement curves predicted by this program have been compared with experimental measurements. These comparisons indicate that the computer simulations were sufficiently accurate for analyzing and optimizing multiple-pass ironing operations.

REFERENCES

17-1. Dieter, G. E., "Mechanical Metallurgy", 2nd Ed., McGraw-Hill, Inc., New York, 1976, p 658.

17-2. Lange, K. (editor), "Study Book of Forming Technology" (in German), Vol II – Massivforming, Chapter 5, Springer-Verlag, Berlin-Heidelberg, New York, 1974, p 227.

17-3. "Rathbone Cold Drawn Profile Shapes and Pinion Rods", Rathbone Corporation, Palmer, MA.

17-4. Avitzur, B., "Metal Forming: Processes and Analysis", McGraw-Hill Book Company, New York, 1968.

17-5. Thomsen, E. G., Yang, C. T., and Kobayashi, S., "Mechanics of Plastic Deformation in Metal Processing", The Macmillan Company, New York, 1965.

17-6. Wistreich, J. G., "The Fundamentals of Wire Drawing", Metall. Reviews, Vol 3, pp 97-142, 1958.

17-7. Blazynski, T. Z., "Metal Forming – Tool Profiles and Flow", John Wiley and Sons, New York, 1976, p 156.

17-8. Hoffman, O., and Sachs, G., "Introduction to the Theory of Plasticity for Engineers", McGraw-Hill Book Company, 1953.

17-9. Rowe, G., "An Introduction to the Principles of Metalworking", Arnold, 1971.

17-10. Brochure of the Standun Company, Compton, CA.

17-11. Subramanian, T. L., *et al,* "Computer Aided Simulation and Optimization of Tandem Cup Ironing Processes", Proc. of NAMRC-VIII, Rolla, MO, May 1980, p 161.

CHAPTER 18
Die Materials and Die Manufacture

The design and manufacture of dies and the selection of die materials are very important in the production of discrete parts by use of metal forming processes. The dies must be made by modern manufacturing methods from appropriate die materials in order to provide acceptable die life at a reasonable cost. Often the economic success of a forming process depends on die life and die costs per piece produced. For a given application, selection of the appropriate die material depends on three types of variables:

(a) *Variables related to the process itself*, including factors such as size of the die cavity, type of machine used and deformation speed, initial stock size and temperature, die temperature to be used, lubrication, production rate and number of parts to be produced.
(b) *Variables related to the type of die loading*, including speed of loading, i.e., impact or gradual contact time between dies and deforming metal (this contact time is especially important in hot forming), maximum load and pressure on the dies, maximum and minimum die temperatures, and number of loading cycles to which the dies will be subjected.
(c) *Mechanical properties of the die material*, including hardenability, impact strength, hot strength (if hot forming is considered) and resistance to thermal and mechanical fatigue.

DIE LIFE AND DIE FAILURE

Proper selection of the die material and of the die manufacturing technique determines, to a large extent, the useful life of forming dies. Dies may have to be replaced for a number of reasons, such as changes in dimensions due to wear or plastic deformation, deterioration of the surface finish, breakdown of lubrication, and cracking or breakage.

As can be seen in Figure 18-1, which shows an example of a die for hot impression die forging, the principal modes of die failure are erosion, thermal fatigue, mechanical fatigue and permanent (plastic) deformation.[18-1]

In erosion, also commonly called die wear, material is actually removed from the die surface by pressure and sliding of the deforming material. Wear resistance of the die material, die surface temperature, relative sliding speed at the die/material interface and the nature of the interface layer are the most significant factors influencing abrasive die wear. Thermal fatigue occurs on the surface of the die impression in hot forming and results in "heat checking". Thermal fatigue results from cyclic yielding of the die surface due to contact with the hot deforming material. This contact causes the surface layers to expand, and, because of the very steep temperature gradients, the surface layers are subject to compressive stresses. At sufficiently high temperatures, these compressive stresses may cause the surface layers to deform. When the die surface cools, a stress reversal may occur and the surface layers will then be in tension. After repeated cycling in this manner, fatigue will cause formation of a crack pattern that is recognized as heat checking. Die breakage or cracking is due to mechanical fatigue and occurs in cases where the dies are overloaded and local stresses are high. The dies are subjected to alternating stresses due to loading and unloading during the deformation process, and this causes crack initiation and eventual failure.

Die life and die failure are greatly affected by the mechanical properties of the die materials under the conditions that exist in a given deformation process. Generally, the properties that are most significant depend on the

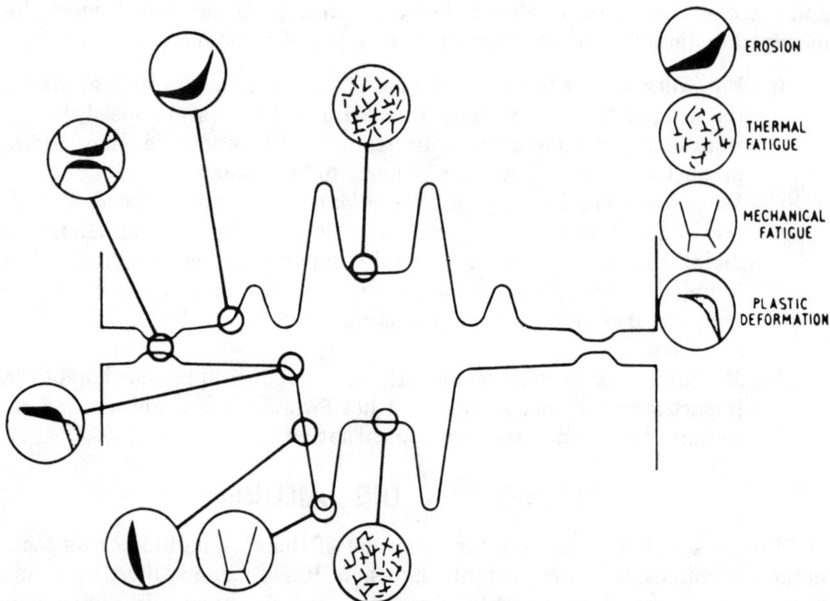

Figure 18-1. Typical locations of various modes of die failure encountered in impression die forging.[18-1]

process temperature. Thus, die materials used in cold forming processes are quite different from those used in hot forming.

DIE MATERIALS FOR HOT FORMING

Die materials commonly used for hot forming can be grouped in terms of alloy content; these materials are listed in Tables 18-1 to 18-3. Low-alloy steels are listed in Table 18-1. Steels with ASM designations 6G, 6F2 and 6F3 possess good toughness and shock resistance qualities with reasonable resistance to abrasion and heat checking. However, these steels are tempered at relatively low temperatures, usually 840 to 930 F (450 to 500 C); therefore, they are suited for applications that do not result in higher die surface temperatures — for example, die holders for hot forging or hammer die blocks. Low-alloy steels with higher (2 to 4%) nickel contents, with ASM designations 6F5 and 6F7, have higher hardenability and toughness and can be used in more severe applications than steels 6G, 6F2 and 6F3.[18-2] The precipitation-

Table 18-1. Low-alloy steels for hot forming

Designation (ASM)	Nominal composition, % C	Mn	Si	Co	Cr	Mo	Ni	V	W
6G	0.55	0.80	0.25	...	1.00	0.45	...	0.10	...
6F2	0.55	0.75	0.25	...	1.00	0.30	1.00	0.10	...
6F3	0.55	0.60	0.85	...	1.00	0.75	1.80	0.10	...
6F4	0.20	0.70	0.25	...	...	3.35	3.00	...	...
6F5	0.55	1.00	1.00	...	0.50	0.50	2.70	0.10	...
6F7	0.40	0.35	...	...	1.5	0.75	4.25	...	...

Table 18-2. Chromium-base hot work die steels

Designation (AISI)	Nominal composition, % C	Mn	Si	Co	Cr	Mo	Ni	V	W
H10	0.40	0.40	1.00	...	3.30	2.50	...	0.50	...
H11	0.35	0.30	1.00	...	5.00	1.50	...	0.40	...
H12	0.35	0.40	1.00	...	5.00	1.50	...	0.50	1.50
H13	0.38	0.30	1.00	...	5.25	1.50	...	1.00	...
H14	0.40	0.35	1.00	...	5.00	...	...	...	5.00
H19	0.40	0.30	0.30	4.25	4.25	0.40	...	2.10	4.10

Table 18-3. Tungsten-base hot work die steels

Designation (AISI)	Nominal composition, % C	Mn	Si	Co	Cr	Mo	Ni	V	W
H21	0.30	0.30	0.30	...	3.50	...	...	0.45	9.25
H22	0.35	0.30	0.30	...	2.00	...	...	0.40	11.00
H23	0.30	0.30	0.30	...	12.00	...	...	1.00	12.00
H24	0.45	0.30	0.30	...	3.0	...	...	0.50	15.00
H25	0.25	0.30	0.30	...	4.0	...	...	0.50	15.00
H26	0.50	0.30	0.30	...	4.0	...	...	1.00	18.00

hardening steel 6F4 can be hardened by a simple aging operation (950 to 1050 F) without any cracking or distortion. In hot forming in presses, heat transfer from the hot stock to the dies causes this steel to harden and to become more abrasion resistant.

Hot work die steels are used at temperatures of 600 to 1200 F and contain chromium, tungsten and, in some cases, vanadium or molybdenum or both. These elements induce deep hardening characteristics and resistance to abrasion and softening. Generally, these steels are hardened by quenching in air or molten salt baths. The chromium-base steels contain about 5% chromium (Table 18-2). High molybdenum content gives these steels high resistance to softening; vanadium content increases resistance to heat checking and abrasion. Tungsten improves toughness and hot hardness; however, steels containing tungsten are not resistant to thermal shock and cannot be cooled intermittently with water. The tungsten-base hot work die steels contain 9 to 18% tungsten (Table 18-3); they also contain 2 to 12% chromium and may have small amounts of vanadium. The high tungsten content provides resistance to softening at high temperatures while maintaining adequate toughness; however, it also makes it impossible to water cool these die steels. High speed steels, originally developed for metal cutting, can also be used in warm or hot forming applications.[18-3] There are two types of high speed steels: molybdenum-type high speed steels, designated by the letter M, and tungsten-type high speed steels, designated by the letter T (Table 18-4). These steels offer good combinations of hardness, strength and toughness at elevated temperatures.

COMPARISON OF DIE STEELS FOR HOT FORMING

Properties of materials which determine their selection as die materials for hot forming are:[18-2]

(a) Ability to harden uniformly.
(b) Wear resistance (this is the ability of a die steel to resist the abrasive action of hot metal during forging).

Table 18-4. Approximate relative rankings of 15 selected high speed steels for three properties[18-3]

Material evaluation	Wear resistance	Hot hardness	Toughness
Highest	T15; M15 M4; M42	T15; M15 T6; T5; M42	M2; T1 M1
Medium	M3; T6; M2 (H.C.) M10 (H.C.); M7 M2; T5	M4; T4 M3	M3; M4 M10; M10 (H.C.) M7; M2 (H.C.)
Lowest	T1; M10 T4; M1	T1; M2 M10; M1 M7 M10 (H.C.) M2 (H.C.)	T4; T5; M42 T15; M15 T6

(c) Resistance to plastic deformation (this is the ability of a die steel to withstand pressure and resist deformation under load).
(d) Toughness.
(e) Ability to resist thermal fatigue and heat checking.
(f) Ability to resist mechanical fatigue.

Ability to Harden Uniformly

The higher the hardenability, the greater the depth to which a material can be hardened. Hardenability depends on the composition of the tool steel. In general, the higher the alloy content of a steel, the higher its hardenability, as measured by the D_I factor (in inches). The D_I of a steel is the diameter of an infinitely long cylinder which would just transform to a specific microstructure at the center, if heat transfer during cooling were ideal, i.e., if the surface attained the temperature of the quenching medium instantly. A larger hardenability factor D_I means that the steel will harden to a greater depth on quenching, not that it will have a higher hardness. For example, the approximate Nominal Hardenability Factors D_I (inches) for a few die steels are as follows: ASM-6G, 15; ASM-6F2, 15; ASM-6F3, 36; AISI-H10, 128; AISI-H12, 88.

Wear Resistance

Wear is a gradual change in the dimensions or shape of a component caused by corrosion, dissolution, or abrasion and removal or transportation of the wear products. Abrasion resulting from friction is the most important of these mechanisms in terms of die wear. The higher the strength and hardness of the steel near the surface of the die, the greater its resistance to abrasion. Thus, in hot forming, the die steel should have a high hot hardness and should retain this hardness over extended periods of exposure to elevated temperatures.

Figure 18-2 shows hot hardnesses of six hot work die steels at various

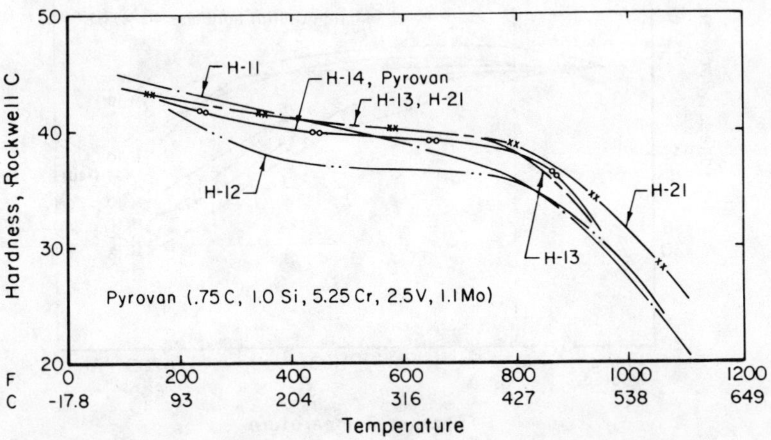

Figure 18-2. Hot hardnesses of hot work die steels (measurements made after holding at testing temperature for 30 min).[18-4]

temperatures. All of these steels were heat treated to about the same initial hardness. Hardness measurements were made after holding the specimens at testing temperature for 30 min. Except for H12, all the die steels considered have about the same hot hardness at temperatures less than about 600 F (315 C). The differences in hot hardness show up only at temperatures above 900 F (482 C).

Figure 18-3 shows the resistance of some hot work die steels to softening at elevated temperatures for 10 h of exposure. All of these steels have about the same initial hardness after heat treatment. For the die steels shown, there is not much variation in resistance to softening at temperatures below 1000 F (538 C). However, for longer periods of exposure at higher temperatures, high-alloy hot work steels, such as H19, H21, and H10 modified, retain hardness better than do medium-alloy steels such as H11.

Resistance to Plastic Deformation

As can be seen in Figure 18-4, the yield strengths of steels decrease at higher temperatures. However, yield strength is also dependent on prior heat treatment, composition and hardness. The higher the initial hardness, the greater the yield strengths at various temperatures. In normal practice, the level to which a die steel is hardened is determined by toughness requirements: the higher the hardness, the lower the toughness of a steel. Thus, in metal forming applications, the die block is hardened to a level at which it should have enough toughness to avoid cracking. Figure 18-4 shows that, for the same initial hardness, 5% chromium-molybdenum steels (H11, etc.) have

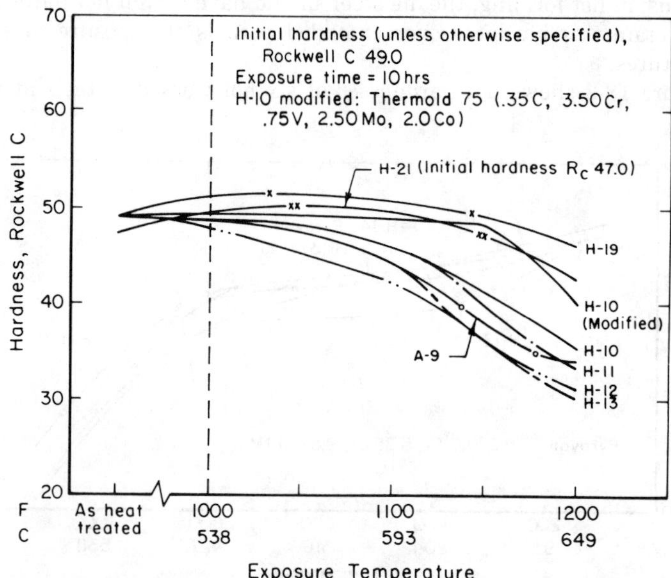

Figure 18-3. Resistance of hot work die steels to softening during elevated-temperature exposure, as measured by room-temperature hardness.[18-5]

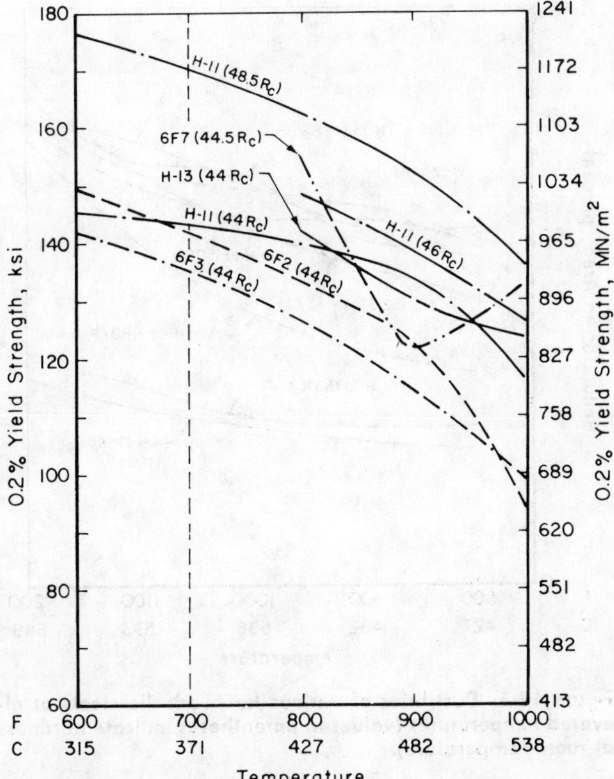

Figure 18-4. Resistance of die steels to plastic deformation at elevated temperatures (values in parentheses indicate hardness at room temperature).(18-5,18-6)

better hot strengths than 6F2 and 6F3 at temperatures greater than 700 F (371 C).

Toughness

Toughness can be defined as the ability to absorb energy without breaking. The energy absorbed before fracture is a combination of strength and ductility. The higher the strength and ductility, the higher the toughness. Ductility, as measured by reduction in area or percent elongation in a tensile test, can therefore be used as a partial index of toughness at low strain rates.

Figure 18-5 shows the ductility of various hot work steels at elevated temperatures as measured by percent reduction in area of a specimen before fracture in a standard tensile test. As the curves show, high-alloy hot work steels, such as H19 and H21, have less ductility than medium-alloy hot work steels such as H11. This explains why H19 and H21 have lower toughness than that of H11.

Fracture toughness and resistance to shock loading are often measured by the notched-bar Charpy test. This test measures the amount of energy

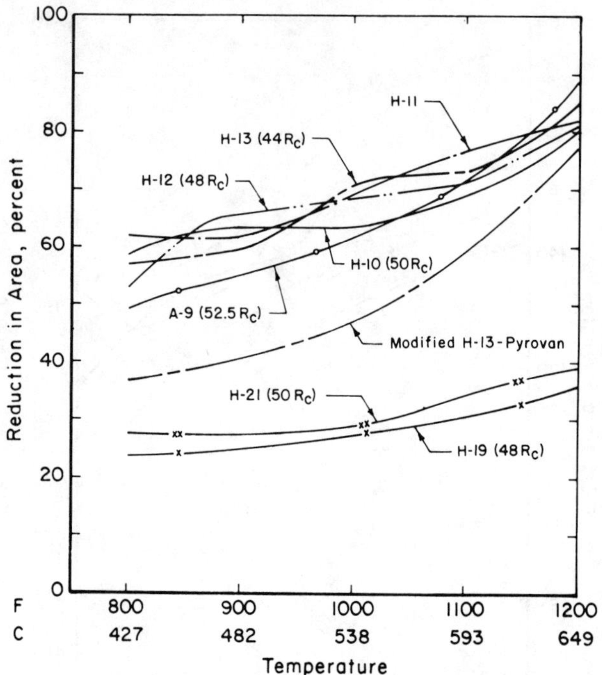

Figure 18-5. Ductilities of various hot work die steels at elevated temperatures (values in parentheses indicate hardness at room temperature).

absorbed in introducing and propagating fracture, or the toughness of a material at high rates of deformation (impact loading). Figure 18-6 shows the results of V-notch Charpy tests on some die steels. The data show that toughness decreases as the alloy content of the steel increases. Medium-alloy steels, such as H11, H12 and H13, have better resistance to brittle fracture in comparison with H14, H19 and H21, which have higher alloy contents. Increasing the hardness of a steel lowers its impact strength, as shown by data on 6F7 steel hardened to two different levels. On the other hand, wear resistance and hot strength decrease with decreasing hardness. Thus, a compromise is made in actual practice, and the dies are tempered to near-maximum hardness levels at which they have sufficient toughness to withstand loading.

The data shown in Figure 18-6 also point to the importance of preheating the dies prior to hot forming. Steels such as H10 and H21 attain reasonable toughness only at high temperatures and require preheating. For general-purpose steels, such as 6F2 and 6G, preheating to a minimum temperature of 300 F (150 C) is recommended; for high-alloy steels, such as H14, H19 and 6F4, a higher preheating temperature is desirable, to improve toughness. For 6F4, a minimum preheating temperature of 480 F (250 C) has been recommended.

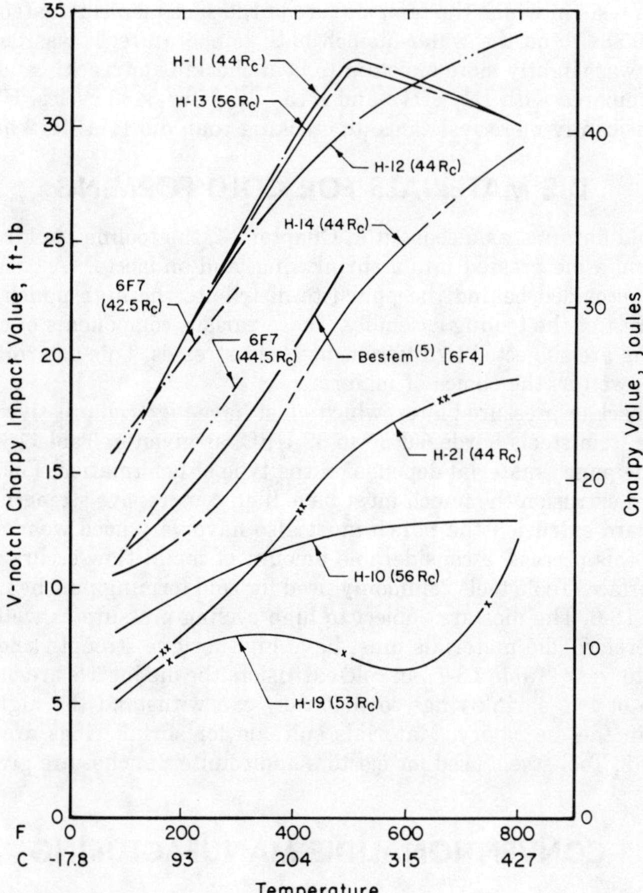

Figure 18-6. Effects of hardness, composition and testing temperature on V-notch Charpy properties of hot work die steels (values in parentheses indicate hardness at room temperature).[18-2]

Resistance to Heat Checking

Nonuniform expansion, caused by thermal gradients from the surface to the center of a die, is the chief factor contributing to heat checking. Therefore, a material with high thermal conductivity will make dies less prone to heat checking by conducting heat rapidly away from the die surface, reducing surface-to-center temperature gradients and lessening expansion/contraction stresses. The magnitudes of thermal stresses caused by nonuniform expansion or temperature gradients also depend on the coefficient of thermal expansion of the steel: the higher the coefficient of thermal expansion, the greater the stresses.

From tests in which the temperature of the specimen fluctuated between 1200 F (650 C) and the water-quench bath temperature, it was determined that H10 was slightly more resistant to heat checking or cracking, after 1740 cycles, compared with H11, H12 and H13.[18-7] After 3488 cycles, H10 exhibited significantly more resistance to cracking than did H11, H12 and H13.

DIE MATERIALS FOR COLD FORMING

In cold forming, as discussed in Chapter 14, the tooling usually consists of a punch, a die pressed into a shrink ring, and an ejector. A back plate is normally provided behind the punch to distribute the high punch pressure into the rest of the tooling assembly. These various components of cold forming tooling are subjected to different levels of stresses. This determines their design as well as the choice of material.

The back or pressure plates, which must have high compressive strength, are made from steels hardened up to 62 HRC, as given in Table 18-5. Selection of the punch material depends on the type of deformation. For example, in forward extrusion the punch must have high compressive strength, whereas in backward extrusion the punch must also have very good wear resistance since, in this process, a considerable amount of metal flow occurs along the punch surface. Tool steels commonly used for cold forming punches are given in Table 18-6. The dies are subject to high cycling pressure as well as abrasion. Therefore, die materials must have high fatigue strength and good resistance to wear (Table 18-7). In cold extrusion, the die inserts are prestressed with one or two shrink rings so that they can withstand the high stresses present in the die cavity. Materials suitable for shrink rings are given in Table 18-8. Tool steels used for ejectors and counterpunches are given in Table 18-9.

CONVENTIONAL DIE MANUFACTURING

For a given metal forming process, die design involves definition of the die geometry, selection of the die material and its hardness, and preparation of a die drawing. In recent years, some companies have started to use Com-

Table 18-5. Tool steels for pressure plates[18-8]

Required strength		Tool steel		
		Designation	Required hardness	
ksi	N/mm^2	(AISI)	HRC	HB
240	1700	A2	58 to 62	...
		D2	58 to 62	...
		D3	58 to 62	...
		O1	58 to 61	...
200	1400	H13	50 to 54	...
		O1	50 to 54	...
155	1100	A8	40 to 44	...
		O1	40 to 44	...
100	700	4340	...	270 to 330
		4140	...	270 to 330

Table 18-6. Tool steels for cold extrusion punches[18-8]

Required strength ksi	Required strength N/mm²	Tool steel: Designation (AISI)	Tool steel: Required hardness, HRC
Forward Extrusion			
300	2100	M2	62 to 64
285	2000	D2	60 to 62
		O1	60 to 62
230	1600	S1	56 to 58
Backward Extrusion			
315	2200	M4	63 to 65
300	2100	M2	62 to 64
285	2000	D2	60 to 62

Table 18-7. Tool steels and tungsten carbides for die inserts[18-8]

Tool steels: Designation (AISI)	Tool steels: Required hardness, HRC	Tungsten carbides: Co (wt %)	Tungsten carbides: Density, g/cm³	Tungsten carbides: Hardness, DPH
D2	60 to 62	25 to 30	13.1 to 12.5	950 to 750
M2	60 to 64	19 to 24	13.6 to 13.2	1050 to 950
		15 to 18	14.0 to 13.7	1200 to 1100

Table 18-8. Steels for shrink rings[18-8]

Designation (AISI)	Required hardness, HB
H13	470 to 530
	440 to 510
	330 to 390
4340	330 to 390
	270 to 330
4140	270 to 330

Table 18-9. Tool steels for counterpunches and ejectors[18-8]

Designation (AISI)	Required hardness, HRC
M2	62 to 64
D2	60 to 62
A2	60 to 62
O1	60 to 62
S1	56 to 58

puter Aided Design and Manufacturing (CAD/CAM) systems for diemaking. In CAD/CAM, the die geometry is already in the computer and can be used for NC machining, this will be discussed later. In most cases, the diemaker must start with the die drawing and select one of the various die manufacturing techniques that are available, i.e., manual machining, copy milling or turning, numerical control (NC) machining, electrodischarge machining (EDM), electrochemical machining (ECM), hobbing and casting. Selection of the preferable (i.e., least costly) die manufacturing technique depends on die cavity geometry, die material and hardness, the number of dies to be produced and the equipment available for diemaking.[18-9]

Manual (Conventional) Turning or Milling

Manual turning or milling is the oldest mechanical process for producing dies. The die cavity is machined, by metal removal techniques, directly into a block of die steel. Therefore, the die steel must be relatively soft to facilitate machining. Axisymmetric dies are easily made by turning on lathes. For manual machining of die cavity impressions that are not round, conventional milling machines are used. The spindle or the table with the die block is moved manually in each of the three directions of feed, and the impression is rough milled according to layout and by use of cross-sectional templates. The efficiency of this operation is largely dependent on the skill of the diemaker, who is highly trained and experienced. After manual milling of a die cavity, considerable amounts of hand finishing and grinding are required in order to obtain an acceptable surface finish of the die cavity.

Copy Milling

In copy milling, the milling machine has a tracer or copying attachment.[18-10] The tracer scans the surface of a model made of plastic, wood, plaster or metal. The model is an exact geometric replica of the die cavity to be machined. Through a hydraulic or electronic system, the position of the tip of the tracer, which moves back and forth to sense the surface of the model, is duplicated by the tip of the cutter of the milling machine (Figure 18-7). Thus, the die cavity, described by the geometry of the model, is automatically generated in the die block. Copy milling requires less skill than manual milling. However, a model must be made first; therefore, the skills of the modelmaker are necessary. Obviously, a single model can be used to produce several dies. Consequently, copy milling is advantageous, compared with manual milling, when more than one die cavity has to be made. As in the case of manual milling directly from a die steel block, the die steel must not be too hard, so that it can be machined at a reasonable metal removal rate.

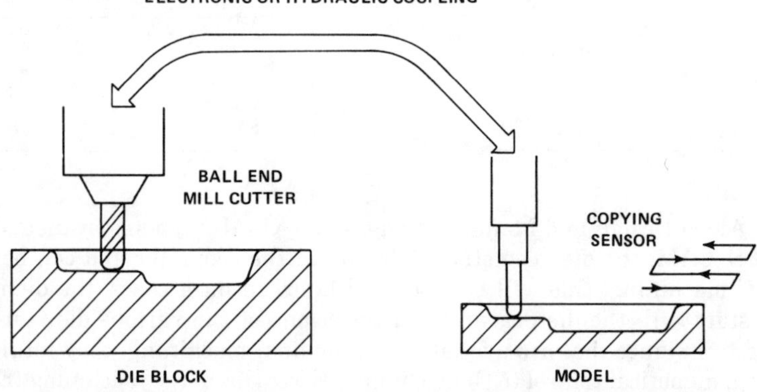

Figure 18-7. Schematic illustration of a copy milling arrangement.

After copy milling of the die, a considerable amount of hand finishing is required to obtain a smooth die surface. This finishing operation is similar to that necessary in conventional milling.

NUMERICAL CONTROL (NC) MACHINING OF DIE CAVITIES

In NC machining, instructions stored on tape or floppy disk, or obtained directly from a computer, control the operation of a metal cutting machine. These instructions are generated by using a computer program and include all geometric data (dimensions; x, y, z coordinates of the positions of the cutter in time) and machining-related information (cutter shape and size, depth of cut, feed, etc.) necessary to activate the machine tool. In NC machining, the die cavity is machined with practically no operator intervention, but surface finishing after NC machining is still necessary.

Preparation of the NC-related information is best done by use of a CAD/CAM system, as discussed at length in the chapters dealing with forging and extrusion. Compared with conventional and copy milling or turning, NC machining offers the following advantages:

- Storage of templates or models is eliminated.
- Changes on dies are easier to make because these changes involve modifications in the computer program statements used to generate the NC tapes.
- Relatively little skill is required of the diemaker.
- The actual machining time is reduced.
- Accuracy and repeatability are increased.

As a result of these potential advantages, the application of NC in diemaking is steadily increasing. NC is particularly advantageous in machining of dies that have repeating geometric features or that are symmetrical about an axis. In such cases, the NC program, written for one portion of the die, can be used to machine symmetrical or repeating geometric features of the die.

ELECTRODISCHARGE MACHINING (EDM)

A schematic illustration of EDM is presented in Figure 18-8.[18-11,18-12] The die block is mounted inside a tank containing a dielectric fluid, which is usually a hydrocarbon oil. The shaped metal or carbon electrode is lowered toward the die block under a servocontrol. Both the die and the electrode are connected to a power source. The power supply provides a voltage potential between the electrode and the die block such that, when the gap between the two is sufficiently small, a spark passes through this gap. The sparks occur at a frequency of 200 to 500,000 Hz, vaporizing portions of both the die block and the electrode. Under optimum conditions, the wear ratio, i.e., the ratio of eroded die block volume to electrode volume, is about 3 to 1 with metal electrodes and 100 to 1 with graphite electrodes. The metal particles removed from the die block are washed away with the dielectric fluid, which is circulated. Thus, spark erosion of die material reproduces the contour of the electrode in the die block.

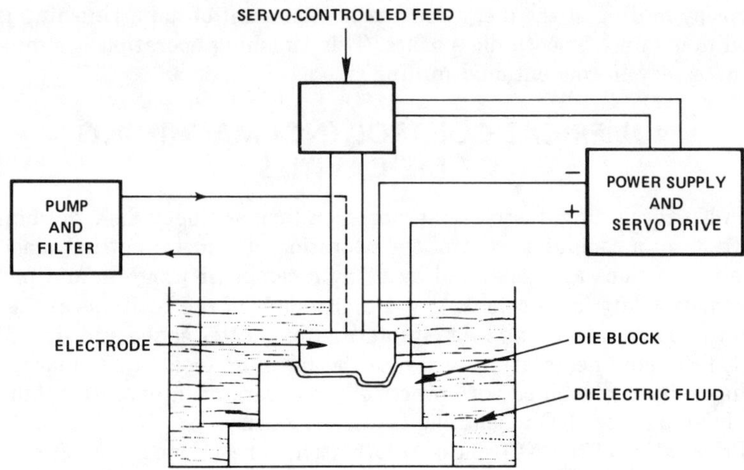

Figure 18-8. Schematic illustration of the electrodischarge machining (EDM) process.

The EDM process is used to produce die cavities with fine surface details and blind or through holes. Some of the advantages of this process are:

- Neither the hardness nor the machinability of the die block steel influences the efficiency of the operation.
- Accuracy and repeatability are very good and exceed most demands regarding die tolerances.
- Finishing of the die surface after EDM requires less effort than finishing of the surfaces of dies made by conventional or copy milling.

Some EDM machines, used for producing shaped cavities or through holes, are equipped for orbiting motion of the electrode. Thus, the electrode moves vertically as well as horizontally. This combined motion provides an agitation in the dielectric fluid; as a result, better flushing and reduced electrode wear are obtained. In addition, by changing the size of the orbit, it is possible to use the same electrode for producing holes of the same shape but of different sizes.

The EDM principle has been further developed in a wire cutting or wire EDM machine, as shown in Figure 18-9. In this case, the electrode is a thin wire which renews itself by unreeling from a spool. After being passed through the cutting zone, this wire is rewound and discharged. Movement of the die material in the x and y directions is achieved by using electronic drive systems, as is done in NC machines. The wire EDM machines are excellent for producing dies with through openings such as those used in extrusion and drawing of shapes.

In using EDM for producing three-dimensional cavities, it is important to have an efficient method of making the electrodes. The EDM electrodes can be made by copy or NC milling. When graphite electrodes are used, the hand finishing necessary after milling requires little work, because graphite

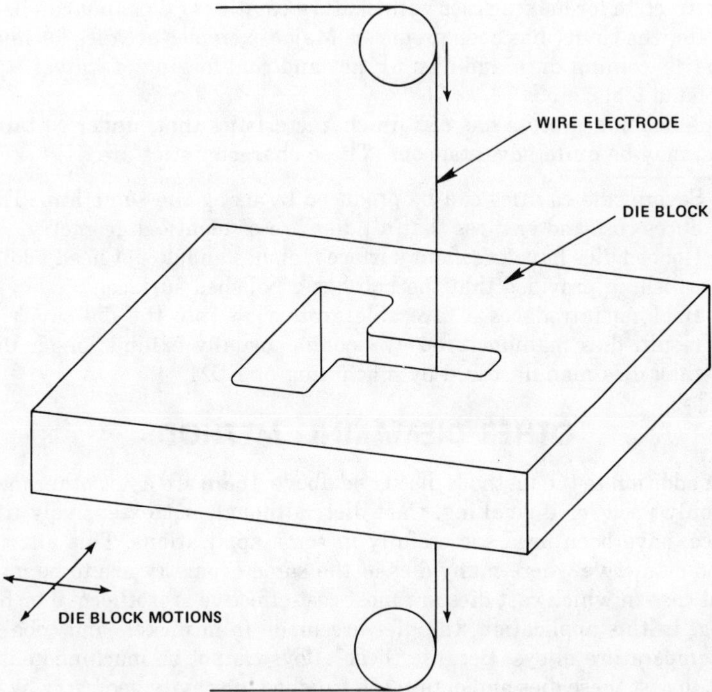

Figure 18-9. Principle of the wire EDM process.

is soft and can be polished quickly with sandpaper to obtain a smooth surface finish. Another method used for manufacture of graphite electrodes is "abrading". In this technique, an abrading die is pressed hydraulically toward a graphite block that is oscillated in an adjustable rotary motion.[18-13] The abrading die is made from epoxy mixed with abrasive particles and has the reverse geometry of the electrode to be produced. A single abrasive die can be used to make a large number of graphite electrodes. Therefore, this technique is very attractive in applications where a large number of electrodes are to be made for the same die geometry.

HOBBING

In hobbing, a tool steel punch hardened to approximately 58 to 62 HRC is pressed into an annealed, soft die steel block, usually in a hydraulic press (as shown in Figure 2-7, Chapter 2). The punch geometry is the "male" replica of the die cavity to be manufactured. Good lubrication is achieved by coating the hob with copper sulfate and by coating the die surface to be hobbed with a high-quality cold forming lubricant, usually molybdenum disulfide.[18-14] The die cavity material may be at room temperature (cold hobbing) or at elevated temperatures (warm or hot hobbing). A single hobbing punch or hub can be used to manufacture a large number of die cavities. This process is particularly attractive for making dies with shallow cavities or dies that can be hardened after the cavity has been produced. Major examples are dies for injection of plastics, coining dies, and dies for hot and cold forging of knives, spoons, forks, hand tools, etc.

The hobbing process has certain characteristics that, under certain conditions, may be quite advantageous. These characteristics are:

- Several die cavities can be produced by using the same hub. This reduces cost and ensures that all dies are of identical geometry.
- Hobbed dies have excellent surface finishes and do not need additional polishing provided that the hob has a polished surface.
- Hobbing introduces a favorable grain flow into the die cavity. As a result, dies manufactured by hobbing usually exhibit longer die life than dies manufactured by machining or EDM.

OTHER DIEMAKING METHODS

In addition to the methods discussed above, there are a few other methods commonly used for diemaking. Cast dies, although not extensively used in practice, have been used successfully in some applications. This alternative may be attractive where many dies of the same geometry are to be made. A special case in which cast dies are most cost-effective is isothermal or hot die forging. In this application, the dies are made from nickel- and cobalt-base high-temperature alloys. Because these alloys cannot be machined easily, it is best to cast these dies and obtain the finished die cavity geometry by EDM.

Electrochemical machining is similar to EDM but does not use sparks for material removal. Only direct current between the metal electrode and the die steel is used for material removal. This method is more efficient than EDM in terms of metal removal rate; however, electrode wear is also quite large and, more importantly, difficult to predict. As a result, this method is used for diemaking only in selected applications.

REFERENCES

18-1. Kannapan, A., "Wear in Forging Dies, A Review of World Experience", Metal Forming, Dec 1969, p 335; Jan 1970, p 6.

18-2. Nagpal, V., and Lahoti, G. D., "Application of the Radial Forging Process to Cold and Warm Forging of Common Tubes", Vol 1, Selection of Die and Mandrel Materials, Final Report, Contract No. DAAA22-78-C-0109, prepared for Watervliet Arsenal by Battelle-Columbus Laboratories, Columbus, OH, May 1980.

18-3. Blackwood, T. B., "The Role of Tool Steels in Extrusion Tooling", SME Technical Paper MF73-565, 1973.

18-4. *Die Steels*, a series of brochures from Latrobe Steel Company, Latrobe, PA.

18-5. *Tool Steels*, a series of brochures from Universal Cyclops Steel Corp., Bridgeville, PA.

18-6. *Hot-Work Die Steels*, data sheets from A. Finkl & Sons Company, Chicago, IL.

18-7. Bens, F. P., and Peckner, D., "Hot-Work Die Steels", The Tool and Manufacturing Engineer, May 1966, pp 68–71.

18-8. Lange, K., "Text Book of Metal Forming" (in German), Vol 2, Massive Forming, Springer-Verlag, New York, 1976.

18-9. Huntress, E. A., "Die Sinking Today", American Machinist, May 1980, p 152.

18-10. Lange, K., and Meyer-Nolkember, H., "Impression Die Forging" (in German), 2nd Ed., Springer-Verlag, Berlin-Heidelberg, New York, 1977, p 219.

18-11. Huntress, E. A., "Electrical Discharge Machining", American Machinist, Aug 1978, p 83.
18-12. Schey, J. A., "Introduction to Manufacturing Processes", McGraw-Hill, Inc., 1977, p 278.
18-13. Ullmann, W., "The Manufacturing of Graphite Electrodes for EDM by Using the Abrading Method" (in German), Giesserei, No. 13, June 23, 1980, p 481.
18-14. Hoischen, H., "The Loading of the Punch in Cold Hobbing" (in German), Industrie-Anzeiger, Vol 91, No. 48, June 10, 1969, p 1090.

CHAPTER 19
Recent Developments in Metal Forming Technology and Application of CAD/CAM

Similar to other branches of manufacturing technology, metal forming has always been under continuous development. During the last decade, research and development in metal forming have resulted in several new advances and cost-effective applications in production. The principal reasons for this trend can be summarized as follows:

- Increases in material and energy costs, especially after the oil crisis of the early 1970's, encouraged manufacturers to form parts to net or near-net dimensions and to reduce machining and scrap losses.
- The low rates of growth in the economies of developed countries and relative reduction of personal income resulted in an increased customer demand for high quality in manufactured products.
- The ever-increasing international competition forced all manufacturers, including metal forming companies, to increase production rates while maintaining quality and improving material utilization.
- Labor costs continued to climb while the lack of skilled manpower, especially in the tool and diemaking trade, continued to exist. This situation forced metal forming companies to automate not only production but also process design and diemaking activities.
- The availability of CAD/CAM systems, which are easy to use and relatively moderate in cost, made computer-aided die design and manufacture a cost-effective alternative for many companies.
- Development of numerical methods and relatively easy-to-use computer codes for die design and process simulation allowed prediction of process variables and reduction of trial and error in setting up new metal forming operations for production.

In this chapter, some examples of the most recent developments and ongoing research efforts in metal forming are reviewed. These examples help to illustrate the status of the advanced state of the art in the early 1980's, as related to the topics covered in this book.

USE OF CAD/CAM AND COMPUTER GRAPHICS

This subject was discussed in Chapter 12 for forging and in Chapter 14 for extrusion. A brief and general review is given here. In the late 1970's and early 1980's, the use of CAD/CAM and computer graphics in the metal forming industry increased considerably. The trend seems to be toward even wider application of this technology for process simulation, die design and manufacture.

There are basically two types of applications of computers in metal forming technology:

- Drafting and numerical control (NC) machining, i.e., preparation of part, die and fixture drawings and generation of NC cutter paths for controlling a CNC machine in order to produce a model (for copy milling), an electrode (for EDM) or a die cavity directly from the die block.
- Analysis of the forming process, i.e., prediction of stresses, metal flow, temperatures, and forming load and energy.

Most companies that have elected to employ computer graphics for metal forming applications use their systems for drafting and NC machining. This application offers immediate increases in productivity although it uses only the experience of the die designer and/or empirical equations, without much analysis (except for calculations of cross-sectional area and volume). The user must learn how to communicate with a CAD/CAM graphics system that consists of hardware (computer/processor, one or more graphics terminals, disk drives, and a plotter for preparing drawings) and software (Figure 19-1). An initial training period of a few weeks is necessary, and additional training and/or hands-on experience is required if the system is to be used efficiently.

In selected metal forming companies throughout the world, computers are already being used, not only for drafting and NC machining but also for analysis and design of metal forming operations. The level of sophistication in the use of analysis techniques varies from user to user. Some companies use hand calculators or desk computers; others use mainframe computers or minicomputers for extensive analysis and simulation of metal forming operations. Use of computers for process design and analysis depends on resources, on the training and experience of the engineering/technical staff, and on the needs of the company.

In introducing CAD/CAM for metal forming applications it is useful to consider the following factors:

- A CAD/CAM graphics system consists of both hardware and software (Figure 19-1). It is imperative that support and maintenance of both be secured for the present and the future, because most metal forming companies do not have extensive in-house computer expertise.
- For most applications, a CAD/CAM system must be capable of (a) describing full three-dimensional geometries with complex sculptured surfaces, (b) drafting with dimensions, tolerances and text, and (c) NC

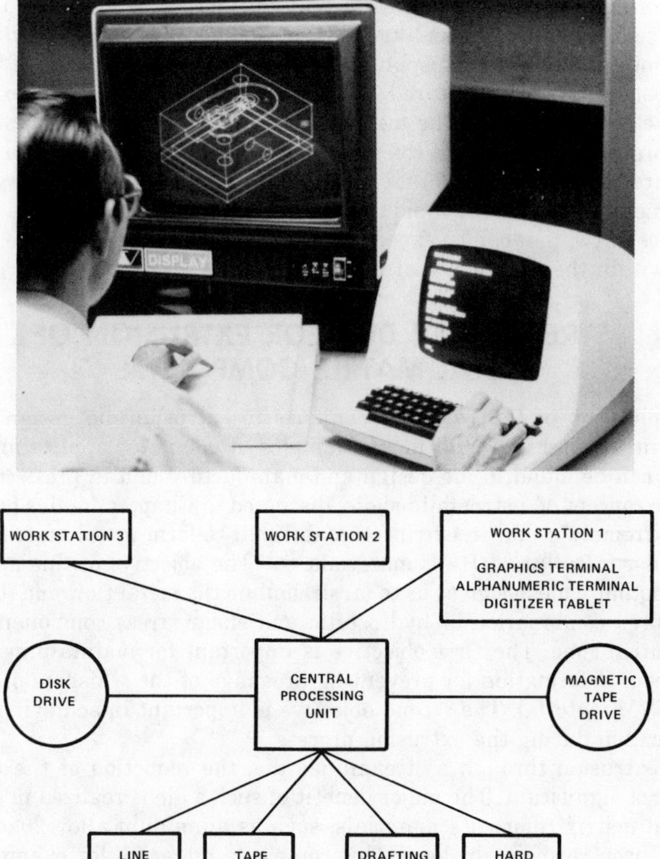

Figure 19-1. A typical CAD/CAM interactive graphics system (by Computervision). Photo shows work station with graphics and alpha-numeric terminals; chart shows system components.

cutter path generation. The 3-D capability is not necessary for 2-D (two-dimensional) die design and manufacturing operations (such as, for example, wiredrawing, extrusion and rolling).

- The trend is toward the use of graphics software hosted on 32-bit processors (such as VAX, Prime or Perkin Elmer) that use unaltered, stand-alone operating systems. These hardware/software configurations allow the computer hardware and operating system to be used also for other engineering and analysis purposes. This feature can be quite advantageous under some conditions.
- For 3-D (three-dimensional) representation of solid objects — for example, forging dies or models — "solid modeling" software packages are available. Solid models can display complex parts on a graphics

terminal by assembling solid building blocks. A graphics display by "solid modeling" looks like a photograph of the real object (with shades and depths). Such a display greatly enhances visualization of the object before it is manufactured. As a result, "solid modeling" is expected to be accepted also in the metal forming industry in the near future. At present (early 1980's), the geometric capabilities of most solid modelers are not quite sufficient for design and manufacture of complex dies and molds, but with the rapid improvements that are being made in graphics software it can be expected that these limitations will be eliminated within the next few years.

STREAMLINED DIES FOR EXTRUSION OF METAL MATRIX COMPOSITES

Application of CAD/CAM techniques to extrusion die design was discussed in Chapter 14. Additional examples of computer applications in extrusion can be found in die design and manufacture and in press control.

The concept of a streamlined die, discussed in Chapter 14, has been found to be extremely useful in extrusion of difficult-to-form metal matrix composite powder metallurgy (P/M) materials.[19-1] The objective of this application was to optimize die design so as to (a) streamline the metal flow and (b) achieve the desired combination of hydrostatic and shear stress components in the deformation zone. The first objective is important for maintaining near-homogeneous deformation for preventing breakage of the whiskers of the composite P/M material. The second objective is important in achieving uniform densification during the extrusion process.

In extrusion through a streamlined die, the reduction of the extrusion load is not significant. The major benefit of such a die is realized in extrusion of metal matrix composite materials, such as aluminum alloy 2024 with 20 vol % silicon carbide whiskers. This composite material, for example, has a higher modulus (nearly twice that of Al 2024) when the aspect ratio of the SiC whiskers is greater than 15. As a result, aerospace structures manufactured from this material are expected to weigh considerably less than those made from the aluminum alloy alone. The streamlined extrusion die minimizes abrupt velocity changes in the material during deformation, thus reducing breakage of the whiskers. The streamlined die concept, described in Chapter 14 (Figure 14-8), cannot be used for designing highly complex dies with re-entrant sections. Therefore, a new technique was developed by using a perimeter (line) mapping technique instead of the area mapping procedure used in earlier studies.[19-1] Examples of complex die configurations obtained with this new design method are presented in Figure 19-2. These dies would be manufactured by EDM using NC machined electrodes, as discussed in Chapter 14.

CLOSE-TOLERANCE FORGING OF SPIRAL BEVEL GEARS

Traditionally, straight bevel and spiral bevel gears (Figure 19-3) are manufactured by machining in special gear cutting machines. Precision forging of straight bevel gears was initially developed in West Germany and is

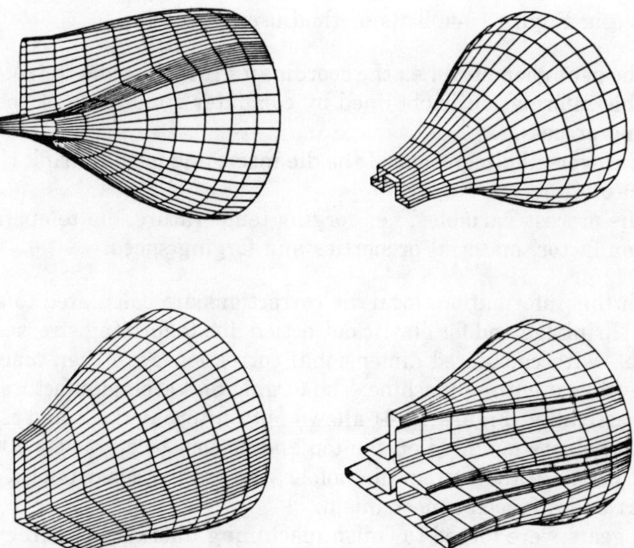

Figure 19-2. Computer-designed streamlined die configurations for extrusion of complex shapes.[19-1]

now routinely used in production.[19-2,19-3] Use of this technology for producing bevel gears offers considerable advantages such as (a) reductions in machining (material and energy) losses and (b) increases (up to 30%) in fatigue life.

Recent studies conducted in West Germany have led to establishment of production methods for precision forging of truck-differential-quality spiral bevel gears.[19-4] A similar development has also been carried out in the U.S. by use of computer-aided design (CAD) techniques.[19-2] The principles of this method, used for design and manufacture of the precision forging dies, are

Figure 19-3. Spiral bevel gear and pinion pair (contact pattern, shown by dark areas, must have required location on teeth).[19-2]

illustrated in Figure 19-4. This method uses as input:

- The gear geometry, i.e., the coordinates that describe the tooth surface. This information is obtained by computer simulation of the gear cutting process.
- The over-all dimensions of the die insert and of the shrink ring (Figure 19-5).
- The process variables, i.e., forging temperature, die temperature, friction factor, material properties and forging speed.

With this information, local die corrections are calculated to account for thermal shrinkage and for elastic deflection due to forming stresses. Graphite electrodes, with calculated dimensional corrections, are then machined in a spiral bevel gear cutting machine. The forging dies are manufactured by EDM. The die assembly (Figure 19-4) allows only internal flash and is contained in the die holders mounted on the top and bottom bolsters of a 2000-ton mechanical press. In the bottom die holder, the tooling consists of a die ring, a die insert and an ejector mechanism.

The gears were forged to finish machining tolerances, thereby eliminating the need for rough machining. The results of this developmental work indicate that it is quite feasible to produce these spiral bevel gears with tolerances such that no machining of the tooth surface is necessary. This method of manufacture, which uses computer-aided techniques for die design and manufacture, is expected to be used in production in the very near future.

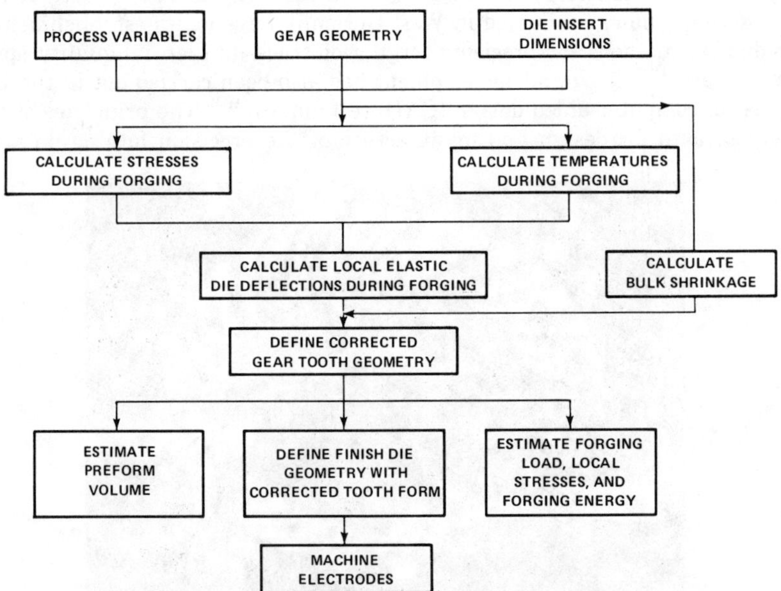

Figure 19-4. Outline of computer-aided design (CAD) procedure for making forging dies used to produce spiral bevel gears.[19-2]

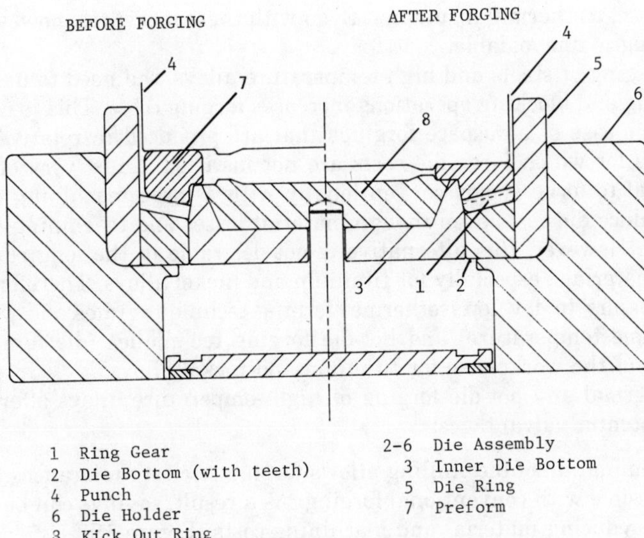

Figure 19-5. Schematic illustration of tooling assembly used for forging spiral bevel gears.[19-2]

ISOTHERMAL AND HOT-DIE FORGING OF TITANIUM AND NICKEL ALLOYS

In isothermal forging, the dies and the forged material are at about the same temperature. Aluminum alloys are usually forged isothermally at around 425 C (800 F), because conventional die materials can be heated to and maintained at this temperature without significant losses in strength and hardness. However, high-temperature materials such as steels, titanium alloys and nickel alloys are forged in the range from 925 to 1260 C (1700 to 2300 F). Therefore, isothermal forging of these alloys requires special tooling materials and lubricants that can perform adequately at these temperatures.[19-5]

In conventional forging practice, as discussed in Chapter 11, dies are heated to about 315 to 425 C (600 to 800 F) to reduce die chilling, i.e., heat transfer from the hot material to the colder dies. Higher die temperatures cannot be used with conventional die steels, because these steels lose their strength and hardness above this temperature range. Die chilling is very significant because (a) the flow stresses of most high-temperature alloys (Ti and Ni alloys in particular) increase drastically with decreasing temperature and (b) die chilling influences metal flow and may cause defects in the forged part. Die chilling may be minimized by selecting working temperatures at which the flow stress is not sensitive to temperature and by employing, whenever possible, fast-acting forging machines, such as hammers, screw presses and mechanical presses. In these machines, the time of contact between the workpiece (the metal part being forged) and the colder dies, during which heat transfer can occur, is reduced. Moreover, in forging of steels, nickel alloys and titanium alloys, glass lubricants reduce the die-chilling effect because they also act as thermal insulators. Even with these measures, however, some die chilling is unavoidable.

In forging of steels and high-temperature alloys, the need to use several preforming and blocking operations increases forging costs. This is especially true in the case of aerospace forgings that are produced in relatively small quantities for which large die costs are not justified. Thus, very often it is economical to forge a part conventionally with a large machining envelope and to reduce die costs even though material losses and machining costs are increased. However, this alternative is not desirable in the long run for expensive materials, especially for titanium and nickel alloys. Therefore, it has been necessary to develop isothermal forging techniques (dies and workpiece at the same temperature) and hot-die forging techniques (die temperature near that of the workpiece) for titanium and nickel alloys.

Isothermal and hot-die forging of high-temperature alloys offer the following potential advantages:

- Elimination of die chilling allows forging to closer tolerances than are possible with conventional forging. As a result, savings can be realized by reducing material and machining costs (Figure 19-6).[19-5]
- Elimination of die chilling also allows a reduction in the number of preforming and blocking dies necessary for forging of a given part; as a result, die costs are reduced.
- Because die chilling is not a problem, a low ram speed, i.e., a hydraulic press, can be used. This lowers the strain rate and the flow stress of the forged material. As a result, the forging pressure is reduced and larger parts can be forged in existing hydraulic presses.

The main disadvantages of isothermal forging are that it requires (a) expensive dies made from special materials, (b) uniform and controllable heating

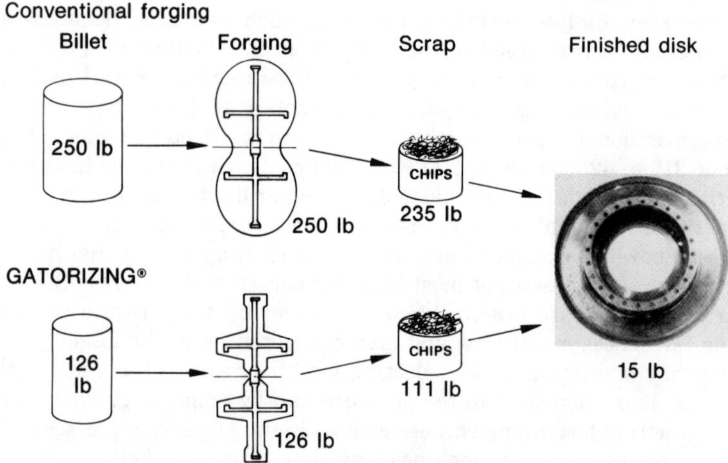

Figure 19-6. Illustration of estimated savings in material and in machining that can be realized by producing a jet engine disk by isothermal forging.[19-5]

systems and (c) an inert atmosphere around the dies and the forging to avoid oxidation of the dies. Much of the early work that established the features of the isothermal forging process was performed at the Illinois Institute of Technology Research Institute (IITRI) by Watmough, Kulkarni and their co-workers in the mid 1960's and early 1970's.[19-5,19-6] Concentrating on titanium alloys, these workers were able to demonstrate the feasibility of isothermal forging of complex titanium alloy aircraft parts in one or two operations. Several of these parts had intricate designs including blades or ribs which could only be produced via conventional, nonisothermal forging in several forging steps. This work also made valuable contributions to selection of die materials that perform satisfactorily at the high temperatures (i.e., about 900 C, or 1650 F) used for isothermal forging of titanium alloys. These die materials included a cast nickel-base alloy, IN-100, which is still widely used today in isothermal forging of titanium alloys.

Isothermal and hot-die forging of nickel-base alloys were pioneered by the Pratt and Whitney Aircraft Company (P&WA) in the late 1960's and early 1970's. Located in Florida, P&WA named this process "Gatorizing"™.[19-7] Developed originally for forging of hard-to-work or cast superalloys such as IN-100, this process often makes use of preforms or starting shapes of fine-grain materials made by powder metallurgy techniques. The starting preform has a low flow stress and high ductility at isothermal forging temperatures and low strain rates, a condition often referred to as "superplasticity". With Gatorizing,™ hard-to-work nickel alloys were forged for the first time. In addition, the higher strengths obtainable in products made from these alloys resulted in high strength-to-weight ratios in parts such as jet engine disks. The invention of this process has also led to the development of techniques for isothermal forging of integral-blade engine rotors.[19-7]

Following the lead of IITRI and P&WA, several other U.S. companies have begun production of titanium- and nickel-base parts employing isothermal as well as hot-die forging techniques.[19-8] In the development of hot-die forging processes for Ti alloys, a wide range of commercial as well as experimental lubricants and various tooling concepts were evaluated. These evaluations included critical examinations of various methods of die heating, from both technical and economic viewpoints.[19-5]

Isothermal and hot-die forging of high-temperature alloys are now well-proven and accepted production processes. In introduction and application of these processes, technical and economic factors, more than in conventional forging practice, must be evaluated, regarding:

- The workpiece material and its flow stress.
- Forging equipment, load capacity and speed control.
- Die material and die design.
- Die-heating methods and temperature control.
- High-temperature lubricants.

DEVELOPMENTS IN FORMING MACHINES AND AUTOMATION

The success and economical application of any forming process requires the appropriate selection and utilization of available machining equipment.

Advances in forming technology are invariably related to advances in forming equipment, tooling and handling devices, some of which are briefly reviewed below.

Hydro-Wedge Press

The hydro-wedge press is essentially a hydraulic press with a wedge drive. A section through a hydro-wedge press is shown in Figure 19-7.[19-9] The ram is moved by a wedge which is actuated by a piston-cylinder unit. The load acting on the ram is supported by the wedge over a large surface area. This reduces tilting of the ram under load. For the upstroke, a pullback cylinder is used. This cylinder is located centrally in the top cross beam of the frame. Its piston lifts the ram, and then the main piston and the wedge move back to their starting positions as a result of the wedge effect. The press is provided with a quick die-changing mechanism. With the aid of a tool-changing carrier, which can be brought to the press on rails, the completely assembled die sets can be fed into the press. By means of keys and hydraulically operated clamping devices, the dies, placed on clamping plates, are secured in the press.

Like other hydraulic presses, the hydro-wedge press is powered either by a water accumulator or by a direct oil-pump drive. Due to its design, the hydro-wedge press offers better ram guiding and off-center loading capabilities than conventional hydraulic presses offer. The largest press of this type built so far has a capacity of 4000 metric tons. This press has a rapid ram-reverse speed of 200 mm/s and a press speed, under load, of 100 mm/s.

Servo-Hydraulic Press

A schematic representation of a servo-hydraulic press is shown in Figure 19-8.[19-10] The ram is hydrostatically guided in the frame (1) and the ram

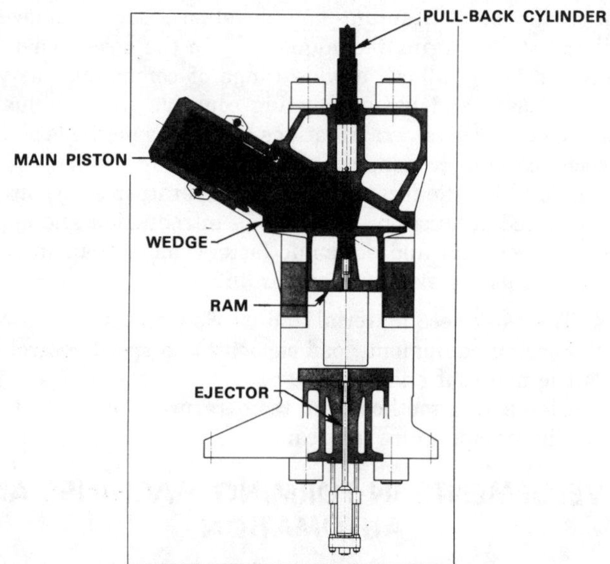

Figure 19-7. Schematic illustration of hydro-wedge press.[19-9]

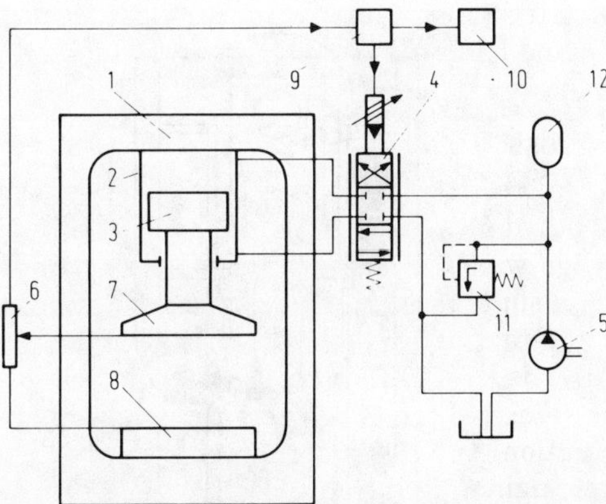

Figure 19-8. Schematic illustration of servo-hydraulic press for blanking or isothermal forming;[(19-10)] see text for identification of components.

motion is servocontrolled. The ram (7) is actuated by a piston (3) in a double-acting cylinder (2). A pump (5) pressurizes the oil into an accumulator (12). The oil pressure is set by a pressure limit valve (11). A servovalve (4) feeds the double-acting cylinder (2). A displacement sensor (6) measures the ram position with respect to the press table (8). The controller (9) compares the "actual" ram displacement (6) with the preset valve (10) and actuates the servovalve (4).

Controlled by this closed-loop system, the ram follows any desired stroke/time function within the limits of the system. The closed-loop control can compensate for the deflection of the press and the workpiece and for the compression of the oil. Thus, this press is well suited for precision forming and coining, for heavy blanking, for trimming, and in particular for isothermal or hot-die forming of rate-sensitive materials such as titanium and nickel alloys.

Hydromechanical Vertical Press

An interesting hydromechanical press drive has been developed in Japan.[(19-11)] The design principles of this press are illustrated in Figure 19-9. This 630-ton-capacity press has an idle speed of 130 strokes/min. The crankshaft (1) is connected to a flywheel and rotates continuously while the plunger (b) moves up and down with a fixed stroke. This plunger (b) is not coupled directly to the press slide (c) but moves within a hydraulic cylinder (a). Between the plunger (b) and the slide (c), there is a hydraulic-fluid cushion (or chamber). This cushion is connected through a control valve (4) to an oil reservoir located on the side of the press. During idling of the press, this valve (4) is open and the hydraulic fluid is circulated through the fluid cushion and the reservoir. At this stage, no pressure is generated on the slide (c). This slide is held in its upper position, while being pressed against an adjustable mechanical stop (2), by hydraulic cylinders (3).

To initiate a working stroke, the control valve (4) is closed when the idling plunger (b) is slightly past the top-dead-center (TDC) position. Thus, the plunger

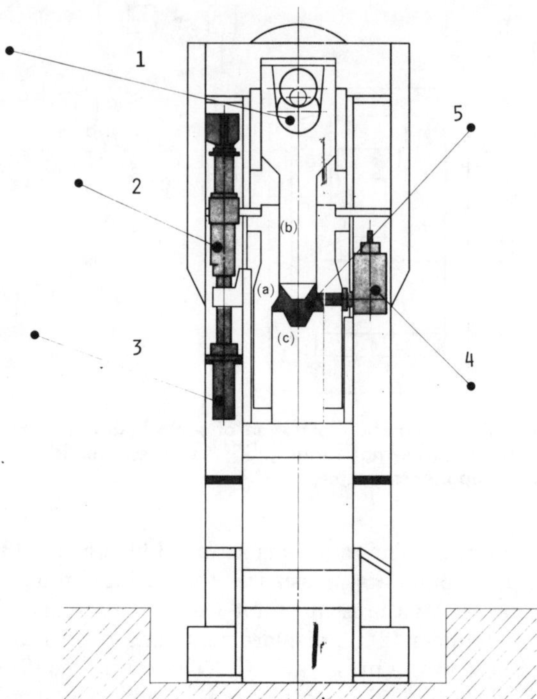

Figure 19-9. Schematic illustration of the recently developed hydromechanical vertical press.[19-11] See description in text.

exerts pressure on the fluid in the cushion and pushes the ram slide (c) down by overcoming the pressure of the lift-up cylinders (3). When the plunger passes the bottom-dead-center (BDC) position, the pressure in the cushion is reduced and the lift-up cylinders push the slide upward toward the mechanical stops (2). During the upstroke of the plunger (5), the control valve (4) is opened and, while the plunger continues its up-and-down motion, the slide stops at its TDC position.

This design offers the following unusual characteristics:

- The fluid cushion between the plunger (b) and the slide (c) acts like a spring. Therefore, this press can be run with "kissing" surfaces without damaging the press. The "nonreproducible" additional force (due to variations in stock temperature or volume) can be absorbed by the hydraulic cushion without causing severe straining of the mechanical press components. Thus, the hydraulic cushion acts as an overload protection mechanism provided that the overload is not very large.
- If a true overload protection mechanism is desired, the fluid cushion can be connected to a maximum-pressure control valve. Thus, when the pressure approaches unacceptable levels, the valve is actuated, the pressure is relieved, and the press and the dies are protected.
- The fluid cushion, compressed during the downstroke, expands during

the upstroke and contributes to the upward acceleration of the plunger and to the rotational acceleration of the flywheel.

- The fluid cushion can be connected to one or more other hydraulic cylinders, which actuate other rams or ejectors, designed to move vertically or horizontally. As a result, multiple-action tooling and forming (in vertical and/or horizontal directions) are available. Thus, this press offers advantages in flashless cold and warm forging of components with internal cavities and undercuts.

Automation in Metal Forming

As in all areas of manufacture, automation is being increasingly emphasized in metal forming applications. Nearly all modern forming machines, presses and rolling mills, for example, are equipped with quick tool/die changing mechanisms to reduce nonproductive downtime of expensive machinery. Handling of billets and formed parts is also automated, whenever economically justifiable, in order to:

- Reduce labor costs by minimizing manual work.
- Reduce the need for skilled operators.
- Increase the production rate (parts per hour).
- Improve quality by maintaining consistency in forming.
- Improve working conditions.

The disadvantages of automation are also numerous and can be summarized as follows:

- Inflexibility and loss of versatility in production.
- Increased downtime due to an increase in the complexity of the machinery.
- The need for a skilled maintenance staff.
- The cost of automation.

The single most important factor in the decision tc use or not to use automation is economics. The economics are, on the other hand, influenced by (a) the type and geometry of the parts formed (whether or not the parts can be mechanically transported) and (b) the size of the production run (the change from one job to another is much more costly in automated operation than in manual forming). Experience has shown that the use of an automated press is restricted to about 80% of the total shift performance, if manual operation is considered to be 100%. This is due to the fact that, when automated, a machine has a greater incidence of breakdown. Thus, the main economic factors for automation can be summarized as follows:

- The parts must have a shape which allows automatic handling without any particular difficulties.
- Automation must provide an increase in production rate of at least about 20%.
- The cost of automation (added to the cost of the existing, normally operated press) and the cost of maintaining the automated press must be compensated for by savings in labor.

In systematically reviewing the possibilities for automation, transport of the material during forming can be divided into three zones. The first zone represents transport to the first die station in the press; the second zone represents transport within the press, from one die station to the next; and the third zone represents transport of the workpiece from the last die station to a conveyor for further processing. Mechanization of the first and third zones is relatively simple. In the first zone, a conveyor belt or a simple actuated mechanical arm may do the job. Similarly, in the third zone, a slide or a swinging arm is needed to push the ejected part out of the press area. Mechanization of the second zone, within the press, requires a sophisticated handling mechanism and has been solved by various material handling techniques, depending on the volume of production.

Robots and Manipulators

The concept of a "robot" is quite vague. The Robot Institute of America defines an industrial robot as "a reprogrammable multifunctional manipulator designed to move material, parts, tools or specialized devices through variable programmed motions for the performance of a variety of tasks". There are basically two types of robots: servocontrolled and nonservocontrolled. The motions of one nonservocontrolled robot are usually controlled by adjustable stops at each axis. This limits the motion capabilities of nonservocontrolled robots but makes them relatively inexpensive and reliable. The servocontrolled robots use feedback devices to measure continuously one position of each axis motion. They generally use microprocessor controls.

Robots and manipulators have been in use in metal forming shops for many years. Most applications involve handling of billets or parts "outside" of the forming machine, because these applications are easiest to mechanize, as discussed earlier. In recent years, mechanization and use of robots have gained even further attention because various types of robots that are reliable for metal forming operations have been developed and tested. Robots available in the market may be classified in the following groups:

- General-purpose robots, used in all types of handling and manufacturing applications.
- Robots or manipulators dedicated to loading and unloading of a one-blow (one-die-station) forming machine.
- Robots or manipulators specifically designed for metal forming operations, i.e., handling of billets and formed parts within a forming machine as well as transporting them from one machine to another.
- Manipulators that are human-operated and that can handle pieces weighing more than 100 lb (50 kg).

For economical and successful operations, robots used in metal forming should have the following general characteristics:[19-12]

- Rigid design and construction because of relatively rough environments and heavy loads.
- Easy programming with high reliability and fairly simple controls, because most metal forming applications require relatively simple motions.
- Flexibility and capability for fast setup for new applications, because

in job-shop-type operations a robot will be used to load and unload various machines, depending on the production program.

- High transfer speed; this is necessary because the robot preferably should be as fast as, or even faster than, the operator who could do the same job.
- Acceptable positioning accuracy and repeatability, on the order of 1.2 mm in most cases, but sometimes even less than 0.5 mm.
- Load capacity in most cases between 20 and 60 lb (10 and 30 kg).
- Required degrees of freedom varying from 1 or 2 to 6; in most cases, however, 1 to 3 degrees of freedom are sufficient.

REFERENCES

19-1. Gunasekera, J. S., *et al,* "Computer Aided Process Modeling of Hot Forging and Extrusion of Aluminum Alloys", Annals of the CIRP, Vol 31, No. 1, 1982, p 131.

19-2. Sabroff, A. M., *et al,* "Application of CAD/CAM Techniques to Close Tolerance Forging of Spiral Bevel Gears", Annals of the CIRP, Vol 31, No. 1, 1982, p 141.

19-3. Kelley, M., and Davis, L., "Precision Forged Gears", Metals Engineering Quarterly, Nov 1974, p 20.

19-4. Mages, W., "Advantageous Application of New Forming Processes in Gear Drive and Manufacture" (in German), VDI-Berichte, No. 332, 1979, p 97.

19-5. Semiatin, S. L., and Altan, T., "Isothermal and Hot Die Forging of High Temperature Alloys", Report prepared for Metals & Ceramics Information Center, April 1983, in print.

19-6. Kulkarni, K., "Isothermal Forging – From Research to a Promising New Manufacturing Technology", Proc. Sixth North American Metalworking Research Conference, published by SME, Dearborn, MI, 1978, p 24.

19-7. Allen, M. M., "Isoforging of Powder Metallurgy Superalloys for Advanced Turbine Applications", Proc. of AGARD Conference on "Advanced Fabrication Techniques in Powder Metallurgy and Their Economic Implications", No. 200, Paper P5, AGARD, France, 1976.

19-8. Coyne, J. E., "Advanced Technology in Superalloy Disc Forging", Metallurgia, Vol 47, No. 11, Nov 1980, p 581.

19-9. Winkler, H., "Hydro-Wedge Hydraulic Forging Press", Metallurgia and Metalforming, May 1974, p 135.

19-10. Altan, T., "Metalforming at 2.EMO", American Machinist, Jan 1978, p 132.

19-11. Kawasaki Yucoh Company, Ltd., "HIMEX Double Action Stamp Forging Press", Brochure of Kawasaki Company, Ltd., Takasago, Japan, 1981.

19-12. Hoerl, A., "Requirements for the Successful Application of Robots in the Forge Shop" (in German), Technical Report prepared for Zahnradfabrik Friedrichshafen A. G., Friedrichshafen, W. Germany, 1981.

CHAPTER 20
Application of FEM to Simulation of Metal Forming Processes

In recent years, one of the most significant advances in analysis and simulation of metal forming processes has been the development and application of the Finite Element Method (FEM).[20-1 to 20-5] Application of FEM was briefly reviewed in Chapter 12, in discussing prediction of metal flow in forging of round parts. The major advantage of this method is its ability to generalize — that is, its applicability to a wide class of boundary value problems with little restriction on workpiece geometry. This is achieved by the proper discretization procedure used in the finite element method. In practical metal forming processes, a number of operations (preforming) are required in order to transform the initial "simple" geometry into a "complex" geometry while achieving desired tolerances and properties. The desired workpiece shapes, in general, are obtained by using dies of various shapes. Therefore, a method of analysis that can treat the boundary conditions of dies is necessary in order to fully utilize the advantage of the finite element method in metal forming analysis. Such a method has been developed for prediction, for practical forming, of the instantaneous velocities, strain rates, strains, stresses and temperatures within the deforming metal. This method has been programmed into a computer code called ALPID.[20-4,20-5] The code ALPID (Analysis of Large Plastic Incremental Deformation) uses (a) higher-order elements, (b) a general and automated description of the die and boundary conditions and (c) an automatic initial guess generation. The details and the theory of ALPID are based on the rigid-plastic FEM developed by Kobayashi and his co-workers[20-1 to 20-3] and are summarized by Oh.[20-4] The assumption of rigid-plastic or rigid-viscoplastic material implies that the flow stress is a function of strain, strain rate and temperature and that the elastic response of the material is neglected. This assumption is very reasonable in analyzing metal forming problems, because the elastic portion of the deformation is negligible in most metal forming operations. The rigid-viscoplastic formulation, however, has significant practical advantages: first, it reduces the effort and computer time required for simulating metal flow; and second, it predicts stresses σ, strains $\bar{\epsilon}$, strain rates $\dot{\bar{\epsilon}}$, velocities V, and temperatures T with sufficient accuracy for practical purposes. In ALPID, the graphic display of FEM input data and of the results is an important part of the FEM analysis, because the analysis involves relatively large amounts of information. For this purpose, ALPID is provided with an interactive display program called FEMGRA.[20-5] Several examples, generated by ALPID and discussed below, illustrate the state of development and capabilities of the rigid-viscoplastic FEM.

SOLID CYLINDER UPSETTING

In upsetting of a cylinder between two flat dies, a bulge is formed on the free surface of the cylinder due to friction between the workpiece and the die. ALPID was used to simulate this process with different degrees of freedom and different types of elements while keeping the process conditions the same.[20-5] The undeformed workpiece was 38.1 mm (1.5 in.) in height and 25.4 mm (1.0 in.) in diameter. The die velocity was 25.4 mm/s (1.0 in./s). The material used for calculation was Ti-6242-0.1Si at 954 C (1750 F). The solutions were obtained in an incremental manner with a step size of 2% of the undeformed workpiece height.

Figure 20-1 shows the quarter section of the deformed workpiece at 40% reduction in height with one and four quadratic elements. The grid distortions are compared with those calculated by using 88 linear elements. This comparison reveals that the flow pattern with one quadratic element shows a minor deviation near the top corner of the side surface. The solutions with four quadratic elements and with 88 linear elements show excellent agreement.

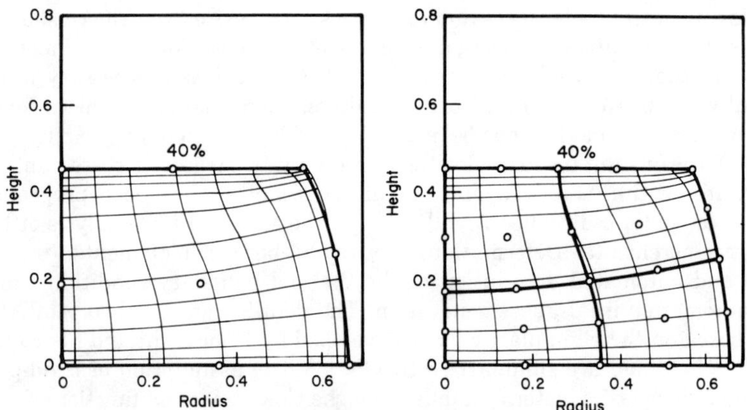

Figure 20-1. Results of solid cylinder upsetting with quadratic elements and 88 linear elements at 40% reduction in height: (left) one quadratic element; (right) four quadratic elements.

RING COMPRESSION

In ring compression, a short ring specimen is compressed between flat dies. The inside diameter of the ring is increased if the interface friction is low, and it is decreased if the interface friction is high. Thus, the changes in the inside diameter of the compressed ring are sensitive to friction at the die/workpiece interface.

Ring compression analysis presents a certain difficulty for FEM analysis because of the unknown direction of frictional stress at the tool/material interface. Recently the rigid-plastic finite element solution of ring compression was obtained by introducing a frictional stress expression which allows a smooth transition of the stress change near the neutral point.[20-3] By use of a similar scheme, ring compression was simulated for different frictional conditions using ALPID.

As an example, Figure 20-2 shows the deformation pattern obtained with frictional shear factor m = 0.6 under isothermal upsetting for a titanium alloy. The arrows in this figure indicate the neutral-point locations. It can be seen that, in this case of relatively high friction, the neutral point is formed, from the start of deformation, between the inside and outside diameters of the ring. The relative positions of the neutral point are reflected in metal flow, indicating a relatively large reduction in inside diameter. These results

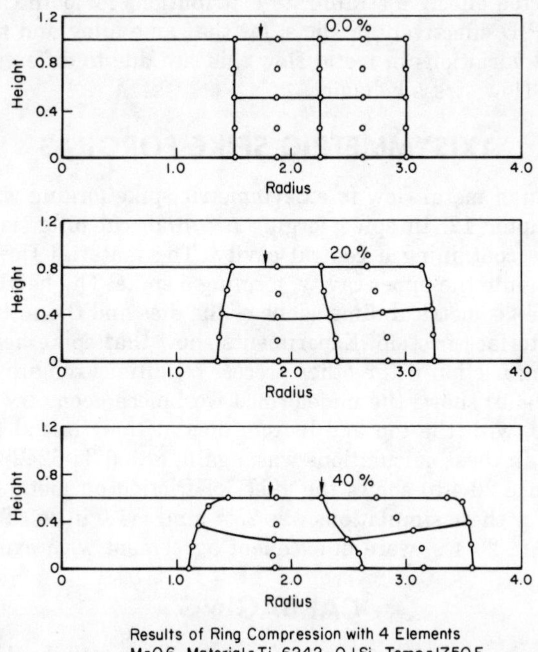

Figure 20-2. Results of ring compression analysis obtained with ALPID using four elements (m = 0.6; material, Ti-6242-0.1Si; temperature, 954 C or 1750 F).

of the ALPID simulation are in concurrence with experimental ring compression results obtained under high-friction conditions.

SIDE PRESSING

In side pressing, a long circular cylinder is compressed sideways (perpendicular to the cylinder axis) between two flat dies. This process has been shown to be very useful in studying flow behavior at hot working temperatures. Experiments show that hot isothermal side pressing of $\alpha + \beta$ Ti-6242 alloy, for example, leads to stable deformation while that of β Ti-6242 produces severe shear bands and unstable flow. This is due to two completely different deformation modes and to the differences between the flow stress behaviors of the two structures — that is, the $\alpha + \beta$ microstructure exhibits a stable strain-rate hardening while the β microstructure shows substantial amounts of strain softening behavior.

In order to estimate the strain concentration, isothermal rigid-viscoplastic FEM-based ALPID was used to simulate the side pressing of cylinders with two different flow stress characteristics corresponding to the two microstructures.[20-5] The diameter of the specimen was 10.2 mm (0.40 in.) and the deformation was assumed to be plane strain. The temperature during deformation was 913 C (1675 F). Figure 20-3 shows the experimentally observed transverse sections of side-pressed cylinders of $\alpha + \beta$ and β microstructures and the predicted effective strain-rate distributions for both cases. It can be seen that ALPID effectively predicts, for the same alloy and forming conditions, detailed variations in metal flow that are due to differences in microstructure and flow stress behavior.

AXISYMMETRIC SPIKE FORGING

Simulation of metal flow in axisymmetric spike forging was briefly discussed in Chapter 12. In spike forging a cylindrical billet is forged in an impression die containing a central cavity. The material flows radially as well as axially into the upper cavity, forming a spike. The height of the spike depends on the geometrical dimensions of the dies and the initial workpiece, and on the interface friction. Experiments show that spike height increases with increasing friction if the other process conditions remain the same.[20-4]

Figure 20-4(a) shows the undeformed workpiece geometry with 16 nine-node elements, with the top and bottom dies at their initial positions. The material used in these calculations was, again, $\alpha + \beta$ Ti-6242-0.1Si at 954 C (1750 F). Figure 20-4(b) shows the effect of friction on metal flow. The die velocity used for these simulations was 25.4 mm/s (1.0 in./s). The predictions shown in Figure 20-4(b) were in excellent agreement with experiments.[20-5]

CABBAGING

Cabbaging was also briefly mentioned in Chapter 12. In the initial stage of backward extrusion, called cabbaging, a round billet is placed in a container. A punch is used to upset and partially pierce one end of the billet. Thus, the outside diameter of the billet is sized, and the pierced recess on top of the billet provides punch guidance for the next backward extrusion oper-

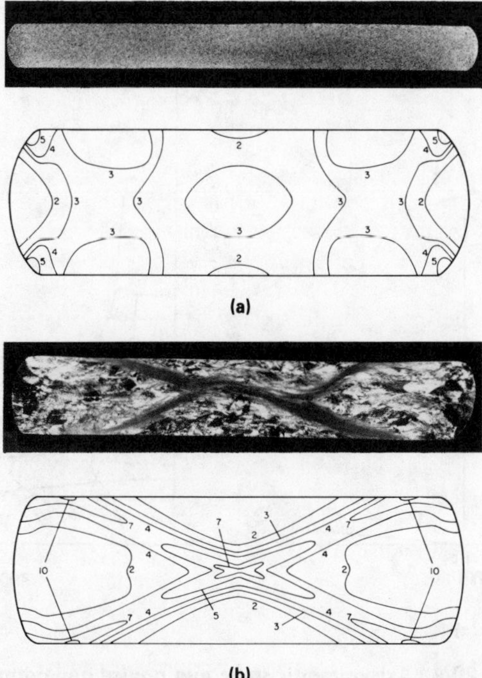

Figure 20-3. Comparison of predicted and experimentally determined strain rate (per second) distributions in side pressing of Ti-6242-0.1Si at 913 C (1675 F): (a) $\alpha + \beta$ microstructure; (b) β microstructure.

ation. The cabbaging operation has been simulated by ALPID using the actual production conditions with minor assumptions.[20-6] The undeformed billet had a diameter of 73.7 mm (2.94 in.) and a height of 354 mm (13.85 in.). The material of the billet was AISI 1046 steel, and the operation was done at 1100 C (1850 F). The frictional shear factor used in the analysis was m = 0.3. The punch speed used for the simulation was 59.3 mm/s (2.3 in./s).

Figure 20-5 shows the undeformed FEM grid line, the calculated grid distortions at various punch displacements, and the predicted curve for punch load versus displacement.

Because of the unusually high strain concentration, the FEM grid near the punch tip underwent too much distortion, as can be seen in Figure 20-5. A partial "remeshing" near the punch tip was done at the punch displacement of 91.4 mm (3.6 in.). In order to preserve the local strain distribution, the interpolated strain values were assigned to the newly generated mesh elements.

COMPRESSOR DISK FORGING

A simulation of a compressor disk forging is illustrated in Figure 20-6; because of symmetry, only a quarter of the disk is shown.[20-7] The cylin-

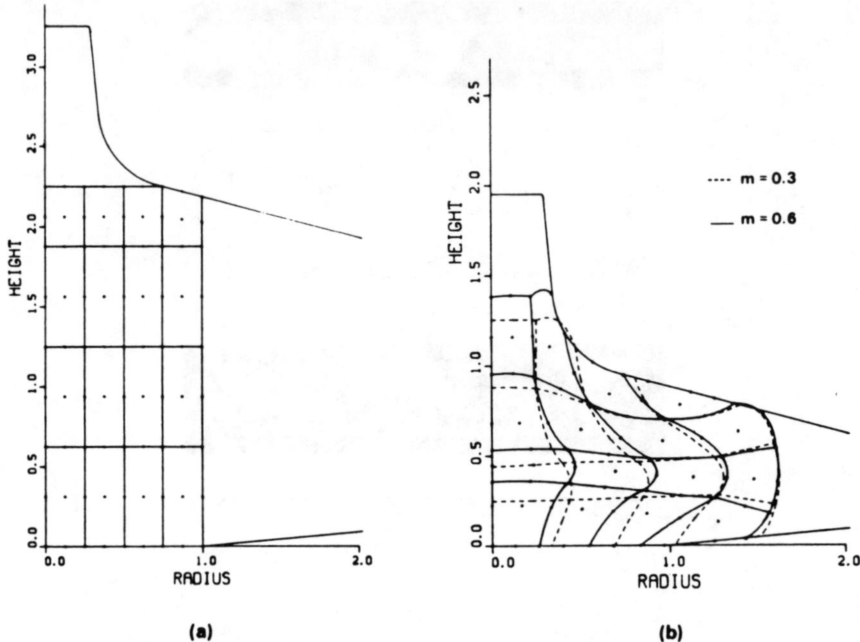

Figure 20-4. Axisymmetric spike forging: (a) undeformed FEM grid; (b) deformation at a die stroke of 0.58H_0 for two different m values (H_0 is initial billet height).

drical preform shape used in this analysis was 158.8 mm (6.5 in.) in diameter and 63.5 mm (2.5 in.) in height. The velocity of the upper die used in the simulation was 5.1 mm/min (0.2 in./min). The bottom die was stationary. Forging was done isothermally at 900 C (1650 F), with an average nominal strain rate of about 0.175 min^{-1}. The results show that this method and the associated code ALPID can be used effectively for simulating disk-type forgings and for predicting strains, strain rates and stresses for a given preform shape.

FLASHLESS FORGING OF A GEAR BLANK AND REMESHING

In practical metal forming operations, deformations are usually very large. As a result, during simulation of a forming operation by FEM-based ALPID, these large strains distort the initial FEM mesh to such a degree that a new mesh (remesh) is necessary in order to continue the simulation. For this purpose a "remeshing" method has been developed.[20-8] This method basically consists of two steps:

1. A new mesh is generated within the boundary of the deformed metal that exists at the last step of deformation prior to remeshing (Figure 20-7).

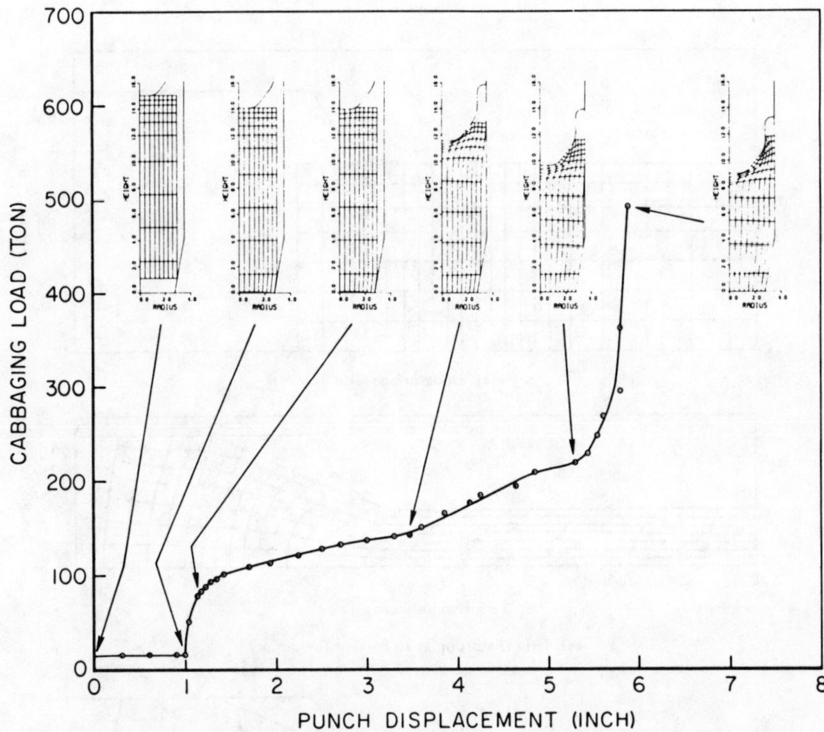

Figure 20-5. Predicted deformed grids, and punch load/displacement curve, for the cabbaging process.

2. The calculated values of V, $\bar{\epsilon}$, $\dot{\bar{\epsilon}}$ and T are interpolated from the old onto the new mesh.

In order to evaluate the remeshing algorithm, an FEM simulation of a gear blank forging was conducted, utilizing the following process variables:

- The undeformed cylindrical billet had a height of 6.66 in. (169.16 mm) and a diameter of 2.755 in. (69.98 mm) (Figure 20-8).
- The billet material was AISI 8620 steel, and the forging temperature was 1100 C (2012 F). The flow stress data for 8620 steel were obtained by performing isothermal uniform compression tests at strain rates $\dot{\bar{\epsilon}}$ = 25 to 30 and 2.5 to 3 s^{-1}. The flow stress $\bar{\sigma}$ was calculated using the expression $\sigma = C\epsilon^m\dot{\bar{\epsilon}}^n$, where C, m and n were calculated as 10.92, 0.0 and 0.134, respectively.
- The velocity of the upper die used for the analysis was 5.0 in./s (127.0 mm/s), and the bottom die was stationary.
- The friction factor used in the analysis was chosen as m = 0.3.
- The non-steady-state deformation of the gear blank forging was analyzed in a step-by-step manner by treating it quasilinearly during each incremental deformation. The incremental displacement of the upper die for each step was chosen to be 0.02 times the original workpiece height.

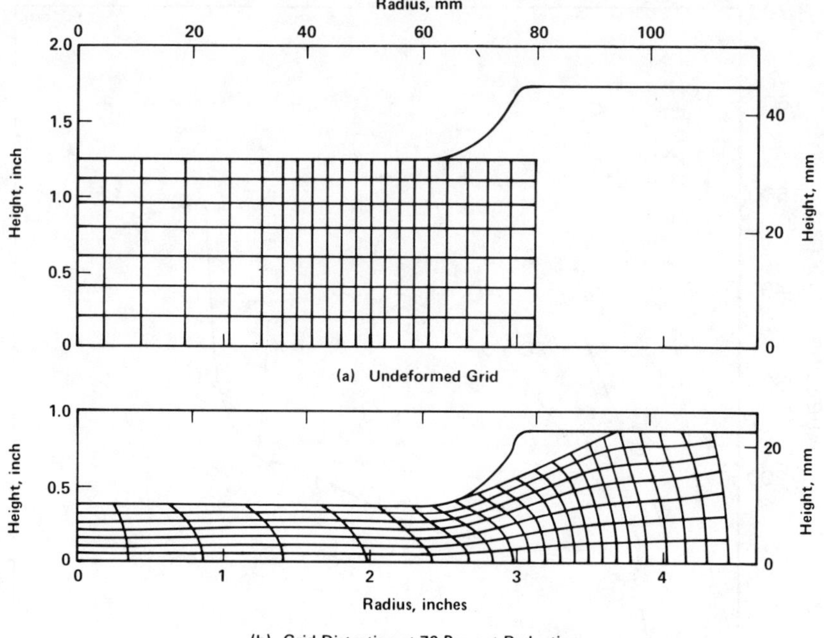

(a) Undeformed Grid

(b) Grid Distortion at 70 Percent Reduction

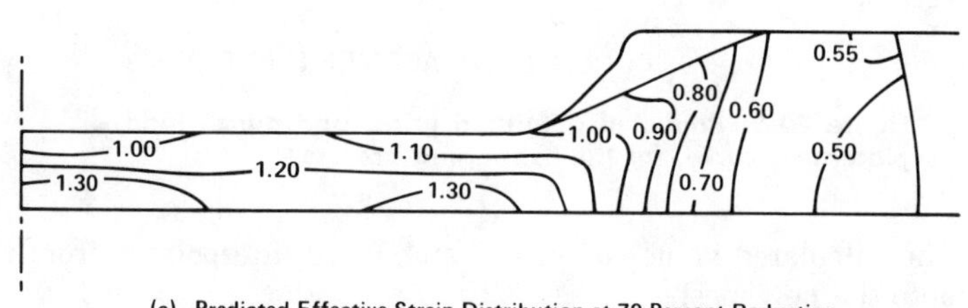

(c) Predicted Effective Strain Distribution at 70 Percent Reduction

Figure 20-6. Results of compressor disk forging simulation.

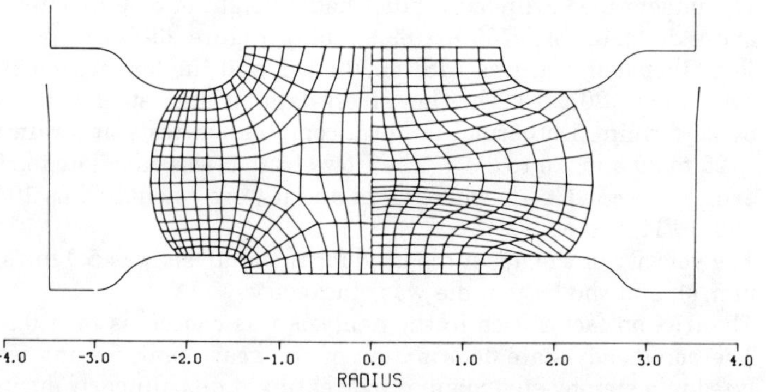

Figure 20-7. Distorted FEM grid (right half) and "remeshed" FEM grid (left half) at 61% reduction in billet height.

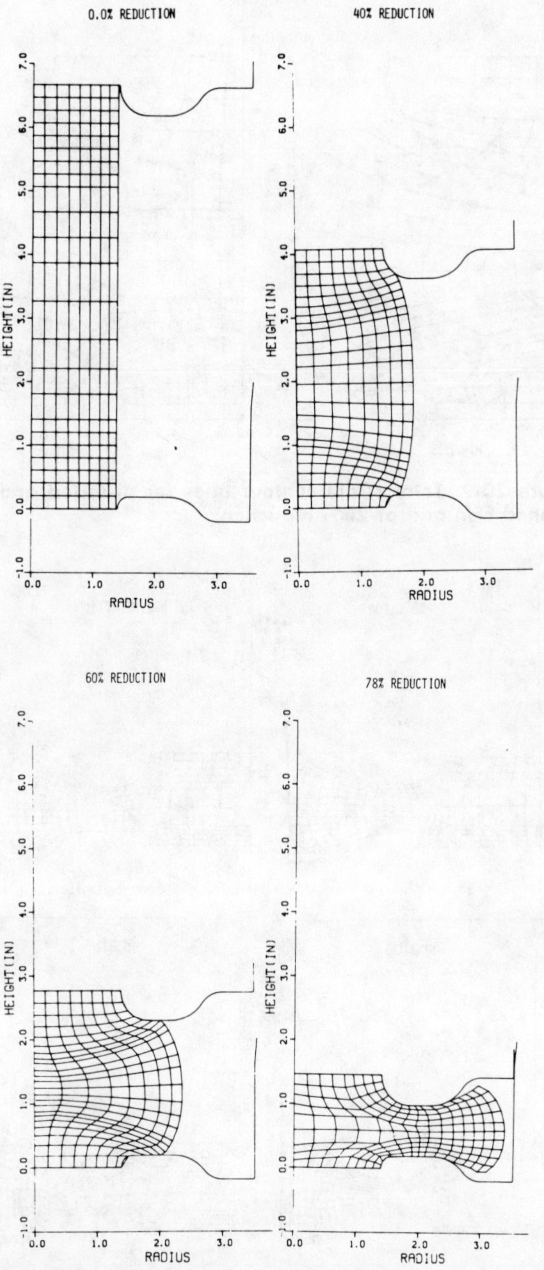

Figure 20-8. FEM metal flow patterns at 0, 40, 60 and 78% reductions in initial billet height.

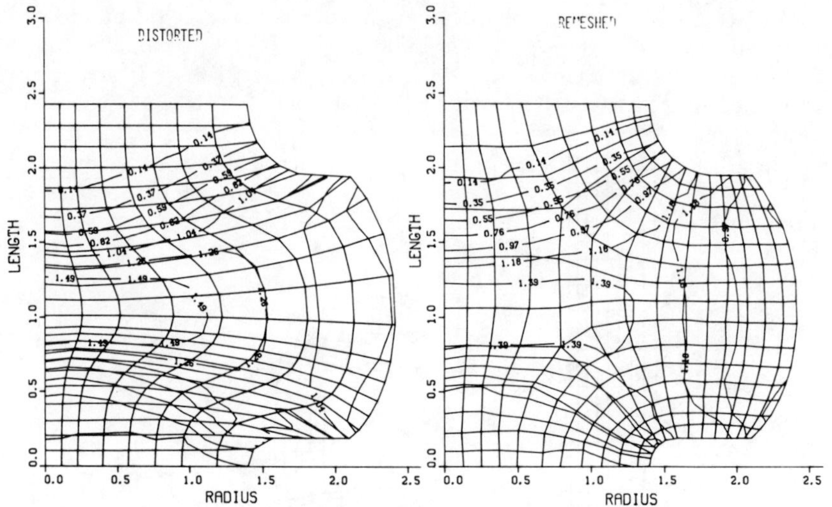

Figure 20-9. Total strain contour lines for distorted and remeshed FEM grid at 28% reduction.

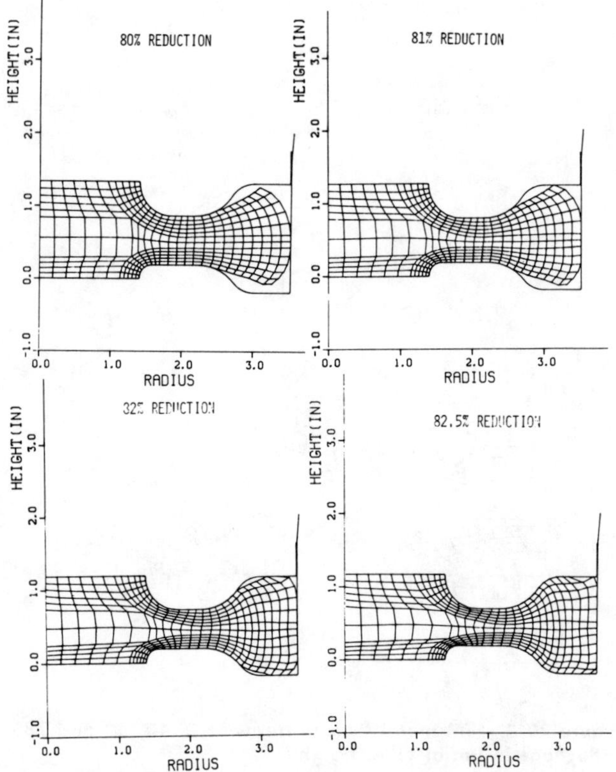

Figure 20-10. Grid distortions near complete die fill.

Figure 20-8 shows the metal flow patterns predicted by ALPID after 0, 40, 60 and 78% reductions in initial billet height. It should be noted that at the 60% reduction the element at the lower right-hand corner is distorted to such a degree that it was impossible to continue the simulation without generating a new mesh. A new mesh was generated at a 61% reduction in billet height, as shown in Figure 20-7. The remeshing program FEMRMS was then used to interpolate the strain values of the last step (at 61% reduction ratio). Contour plots for the total strain distribution before and after remeshing are shown in Figure 20-9. Figure 20-9 demonstrates that the accuracy of the remeshing program is acceptable for practical engineering purposes. The simulation was then continued using the fresh mesh as an initial mesh. Two other remeshings were necessary to complete the simulation up to the complete die fill and to obtain the results shown in Figure 20-10.

FUTURE DEVELOPMENT AND APPLICATION OF FEM IN METAL FORMING

The FEM-based ALPID code offers significant potential for simulation and design of forming processes. ALPID has been applied to two-dimensional forming operations and surely will be expanded to simulate 3-D forming operations. Present developments are being directed toward automation of the FEM simulation procedure to the greatest possible degree, so that the following steps may be conducted automatically or semiautomatically with a minimum amount of user effort:

1. Generate the die geometry, i.e., upper and lower die surfaces. This is best done by means of a CAD/CAM system used for computer-aided design (CAD) of dies.
2. Generate the geometry of the billet or preform that will be placed in the die and deformed. At this stage it is also necessary to generate a mesh on the preform as input to ALPID. This mesh is best obtained from a separate mesh-generating program or within the CAD/CAM system, because most of today's CAD/CAM systems have mesh-generating modules for FEM analysis.
3. Transfer the die and preform geometry, as well as the FEM mesh, into the ALPID program.
4. Run ALPID and remesh automatically as often as necessary. As discussed above, the remeshing consists of:
   (a) Construction of a new mesh within the boundary of the deformed preform that exists at the last step of deformation prior to remeshing (Figure 20-7).
   (b) Interpolation of calculated results (values of velocity, stress, strain, strain-rate and temperature fields) from the old to the new mesh. This interpolation is done by a special module of ALPID that has been developed for this purpose.
5. Postprocess the results of ALPID. A given simulation may require several remeshing/interpolation steps. The results of the simulation for selected steps are stored in a special format. These results must be displayed to the user in an easily interpreted form, such as color contour plots, color displays, isometric views, etc.

Automation of the above-listed steps, such that the user of the ALPID code does not have to be concerned with the details of this entire procedure, will make application of FEM to metal forming truly practical. Considering that research toward this goal is in progress, it can be expected that the FEM-based metal flow simulation techniques will be used within the next five years for:

- Practical design of metal forming dies.
- Optimization of preform shapes for cold and hot forging.
- Prediction of local microstructures and properties of formed parts from the calculated distributions of strain, strain rate and temperature.
- Optimization of metal forming process sequences for desired metal flow and product microstructure.

REFERENCES

20-1. Lee, C. H., and Kobayashi, S., "New Solutions to Rigid Plastic Deformation Problems Using a Matrix Method", Trans. ASME, J. Engr. for Ind., Vol 95, 1973, pp 865-873.
20-2. Kobayashi, S., "Rigid Plastic Finite Element Analysis of Axisymmetric Metal Forming Processes", Numerical Modeling of Manufacturing Processes, ASME, PVP-PB-025, 1977, pp 49-68.
20-3. Oh, S. I., Rebelo, N., and Kobayashi, S., "Finite Element Formulation of the Analysis of Plastic Deformation of Rate-Sensitive Materials for Metal Forming", Metal Forming Plasticity, IUTAM Symposium, Tutzing, Germany, 1978, p 273.
20-4. Oh, S. I., "Finite Element Analysis of Metal Forming Problems with Arbitrarily Shaped Dies", Int. J. of Mechanical Science, Vol 17, 1982, p 293.
20-5. Oh, S. I., Lahoti, G. D., and Altan, T., "ALPID – A General Purpose FEM Program for Metal Forming", Proceedings of NAMRC-IX, May 1981, State College, PA, p 83.
20-6. Oh, S. I., Lahoti, G. D., and Altan, T., "Analysis of Backward Extrusion Process by the Finite Element Method", Proceedings of NAMRC-X, Hamilton, Canada, 1982.
20-7. Oh, S. I., Park, J. J., Kobayashi, S., and Altan, T., "Finite Analysis of Compressor Disk Forgings of Ti-Alloys", accepted for publication in Trans. ASME, J. Eng. for Ind., 1983.
20-8. Oh, S. I., Badawy, A., and Altan, T., "A Remeshing Technique for the FEM Simulation of Metal Forming Processes", to be published in Proceedings of 1983 ASME Int. Comp. Eng. Conf., Chicago, 1983.

Index

The symbol (F) following an entry signifies that information is presented in a figure; the symbol (T), in a table.